BUILDING A LIFE
BY
CARPENTER JESUS

The Divine Teacher's
Seven Steps to Wholeness

With
Supplementary Wisdom from both
Western Classical and Eastern Sages

JERRY DELL EHRLICH

ACADEMIC CHRISTIAN PRESS
P.O. BOX 80247
SAN DIEGO, CA   92138-0247

(TELEPHONE) 619-422-8701
(FAX) 619-422-8749
E-MAIL acachrprsjdehr@msn.com

Copyright © 2003 by Jerry Dell Ehrlich

Published by Academic Christian Press
P.O. Box 80247
San Diego, CA 92138-0247

Library of Congress Cataloging-in-Publication Data

Ehrlich, Jerry Dell
   Building a Life by Carpenter Jesus: The Divine Teacher's Seven Steps to Wholeness, with Supplementary Wisdom from both Western Classical and Eastern Sages.
   Includes bibliographical references, glossary, and index.
   ISBN 0-9710000-1-8 $24
1. Humanity's Great Teachers. 2. The Goodness of Life. 3. The Anxieties of Living. 4. Taking Control of One's Life. 5. Finding Oneself. 6. A Rational Life Plan. 7. Friendship. 8. Love and Justice Extended. 9. Goodbye to Judgmentalism.

Library of Congress Control Number: 2003093848

10 9 8 7 6 5 4 3 2 1

TO

ALL THOSE WHO SEEK

THE

LIFE MORE ABUNDANT

Also by Jerry Dell Ehrlich

PLATO'S GIFT TO CHRISTIANITY:
The Gentile Preparation for and the Making of the Christian Faith

Academic Christian Press
San Diego, CA: 2001

ISBN 0-9710000-0-X $32.00

GRATITUDE

As man travels his physical and spiritual journey through life, he receives many blessings that are both recognized and unrecognized, and, therefore, it is always impossible in a brief space to say "Thank You", by name, to all those who have brought some form or other of human sweetness into one's life. To them, at least now, I do say "Thank You", and in the "Cosmic Book of Human Kindnesses" your actions will surely be registered. I also realize that those kind deeds you did for me and for others enhanced your own dignity and goodness, and for that too I am thankful. For I do believe that goodness and virtue do have their own rewards, and this book is based upon that very idea; that only the good can be happy and whole. Still there are some people who play such a great and beautiful role in one's life, that even the most weak at mind can readily recall them quite easily. First of all, I want to thank my parents: my father, Mr.Carl Ehrlich, who taught me the value of work, discipline, and the power of numbers and my mother, Mrs. Elizabeth Manweiler Ehrlich, who taught me human kindness and the spiritual blessings of love and devotion. They were my primary teachers in life. Secondly, I thank all those teachers in schools, institutions, and universities that pushed me a little extra that my life would be so deepened that I would be able to appreciate the wonder and beauty of life itself. Finally I would like to thank those who have offered me incredible friendships that have lasted throughout my years: my brother Mr. Robert A. Ehrlich and his wife, Gerri, where food and talk are always available; my sister, Ms. Sheila K. Ehrlich who enhanced my affection for the animal world. Dr. Rodger I. Meinz with whom I have enjoyed many wonderful and enlightening conversations; Dr. E. Robert Borchert whose tender care for those suffering and whose spiritual openness have been a delight to me; Mr. David and Mrs. Jean Faszholz whose friendship and hospitality have brought me encouragement and laughter; and finally Ms. Letitia E .M. Noordhuizen whose spiritual embrace of people everywhere, and whose personal hospitality to me have been a beautifying element in my life.

Jerry Dell Ehrlich, M.Div., M.A., Ph.D.
2003

CONTENTS

CONTENTS

CONTENTS

CONTENTS

CONTENTS

CONTENTS

CONTENTS

CONTENTS

INTRODUCTION

There are many books on the market that propose various ways of structuring one's life in such a way that he or she will find happiness, as happiness or wholeness is the acknowledged *summum bonum* of human existence. Yet, I find that most of such books do not take into account the depth and power of theological and philosophical wisdom and present it in a rational way in which one can actually build his own person into wholeness. In the Christian market there are an overwhelming amount of books that point to Jesus' teachings, at least in theory, but, in general, are either too simple and shallow, presenting happiness as an easy quest based upon an emotional decision, and not upon good and rational theology. Also, even if they do show the life giving sparks of scholarship, they almost always neglect the great Eastern Sages, thinking that they are irrelevant, as well as the classical Greek and Roman wise men, classifying them simply as "pagans". This is the very narrowness that the Church has often accused other religions and philosophies of being. Simplistic ways to an abundance of joy also permeate much of the secular self-help market. The reason I have given the title to this book that I have is because I wanted to declare up front that it takes a building process, full of discipline, reason, and commitment to become a good person in thought, word, and deed; and that that goodness is the only basis upon which a man can establish a life of fulfillment or wholeness. The great teachers of mankind have survived and been honored by many generations of people who can see the wisdom in their teachings, and the power therein to bring men to a higher thought and moral level in which he finds in man the seed of the image of the Divine. Then with the birth and growth of that spiritual seed his life is changed step by step into an ascent that lifts the soul to a transcendental level; and it is there in the greatness and power of the Good that he finds, first himself, and then what love, joy, kindness, justice, courage and self-control are and how they, of their very nature, reach out to make other people's lives as beautiful as his own has become. In the First Chapter I have pointed the reader to those very teachers of humanity whose goodness and wisdom have penetrated the minds and souls of the many and planted those very seeds of joy. I start with Jesus because in terms of world influence and the number of his followers, his words and teachings have given more to the spiritual joy and wholeness of humanity than any of the other teachers. But wisdom has many ways of being expressed and presented, and to neglect the many others who have deepened life for millions of people, and some of them before Jesus -- especially those who had an influence upon him and the way the people of his age thought--, would be irresponsible and even dishonest to the actual flow of thought within the development of human history. All such wise teachers I have tried to honor because of the great value they have given to human existence. The Second Chapter is a manifestation of the goodness of life on earth in the very fleshly body that we have. For far too many, who are either wrapped up in human misery here or are overly intoxicated with the transcendental world that awaits them, do not appropriately appreciate the miracle of life now and all its almost magical joys that accompany it. Bodily, yes fleshly, life is good to the core, and should both be appreciated and lived to its fullest. The Third Chapter presents the causes why some find life so unhappy or without purpose or even downright evil. Man creates for himself his own miseries, and he must acknowledge that fact before he can start climbing to the mountain of wholeness, for he has simply no path to follow, no goal to reach, anxious about his nothingness of being, and lives in both anxiety, mostly of death, and even hatred of himself and others. Once he accepts the fact that he is lost and needs a path to his cosmic existence, then he will be able to take the first step to wholeness. Chapter Four presents that first step in which man can find meaningfulness within his earthly finiteness by 1) unattachment to the past, things out of his control, and to unnecessary material and social passions, and 2) by taking control of his life by releasing certain passions, letting the past begone, balancing his life, adapting to difficulties, and by simple gratitude for the obvious blessings he is presently receiving. Chapter Five, step two, opens up the cosmos, with all its beauty, to him, and lets him know that it is a wonderful and friendly home, and his spirit is deeply connected with it. Chapter Six, step three, presents the ability of the individual to find himself in this time in history and his participation in the universe, and accepting that he is a child of the Eternal. Chapter Seven, step four, calls the reader to rationally organize and prioritize his life, and to give up those irrational passions or excuses that keep him from reaching his goal of wholeness. Chapter Eight, step five, directs the reader to the power, beauty, and wonder of friendship, which is truly the blossoming of the flower of human existence. While the first four steps help build man's own personal being into one of identity and independence that he might be a truly good human being, this step, the fifth, directs him towards friendship: for friendship was not available to him before he first was made good by his quest for inner goodness, for only good people can receive or give friendship. Friendship is impossible between indecent people. Chapter Nine, step six, extends the person's inner love from himself (steps 1-4) to friends (step 5) and then to the world at large (step 6) where human barriers all break down in the presence of his love for others. This step fulfills his soul as he casts his love and happiness towards all his human and animal brothers and sisters, knowing that no man is an island, and his participation in their joy is a strengthening of his own happiness. The final chapter, Chapter Ten, shows that he has been liberated from both sin, i.e. "missing the mark in life", for now he has his path, and from judgmentalism which has hithertofore hindered him in his quest for a soul opened to all humanity. He says, then, in his wholeness, "Goodbye to all that."

This is a book about human happiness and the great teachers that help us get there by their wisdom spelled out as different pathways and routes by which to travel. Its "doctrines" are inherent in their ethical teachings, and it has no desire to pit one "divine master" against another. Also the book speaks of those attitudes and actions that are profitable for this very life that one is now living. Abstract doctrines of past reincarnations or future salvation have not been used to explain or excuse one from avoiding what I consider the necessary ethical standards one needs to be a good person now. For example, I do not permit the doctrine of past Karma and reincarnation to excuse the caste system nor do I permit the doctrine of eternal salvation to excuse the torture and even execution of people for the purpose of bringing them into the "true faith" by which they can save their eternal souls, and its explanation that a little suffering now for an eternity of blessing is a small price to pay for a heretic considering the reward of eternal life for getting his thinking straight. I understand such defenses that certain religions have had for such actions, but I find them contrary to the teachings of the truly great Teachers and

Divines that I have presented in this book. Likewise, I personally find such excuses abominable. All people living today have the right and equality before God and his fellowman to pursue happiness and wholeness in the most pleasurable way available to the whole of mankind. For this life in itself is a magical blessing given to each person. Let each person live, laugh, play, and seek the good life of joy and happiness, but always knowing that it comes from his own internal goodness which he himself has built as a foundation upon which such joy and happiness can be erected. From the Rig-Veda and Lao Tzu in the East, from the Egyptian Book of the Dead in the South, from the Vikings in the North, from the Mesopotamian area in the Mideast, from the Greeks and Romans in Europe, and from the Buddhist's Canon, the Four Christian Gospels, The Sufis, and the Western scholars and mystics, paths have been given for the sake of light, wisdom, liberation, happiness and wholeness.

Jerry Dell Ehrlich, M.Div., M.A., Ph.D.
2003 AD

ABBREVIATIONS

FCL   Family Classical Library. A.J. Valpy; Henry Colburn and Richard Bentley. New Burlington St. London.1830-1833.

GBWW   Great Books of the Western World. Associate Editor, Mortimer J. Adler. Encyclopaedia Britannica, Inc., London.1952.

LCL   Loeb Classical Library. Harvard U. Press. Cambridge, MA.

LAT   Los Angeles Times.

OCR   Orange County Register.

QUOTATIONS

All quotations from Plato's Works are from B. Jowett's translation of 1892, except where noted.

All translations of Bible are from the Academic Christian Press, unless otherwise noted.

Except where noted, all quotations from Cicero, Demosthenes, Hesiod, Horace, Juvenal, Ovid and Sophocles are from the FCL (sometimes with slight adaptations).

All translations of Kant, Goethe, and Schiller are from Academic Christian Press, unless otherwise noted.

All translations, with occasional modifications, of Lao Tzu, Confucius, Mencius, Kwang Tzu are by James Legge.

All quotations of the Dhammapada are from the Max Mueller translation.

Brackets [..] within a quotation are my added comments.

CHAPTER ONE

JESUS, THE TEACHER

The genre of "Spiritual Self Improvement Books" contains an enormous number of books, and the reader may ask why another? and what makes this one special or even worthwhile reading? Despite the benefits and the many people who have been helped by these popular psychology and advice books, there are not only a few that promote a far too simple method of thinking as an easy way to get "what you need and deserve" either from another or from society itself. Such simplicity can lead to disappointment and self-centeredness simply because the courses of introspection that they chart do not lay a sufficient foundation that is needed for a radically thorough change of mind-set that is necessitated. This concept of a total change of mind-set is as old as Plato who called it, in Greek, METANOIA, and possibly was reflected in Socrates' platform of advice that he received from the Oracle of Delphi in the two commands "Know yourself" and "Nothing too much". In the New Testament this Platonic term METANOIA is used often but is usually translated either as "conversion" or "repentance". Another way in which Plato expressed the quest for wisdom and personal fulfillment was his teaching that one, in his expression, needs to think "above the divided line". The wisdom that was to be sought was that of the eternal goodness, beauty, and perfection that was brought together into a unit in the person of God, and therefore to be like God as much as possible was the only way to participate in wholeness, happiness, goodness, and beauty. Jesus, in his teachings and his life, brought forth these redemptive thoughts, not within the walls of the Academy, but among the people in the streets, in their homes, at the synagogue, at the foot of hills and mountains, by the sea shore, and in the temple area that all, even the "untouchables of the day" could hear the "good news" of spiritual realization and the warm feeling of living in a friendly universe with a loving Father in heaven. The people felt something deep within and their lives were changed as they heard him, so that they were astonished and glorified him as they contemplated with wonder the charismatic and gracious words. They asked, "From where is this One and from where is His wisdom? Is not this man the carpenter, the son of Joseph and Mary? From where did all this wisdom come to this man?(Mt 13:55-57).

Jesus, without parallel in history, based on universal influence, the most diverse and integrated followers, the sheer number of people who claim him to be the Incarnation of Divine Wisdom, the book containing his life and teachings (New Testament) being the world's best seller, and the division of human history based on the approximate year of his birth, is certainly a person whose teachings are most worthy to be the basis and backbone of a spiritual self-help course of building a foundation of happiness and wholeness, that, in turn, blossoms into a beautiful and fulfilling life. He sought with his full heart that the people he so loved would get the seriousness of his message: AMEN LEGO HYMIN (Truly I say to you) appears 75 times in the Four Gospels, and every time it appears, it refers to the sayings of Jesus and no one else.

"Wisdom is justified by its fruits" declared Jesus, and the great acceptance of his wisdom mentioned above is in itself the verification that his wisdom has born many fruits and blessing as they lifted up generation after generation to happy and fulfilling lives. Alex Osborn in his book Wake Up Your Mind, written in 1952, makes this statement:

> Ministers' sons represent far less that one per cent of our popula-
> tion, and yet, in Who's Who in America nearly 10 per cent of
> those listed were sons of clergyman. England has far more lawyers
> than clergymen; and yet, in England's Who's Who, sons of clergy-
> men outnumber sons of lawyers two to one; and they outnumber
> doctors' [physicians] sons by three to one. 1.1

Jacques Maritain in his Education at the Crossroads stated:

> We may now define in a more precise manner the aim of educa-
> tion. It is to guide man in the evolving dynamism through which
> he shapes himself as a human person--armed with knowledge,

strength of judgment, and moral virtues--while at the same time conveying to him the spiritual heritage. 1.2

This book not only presents and explains the teachings of Jesus, but puts them in a step by step order, and supports them with the wisdom and teachings of human history's other great philosophical and theological religious teachers from Lao Tzu to Dietrich Bonhoeffer.

I. JESUS, THE TEACHER

Jesus was the Teacher of wisdom throughout his ministry, and it would be well to remember that, although he also preached and healed, he was always addressed as The Teacher. He went about his homeland teaching, preaching, and healing--always in that order: teaching was always mentioned first. He was never addressed or referred to as preacher or healer, or even Savior or Redeemer, but as The Teacher. When he needed a place to celebrate the Passover with his disciples in Jerusalem, he sent for reservations and reminded those sent that all they had to say was that it was for The Teacher. On the first Easter, after Mary recognized him, her only word was "Teacher". The Carpenter Jesus came to teach us about the building of our lives into joyous and abundant ones: socially, economically, and spiritually. 43 times in the Four Gospels was he referred to as Teacher (DIDASKALOS), 13 times as Rabbi, and in a parallel thought, he himself used the word Master in the sense of Teacher (Mt 23:8-11). Jesus, in three different ways, declares himself to be man's Teacher, and every type of person in the Gospels addresses him as such: the frightened disciple at sea (Mk 4:38 "Teacher, do you not care if we perish?"), a scribe came to him and said "Teacher, I will follow you wherever you go."(Mt 8:19), one in a crowd who was looking for help for his dumb child "Teacher, I have brought my son to you..."(Mk 9:17), a perplexed Nicodemus, a leader among his people, addressed him thus "Teacher (RABBI), we all know that you are a teacher (DIDASKALOS) from God (John 3:2). The disciples seem to know no other way of addressing Jesus than by calling him either Rabbi or Didaskalos: Judas addressed him as such (Mt 26:25), Peter (Mk 9:5 and 11:21), Nathanael (J 1:49), and the disciples as a whole many times (such as J 4:31, 6:25, 9:2, 11:8 etc).

Christians have a natural tendency to call Jesus, "Christ", "Savior", "Redeemer" and other names that convey many blessings in themselves, and while this is proper, they seldom mention him by the name of the people in Gospels, "Teacher". Yet, Jesus was adamant that this is the name by which he is to be known and addressed--BECAUSE it was his teachings that were the Word of Life, and he demanded that those only who follow his teachings have a right to address him as Lord. "Whoever does the will of my Father in heaven [as expressed in Jesus' teachings] is my brother, and sister, and mother"(Mt12:59). Happiness is not found in just calling Jesus one's savior, it is only in following his teaching that one can find wholeness: "If you continue in my reasoned declarations [LOGOS from which we receive the word "logic"], you are then my real disciples, and you shall know the truth [of life], and that truth will make you free [of anxieties and fears]."(J 8:31-32). For blessings come to those who love him and keep his commandments (J 13:17; 14:12-15' 15:10,14). Only those who digest him (i.e. His teachings) can eat the "bread of life" and have their hunger satisfied (Mt 5:6). Throughout the Sermon on the Mount (Mt 5-7) Jesus was emphasizing that those are the blessed ones who build their lives upon his teachings, which are the basis (the rock foundation) of a stable and happy life. They are to learn from him and receive rest for their souls. "Come to me, all you who work hard and are broken down, and I will give you rest. Be yoked to me, and learn from me; for I am gentle and have a humble heart, and you will find rest for your souls"(Mt 11:28-29). Jesus spoke to everyone: individually, in groups--both small and large, to professional scribes and devout Pharisees, and sometimes alone with his disciples. The Gospels record 28 personal (to an individual) conversations that Jesus had, for no one person was too "small' or "unimportant" to him. Unlike some of the great teachers he was not a court philosopher (as was Confucius) nor a professional priest, but rather he was more like the Hebrew prophets or the Greek school masters and philosophers. He was not a judge of disputes over material possessions, nor a military leader, nor a political figure, and he did not talk of the distant future (the end time was left to the will and knowledge of the Father), but rather the immediate concern for the welfare of the people, for in his presence thought was provoked and existential decisions were called for. As C.H. Dodd has said:

In the Jewish society of his time Jesus found his place, to begin with, as a teacher of religion and morals. He was addressed as "Rabbi" (Master), and not only by his immediate followers, but also by strangers, including some who would themselves have claimed the same title.1.3

K. Weidel expressed the lovely beauty, personal charm and care, and his power of attack on those imposing harm on others with which Jesus taught:

> The form of the teachings of Jesus, the way in which he clothes
> his interior life in words, indubitably possesses an artistic char-
> acter. The wealth of the style is remarkable. Jesus, could tell a
> story in a very living, simple, and arresting way; he knew how
> to stir the minds of his hearers with vigour; if necessary he could
> pour forth scorn with unmistakable energy, he could console with
> gentleness, humiliate with biting sarcasm, blame with bitterness,
> be indignant with intense vigour, and rejoice intensely. Everywhere
> he manifests his creative originality. Everything is brief, every
> word hits the target, all is concrete. There is never a word too much.
> 1.4

Jesus mentioned that wisdom is known by its effects (fruits), and from human history his wisdom is preeminent among the great teachers of the world in terms of changing and giving fulfillment to people of all rank, color, wealth, and education. Anton T. Boisen gives the following personal creed in his book The Exploration of the Inner World: A Study of Mental Disorder and Religious Experience.

> I believe in the Love which came to my rescue on that Easter
> morning long years ago...I believe that this God [of love] was once
> perfectly revealed in the life and character and teachings of Jesus
> of Nazareth...and this process [of his love among men] has been
> going on for nineteen centuries.1.5

Therefore, the divine teachings of Jesus will be the basis for this book, however the other great teachers of humanity shall not be neglected for their great contributions of rational, caring, spiritual, and uplifting concepts and ideas to the people of the earth.

II.   TEACHERS, GOD'S DIVINE GIFTS TO MANKIND

We can think of a poor country man who has been isolated from the big city for his entire life going to a metropolis with which he is totally unacquainted, has no friends there, and has never even rented a room at a hotel or motel. He finds himself there and feels lost, even though he is fascinated with the great amount of people, huge structures, rapid transit, hot dog stands and everything else. However, if he is to make his home there, he must find his way around, get to where he can find a place to stay, employment, and a friend or two to trust. He needs an introductory map to the city that he might be able slowly to find his way.

Humankind is that man, and the great metropolis is the universe which overwhelms him with its unthinkable depth and spectacular night skies. He wants to find his way and to find himself in this cosmic metropolis, but he needs help. He needs a teacher to map out for him the beautiful existence before him, how he can best participate in its goodness and find himself at home in it. Teachers are among the finest gifts of God, for they show us the map of living and how to read it and follow it. They are seldom honored by the masses, who, themselves, enjoy a good life because of the teachers who helped them through their learning years. But through the history of mankind, there have been given to men many teachers, some of magnificent and divine stature, and they have brought their people to a higher and more beautiful plain of existence. God dispersed them in all parts of the world, for God so loved the world that it was his natural graciousness to give such to every part of mankind. In this section, some of those wonderful teachers, and some of the thoughtful words in their praise will be presented.

A. PLATO

Plato, 427-347BC, was a fortunate man who lived in Athens, Greece amidst many other fine teachers, including Socrates, the Mid-Wife who brought to birth the quest for the knowledge that gave life meaning and virtue, which in turn led to happiness. Socrates was the gad-fly sent from God to direct the Athenians from thinking, not only of wealth, the games, physics, and rhetoric, but to thinking about themselves and their personal value--to know themselves in this cosmic metropolis, and to participate in the beautiful, the holy, and the eternal. Plato, his even more brilliant student, recorded from memory much of what Socrates had taught, but as Plato grew into middle age he himself became the   greatest and most influential secular teacher of the Western world, beginning with his establishment of his university: the Academy, which survived longer that any other academic school in human history, well over 900 years until it was closed by Justinian, the Christian Emperor (a terrible act of intolerance). Plato taught that all human happiness was based on eight virtues: four divine and four human, the four divine being first and the basis of the subsequent and inferior human virtues. The four divine virtues were: wisdom, temperance (self-control), courage, and justice. The four human virtues were: health, comeliness, strength, and wealth--in that order. If a person had all four human "virtues" but not the divine virtues, he would be insecure and utterly miserable. As an example, if a person had wealth (the least of even the human virtues) but had bad health, was hideously ugly, or so weak he was not mobile, then his wealth had no possibility of giving happiness. Even if he had all four of the human virtues, but had no wisdom--all would be quickly lost: he would not take care of either his body or his wealth (a fool and his money are quickly parted). Plato taught that the divine virtues had an order of importance also: wisdom first, courage second, and self-control third, and justice, that is the spiritual harmony within a man's soul would come into being with the proper balance of the first three--as justice was a harmony of the people within a city that balances the three groups of people: the thinkers (we might say congress, and the executive and legal branch), the courageous (the military branch), and the workers of industry (the laborers and tax-payers). When all three are balanced then the city has justice. Plato constantly drew parallels with the happy soul and the happy city, especially in his political works (Republic, Laws, and The Statesman).

For complete harmony of the soul man had to follow his love (EROS) for the beautiful, the good, the eternally unchangeable One, who was God. For within man there was a daemon (a "good" being in Plato's works) which pushed man towards God and would not let him find rest until he found himself at one with Absolute Beauty and Goodness, God himself. The following is my paraphrase of Plato's Symposium 211-212:

> When the love which is implanted into our soul seeks to behold Absolute Beauty, it starts its ascent upwards by acknowledging the beauties bound into this world's order, but perceiving that they are not the ultimate fulfillment, discards them, and resumes its quest for Ultimate Goodness, and stepping upwards, one step by one, seeks that which is the Eternal Good and Absolute Beauty, knowing that what it has left behind will never fully satisfy it. When it finally meets Beauty itself, face to face, that Beauty that never decays or changes or fades, but gives its goodness to all reality, always and never wavering, than that soul knows he has become a friend of God, beloved and uplifted by the Same to his eternal home.

Plato used the word THEOPHILES (friend of God, or beloved of God) 22 times in the dialogues of his maturity. A great teacher himself, he, at his Academy, attracted 22 students who spent many years learning from him (Aristotle was his pupil about 20 years), and those disciples went on and continued to teach mankind the value of human existence and point out the way to travel the cosmos and to find virtue, happiness, and, eventually, the Eternal One. Of his disciples there were Lastheneia of Mantinea and Axiothea of Phlius, two women. In his writings he insisted that men and women were to be equally educated, according to their individual talents, and that the priesthood as well as the Thinkers or Guardians of the state that made all ultimate decisions should have members of both sexes. It is no wonder why some of the early Church Fathers, Renaissance educators, and Erasmus all referred to him as the Divine Plato.

B.   THE BUDDHIST CANON

In the Buddhist canon one who is seeking a path in the cosmos is cautioned in the selection of a teacher by checking out the men thoroughly oneself before choosing, and not depending on other reports, traditions, hearsay, or by the mere recital of doctrine and mere logic and inference. Rather one is to converse with and feel the charm, the openness of mind and heart, the purity of character, the element of compassion, and the power of contemplation of the prospective Master. The teacher is to show wonder and a marvelous desire to find truth, a soft soul, and a radiant personality. For it is this teacher that will awaken the mind, cause a Way to arise which has not arisen before, so that one may grow and be freed by wisdom. I-Tsing, a Chinese monk and traveler (634-713AD), listed seven qualifications for a teacher:

1. The breadth and depth of the teacher's learning
2. The ability of the teacher to write, teach, and explain
3. The teacher's intelligence
4. The teacher's liberality
5. The teacher's loving-kindness
6. His devotion to work
7. His knowledge of cause and effect in the decisions of life 1.6

The Dhammapada encourages its readers that when they find a worthy teacher they must let him teach because we are what we think and we think what we have been taught and learned.

If you see a man who shows you what is to be avoided, who admin-isters reproofs, and is intelligent, follow that wise man as you would one who tells of hidden treasures; it will be better, not worse, for him who follows him. Let him admonish, let him forbid what is improper! -- he will be beloved of the good, by the bad he will be hated.1.7

All that we are is the result of what we have thought; it is founded on our thoughts, it is made up of our thoughts. If a man speaks or acts with a pure thought, happiness follows him, like a shadow that never leaves him.1.8

The word DHAMMA (Pali) or DHARMA (Sanskrit) is a flexible word that has various specific meanings, but they all stem from correct teaching, correct thoughts, and correct living: good conduct, moral instruction, teachings of Buddha, and cosmic law (universal natural law). It is the way or the path to virtue and happiness, and one is mentored into its mind-set by one's teacher, for happiness is virtually impossible unless one has been taught Dhamma. Therefore, the value of teachers is comparable to that of parents in a person's life. In the Buddhist work, The Tibetan Book of the Dead, the prayer beseeches the help of the Gurus and Dakinis:

> O ye Gurus and Devas, and ye Dakinis, the Faithful Ones,
> Hearken now out of great love and compassion:
> Obeisance, O ye assemblage of Gurus and Dakinis;
> Out of your great love, lead us along the Path...
> May the Gurus of the Inspired Line lead us.1.9

For it is the great teachers who give enlightenment that liberates man in his soul, parting him from his fears and anxieties, and giving to him the peace that comes from correct teaching. In the Conversion of Sariputra we see his joy that comes from the new mind-set:

> Struck with wonder, O great Leader,
> And amazed I heard your voice.
> All my perplexity has passed away,
> Fully ripe I am for this superior vehicle.
> ...
> For in the past I have clung to false views.
> ...
> When from all those false views I had become free,
> ...Then I thought: 'I am at rest.'
> ...
> All my former cares have now been removed,
> Since I have heard your call.1.10

There are many other texts which praise the teachers, gurus and Bodhisattvas.

C. CHINA'S SPIRITUAL EDUCATORS

There are many well known teachers of China, and they too, were held in the highest esteem by their disciples: Lao Tzu, Confucius, Mencius, Mo Tzu, Han Fei Tzu, Hsun Tzu, and Huang Po to name only a few. However, their words of wisdom will appear throughout the following pages and their wisdom will be freely and honorably given to the reader for his growth into wholeness. This section will be limited to the respect and praise that is given by them to the teachers of mankind.

A teacher is in love with teaching, not the money, and he will turn away no one. About Confucius (551--479BC), the Analects state:

> The Master said, "Am I indeed possessed of knowledge? I am not knowing. But if a poor person, who appears quite emptylike, ask anything of me, I set it forth from one end to the other, and exhaust it.1.11

The learning of knowledge from a Master Teacher was of utmost importance for a life of well-being; from the Analects:

> There is the love of being benevolent without the love of learning; -- the beclouding here leads to a foolish simplicity. There is the love of knowing without the love of learning; -- the beclouding here leads to dissipation of mind. There is the love of being sincere without the love of learning; -- the beclouding here leads to an injurious dis- regard of consequences. There is the love of straightforwardness without the love of learning; -- the beclouding here leads to rude- ness. There is the love of boldness without the love of learning; -- the beclouding here leads to insubordination. There is the love of firmness without the love of learning; -- the beclouding here leads to extravagant conduct.1.12

Confucius here, of course, is saying that wishful thinking without the discipline of study and mental exercises, is not only nonproductive, but it actually is destructive. There are no ways to virtue without rational learning and thought. Teachers help us how to think properly.

About being a teacher, Mencius (379-330BC) declared:

> There are five ways in which the superior man [master] effects his teaching.
> 1. There are some on whom his influence descends like seasonable [needed and timely] rain.
> 2. There are some whose virtue he perfects,

3   and some of whose talents he assists in developing.
4. There are some whose inquiries he answers.
5. There are some who privately cultivate [with the aid of my teaching] and correct themselves.1.13

Sometimes the Teacher is limited because people are different, some are hard ground and to plant wisdom into their souls is almost impossible, while others rejoice at and devour the teachings given to them. When asked about this, Mencius gave this illustration, which reminds one much of Jesus' Parable of the Sowing of Seed in Matthew 13:18-23:

There now is barley. -- Let it be sown and covered up; the ground being the same, and the time of sowing likewise the same, it grows rapidly up, and when the full time is come, it is all found to be ripe. Although there may be inequalities of produce, that is owing to the difference of the soil, as rich or poor, to the unequal nourishment afforded by the rains and dews, and to the different ways in which man has performed his business in reference to it.1.14

Teachers, regardless of how good, how patient, or how inspired--even from above, will have different results with different people, but he or she must continue the quest to lead mankind to, not only a functional life, but one of beauty, wholeness and happiness.

D. INDIA'S GREAT TEACHERS

In the Laws of Manu (put into writing before the Second Century AD, but were preceded by a long oral history) a teacher was to be honored as being in the inner-most group of the disciple--equated in value to the members of his family:

He who defames his mother, his father, his wife, his brother, his son, or his teacher, and he who gives not the way to his preceptor, shall be compelled to pay one hundred (panas). VIII.275

Carnal intercourse with sisters by the same mother...with the wives of a friend, or of a son, they declare to be equal to the violation of a Guru's bed...Slaying kine, sacrificing for those who are unworthy to sacrifice, adultery, selling oneself, casting off one's teacher, mother, father, or son...etc.XI.59-60

Shankara's first words in his work Crest-Jewel of Discrimination are "I prostrate myself before Govinda, the perfect teacher," and his idea of a teacher, actually a good teacher, are as follows:

A teacher is one who is deeply versed in the scriptures, pure, free from lust, a perfect knower of Brahman. He is upheld continually in Brahman, calm like the flame when its fuel is consumed, an ocean of love that knows no ulterior motive, a friend to all good people who humbly entrust themselves to him.

The Katha Upanishad warns its readers to avoid at all cost a bad and unqualified teacher.

Fools dwelling in darkness, but thinking themselves wise and erudite, go round and round, by various tortuous paths, like the blind led by the blind.(I.ii.5) (see Mt 15:14 where Jesus is quite critical of the Pharisees as teachers).

E. TEACHERS OF THE CLASSICAL WESTERN WORLD

Ancient Greece was the leader of the entire world when it came to developing teachers and finally even developing the structure of teaching and establishing stationary schools where pupils could go for instructions for all the arts and sciences of the day. It produced philosophers for physics and sophists who taught the art of living and achievement within society. From Thales to Parmenides physics reigned as the topics of the Greek philosophers, and from the earliest sophists to those of the late 5th Century BC (Gorgias, Antiphon, Protagoras, Prodicus, Hippias etc) the sophists gathered small groups of students wherever they could find them, as the wandered place to place, and taught them the art of politics, dialectics, rhetoric, and ways to think about succeeding in their culture as well as possible. Most did it for a fee, with Protagoras probably being the most famous and expensive under whom to study (Socrates says he was quite disappointed when he heard the famous Protagoras and his concept of mind, NOUS, expecting much more than what was said, and part of his disappointment was probably aimed at the fact that to study a few years under Protagoras was so expensive--Socrates was quick to point out that he himself did not charge a fee). And Socrates himself was one of the last and undoubtedly the greatest sophist. He was also immensely popular and after him, through Isocrates first and then Plato, came the establishment of stationary schools. Isocrates school was more like a school from clementary through high school and taught people the basic things which the sophists had taught, and Plato's school was for the more advanced in all the same subjects with an additional stress on the search for truth by means of dialectic and mathematics which made a basis of strength from which the student could move to advanced thought, especially in what we would call the abstract and ultimate truths that guide the workings of the universe. He even required a high efficiency in mathematics to enter his school, the Academy (so named because it was dedicated to the god Akademos), and over its entrance he put the words "If you do not know geometry, do not come in". Plato, in his own works, stressed education and the qualifications of teachers throughout his works, especially his political works to the extent that music, children's toys, the plastic arts, the religious ceremonies all had to pass a test to see if they were teaching, first the children and then all society, the education that one needed to be good and to make society good. Frivolous, mythical (if there were no truth to be found within the myth), untrue, and negative stories were all to be forbidden, as they confused and misled the young and hindered true knowledge for the more serious older students. Plato did not shy away from censureship.

After Plato died in 347BC, his most famous student (of 20 years), Aristotle, also founded a stationary school, also in Athens, and added much to the curriculum in the physical studies realm (botany, zoology, the plastic arts, mechanics, and physics in general), as well as economics and extended explanation of logic. The Lyceum never became as famous as the Academy, but the canonization of Aristotle's and Theophrastus' works had an almost unbelievable influence upon both the West and the East (including the Arabs) in the subsequent centuries. Without doubt Aristotle was one of the greatest teachers of mankind, both in depth and breadth and the wide spread influence he exerted until the time of Francis Bacon, when a new "instrument" for thinking was developed. There is little doubt that the thinking of modern men go back to ancient Greece, and especially Socrates, Plato and Aristotle. Teachers who pushed mankind forward and upward were they and their Hellenistic followers who spread their works as well as extending them in depth and quality to the entire Mediterranean World.

Some of those other great teachers were:

In Medicine: Hippocrates and Galen

Cosmology and Astronomy: Aristarchus of Samos (310-230BC) who taught the solar system

Hipparchus of Nicea (late 2nd Century BC) who calculated year at 365 ¼ days

Eratosthenes who taught the circumference of the earth to 24,662 miles within 195 miles of the correct figure.

Poseidonius who calculated and taught the size and distance of the sun to within 3/8 and 5/8 of the correct figures--when the rest of the world believed the earth was larger than the sun

Geography: Greeks were the first map makers: Anaximander and Eratosthenes

Historians: Previous peoples had annals, the Greeks invented history, that is, they provided a rational approach to, not only the fact that things happened (annals) but why they happened, how they happened, and the decision making qualities of those who made them happen. The word HISTORIA in Greek means "inquiry", for the Greeks wanted to know why and how. In brief, they were teaching the world how to think as they applied this why and how to all other studies.

Mechanical arts: Ctesibius and Archimedes.

Philosophy, metaphysics, ethics, and happiness: the number of Greek teachers are overwhelming: but to name a few: Zeno the Stoic, Plutarch the Platonist, Epictetus the Stoic, Plotinus the Platonist, Ammonius Saccas the Platonist, Epicurus, and Diogenes the Cynic.

If the reader wants a more extensive showing of the Greeks as our Teachers, he can so read the second chapter "The Greek Brilliance" in my book Plato's Gift to Christianity.

The Ancient Romans also offered to the Western World many wonderful teachers who both passed on what the Greeks had taught us and also broadened the teachings for a greater audience within their empire. Livy who wrote about Roman history; Cicero who developed the Roman language enough to be capable of philosophic thought which helped all the teachers in the Romance languages of the subsequent twenty centuries discuss the philosophical, theological, and abstract; Seneca, the reflective stoic; and Quintilian that teacher and educator who established a school in Rome and directed its curriculum. H.I. Marrou in his A History of Education in Antiquity states "The school depicted at the end of the fourth century by Ausonius, by St Jerome and St. Augustine, was still on the whole the school of Quintilian's."1.15

F. THE CHRISTIAN WEST

The Christian West was very fortunate to inherit the structure of the ancient Greco-Roman world, and it is to that structure and much of its philosophies that the early fathers of the Church owed their education and power of thought. They used it well, especially in Hellenized cities like Antioch and Alexandria, and later in Rome and Constantinople. But when the collapse of the Greco-Roman world took place, the Christian Church fell behind, as the structure upon which it was built was no longer there. "Orthodoxy" also took its toll, as many Classical writers were forbidden (this happened even before the fall of the West), and after the fall of the West, the East, under Justinian, closed the "pagan" Academy of Plato. Much of the intellectual set-back of Christianity during the "dark ages" was self-inflicted, and there was a struggle to survive intellectually until a rebirth (French=Renaissance) of the Ancient Western Classical Thought started in Italy, and even that was hindered by the Church as censorship and heresy trials did much to keep the earth flat and at the center of the universe.

But gradually the Church opened up slightly, and then much more with the Reformation. All of Plato (not just the Timaeus) would be taught, all of Aristotle (not just the logic) would be taught, Copericus would read Aristarchus and claimed with him that the sun was the center of the planetary system. But the Teachers of Truth, the Seekers of Wisdom, pushed the West forward to where it is today. Yes, there were teachers in the "Dark" and "Middle" Ages, but many were limited to the basics of teaching to read and write, save church documents, and promote the Orthodox faith. But overall, the Renaissance saved the West and brought to it a superiority over the rest of the inhabited world in every scientific area--because of its teachers, who often suffered poverty, disgrace, and rejection. Jesus certainly was acquainted with such experiences himself. But the drive, the honor, the courage, and the committed wisdom of the teachers of the West have given to us what we have in our freedoms and standard of living today. Perhaps we, as the ancients can understand the value of the term "teacher" that was given to Jesus by those who were taught by him and loved by him. It truly is the teachers of humanity that have given us that map to find our selves and our way in this wonderful and majestic universe.

III. JESUS' MANNER OF TEACHING

A. THE CARPENTER

Most of the time when it is mentioned that Jesus was a "Carpenter", it is implied that this meant he was a common day worker who simply took orders from someone else and did his blue collar work. However, in both Greek thought and Hebrew thought at the time of Jesus, "carpenter" symbolized a wide field of architectural and constructional talents in both wood and stone. Joseph and Jesus probably like Peter and Andrew as well as James (Jacob) and John, formed small partnerships with other locals or went into business for themselves. Biblical testimony calls both Jesus and his father, Joseph, carpenters. In fact, carpentry was more like the 'art of building", and as a result, both in Hebrew and Aramaic, according to Michael Grant, "word with this meaning was used figuratively to signify 'wise man' or 'scholar'." This made sense when one considers what a carpenter did. He planned (drafting/blueprinting), he measured (mathematics), he considered the cost of building (economics), the strength of the wood, metal, or stone with which to build (architectural physics), the foundation (foolish is the man who does not build upon rock), whether or not his partnership could handle the job, the length of time it would take to finish the project, and where to purchase the materials needed. One who would take the same approach to planning his life, its economic, social, and spiritual needs would indeed be considered a wise man. Jesus' teachings constantly show the wisdom needed for many building activities as well as building one's future and where man's real treasure (home) is.

In addition to the simple business of building a house, landscaping the surrounding area, finding both the suitable foundation for the house as well as soil suitable for the garden outside, the places where Jesus did other work of carpentry added to his cultural and spiritual depth (Luke mentions that he grew in both stature and wisdom, and in favor with both God and man: Lk2:52). Since there is no indication that Nazareth offered much work for carpenters at the time of Jesus' life, and only three miles away was the capital of Galilee, Sepphoris, built during Joseph's years and most of the years of Jesus' life by Herod Antipas, the Hellenized son of Herod the Great, whose own massive buildings raised Jerusalem and all of Palestine to a high cultural level, it is obvious that to stay in business Joseph and Jesus would have done the majority of their work in Sepphoris. Carpenters went where the work was as shown by a passage in The Infancy Gospel of Pseudo-Matthew: "Joseph was in Capernaum-by-the-Sea on the job; he was a carpenter. He stayed there for nine months." As in the case of his father's building programs, Antipas also built a Hellenized city which Jews, Samaritans, Galileans, Greeks, Phoenicians, and some Romans would live in in order administer his Tetrarchy. The official language would, of course, been Greek. This cosmopolitan setting gave Jesus, not only the need to learn Greek for his livelihood, but also to learn Greek for any exchange of ideas or theological discussions in which he would participate. The buildings which themselves were the means of spreading Hellenism had to intrigue Jesus: the palace of Antipas and his Hellenized aristocracy, a 4,000 seat theater in which the plays of Sophocles, Aristophanes, Aeschylus, and Euripides were performed in Greek (never was a Greek or Latin literary work translated into Aramaic--culture, linguistically, was a one way street: towards the Greek language), public baths and gymnasia, in which politics and philosophy were discussed, and other places such as the market square (AGORA), pools and fountains, and other buildings for storage of good and administrative functions were all places which had to be built, but also, once built, were avenues to all the locals of the great Greek language and culture. It is impossible to imagine that a person like Jesus would not have relished such an opportunity to reach out to men's souls by means of conversation, by which he himself became a part of the greater Hellenized world. Thus we can answer the bewilderment of some of his Jewish followers: "Where did this man get this wisdom..Is not this the carpenter's son? Is not his mother called Mary...Where then did this man get all this?(Mt 13:54-58"). Luke adds, "And the child grew and became strong, filled with wisdom; and the favor of God was upon him (this was recorded about his life when he was only 12 years old)..."and all who heard him were amazed at his understanding and his answers...(and referring to his teenage years) "And Jesus increased in wisdom and in stature, and in favor with God and man" (Lk 2:40,47,52).

From the secular world we can learn a little more about the houses and accompanying gardens of the Greeks and Romans. Pliny the Elder in his Natural History (HISTORIA NATURALIS) stated:

> Epicurus, that connoisseur in the enjoyments of a life of ease, was the first to lay out a garden at Athens; up to his time it had never been thought of to dwell in the country in the middle of town. At Rome on the other hand the garden constituted of itself the poor man's field, and it was from the garden that the lower classes pro-cured their daily food.l.17

In the Gospel of Philip it is stated that: "Joseph the carpenter (referring to the father of Jesus) planted a garden because he needed wood for his trade." Mencius (c. 379-330BC) tied together the concept of equating the work of a carpenter with the work of a prince in that the same careful planning was needed to make a good physical thing that was needed to make a good government: one made the works of a carpenter the other the works of a sage, one for good furniture and the other for good people and happy people who lived harmoniously. "The compass and square produce perfect circles and squares. By the sages, the human relations are perfectly exhibited [made]"(4.1.2). "When the sages had used the vigor of their eyes, they called in to their aid the compass, the square, the level, and the line; to make things square, round, level, and straight: -- the use of the instruments is inexhaustible...When the prince has no principle by which he examines his administration, and his ministers have no laws by which they keep themselves in the discharge of their duties...(4.1.1). In this Mencius was showing that to build a life or build a happy city, it is important that the very principles and high standards of measuring and accuracy were needed as the carpenter utilized in making sturdy structures or beautiful furniture. In other words, both Jesus and Mencius were telling their hearers that at least take as much time and thought in making your life as a carpenter does in building a house or planning a landscaped garden. Your life is worth immensely more!

Wilhelm Reich used such a comparison for a man who wants to build his own or humanity's future: "You have to give proof the same way a contractor who builds a house has to. The house must be there and it must be livable".1.18 Aristotle stated in his Nicomachean Ethics that the art of carpentry can be a standard by which we can pursue other activities in our lives. Likewise he, speaking about happiness, stated that it was important first to concentrate of the basic structure first and then add furniture. "...implying a rational principle...for we must presumably first sketch it roughly, and then later fill in the details" (Bk I. Ch.7). Do not get loaded down by anxiety about the little things in life, but build the structure of your life of goodness first and the little things will fall in place. He goes on to say that a carpenter and a mathematician will both work with right angles, but one does it to build and the other to know the truth about numbers: they apply what they know in different ways. The man wanting to be complete in virtue and to control the circumstances about him that he has the capability to control for the sake of happiness, must build his life with the same practical and theoretical truth that the carpenter and mathematician or geometrician have.(1097-1098).

Jesus made it very clear that he was trying to give his listeners the words and directions, basically the blue-prints, that were necessary to build a life of wholeness and happiness; but also said the words must be heard, that is, obeyed and followed for there to be any good at all, simply calling Jesus Lord is of no value.

"Why do you call me 'Lord, Lord,' and yet not do as I say? Each
of those who come to me, and hears my reasoned words, and then
does them, I will show you what he is like: he is like a man, who,
building a house, dug and deepened and laid the foundation upon
a rock base. But he who hears me and doesn't do as I say, he is like
a man who simply builds upon the dirt of the earth without any
foundation, and when the river breaks forth upon his house, it will
quickly collapse, and be totally destroyed"(Lk 6:46-49).

It is interesting that the Vedanta-Sutras (III Adhyaya, 4 Pada, 50) also
speak of building one's life as one builds his house: "go build your
house" was the way the Master Teacher was telling his disciple to go get
his own life now and build on it.

Sometime ago I read an article in Bunte, a German magazine, in
which the people were asked what particulars they preferred to have in a
house; which included the location, price, or financing (which, of course
had the higher percentages of preference--these and some others where
included in 18 living-desires). I will present the percentages of just the
first seven of the 28 additional features (total of 46) that were wanted to
show to what lengths people prize their most precious material
possession.

Kamin in Wohnzimmer	(fireplace in the living room)	46%
Wintergarten	(winter garden)	41
Gaestezimmer	(guest room)	34
Separates Gaestebad	(separate guest bathroom)	34
Fussbodenheizung	(floor heating)	33
Sauna	(sauna)	32
Bad/Toilette getrennt	(separate bath & toilet)	32

One interesting desire of 31% of the people was solar heating, even
though it was available in less than one percent of the houses build. In
our very materialistic world these same desires are probably present in all
who seek their dream house; in fact, owning a house in the United States
is often called the "American Dream". The point Jesus, who himself
owned no dwelling at all, was desperately trying to make is that our lives
as a whole are much more important than the house we built or live in.
Building our lives should take preference to all other things, since our

lives are really what we are, and if we expect to be happy that is where we must put our time and effort. As a carpenter Jesus probably helped his father build some houses for people who were not very happy at all and in some ways desperate for some meaning to their lives which they would find in a lovely house. As Jesus encouraged Peter, Andrew, James and John to leave their nets and become fishers of men, he was merely asking them to follow what he had done, leave his carpenter tools to become a builder of men. As a carpenter knew all the rules for building a physical edifice, so Jesus knew the rules, guidelines, and wisdom to help men build their lives. As the man who was not trained to be a carpenter would perhaps throw together some poorly cut boards stuck into the sand near a forceful river, and then brag about how easy or cheaply he was able to build himself a house, so also some people build their lives in the same haphazard way, and wonder why things seem to collapse around them, why nothing goes right, and why they are always unhappy and at the "bottom of the barrel" of life. Sadly this is often the man who is proud of the way he does things, will not listen to others, judges others to be inferior. And laughs at those who "follow all the rules", until his house collapses, and then he blames others or cries "victim". Indeed great will be the collapse of that house, and all will be lost.

In brief, to summarize this section, seven basic steps from a carpenter's vocation:

1. Planning ahead (drafting/blueprinting): Where am I going and where do I want to go in life? What do I need to do to get there? What is my vision? What kind of contribution or vocation do I wish? Single/married, w/wo children, travel, and where to settle?

2. Measuring (mathematics & geometry): Count your days on earth, plan by measured time and enjoy the times and the passages from youth to middle age to maturity and retirement.

3. Cost (economics): Having the money to do and experience what you consider important while both having the basic necessities and assuring a comfortable retirement.

4. Strength of materials (architectural physics): with what am I building in my financial, physical, social and spiritual lives? Are my values durable enough to hold up under crises and broken dreams?

5. Foundation (rocky or sandy): What are my ultimate values in terms of both life and death? Is my universe friendly and do I have a God of gracious love and compassion?

6. Partnership capability: Do I appreciate and properly learn from and use the wisdom of my teachers and mentors? Do I value friendship and have trusting and helpful companions?

7. Finally, do I have the divine virtues to give life and strength to the human virtues and do I make them a priority?

B. PROVERBS, MORAL PRINCIPLES, AND PARABLES

Jesus asked men to follow his teachings, so it is rather natural to see in what forms his teachings were presented. Basically, they were down to earth sayings with a certain point or principle that was highlighted and often came in simple, sometimes delightful and sometimes witty and biting, stories called parables. A man might ask him a question and Jesus would reply, "Let me tell you a story. There was this man who..." Often he was quite blunt with his critics, but his point was always quite clear. He had tolerance, but was quick to criticize those who knowingly hurt others for their own advantage, especially if they themselves posed as teachers of the law of Israel. About his parables, in addition to making obvious references to his carpentry wisdom, he also used the basic illustrations from a common life of family, community, and work. John Sutherland Bonnell writes these words about Jesus' teaching:

> The parables of Jesus give us glimpses of his family life. He told of women grinding wheat with the primitive stones of that early period; of the housewife putting leaven into the meal; of a little boy asking his father for bread, or for an egg, or for a bit of fish. These were the cheapest foods available in Palestine. He tells of a thrifty mother patching old garments, or searching diligently for one small coin

that has been lost. Who can doubt that in some of these parables
we have a portrayal of Mary, his widowed mother? We gain insight
too into those early years through the words of Jesus spoken during
his ministry: "They that are gorgeously appareled dwell in kings'
houses."1.19

One must always remember, however, that these very human stories also
had a heavenly and ultimate meaning to them and offered both advice
and a challenge to reach for heaven and friendship with God, and
therefore were not so easy because they demanded the entire person in
response. A Divine Teacher cannot demand less, and all other pursuits in
life must be put secondary to his way. This was true of all those who
became founders of a religious or philosophical group. Some have
criticized Jesus for telling his followers to put all things and even their
families second to his calling (this did not necessarily mean they had to
leave all or give away all to accept his call to the soul's quest for a
beautiful life here on earth and will be discussed in the next section). But
listen to the same criticism of Mencius and his response:

> Kung-sun Ch'ow said, "Lofty are your principles and admirable,
> but to learn them may well be likened to ascending the heavens,
> something which cannot be reached. Why not adapt your teaching
> so as to cause learners to consider them attainable, and so daily
> exert themselves." Mencius replied, "A great artificer does not, for
> the sake of a stupid workman, alter or do away with the marking
> line. He does not, for the sake of a stupid archer, change his rule
> for drawing the bow."1.20

Jesus once spoke of a banquet that was freely offered to those in the
highways and the byways and were compelled to come in, yet he sent
away one who was not wearing the proper garment for such an occasion.
This seems to infer that the person was an impostor who was coming to
the banquet under false pretenses and for the wrong purposes: the proper
garment referring to his values being expressed in words only and not in
the true substance of a man hungering for righteousness. Epictetus
attacked some of the superficial philosophers of his day for much the
same reason--a lack of genuine hunger for truth and virtue, ones who
simply wanted to speak the words of piety.

But you publish and divulge them out of time, out of place, without
sacrifices, without purity; you have not the garments which the hier-
ophant ought to have...nor have you purified yourself as he has: but
you have committed to memory the words only, and you say:
"Sacred are the words by themselves. (Discourses, Book
III, Chapter21)

When Jesus spoke he lamented when those about him "hear, but do not
hear", for in all cases to the larger groups he sought simplicity and true
understanding that they might take his message to heart and refocus the
meaning and direction of their lives.

C. JESUS' LIFE EXAMPLE

The Gospel of John says that Jesus was the LOGOS (Word or
Rational Expression) of God, and that could be through both his verbal
teachings and his life example: to make audible and visible the thinking
of God was his mission. The sheer depth and beauty of his life that
brought acceptance and forgiveness to the widest range of people that
any holy man every brought forth glowed with graciousness and love. He
had absolutely no prejudices at all; he was no respector of class, race,
gender, nationality, wealth or poverty, vocation, heath, or education.
While other religious leaders, with the exceptions of Siddhartha Gotema
and Mo Tzu, usually one saw obvious limitations to full acceptance
because of a caste system, a racial system, a system of exile for the
unhealthy, a system of purity or sacramental or ritual separation, or a
national system. But in his life Jesus never saw anyone, except the
vicious, proud, and evil ones, that repulsed him in any way. In the Gospel
of Matthew from the Eighth and Ninth Chapters one sees the sparkling
love of Jesus for all people to whom he ministered: 8:14 a leper (who
was considered by his society as so unclean than he was forbidden to
enter the city and had to shout to passers-by that he was unclean); 8:5-13
he helped a dear servant of a Roman centurion (the hated enemy and
oppressors of Israel); 8:14-17 he cared for Peter's mother-in-law; 8:23-27
he comforted his disciples in a storm; 8:28-34 he ministered to two
demoniac Greeks from Gadara; 9:1-8 he ministered to a paralytic; 9:9 he

called for Matthew, despised tax collector for Rome; 10:2-4 he chose a variety of people for his disciples; 9:10-13 he socialized with those despised by the "good" people--tax collectors and people who did not keep the law, some of whom were probably women who sold their bodies willingly for money; 9:14-17 he broke traditional laws (Sabbath) and social molds in order to establish a new way of acting (he wants new ways not to be poured into old wineskins or sewed on old garments); 9:18-26 he cared for a local ruler's daughter and an "unclean" woman; 9:27-31 he ministered to two blind men and restored them to usefulness; and 9:32-34 he cared for a dumb demoniac. One of the Christian Church's failures throughout history has been its inclination to judge others who did not follow "proper" rituals, "proper" doctrines, and lived outside of "orthodoxy's" purity laws--often even inflicting death upon the people, when shame and prison did not work. The Church certainly did not learn much from Jesus in such matters, and the main reason for this book is that both Christians and non-Christians can learn from Jesus as well as the other divine teachers. By presenting them, I am trying to present the "divine" way or path that leads to a life more abundant. To imitate Jesus, as much as possible, is to show that we have learned something from The Teacher, and in so doing, not only make other people's lives more beautiful but lift up our own towards God's beauty where alone there can be a true wholeness and happiness. For when Jesus says "Follow me" he meant to give us a new perspective, a new mind-set, towards how to live, that would involve the total complex of the human personality, resulting in a new creation of a richly satisfying wisdom, courage, love, a sense of justice, control of the emotions, faith and hope. One can be that flower that brings tenderness and beauty into the heart of another whoever that person may be. One can be a lighted candle to one who has lived his life as though there were only gloomy and hopeless darkness. Why be an arrogant judge of others when one can bring the other person a flower or a light that lifts up his spirit to the Eternal One? When the people questioned Jesus as to what and who he was, he directed them to the way he worked with people "My works bear witness to Me"(J 10:25). When Jesus said that we should believe in him, that meant that his words and his life were to lead us into actually following his example. Otherwise we do not harmonize our lives and both appear as hypocrites to others and deprive ourselves of the virtues upon which spiritual happiness depends. Word and Deed must harmonize. Plato, in the Laches, puts into the mouth of Laches: "But a man whose actions do not agree with his words is an annoyance to me, and the better he speaks the more I hate him"(Laches 188e). J.S. Bonnell wrote of Jesus:

> He was always in command of himself and of every situation. He was never embarrassed or taken by surprise, always poised and self-possessed. He was never in haste...never jealous or impatient with anyone. As he moved among men and women exercising his ministry of redemption and healing, he brought to them unfailing-ly a sense of God's presence and power.1.21

Jesus says, "Follow me...you are the light of the world." It has been said many times that the light that shines the brightest is the one that is strongest at its source.

IV.   LEVELS OF DISCIPLESHIP

Often when people read the teachings of Jesus they feel that he is asking them for the impossible: "leave all and follow me", "sell all that you have and follow me", "when one asks for your coat, give him your overcoat also", "if a man hits you, turn to him the other cheek also", and many more such statements. Most religious movements have different levels of commitment for different groups of followers: Buddhists have different commands for their monks than for the general believer, and different statutes for the men than the women; Hindus have four different castes with differing obligations--the Brahmin is called in a different way than a warrior or a "non-touchable"; and Christian monks, nuns, priests and clergy have different standards of behavior than the average believer. Jesus seemed to make much greater demands on those who wanted to follow him as a member of the inner circle (a disciple) than he had for other believers like Mary, Martha, and Lazarus, and even they perhaps a little different than the general believers. The most "hard sayings" are directed towards his disciples, and the average Christian should not feel that he is a lesser Christian because he does not sell all that he has and become a clergyman--Jesus and the disciples could not have been supported in their ministry unless some, like Mary and Martha, had dwellings to accept him and money to support him. "And the twelve were accompanying him, and also some women who had been cured of evil spirits and physical infirmities: Mary, called Magdalene, from whom seven demons had gone out, and Joanna, the wife of Chuza, Herod's steward, and Susanna, and many others, who provided for them [Jesus and the disciples] from their own money [possessions]. They did not leave all to follow him, but they shared their possessions to help make his mission possible. There are different levels of commitment. In the teachings of Jesus that will appear in the following pages of this book, this distinction should be made by the reader. The main backbone of goodness, generosity, love, justice, non-aggressiveness, kindness, trust, faith and hope are the general foundation upon which to build a life of virtue and happiness for all those who call Jesus, "Lord". Sincerity, honesty, and loving kindness must constitute all one's actions and thoughts or else the confession of faith means absolutely nothing. To shout "I am born again, are you saved?"..."Jesus is my Savior, hallelujah."...or say the Apostles Creed in church, are not, in themselves indicative that you are a follower of Jesus on any level. Jesus warns his hears not to make empty statements of faith if there is no functioning substance of a man truly committed to the Way of Heaven, the Father's Will.

> Not everyone who says to me, 'Lord, Lord', will enter the kingdom
> of heaven, but he who actualizes in deeds the will of my Heavenly
> Father. On that day many will say to me, 'Lord, Lord, did we not
> by means of your name prophesy, and by means of your name cast
> out demons, and do many other great things by your name?' And,
> at that time, I will declare to them, 'Never did I know you; away
> from me, you are evildoers.(Mt 7:21-23)

These people put on a show about being Christians, but they do not have the substance of spirit that puts into effect the day by day love and kindness which Jesus showed us in his own life. At any level of a Christian's calling, the basics of the spirit of Jesus are necessary, and that is what is being addressed in this book. While not all the teachings of Jesus are totally applicable to all who love him, the spirit in which they are molded is the necessary substance and foundation upon which virtue, wholeness, and happiness will be built. Listen to, feel the spirit, and seek the likeness of the proclamation of Jesus in both his teachings and his life, and then build your house.

CHAPTER TWO

THE GOOD EARTH

GOD'S BEAUTIFUL GIFT

I. JESUS' TEACHINGS

Often in the teachings of the transcendental religions where man's final home is beyond his earthly experience, the life in the body is unfortunately seen as being a type of hindrance to the ultimate good, and therefore is, not only unappreciated, but seen as something miserable or downright evil. While this is most common in the Indian based faiths, it also is not uncommon in Christianity, a view which is certainly contrary to the life and teachings of Jesus. The earthly life is good and beautiful, a marvelous and miraculous gift, that is to be lived to its fullest with joy being felt in all the "fleshly" experiences that come to us by "being in the body." Yes, in Jesus' teachings it is always secondary to eternity, but it is always a good. It is sad to hear people singing hymns about the miseries of "this vale of tears" for it shows a basic and brutal ingratitude towards the Creator for giving us this "wonder of life on earth". Jesus himself displayed a joy of living, eating, drinking, attending suppers and banquets with both those of high status in the community and those of lower status, and in the Garden of Gethsemane he is not very anxious to leave this life, only consenting to his immanent death after a long prayer session in which he gave up his will to live on earth for the sake of the will of his Father in Heaven. He wept when he heard that his friend Lazarus had died, and mourned and ministered to others who faced the loss of loved ones. He wanted the good earthly life for those who were driven down: "blessed are the meek for they shall inherit the earth". He taught his disciples to pray for daily bread and to have the spirit to live on earth as the angels do in heaven. Did not he teach that God also cares for other beings with less intellectual stature than mankind? God cares about the sparrows and the ravens, he beautified the earth with grass and lilies, and even has a knowledge of the number of hairs on our heads. The body is more sacred than the covenantal laws of his people (he healed sick and picked grain to eat on the Sabbath). The Fourth Gospel even declared that there is no evil at all in the "flesh", for he proclaimed that the LOGOS of God became flesh. To be human and to be flesh does not necessitate one's doing evil. The followers of Jesus are to imitate him in his most joyous moments as well as his sorrowful moments when he is called to the duty of physical sacrifice. His followers, to fully appreciate him, will do well to celebrate weddings, have banquets, enjoy friendships, family, and fellowship with others. The Passover was celebrated by Jesus (a celebration of a purely earthly liberation from slavery) with singing and wine. The wedding of Cana probably lasted a few days, maybe even a week, and when they ran completely out of wine, he even used his spiritual powers to created more--not only more but six large stone jars, each containing between 20 and 30 gallons; and this after the people already were well drunk, for it was a time of celebration. Jesus, a prude about enjoying the material life?--never! "When the wine ran out...Jesus said to them 'Fill the jars with water.' And they filled them to the brim...When the steward of the feast tasted the water now become wine...the steward of the feast called the bridegroom and said to him. 'Every man serves the good wine first; and when men have well drunk, then the poor wine; but you have kept the good until now.'(J 2:1-10)" The author of the Gospel calls this a sign given by Jesus, not only that he has control over material things, but that material things in abundance can be enjoyed at a feast. It is no wonder that his critics complained that he enjoyed things too much to be a prophet like John the Baptist, for Jesus came eating and drinking and enjoying feasts and celebrations and even used his miracle energy to lengthen and deepen the celebration, and in doing such was not very "discriminating" in the company with which he choose to keep and celebrate. He taught us to love this life, enjoy this life, and celebrate it with others.

II. CONCURRENCE

   In the Hebrew book of Genesis, the very first thing that is declared is
that material life is good, both for all the living creatures as well as
mankind; and that man, in some way, was a replica of God himself. "And
God saw everything that he had made, and it was very good."
   In the creation and flood story of Ovid, man was made of clay that, by
means of the gift of breath, was brought to life; and after the devastation
of the flood, man was again recreated, but this time with more durability,
as both male and female were made from stones (Ovid: Deucalion and
Pyrrha 358-395). Again it was by the good will and blessing of heaven
that man was given life, and it was good.
   From Plato's delightful creation story, perhaps the most beautiful one
ever written, I will present these quotations:

   Every one will see that he [God] must have looked to the eternal;
   for the world is the fairest of creations and he [God] is the best of
   causes. And having been created in this way, the world has been
   framed in the likeness of that which is apprehended by reason and
   mind and is unchangeable, and must therefore of necessity, if this
   is admitted, be a copy of something [eternal and perfect] (Timaeus
   29a).

   Let me tell you then why the Creator made this world of generation.
   He was Good, and the Good can never have any jealousy of anything. And being free from jealousy, he desired that all things
   be as much like himself as they could be. This is in the truest sense
   the origin of creation and of the world (KOSMOS),...God desired
   that all things should be good and nothing bad, so far as this was
   attainable (Timaeus 30b).

   When the Father and Creator saw the creature [the living world--
   cosmos] which he had made moving and living, the created image
   of the eternal...he rejoiced, and in his joy determined to make the
   copy still more like the original; as this was eternal, he sought to
   make the universe (cosmos) eternal, so far as might be (Timaeus
   37d).

The Maker and Father of the universe was good, and not envious in any way, and decided to share existence by creating a beautiful universe in the empty space and fill it with movement and life of all kinds. He wanted it to be as perfect as possible and therefore worked from a pattern of eternal perfection (perhaps a blueprint in his mind). God used this model of eternal perfection by which to construct a material universe, which Plato called the cosmos (KOSMOS), which means the beautifully ordered one (hence our word cosmetics which give beauty and order to one's face). God gave this beautifully ordered universe movement and life (soul), and directed its movements in harmony that all might see His own beauty in the beauty of the cosmos, and he did it for the enjoyment that mankind might have, from his gracious goodness and care, the experience of life. The creation, then, was a loving and generous gift of a good and non-envious God, who delighted in sharing life with all his creatures. Man was implanted with a soul that sought to enjoy the beauties of the creation and with a longing for the Eternal Beauty, God himself, the true Father and Maker of all, who rejoiced in man's existence and in his longing for Him.

Sophocles has a Chorus in his Antigone sing the praises of the created man:

> But surpassing all [in nature] in wisdom and in art,
> Superior shines inventive man...
> On him, unwearied Earth, with lavish hand,
> Immortal goddess! All her bounty pours;...
> Man crowned with science, explores all
> With depth of thought profound (291ff).

A messenger declares "Now all is gone: when pleasure is no more, man then is but an animated corpse, nor can he be said to live." (Antigone 1052ff).

Goethe begins the Second Part of his Faust with a lovely section called "A Pleasant Landscape" which describes the beauty and loveliness of both the night and the new day which follows. He speaks of the twilight which gently closes the day by bringing with it the sweet fragrance that softly whispers peace...and rocks the heartfelt concerns to a childlike rest, closing softly the eyelids, gates of daylight. The stars begin to appear, some brightly, others dimly, and with them and their gleams from afar appear their reflections that glitter upon the lakes. While man is enjoying his deepest rest, the moon lights up the heavens and manifests its full majesty. Daybreak approaches and man, who is refreshed anew, sees the beauty of the sunrise, and this new fresh adorning of nature 'wraps me round with gladness thrilling'. All earth comes alive and even the deepest gorges are given the light from heaven to awaken the flowers of earth: 'all around me is a Paradise appearing'. He feels a hope that is supreme and transcending so that he experiences a great flame with wonder burning within, calling out to it "embrace me", viewing it all with rapture growing in amazement. He views with joy the many-colored rainbow as it slowly changes and mirrors human goals and activities: "Think, and more clearly will you grasp it, seeing life is but light in many-hued reflection". What loveliness of thought Goethe has given us! Let us be absorbed therein!

Cicero, who himself thoroughly enjoyed banquets and the fellowship of friends declared that all the good things should be enjoyed, as long as they do not conflict with goodness itself (Discussions at Tusculum V.15:43-44). A person seeking wholeness must begin with the basic thought that his own existence and the creation of the world for his benefit are good and are to be experienced and enjoyed. Unless this attitude of gratefulness for such a life is felt deeply, then the reader will have little chance of mounting the first step to wholeness which begins in Chapter Four.

III. THE GOOD EARTH TO BE SHARED

While it is quite obvious that among humans each needs his own space, freedom, and dignity, it is less so among men that they should share the earth with God's other creatures--which was implied by Jesus' referring to the care God took for the welfare of the ravens and sparrows and even the plant life of grass and lilies. Some religions even feel that they are human beings in the process of developing worthy karma through the system of a series of reincarnations, such as the Hindus, who respect the animals as they would a grandparent or relative. Such is much to their credit, as credit also is to be given to the Buddhists, as many of them feel it is wrong to "kill any living being." Siddhartha and Francis of Assisi are truly the bright lights of humanity in terms of seeking to share the earth with God's other creatures with "soul". It is not only man's selfish overpopulation of the globe that poisons the land, the rivers and the oceans off of or out of which the animals receive their substance of nourishment to survive, but his arrogant and condescending attitude towards them by which he uses them for deadly experiments for the sake of an expensive perfume or worse to kill them as a "sport". Ike Nwankwo, a rookie tryout for the Cleveland Cavaliers basketball team, who had played the previous year in the pro league of Turkey, told how repulsed he was when a goat, he thought was a mascot, was slaughtered before his eyes, and the players put its blood on their heads for good luck. He refused to do it, and stated "They looked at me as if I were crazy"(LAT 10/17/2002). Newsweek Magazine using information provided by the Humane Society of the United States told of an artificial and cruel "hunting-ranch industry" in which animals attained from zoos, private collectors and exotic breeders were fenced in and gunned down by "gamesmen" (some game) for prices ranging from $800 for a Zebra to $20,000 for a rhinoceros. Christianity has not yet very well addressed this issue, this crime of selfish arrogance against the animal world. Some of the ancients of the West and the religions of the East can be our teachers--let us beware that we hear but do not hear. The Jainist, Akaranga Sutra 1.3.2.3, declared:

> Killing (animals) he thinks good sport,
> And derives mirth from it;
> Away with that fool's company,
> He increases his own unrighteousness.2.1

Dolphins in antiquity were loved and honored as a friendly and helpful mate to mankind and their many attempts at saving drowning humans were so well known that it was almost proverbial to speak of them as man's friend at sea. Plato puts into Socrates' mouth these words while speaking to Glaucon: "Then we, also, must swim and try to escape out of the sea of argument in the hope that either some dolphin will take us on its back or some other desperate rescue"(Republic V.453d). In the mythology of many ancients the progenitor of a hero race himself is often cared for and fed by animals. This is not so absurd as some might think, for today we find one species of animal nursing an infant of another animal, and most people in America witnessed via television an ape who cuddled a human child that fell several feet to a hard surface and lay unconscious in the bottom of the area set aside for apes in the zoo. He was absolutely tender with the child and turned him over to the zoo keeper. Jacob Grimm in his massive study entitled Teutonic Mythology stated:

> A widely prevalent mark of the hero race is their being suckled
> by beasts, or fed by birds. A hind offers her milk to Siguror
> when exposed, Vilk.saga 142; a she-wolf gives suck to the
> infant Dieterich (like Romulus and Remus) together with her four
> blind whelps, hence his name of Wolfdieterich...The Servian hero
> Milosh Kosbilitch was suckled by a mare...in distress and danger
> also, swans, ravens, wolves, stags, bears and lions will join the
> heros.2.2

Pliny the Elder, in praise of the loyalty of dogs mentions several occasions, some during his own life time, when dogs risked their own lives in defense of their masters or died trying to save them from a hopeless situation:

> A dog to which Darius gives the name of Hyrcanus, upon the fun-
> eral pile of King Lysimachus being lighted, threw itself into the
> flames, and the dog of King Hiero did the same. Philistus also gives
> a similar account of Pyrrhus, the dog of the tyrant Gelon...Among
> ourselves Volcatius...as he was riding on his Asturian jennet
> towards evening from his country-house was attacked by a robber
> and was only saved by his dog...(about another dog who was howl-
> ing next to his dead master) when some one threw a piece of bread
> to it the animal carried it to the mouth of its master...the dog swam
> into the river (his dead master had been dumped into it) and endea-
> vored to raise it out of the water.2.3

> There is a very famous story about an eagle at the city of Sestos.
> Having been reared by a little girl, it used to testify its gratitude
> for her kindness, first by bringing her birds, and in due time
> various kinds of prey: (she died as a child and her body was
> in the process of being burned)...and the bird threw itself on the
> lighted pile and was consumed by the fire (in an obvious attempt
> at rescue despite the flames).2.4

Pliny the Younger in his letter to Caninius Rufus tells the story of a dolphin that came to shore and entertained the children there, and eventually letting them swim with him and even touched and stroked it. One boy in particular formed a friendship with the dolphin and even mounted it, and one day the dolphin took him out further into the sea and then returned him to shore in the company of another dolphin:

> ...the boy, in particular, who first made the experiment, swam by the side of him, and leaping upon his back, was carried to and fro in that manner: he fancies the dolphin knows and is fond of him, and he returns its fondness...All the magistrates round the country flocked hither to view this sight, the entertainment of whom upon their arrival...was an additional expense [when Roman officials came to a town, the town had to feed and shelter them at the town's expense]...which this little community could ill afford. It was thought proper therefore to remove the occasion of this concourse, by privately killing the poor dolphin. And now, how will your genius adorn and heighten this moving story! Though, indeed, it does not require any fictitious embellishments.2.5

When King Asoka (274-232BC) was converted to Buddhism he issued many edicts to try to bring his kingdom up to the Buddhist ethical standards. Rock Edict I reads:

> Many hundred of thousands living creatures were formerly slaughtered every day for curries in the kitchens of His Majesty. At present, when this edict on Dharma is inscribed, only three living creatures are killed daily, two peacocks and a deer, and the deer is not slaughtered regularly. In the future, not even these three animals shall be slaughtered.

Pillar Edict V stated:

> Twenty-six years after my coronation I declared that the following animals were not to be killed: parrots, mynas, the aruna, ruddy geese, the nandimukha, pigeons, bats, queen ants, terrapins, boneless fish,...(many more animals including she-goats, ewes, sows,

cocks, et cetera are mention)...Living animals must not be fed to other animals.

<u>Immanuel</u> <u>Kant</u> (1724-1804AD) in his <u>Vorlesungen</u> <u>ueber</u> <u>Moralphilosophie</u>: <u>Ethica</u> (in the section titled <u>Von</u> <u>den</u> <u>Plichten</u> <u>gegen</u> <u>Thiere</u> <u>und</u> <u>Geister</u>) takes an indirect approach in his judgment of man's neglect of duty to animals, for he feels that animals are to be respected indirectly because of the human traits which they exemplify. But even this indirect duty of man is a powerful teaching of human morals towards animals, and it is much more as one can see from his words.

> We have towards the animals directly no duties, but the duties to-
> wards the animals are indirect duties toward mankind. Because
> the animals are relatives (relative to man -- 'analogon')of mankind,
> we observe our duties towards mankind, when we also observe our
> duties to these same relatives (analoga), and by means of such duties
> to these same animals we carry out our duties to mankind. For ex-
> ample, when a dog has long and faithfully served his master, in that
> very manner it is an analogy of having his rights to wages; and on
> account of that very service I must reward the dog, even if he no
> longer can serve, and maintain him until the end; therewith I have
> then observed my duty to humankind...Likewise if someone shoots
> dead his dog, because he cannot serve him anymore, he acts not at
> all against his duty towards the dog, because the dog cannot play
> judge, he only harms, through such action, the affability (Leutseel-
> igkeit) and humanness in himself, which he in regard to his duty to
> humanity should exercise. Therewith man should not destroy, rather
> he ought to practice goodness towards the animals. For a man who
> readily practices such cruelty towards animals, is also in the same
> way hardened against mankind. Man can already know the human
> heart of another as he considers his actions towards animals.(tr.JDE)
> 2.6

Kant then goes on to refer to a cooper engraving of Hogarth that pictures the stages in which a child, from abusing a dog or a cat escalates, with the years, his type of cruelties until he ends up murdering someone. He continues by pointing out the tenderness of animals towards their young, yes, even the wolf. Man would do well, said Kant, to acknowledge that if we have genuine feels of kindness for the animals, we also will have similar feelings towards other humans. Kant, then, develops here two themes: how we treat animals is the way we treat human beings, although it is indirectly; and how we treat animals is how we develop our own virtue and dignity as human beings. One then easily concludes that man harms himself spiritually and psychologically when he harms an animal, and this harm deposits nourishment to his evil nature and thereby excludes him from moral goodness and with that eliminates any chance for personal happiness. We are all familiar with John Donne's statement that no man is an island, Kant is telling us that no animal (man is one species of animal) is an island. When an animal dies, the bell tolls for mankind also.

<u>Wilhelm</u> <u>Reich</u> in his book <u>Listen, Little Man</u> says this to the "little man":

> You remember the beautiful afternoon when, this time as a woods-
> man, you came to my cabin, looking for work? My puppy dog
> sniffed you and joyfully jumped up at you. You recognized him as
> the pup of a splendid hound. You said: "Why don't you put him on
> the chain, so he gets vicious? This dog is much too friendly." I
> said: "I don't want him to be a vicious dog on the chain. I don't like
> vicious dogs." My dear little woodsman, I have far more enemies
> in this world than you [Reich speaks quite truly here], but I still pre-
> fer the kindly dog who is friendly with everyone.2.7

While man has never had a state of perfect harmony either with his fellowman or his fellow creatures, the man who in his own life can live such with other men and the animals will be a good man who will experience a wholeness and happiness which the man at odds and in conflict with all other creatures can never have--because he can not share. It is a common phrase that "man's best friend is his dog", and while that may convey a good and positive statement, it is limited, because there are many animals that have the capacity to share affection with human beings, as I have tried to show above. Man, being the more intelligent and the more able to use power, is therefore the one obligated to initiate friendship with the animals. It is his duty as a fellow creature of God to share the earth and his personal care with the animals. In 1983 the Los Angeles Times (10/04/1983) reported that a man in North

Carolina who had tried to save his son from drowning off of the beach noticed a group of porpoises gathered around the boy and together pushed his body right up to the beach. The report was confirmed by several witnesses. Just last year a cockatoo bird was killed trying to defend his owner from two murderers, and while it was unsuccessful in the defense of his master, he drew enough blood from both of the assailants that by means of DNA both were caught for trial and were prosecuted. The prosecutor, George West, stated that "Bird (the name given to the cockatoo) was valiant." (LAT 9/05/2002).

IV.   HONORING WORK AND INDUSTRY

Work is really honoring our obligation in life to make life better for ourselves and others, and is thereby a noble enterprise which takes many different forms according to the needs of society as a whole. Jesus as a carpenter certainly was acquainted with work, as was his father. His parables constantly refer to people who are working: a man went out to sow some seed; a man went to build a tower; the shepherd who cares for his sheep; the woman who sews, grinds, cleans, and bakes; the man who plants a tree; the teachers who teach; the fishermen who fish; even the tax collectors and foreign soldiers; a merchant in search for pearls; a scribe; a man who builds a house upon a rock; a servant in charge of his master's household duties; and the trader of the 'five talents". Indeed almost every story tells of the person's vocation, and many such as used in the comparison of the kingdom of earth and the kingdom of heaven. To have a vocation and do something for the benefit of others was simply accepted by all, even the king had to oversee and administer his kingdom, and the owner of a vineyard had to teach and monitor his workers. Work is part of the good life which brings personal value and wholeness, and those who flee it will lose themselves in obscurity and emptiness. Most of the world's great religious teachers and leaders had manual vocations at one time in their lives: Jesus as a carpenter, Peter and Andrew as fishermen, Confucius was a granary clerk, Paul of Tarsus was a tentmaker, Gandhi was a spinner, Schweitzer a physician, Moses was a shepherd for his father-in-law (Jethro), and many others worked in executive and leadership positions like teachers and tax-collectors. Among the Greek gods Hephaestus was the true working man, the smith.

In Germanic stories the hero of the working man was Walter der Schmied. Luther was the first one to refer to the common man as having a vocation (vocatio in Latin means a 'calling')--before him a 'calling' was just for the royalty and priesthood, for Luther knew that every working man was a dignified and called servant of God. Paul Tillich reflects his Lutheran background when he stated in his Theology of Culture:

> The universe is God's sanctuary. Every work day is a day of the Lord, every supper a Lord's supper, every work the fulfillment of a divine task, every joy a joy in God. In all preliminary concerns, ultimate concern is present, consecrating them. Essentially the religious and the secular are not separate realms. Rather they are within each other.2.8

In becoming whole a person needs to see the beauty of his working and what it means for himself and his community. Industry is another element in the foundation upon which a person will build his seven steps to wholeness and happiness.

V.   PHYSICAL PLEASURES ARE TO BE ENJOYED

One of the common misconceptions is that if you are religious then you will not have any "fun" in life, and, unfortunately, religion itself is often to blame for such a distortion. Above we have seen how Jesus himself enjoyed people, banquets, fellowship, wine and undoubtedly many other of the pleasures that are available to us in this life. Even in my own youth I was taught about all the evils of any kind of dancing, and playing cards was also quite suspect. Some had guilt feelings about having to work on Sunday, and, of course, in America all the statues of people must have a fig leaf covering the sex of the symbolized being. Of course that was in keeping with the centuries long "sex is ugly" doctrine of the church, and even coition for the sake of propagation was deemed evil if the participants found some pleasure in the act. Of course, much of it was sheer hypocrisy by the church: earthly wealth is not to be sought they taught while bringing in massive amounts of money through indulgences (which people gladly paid, even if their children--no birth control permitted either--were not well fed, because their consciences had been poisoned with guilt and their hearts filled with fear of hell). Likewise, sex was seen as detrimental to salvation, and chastity was the more secure way to attain heaven. From Gregory the Great's letter to Augustine (the British Augustine in the years surrounding 600AD) with so many sexual prohibitions that the Saxon kings of England postponed their conversion for a couple of generations. This can be read in Bede's A History of the English Church and People where it is clearly declared that sexual mating is such a contaminate that the person should go through rites of cleansing before he can enter the church after sexual intercourse.

It was always the ancient Roman usage for such a man to seek purification, and out of reverence to refrain awhile from entering a holy place. In making this observation, we do not condemn marriage itself, but since lawful intercourse must be accompanied by bodily pleasure, it is fitting to refrain from entering a holy place, since desire itself is not blameless....
In saying this, he does not term the union of married people iniquity, but the pleasures of such union. For there are many things that are lawful and legitimate, and yet in the doing of them we are to some extent contaminated...
Lawful intercourse should be for the procreation of offspring, and not for mere pleasure; to obtain children, and not to satisfy lust. But if any man is not moved by a desire for pleasure, but only by a desire for children, he is to be left to his own judgement either as to entering church, or to receiving the Communion of the Body and Blood of our Lord.2.9

Pope Gregory would probably have even shamed the Puritans and Queen Victoria herself, although it seems as English people they heard the Pope only too well. Meanwhile the monasteries and convents were filled with sexual activities which were reaping havoc upon the inner structure of e church (its very soul was being contaminated), and at the Vatican things were not any better. As early as the reign of Commodus (180-192AD) Hyacinthus was saving 'exposed' female infants who probably would have been adopted (exposure often was a form of an adoption system, as certain places were designated and those wanting a child would frequent those places, sometimes staying there until a child was offered), and Hyacinthus, the Christian, raised the little girls--OK so far--but then when they reached maturity (about 12 or 13) they would be sold to either harems or brothels. The history of the Papacy, and the way it was purchased throughout the ages and its accompanying nepotism was bad enough, but when sexual corruption entered it from 440AD (during Pope Sixtus III) onwards, new lows in morality became very common in the history of the church. Nigel Cawthorne's book Sex Lives of the Popes tells the long sad history of such corruption. But even worse was the pious declarations that made all the sincere believers carry a tragic burden of guilt with them in their lives for merely enjoying the natural pleasure experienced in sexual activity that God built into our bodies for our benefit. Bernard of Clairvaux, not only despised himself--so badly was his conscience manipulated--but taught others to despise themselves also. "Humility is that thorough self-examination which makes a man contemptible in his own sight" he declares in the first chapter of his book The Steps of Humility.

Paul Tabori is correct in claiming that many have rebelled against the church for this very reason, and, unfortunately gone to the opposite extreme, He stated: "The religious cults of the ancient world were usually for the freedom of physical pleasures. But Christianity and Buddhism are definitely ascetic faiths. For them the whole subject of sex is a cause of suspicion and danger...the main reaction was that of protest."2.10

Today, as we enter the 21st Century, we know that those "wet dreams" that men have, commonly called nocturnal emissions (of semen), in which an ejaculation of semen takes place while a man is sleeping, are the body's normal reaction to a build up of unused semen in the system. A man who is sexually active or masturbates will not experience them as such, but pious monks and others who feel that such activities are in some way sinful (it is still taught in some churches that masturbation is a "grave" sin) have battled with the guilt that some of the Church Fathers instilled in their consciences. John Cassian (360-435AD and sainted by the Church) in his work On The Eight Vices instills guilt in the sensitive men with these words:

A sign that we have acquired this virtue perfectly is that our soul ignores those images which the defiled fantasy produces during sleep; for even if the production of such images is not a sin, never-theless it is a sign that the soul is ill and has not been freed from passion. We should therefore regard the defiled fantasies that arise during sleep as proof of previous indolence and weakness still existing in us, since the emission which takes place while we are relaxed in sleep reveals the sickness that lies hidden in our souls.2.11

Gandhi in his wisdom desired that man would develop a strong self-control over all of his desires, for this liberates him to rise to greater spiritual heights; yet he also knows that what is a natural desire is more fulfilling in the body than just the thought of it.

It is better to enjoy through the body than to be enjoying the thought of it. It is good to disapprove of sensual desires as soon as they arise in the mind and try to keep them down, but if for want of physical enjoyment the mind wallows in thoughts of enjoyment then it is legitimate to satisfy the hunger of the body. About this I have no doubt...As long as you derive inner help and comfort from anything, you should keep it. If you were to give it up in a mood of self-sacrifice or out of a stern sense of duty, you would continue to want it back, and that unsatisfied want would make trouble for you.2.12

Life in the body on earth is a good life, given by God as a gracious gift to us that we can see his goodness for us. In moderation, all that is good is to be enjoyed. Because of the great stress on karma within the Hindu system, sometimes in seeking a better and higher station in the next incarnation the devout person becomes so spiritual that he can not enjoy this life nor is he sometimes acting responsible in terms of earthly duties. However, within the liberality of the Hindu faith, many "heresies" (that is, teachings that do not agree with the mainstream) arise, without persecution, to bring teachings for certain needs that are neglected by the more accepted traditional views. One such group is the Carvaka system of thought which strives for material development and the using of all material resources for man's bodily comfort as he goes through his earthly journey. It also lays stress on one's emotional and economic well-being and the subsequent development of a higher culture by which man's image as a fleshly being is held in higher honor. This more "balanced life" is called MOKSA.

Carl R. Rogers agrees with and quotes Maslow's statement that:

> Self-actualized people have a wonderful capacity to appreciate again and again, freshly and naively, the basic goods of life with awe, pleasure, wonder, and even ecstasy, however stale these experiences may be for other people.2.13

In my youth, other than a good night's sleep, my greatest bodily pleasure came from playing sports, and I tried most all of them. To be utterly exhausted after a 200 meter dash (220 yards in my day), a basketball game, or a long swim (I foolishly swam from Balboa (CA) to the island by myself once--got a cramp at the half way mark and had to hold onto a life-buoy for about 30 minutes--I wasn't a brilliant kid, but I had fun) was, for me, a tremendous physical pleasure and sports remained the one great bodily pleasure for many years. But I never became a connoisseur of the palatal pleasures. In fact sometimes I envy the lovers of wine like Silenus in Euripides' The Cyclopes who happily proclaimed: "For if a man rejoice not in his drinking, he is mad; for in drinking there is love with all its frolic, and dancing withal, and oblivion of woe (180ff)". But, I did, finally reach the mental pleasures (energy and food always come in life before wisdom arrives). Give me my moments of the lofty soul of Bach, the gentle beauty of Mozart, the deep soul-searching of Beethoven and a night reading a Platonic dialogue and I thank God for the pleasure of the five senses of my body as well as the rational sense of the soul. Socrates was told by the Delphic oracle "Nothing too much". But great pleasure, as a relief from the seriousness of adulthood, is a gift. I like the words with which Joseph Campbell ended a lecture called "The Historical Development of Mythology":

> From the position of secular man (Homo sapiens--wise man), then, we are to enter the play sphere of the festival, acquiescing in a game of belief, where fun, joy, and rapture rule in ascending series. The laws of life in time and space---will dissolve...we are to carry to the point of view and spirit of man the player (Homo ludens--playing

man) back into life: as in the play of children, where,..the sheer
delight of play, transubstantiates the world.2.14

Excess in anything is self defeating, even natural pleasures, as Socrates
said: "Nothing in excess". Men and women who commit adultery for the
sake of pleasure and fun are putting their desires for pleasure above their
oaths of fidelity, that is, if such oaths were part of the marriage
agreement. Fraud, lies, dishonesty towards a loved one is always a
negative step in one's quest for wholeness and happiness. Any form of
consenting and voluntary sexual relations between adults can be most
pleasurable -- if it does not involve using or misleading the partner or the
betrayal of an oath or trust of a beloved. Likewise, in terms of excess,
one should ask himself if he is not edging towards an addiction to the
passions that overthrow one's reason and psychological balance of mind
and soul. "Yes, that's correct -- 20,000 different ladies. At my age that
equals out to having sex with 1.2 (different) women a day, every day
since I was 15." (Words of Wilt Chamberlain: Newsweek 11/11/1991).
This, even with consenting partners, to me at least, seems to be a sign of
addiction to that particular physical pleasure. Also pleasures at the
expense of the young, especially when a certain trust is betrayed, is a
very unhealthy thing, and for the young often a planting of shame and
psychological degrading: "Panel Finds Priest Sexually Abused 34 Boys
at Seminary" (LAT 11/30/93). And, of course, the worst of all sexual
sins, is that of forced sexual favors -- rape is so utterly degrading to both
the victim and the raper: "Where are all the pretty girls for us to rape"
were the words of a Serb (Orthodox Christian) in the literal rape of
Kosovo Muslim women. Yes, the Serb warriors actually felt they were
the victims, as they were deprived of raping pretty girls -- they had to
settle for the average girl (Newsweek 11/08/1993). War, Glorious War!!
But these evil deeds of sexuality must not be used to fence in and
make free people feel ugly when they practice sexual pleasures. And to
legally or socially enforce a artificial or guilt ridden restraint on sexual
pleasure is in itself an evil and vicious act. One of the most powerful
examples of this arrogant imposition to take away natural sexual pleasure
is the practice of "female circumcision" that is so common in Africa. It
is, of course, male instigated so that women would be faithful to their
men, since there were no longer any pleasurable feelings experienced in
the sexual act. Unbelievable sexual cruelty! This sexual "genital

mutilation" of young African girls shows how ugly tradition and sacred rites can get when imposed by certain power-people upon the rest of society. While the Christian Church has never gone this far, yet some pretty evil things have been imposed upon the believers by the Church Hierarchy throughout history (I deal with this much more in Chapter Ten). Jerome, the Monk, thought that one, if he loved his own wife too much, was committing adultery, and John Chyrsostom would talk about women being a lot of phlegm, blood, bile, and the refuse from used food to divert men away from a woman's natural outer beauty and attractiveness. And in Milan at a council in 390 AD a monk was excommunicated because he would not agree that "virginity is more meritorious than marriage". But <u>Luther</u> had a more natural and honest view. When told of a Waldensian minister by the name of Lawrence, who castrated himself to avoid sexual temptation, Luther replied that "For my part I'd rather have two pair (of testicles) added than one pair cut off." This is a far healthier attitude than that of <u>Teresa of Avila</u>, a frail nun of the 16th Century, who was deeply devoted to the service of God, but had to go through endless guilt because she was intimate sexually with other nuns. She was quite a sickly person who seemed tormented with her basic sinfulness before God, but she found comfort in the embraces and in the sexual pleasure shared with others. But because the teachings of the Church plagued her with the guilt indictment against sexual pleasure, her faith was almost destroyed, and she eventually gave up the human pleasures available to her to be pure before the "Lord" as the Church presented him. She participated in an act that neither Jesus nor the Hebrew Scriptures condemned, yet listen to her repentant words: "I entered into relations with that person once again...I got to know other people in the same way; and I spent many years in this <u>pestilential</u> <u>pastime</u>,...<u>I had merited hell</u>."2.15

The earth is good and beautiful and so is this life in the flesh. It is a wonderful gift of God and to depreciate it in any way, is to be ungrateful to God. To work within it to make life more wonderful for both our fellow human beings and our animal brothers is our calling, that in sharing the good and the beautiful, we ourselves will enjoy it the more.

CHAPTER THREE

ANXIETY AND PROBLEM CREATING

I.   ANXIETY, FEAR, AND DREAD

In Chapter Two the good and beautiful life on earth and in the body were presented at length to show the great and wonderful opportunity that is presented to those of human birth. Yet, this generation has been called the Age of Anxiety. Exactly what anxiety is and how it relates to fear and dread has been debated by many and the arrangement as to which is more dehabilitating by many others. My arbitrary order is that anxiety is first to appear, which in turn develops into a phobia (fear) and that in turn, if not controlled, leads to dread which is so strong a power within the individual that he or she is incapable of maintaining any purposeful control over his life and obligations to others. If life is good and the place we experience it, earth, is good, and the body in which we experience it is good, then why all the anxiety? Paul Tillich's suggestion that it is in our mortality and the recognition that all this good life and the body in which we live is headed for death that we find the source of our anxieties. The limitations of all this good so powerfully controls our ultimate thoughts that functioning can sometimes be difficult, if not impossible for some. He stated in his work The Courage to Be: "The first assertion about the nature of anxiety is this: anxiety is the state in which a being is aware of its possible nonbeing."3.1 He continues, declaring death to be a personal existential dilemma and is in reality part of our own being--this knowledge causes anxiety. For it is not in the fact alone that it is a universal reality, but that this transitoriness is part of our own fate, and we surely have the awareness that each one, we, (or myself) is/are going to die. This limitation brings us to a state of finiteness while all that we see in the earth with it's constant regeneration and all that we see in the heavens, by contrast, seem so infinite, and we are not. To many this brings a sense of hopeless, as well described by Albert Camus who sees life as trying to live within a plague that is killing everyone. In his book The Plague in which the plague is a microcosm of our brief life, he presented his hopelessness: "At thirty one's beginning to age, and one's got to squeeze all one can out of life." Later in the book as the people were all gradually dying, he stated that "the habit of despair is worse than despair itself", and again:

> Without memories, without hope, they lived for the moment only. Indeed, the here and now had come to mean everything to them. For there is no denying that the plague had gradually killed off in all of us the faculty not of love only but even of friendship. Natur- ally enough since love asks something of the future, and nothing was left us but a series of present moments.3.2

The Hebrew book of Ecclesiates expressed the emptiness of man's brief life, even if one is the son of a king.

> The words of Koheleth, son of David, king in Jerusalem.
> "Everything is empty of value, total vanity!
> Futility upon futility!
> What does man actually gain from all his work,
> All those days of labor in the sun?
> One generation of men die, another takes their place,
> But the earth remains forever.
> ...one fate comes to all men, and...the living must ponder death.
> Man is no better than the beasts, for both return to dust.

For man is no better than the beasts, even worse because while alive, he thinks of death. Both return to the dust... But a living dog is better than a dead lion, he too dies soon, but does not think about it. "And I thought the dead who are already dead more fortunate than the living who are still alive; but better yet than both is he who has never been born"(4:2-3)

Aristotle listed many things that a man is prone to fear, but he also focuses on death as the ultimate concern: "Now death is the most terrifying of all things; for it is the end, and nothing is thought to be any longer either good or bad for the dead" (3.6.25-27 / 1115a.25-27)

The Chorus ends <u>Sophocles'</u> <u>Oedipus</u> <u>The</u> <u>King</u> with these words: "Let mortals, hence, be taught to look beyond the present time, nor dare to say a man is happy, till the last decisive hour shall close his life without the taste of woe." Such comments are common also within the plays of the two other canonized tragic playwrights of the ancient Greeks, Aeschylus and Euripides.

A poem in <u>Sanskrit</u> that declares the very basic natural pleasantries of the most simple life also adds that such are bound by the thought of death. For a man can travel and behold the world, feel at home below the heavens, enjoy the wind and the quiet moonlit evenings, yet, even in all this, he is anxious for his life.3.3 Here is a man who would be happy without one possession other than life itself, and yet that is the one permanent possession he can not have. The experience of life, even in its most basic and simple form, is a delight for him; but it is an experience, not a possession, and that thought keeps him from "sleeping like a king". A <u>Viking</u> <u>poem</u> reflects the idea that man must accept his fate and not try to "hog it all" for he can not have it all, and to complain or worry about his fate is a sign of stupidity--that is, he must accept what he has no chance of changing.

> Don't cling to the cup   but drink your share,
>   speak useful words or be silent;
> no one will blame you   for bad manners
>   <u>if you go to bed early</u>.

> A stupid man   stays awake all night
>   pondering his problems;
> he's worn out   when morning comes
>   and whatever was, still is.3.4

<u>Retire early to bed</u> sounds like a Stoic statement that if you do not like life, check out and go to sleep. However, to cling to life and then grab an excessive amount of wine that takes someone else's share while living is certainly bad manners, but if you leave the party of life early--those bad manners you will not be blamed for. Likewise, to worry all night about something you can not change, is stupid, because in the morning nothing

will have changed despite your anxiety. Yes, the Vikings too philosophized of death; one must not forget that Odin gave up an eye for wisdom.

Chuang Tse speaks of a man who is constantly restless about everything "striving and struggling with the immediate circumstances", and frightened over all petty fears and disheartened and dismayed that something terrible might happen to him. The end result is that he is imprisoned in such fear and dread. Chuang Tse tells his students that this is all foolishness because death is going to terminate their entire existence anyway. So if they are to live in despair, at least it should be death that they fear and not petty and momentary things.3.5

Tu Fu laments the shocking brevity of life in a letter to Wei Pa. For being young and healthy and strong is a state of being that does not last very long. Even conversation is controlled by such fate, for most of the people that man talks about quickly become "ghosts", and the decades pass by in unthinkable rapidity.3.6

Boethius, in his complaint to Philosophia, argues that all is so finite, insignificant and temporal that of what value can life be, for even fame long after one's death departs from the legacy of humanity. "And anyway how short-lived all reputations are! Books, like their authors, are mortal. No one now knows where the bones of Fabricius lie."3.7

II. JESUS' RECOGNITION OF MAN'S ANXIETY

Jesus recognized the heavy anxiety of the people about him and of people in general, and spoke much of such anxiety, and ultimately it was to this anxiety, especially of death, that he addressed with his gospel. In Matthew 10:28 he comments on the fear of dying, the death or killing of the body, and in the Sermon of the Mount in Matthew, 6:25, he tells the people not to be anxious about their lives. The Greek word for anxiety (MERIMNA) is used 4 times in the Gospels, and the verb for being anxious (MERIMNAO) appears 11 times in Matthew and Luke. But even more important the word "to cause fear or terrify" (PHOBEO) occurs a total of 36 times and is present in all Four Gospels. The Good News or Counsel which Jesus gives will be presented in Chapter Four, but first let us look at how humanity misses the mark in the many ways in which it handles its finiteness.

III. ANXIOUS MAN CREATES PROBLEMS WITH HUMAN VANITIES

The anxiety driven man, with his motto "you only go around once in life, therefore it is necessary to get all the 'gusto' you can", tries desperately to enhance the beauty and meaning of his life with human vanities, which in turn add to his fears of not being "successful" in his finite experience. He feels he has only "one turn at bat" and must hit his home run so that he can at least have a sense of superiority over those who "just settle for playing the game" but "never amount to anything". But this, of course, is only the attitude of a desperate man living off of some kind of scorn for others and a false sense of personal grandiosity. Life itself, in its own simplicity and innate beauty, is not enough, he must round the bases and score big. That lust and desire is the evidence that he has not come to terms with his time-limited life on earth.

A. The General Classification

In speaking about these matters the world's great teachers and sages often simply speak about the desires, passions, appetites, or obsessions that man creates in this life, only to find out that those very emotions which he has created have become tyrants that, in turn, control him. Plato describes them as the lowest part of the soul of man, and must be conquered by the spirited and rational elements of the soul, otherwise man will throw himself into a pit of self-destruction. This battle within the soul of man is the chief battle man has in life; to conquer one's emotions is the only way to bring harmony to the soul. Such tyrants must be cast out of the soul as one would want them to be cast out of the city in which one lives: only the emotional tyrant is worse, because it poisons one's life wherever he is and whatever he is doing. Epictetus, the "Prince of the Stoics", stated: "Can we, in a word, abolish the acropolis which is in us and cast out the tyrants within us, whom we have daily over us, sometimes the same tyrants, at other times different tyrants", and "The difficulties of all men are about external things, their helplessness is about externals" (Discourses: Book Four). The Tibetan Book of the Dead calls these tyrants "illusions" because they are the bearers of vanity and emptiness: this is a common word used by many of the Buddhist teachers when expressing man's misdirected thoughts; avoid illusion. One of the Four Great Vows of Zen Buddhism is "However inexhaustible the passions are, I vow to extinguish them". The Hindu Srimad Bhagavatam declares that man ought to worship him (that is, the God of Love) alone, and to avoid the six passions: lust, anger, greed, pride, delusion, and jealousy-- "which are like ferocious sharks in the ocean of the world"(Chapter III). Likewise, the Bhagavad-Gita in Section Two "The Yoga of Knowledge" warns about the attachment to sense-objects, for they cause confusion in the mind and keep it from thinking about ultimate concerns and reality.

Hsun Tzu warned man about the dangers of obsession, especially about little things, which are of small importance, yet, if one is attached to them, they control and split the mind away from that which is truly important. All things: desires and hates; projects and relationships started and finished; both distance and present matters, and even worry about the past; all such things fill the mind so that it cannot have liberation from them and the delusion that comes with them.3.8

Cicero speaks of our appetites that, if indulged in, throw us out of control:

> But, generally speaking, the great source and fountain of all
> such injustice is the satisfying some irregular and exorbitant
> appetite; and in a more especial manner, the desire of riches.
> (Offices: Book One, Section VII)

Let us now move on to these particular appetites and passions which compound anxiety and fear, instead of bringing harmony, happiness, and wholeness into our lives. Acknowledging them and seeing how they throw a person out of control of his life, we then can move one to the first step upwards in our quest for happiness and wholeness.

B.   GREED (THE LUST FOR FINANCIAL POWER)

Greed and the building of great treasure has been a lure of happiness and security for men throughout the ages, but Jesus told a multitude that the quest for riches or the having them is not the basis of happiness or even security. For a rich man who was well blessed so much so that he tore down his barns and built bigger ones; after which he congratulated and comforted himself because he now had ample resources for many more years, only to die that very night (Lk 12:13-21).

Plato was amazed that people would be dishonest for the sake of financial gain, for he sells the glory and honor of his soul for a small piece of gold:

> ...but all the gold which is under or upon the earth is not enough to give in exchange for virtue. In a word, I may say that he who does not estimate the base and evil, the good and noble...and abstain in every possible way from the one and practice the other to his utmost of his power, does not know that in all these respects he is most foully and disgracefully abusing his very true self, the soul, which is the divinest part of man (Laws V.728a).

The ancient Greek myth of Midas was a rather humorous way of showing the foolishness of thinking that gold was the most important thing a person could have, for Midas desired that everything he touched would turn to gold. It was granted to him, and all was going well as the several objects he touched became gold; until he reached for a piece of fruit because he was hungry and it and all other food he touched became gold. He realized his folly and begs the gods to release him from his former request, being very happy to eat food again. Plato is saying that the same applies to such folly of seeking gold instead of virtue, because it will starve the soul, which is truly the divine spark that makes life worth living.

Anacreon, a Sixth Century BC Greek poet realized that there are other even worldly things he would much prefer than wealth, as seen in the words of his 23rd Ode, The Vanity of Wealth, which follows in its completeness:

> Could glittering heaps, or golden store
> Life preserve, or health restore,
> Then with ceaseless, anxious pain,
> Riches I would strive to gain,
> That, should death, unwish'd for come,
> Pointing to the dreary tomb,
> I might cry, in springhtly tone,
> "Here's my ransom, Death! Begone!"

But, alas, since well I know
Life can not be purchased so,
Why indulge the useless sight?
Fate decrees that all shall die.
Vainly to our wealth we trust,
Poor or wealthy--die we must.
Present joys then let me share,
Rosy wine to banish care;
Cheerful friends that faithful prove,
Beauty's smiles and blissful love.(tr.by Thomas Bourne)

Ovid in Book One of his Metamorphoses in the section of the "Four Ages" in which man falls from paradise, declared that during the Bronze and Iron Ages man fell into greed for the metals, but especially for gold.

Iron succeeded then,
And stubborn as the metal were the men.
Truth, modesty, and shame, the world forsook;
Fraud, avarice, and force, their places took.
.....
But greedy mortals, rummaging earth's store,
Digged from her entrails first the precious ore
(Which next to hell the prudent gods had laid)
And that alluring ill to sight display'd
Thus cursed iron, and more accursed gold,
Gave mischief birth, and made that mischief bold;
And double death did wretched man invade,
By iron assaulted, and by gold betray'd.
Now (brandish'd weapons glittering in their hands)
Mankind is brokenloose from moral bands;
No rights of hospitality remain;
The guest, by him who harbor'd him, is slain;
The son-in-law pursues the father's life;
The wife her husband murders, he the wife;
The step-dame poison for the son prepares;
The son inquires into his father's years;
Faith flies, and piety in exile mourns;
And justice, here oppress'd, to heaven returns.

The desire and lust for wealth never made mankind better or an individual man happier. The above verses are so familiar to us today, as then. The Letter of James in the New Testament reflects the same age and the same desires of the vanities that Ovid expressed. "What is the source and reason you have wars and fighting among yourselves? Is it not from this, that you are filled with inner lusts which war within your own souls? You have a passionate desire for something that you do not have; and for it you murder and are jealous, and if you are not yet able to attain the objects of your passions, you fight and go to war" (James 4:1-3). Juvenal, in his Satires, ridicules the idiocy and vanity of those doing anything they can to become wealthy, even gambling away the money they already have:

> For when did vice so boldly raise the head?
> When were the sails of avarice wider spread?
> When did such dire infatuation fly
> To the swift mischief of the falling die?
> With common stakes too long the gaming might last,
> For all or nothing now the throw is cast!
> The chest entire, the guerdon of the strife,
> On! On! They madly rush for death or life!
> What! Is it mere and common frensy, say,
> To lose ten thousand sesterces at play...(Satire One: 117-125).

It seems that these men actually live in the United States of American at the present time: CEOs who cast away any possible crumb of virtue for wealth; the entertainment industry sponsoring the Sonny Bono Act for the sake of greed; the "needy poor", using welfare money taken from the other working people legally to give them goods, play the lotteries faithfully with money not even morally their own; trial lawyers who grossly exaggerate the needs of their clients--as well as the silly and irresponsible juries--in order to receive billion dollar claims; from politician and used car dealer to telemarketing and television frauds who offer either something free or a reading of your future for only $5 a minute; there is greed. Sadly enough, greed even is well rooted in the hearts and minds of our "spiritual" leaders who beg their audiences for money so that they can continue to carry on the ministry of "Our Lord". The Roman satirist Petronius in his work The Satyricon presented a delightful satire on a newly wealthy, but totally uncultured and illiterate, boorish man who gave a dinner to the Roman elite to flagrantly show off his wealth, but only succeeded in showing himself to be humorously low class, full of folly, and downright crudely odious. Unfortunately the man today who is in constant quest of wealth appears the same way, this ignorance of what other's think is added to his list of boorish and vain personality. The <u>Viking</u> <u>Poem</u>, <u>The</u> <u>Lay</u> <u>of</u> <u>Regin</u>, mourns the knowledge that (in Loki's words) "Worse yet, my wisdom tells me, will be the clash of kinsmen; by the gold's power, princes not yet born will turn their hearts to hate". Greed rates as one of the three great evils in <u>Buddhist</u> teachings (LOBHA, DOSA, MOHA: greed, hatred, and illusion). Two stories that describe the danger and vanity of greed are among my favorites. The first, rather well known, is the story told by <u>Tolstoy</u> of a man who was promised all the land that he could circle in one day's walk (that is from the time the sun came up to the time it set). The night previous to his 'walk' he spent planning exactly the route he would take, balancing the time he spent walking, running, and resting in between. When the day came he set off confidently upon his journey, but as he was following his mapped out route, his greedy heart convinced him that at certain place he could make the circle alittle bigger, and so he kept broadening his circle, but it soon became evident that he would have to give up some of his rest periods and even some of his walking periods, and he subsequently kept pushing himself harder and harder, feeling his heart pounding within his chest and his body taking on heat to the point of fever and pain, even in his legs, but he pushed on and finished his circle just before the sun set,...and then died from exhaustion. The other story I read in a newspaper some twenty years ago in which a rich man was buried in his Cadillac (who says you can't take it with you), and one of the gravediggers humored by the event, smiled and said, "That's living". On a trip to Mexico City I went to see a show something like our comedy shows, so popular in Southern California. In one scene of only two men, a rich man who was very well dressed and had a high standard of living, needed more money to stay at his accustomed standard of living, and bowed down before the altar and started to pray to God for one million pesos for that would be sufficient to satisfy his present desires. He was praying fervently when a poor, dirty, unshaven man dressed in pitiable rags came in and shared a space with the rich man before the altar and began to pray with great fervor that he wanted only one peso for his daily bread. He prayed so desperately and loudly that the rich man feared the other was going to attract God's attention and God would then be distracted from his own prayer. In anger he got up, went to the poor man, gave him his wanted peso and chased him out of the church. Then he returned to the altar to continue his prayer, muttering that the poor man had his nerve bothering God for one little lousy peso. The play ended with the rich man still at the altar, and the poor man smiling while eating his bread. Yes, it was the poor man that had his prayer answered. Greed kills everything, and offers only emptiness, corruption, and vanity. It may appear to bring happiness, but it is a deceptive vacuum that engulfs its victims.

C.   ENVY (A FORM OF HATRED)

The envying or coveting of those things which properly are assigned in life to another has long been condemned as both a personal and social disruption of values and harmony. Envy is different than jealousy in this sense: jealousy is the expression of one fearful that he will lose what he has, and envy is the desire to take what another has. Therefore, they are related to each other but from different motives. Only envy will be discussed here, as the greater of the two evils that disrupt man's happiness is that of envy. Even though we in the West are most familiar with its prohibition because of the Jewish Torah's '10 Commandments', it is prohibited in most laws and moral codes of humanity and often related to the actualization of the desire, stealing or defrauding, or in the case of a wife or servant, of luring away from or seducing into acts of unfaithfulness. Such a desire naturally causes friction among men, and if the perpetrator has any virtue at all, a sense of shame or guilt, and if he has no virtue, at least the fear that another acting like himself will take away from him what he has and prizes. Plato in his Laws, while encouraging competition in various forms of man's excellency, whether in the arts, physical competition, or production, declared that there should be no envying of another who excels. For the envious man ceases his quest to excel in his own right, but concentrates on hindering the other person in his quest to be the best he can be; thereby injuring himself and doing damage to the community also. "Thus he cripples the whole society which is seeking, as in a race, virtue itself, while at the same time he lowers what virtue lies within himself" (Laws V. 731a-b).

Plato puts into Socrates' defense of himself the idea that the accusers who brought Socrates to trial were motivated by envy and love of slander. Socrates then lost his life, and Athens lost Socrates; the accusers subsequently lost their fame and they and their followers were excluded from Plato's Academy. Envy is a form of hatred at the good fortune or standing of another, and a desire to harm that person in the process of attaining that which in no way is proper to oneself. It diminishes fellowship, love, and mutual respect within one's community. It has absolutely no redemptive elements within its being. Lao Tzu taught that if one follows The Way of Tao then one has a natural cleanness to his soul: "By the simple unnamable cleanness through which men cease from coveting, and to a land where men cease from coveting peace comes naturally."3.10 Mencius taught that a man who is filled with virtue will have no room left within himself for envy, for virtue brings happiness but envy brings self-destruction (Book VI.A.17). Ovid in his Metamorphoses often refers to the destructiveness of envy, for it not only does not bring benefits, it destroys what harmony is already there. He describes the personalized concept of envy as a goddess who seeks desperately to destroy any beauty of life in a man or a woman. His anthropomorphic presentation of Envy goes like this: she is a half-eaten snake on the ground, sickly and pale, skinny, squint-eyed, violent, her teeth (for a snake?) are rusty and reddish, her breast green with gall, her tongue filled with poison, she laughs only when a person is in deep pain, eats her heart out in secret and she herself is always anxious. To invite envy into one's life for an antidote to one's mortality is the extreme of folly, and takes away even that joy that man has in his finiteness (768-815).

D.   EGO AND ONE'S OWN FEELING OF GRANDIOSITY

Jesus taught that one should love his neighbor as himself (Mt 19:19), and thereby declared that self-love is natural and good, and even a basis by which to gauge one's actions towards another. What I am talking about in this section is a self-centeredness that excludes the feelings and dignity of others in pursuing one's own desires, claiming to have privileges above and beyond the rights of others, and placing oneself into the center of life in which others are simply the byproducts of one's own existence. "I am Number One and there is no other" is not an uncommon reaction of many who have trouble dealing with their mortality and finiteness. It is basically an illusion that one is the whole substance of reality, and if that one dies all dies with him, or if it does not all die with him, why should he care? This life expression of grandiosity is quite evident to others, and it ultimately destroys any hope of enjoying a friendship or a lasting intimacy with another--because it is quite repulsive. In many ways it is more ugly than arrogance and pride which seem to make one think that he is more worthy than others, but egoism on the grandiose level even excludes the possibility that others can have some ultimate value. "It's all me" is stretching self-love far beyond its appointed value. One can completely "loose his bearings" when infected with this self grandiosity. In the Tibetan Book of the Dead the person's soul after death is wandering and completely lost and asking for guidance because of such self-centeredness: "Alas! when wandering in the SANGSARA because of the power of violent egotism" is the cry of despair from one who is caught in between that which he left and the Nirvana toward which he desires to go (Book I, Part II, The Third Day).

William James in his Essays on Faith and Morals presents egoism as a fall into a spineless illusion of reality, which ultimately leads to one's self-destruction: "--and at what point on the downward slope are we to stop? In theology, subjectivism develops as its 'left wing' antinomianism. In literature, its left wing is romanticism. And in practical life it is either a nerveless sentimentality or a sensualism without bounds. Everywhere it fosters the fatalistic mood of mind"(The Dilemma of Determinism). In a statement that covers much ground, Reinhold Niebuhr in his Beyond Tragedy (p.139) said: "All mature moral conduct is therefore infected with an element of dishonesty and insincerity. The lie is always intimately related to the sin of egotism." In the Mystical Fathers of the Greek Orthodox Church "self-esteem" is seen as an evil closely related to egotism, while in current usage in the United States it is considered a healthy and necessary state of mind upon which a person can build his self-dignity by some, but not all psychologists. Evagrios taught his monks "let us day by day rid ourselves of all that fills us with self-esteem...In the whole range of evil thoughts, none is richer in resources than self-esteem" (On Discrimination). Let us also beware of too readily desiring the "necessary self-esteem" we feel we need to succeed in life, for it is but a short step towards grandiosity and the crippling attitude that one is above, or has the right to be above, life's difficulties, and when such come, he cries out "Why me? Why me?, others yes, but Why me?" All natural hardships are then magnified into "the terrible acts of fate that have burdened me in life". Since the grandiose person believes he deserves more than others, it is totally embarrassing and confounding to see another prosper while he himself must endure the hardships of life. Complaining, melancholy, sadness and even paranoia sets in. This vanity is also a strong vacuum that sucks one into emptiness and despair. In America we seem to have higher rates of disillusionment about life than in other countries: more women suffer postpartum depression, more of our teenagers see no value in life and are bored, our jobless feel that it was the circumstances and not themselves that "caused them to rob a bank", and our homicide and gang crime exceeds the rates in other industrial nations. The old Western ethic of finding a plot of land and with hard work make a life is seemly gone. Are we so rapped up in our egoism as individuals that life's natural hardships seem a curse, a disease, or a neurosis? Our finiteness is made even more finite because of our silly and self-centered grandiosity.

E. LUXURIES AND THINGS (ADULT TOYS)

In trying to gain some significant identity through a show of things for the sake of claiming a status above the rest, with the implication that one is happier or having more fun in life, many accumulate luxuries, things, automobiles, and grand houses. Current corrupt CEOs have included large yachts and 20,000 square foot houses (the last one is a loop hole against justice because such a one may be able to keep his house, so that he is not cast out to live among the homeless-- ugh!). But this trait to find happiness in things is common to all levels and classes of society. A man lives in a very small apartment, but buys a BMW to flash around town and thereby convince himself that he is happy, or a woman may adorn herself in expensive clothes and jewelry to try to gain a status among others. People give up good food, the proper insurance for the family, a personal library, family outings, personal and children's educational opportunities, all for the sake of having and being able to show others their toys. This infection comes into the lives of people of every station in life, and brings grief when the toys grow old but the bills keep coming (as so many pay for them on credit against their future livelihood). Yet the money spent so frivolously is sorely needed by the family for essentials, if not for better and longer lasting life enhancing experiences. Dale Carnegie, a half a century ago, in his book How to Stop Worrying and Start Living, at the beginning of Chapter Thirty stated: "Seventy per cent of all our worries, according to a survey made by the Ladies Home Journal, are about money". The quest to have and show one's toys add to that already serious problem. Families argue over money and one of the chief reasons is that they all want their toys. Are they that bored or are they that anxious to keep up with the "Jones'" at any cost? From one sickness to another. The sages and teachers of humanity have always warned of this, yet every generation seems to have an addiction to things. The simple things in life are a gift of the earth, yet we despise them lamented Persius in his Fourth Satire:

> How truly fair was bounteous Nature's plan!
> How wisely suited to the state of man!
> For him her hand had traced a flowery way;
> Mild was her reign, and gentle was her sway:
> But fury passions, owning no control,
> Seized on her empire, and usurp'd the soul.
> Then simple Nature charm'd mankind no more,
> Her pleasures vanished, and her power was o'er.

Destroy the mountain and the stream,
Pollute the soil and poison the ocean,
Mankind into each eye puts a beam,
He wants his toys as a magic potion (JDE).

The Younger Pliny complains to Julius Valerianus that things are more attractive when you do not have them, but a down right pain when you actually own them. His mother's property which he inherited is consuming too much time and effort and he keeps it only because it was his mothers: "Are you pleased with the new property now that it is yours? It rarely happens--nothing is quite so attractive in our possession as it was when coveted." There is an ancient story among the Greeks that a man fell in love with a beautiful vase with its lovely painting of objects so carefully done, so he sold half of his property to buy it. But then, in great fear that someone would steal it at night, he had trouble sleeping for months. Finally, someone did steal it, and that following night he had his first good night of sleep since he had purchased the vase. He laughed at his vanity, and then laughed again saying, "Now let the thief have restless nights for the next few months." Another Greek proverb makes it clear: man does not own things, things own men. Cicero, aware that he was echoing "Pythagoras and Socrates and Plato" in his Fifth Discussion at Tusculum said critically of those posing as sages:

> For since they are so keen on this fine and imposing epithet 'wise',
> it is imperative that they should also make every effort to stop being
> dazzled by physical strength...beauty, riches, honors and possess-
> ions. They must view these things with contempt instead. If they
> succeed in doing this, they will be able to disregard the so-called
> 'evils' that the opposites of those alleged advantages.3.9

The Confucian Hsun Tzu reminded his students that those who attach great importance to external material things are always inwardly anxious, but the simple sounds of nature, the smell of vegetable soup, and warm clothes make a man's mind joyous and peaceful, and it is in this way that man makes material things one's servant, instead of one's master. Seneca warned also of the slavery of wealth and other things, for if one seeks true freedom, he must "take the yoke off of his neck" and diminish the value of all other things. (Letter CIV). In his exile by Claudius' command, he wrote to his mother, Helvia, and in that letter, he consoled her over any financial loses Claudius had caused him by telling of the addiction to money of one Apicius, who had 20 million dollars and wasted it all on things, especially a grand kitchen that he had built. Startled to see how much everything had cost, he examined his accounts, and realized he only had two million dollars left. He felt that at two million dollars he was on the verge of poverty, and not wanting to die in the future as a pauper, he ended his life then by drinking poison. Wall Street free-falls have caused similar reactions here in United States. If man seeks to find happiness in the things he owns, he only makes his unhappiness greater and becomes a slave of the very things themselves. The passion for luxury is an empty quest with a self-destructive ending. I end this section with the words of Epictetus' plea to his followers:

Cease, I adjure you by the gods, to admire material things. Cease to make yourselves slaves, first of things, then on account of things slaves of those who are able to give them or take them away (Discourses, III.20).

F.   THE ROMANTIC OBSESSION

Romance is undoubtedly one of the most deeply felt pleasures a person can experience, but, unfortunately, also one of the most prone to come and go with great velocity. Romantic love, stability is not thy name! While it can take a man or a woman to heavenly heights it can also plunge a person's spirit into a psychological hell. It is not evil as many of the above emotions are, but it has great power to overthrow the reason in man, that reason, the very thing that separates us from animals, is dethroned when the obsession of romantic love invades a person's soul. Thus a person becomes no different than the lion, the walrus, or any other male animal who protects with his life his harem of females. Thus romantic love and the threat of losing it can be as reason and self-control destroying as the egotism, love of money, envy, and lust for things can be. It is surely not the basis of a happy and harmonious life. Common sayings like "He needs a good woman" or "She needs a good man" are misleading when they presume to be the one thing lacking for an otherwise unhappy person. In Homer and much of Classical Mythology the gods fight over male-female relations constantly. Homer blames the Trojan War on a fight over Helen, and romantic love jealousy prompted Agamemnon to cry out for total annihilation of the Trojans, "Let us not spare a single one of them--not even the child unborn and in its mother's womb; let not a man of them be left alive, but let all in Ilius perish, unheeded and forgotten" (Iliad VI.51-60). Likewise, Achilles refused to fight for the Greeks because Agamemnon took the girl Briseis from his tent; Achilles refusing to replace her with the twenty other women plus one of Agamemnon's own daughters which were offered to him. Perhaps as a result of Achilles' not fighting, his best friend Patroclus was killed, and that filled him with even greater anger. When one is possessed with a romantic obsession, self-control of all other emotions is lost. The ancients often played the "blame game" by accusing the god of love (Eros in Greek and Cupid in Latin) to plant such a lust into man's heart for another that it was humanly impossible to resist. Anacreon's Ode

<u>XIV</u> (On Eros) presents one succumbing to the poison of irrational obsessive love"

> I waited till the foe (Eros/Cupid) drew near.
> His bow-string twang'e--then seized with dread,
> My courage failed--I trembling fled.
> He plied his darts till all were spent;
> Nor did his anger then relent:
> Himself he changed into a dart,
> And shot like lightning through my heart.
> Ah me! I felt my life-blood flow;
> I sunk beneath my conquering foe.
> How vainly defensive arms I bear;
> For victory who can hope to win
> While fiercely burns the war within?

Today, being just as dramatic, people declare "I couldn't help it, I just fell in love, and love does those types of things to a person." Ugh! Mindless creatures without thought or self-control and they want to be known as a species called Homo Sapiens (the wise human-animal). <u>Ovid</u>, in his <u>Metamorphoses</u> presents many myths of men and women who were controlled by love obsession to the point where they were so self-destructive that the gods had mercy upon them by changing them into an animal, vegetable, or mineral being, for they no longer had the capacity to be a rational being. <u>Tibullus</u>, who wrote many love poems, likewise excuses the loss of reason when "love" comes:

> Slavery confronts me now, and a mistress--
>   Farewell, my inheritance, Liberty!
> Worse! Slavery unrelieved, and chains:
>   Love never eases his victim's bonds;
> He burns them, innocent or guilty;
>   Remove the firebrands, cruel girl; I am in flames.
> To be free from the sensation of such pain,
>   How preferable to be a stone on a frozen mountain (II.iv.1-10)
>   (tr.P.Dunlop)

Indian love poems are no different, passionate love is pleasant and sensual, but brutally obsessive making one helpless and deadens reason or any power of resistance, even if one knows it is slavery and temporary.

> We listened; knew not whether they went
> On love or hunger the more intent.
> And under your kisses I hardly knew
> Whether I loved or hated you.
> But your words were flame and your kisses fire,
> And who shall resist a strong desire:
> Not I , whose life is a broken boat
> On a sea of passions, adrift, afloat.
> And, whether I came in love or hate,
> That I came to you was written by Fate
> In every hue of the blood-red sky
> In every tone of the peacocks' cry. 3.10

Sappho wrote about a poem about a man whom, she said, appeared in looks to be equal to a god, and naturally she lost all control. She felt the pounding of her heart that love brought to her, her trouble speaking, the flame inside her is so hot, yet she breaks out in a cold sweat, and she even loses the natural color in her cheeks.3.11

The Kama Sutra expresses the loss of control when a woman fears or confronts the idea of a competitor for her chosen's love:

> A woman who is very much in love [obsessed with love] with a
> man cannot bear to hear the name of her rival mentioned, or to
> have any conversation regarding her, or to be addressed by her
> name by mistake. If such takes place, a great quarrel arise, and
> the woman cries, becomes angry, tosses her hair about, strikes
> her lover, falls from her bed or seat, and casting aside her garlands
> and ornaments, throws herself down on the ground (Chapter Ten).

Now does this sound like a person out of control or what? Is this what men and women think will make their lives harmonious and stable? Such "love" (romantic obsession) is sometimes as short as the time of the flight of one of Cupid's arrows. Chaucer puts the same dementia of love into the mouth of Troilus in his "love" song who, although he seems to sense the destructiveness of such "love" still wants to experience more of it: "if it is wicked...and gives me torment and adversity...why do I yet thirst of it and want more to drink of it...it is a living death, so why am I consenting to it?...it is leaving me rudderless and causes a strange sickness in me." But perhaps the most powerful story ever written about a person who was so possessed of the obsession of romantic love is The Sufferings of Young Werther by Goethe. Werther was a brilliant young man who loved the beauty of nature and the glory of life itself, until he met Charlotte (Lotte) and went into an obsessive love frenzy for her, becoming convinced that if this romance for her does not become realized in her being his love for life, then life and all other beautiful things of the creation and all arts and culture become valueless. Her offered friendship was not enough! She must leave Albert and become his alone! Three together can not exist; either he or Albert must go. Here Goethe shows how delusional Werther was becoming, for Lotte had made it very clear that Albert was her chosen. His dementia showed itself further when he declared to Lotte that he wanted to die, and he claimed he was saying this 'without romantic exaggeration (Ueberspannung)', like a man drowning without realizing he is in water. Only death seemed available to him... "this night has made fast my decision, it is appointed: I want to die (Ich will sterben)...in frightful rebellion against my mind, everything was pressing on my heart and my hopeless, joyless existence seized me in shocking coldness...I want to die! I lay myself down, and in the morning, my decision still stands fast, still strong in my heart: I want to die." Since he has her captured in his heart, he decides to kill himself with a gun, and then in heaven wait for Lotte there and it will be heavenly ecstasy. Before he kills himself he utters a prayer:

You are from this moment mine! mine, O Lotte! I am going before you! I go to my Father, to your Father. To him I will complain, and he will cheer me up until you come, then I will fly to meet you and hold you fast and remain with you before the face of the Infinite in eternal embraces. I am not dreaming, nor have I lost my mind in a delusion...we shall be! We shall see each other again (wir werden uns wieder sehen). (tr.JDE).

Yes, he was delusional, so much so that he believed even God would rush to his comfort and keep him company in heaven until Lotte arrived, and then before God himself they would enjoy each other in "eternal embraces". In other words, the universe and its God is controlled or at least responding to my romantic love obsession for Lotte. Ugh! Did this work have appeal? Most certainly. In Germany it was an instant sensation and the first decade almost 2 editions a year were published, and in England and France the production rates were similar, and even the clothes he was projected to have worn were popularly known as the "Werther Costume". Romantic obsession is a powerful force that all of us have become aware of and most of us have, at least a little, experienced it. But to put all one's eggs of happiness into this basket will truly make one a "basket" case. Breakups and divorces often end in the tragedy of someone's death, and even the children are sometimes murdered as an act of vengeance. To build one's happiness totally upon a relationship of intimacy with another is not the "rock" upon one should build his house.

G.   ANGER AND PRIDE

Anger is another emotion that deprives us of any rational activity, and "cool down before you decide anything" is the best of advise. This choice of being angry is usually blamed on someone else "you make me so angry" is often heard when the person who chooses to be angry does not want to face up to the reality that he simply is unable to control his emotions at certain difficult times. I am mortal, I know, but my doctor told me today that I will die in six months "of course, I am angry". The ancient Greeks had a saying that a truly wise man practices dying every day, so that when its reality closes in upon a person, he is prepared for it. But many in their quest for romantic obsessive love or their adult toys do not have time for that "philosophy crap". They can always choose to become violently angry. Choosing to be angry, especially at someone else, is dangerous because of what it does to the soul and how it makes ugly our basic nature. Jesus thought it not to be a little problem: "But I say to you that everyone who is angry with his brother will be liable to judgment; whoever says Raca (term of abuse) to his brother will be liable to the Sanhedrin (highest Jewish court) and whoever says, 'Moron' will be liable to the fire of Gehenna (a trash site where things were burned to destruction" (Mt.5:22-23). Chapter XVII of the Dhammapada is a series of 14 statements warning about the dangers of anger and encouraging the reader to calm the emotion when it first makes its appearance: Let man put away his anger...He who holds back rising anger like a rolling chariot, him I call a real driver; other people are but holding the reins ...overcome anger by mildness...do not yield to anger...Beware of bodily anger and control your body...Beware of anger of the tongue and control your tongue...Beware of the anger of the mind and control your mind.

Sophocles presented Electra as being so angry that she lashed out irresponsibly towards those who had caused her woe, and in so doing only complicated her life:

> Chorus: Despair not, daughter; Zeus is yet in heaven,
> The God who sees and knows, and governs all:
> Patiently to him submit, do not let your rage
> Too far transport you, nor oblivion drown
> The just remembrance of your matchless woes...
> Cease your complaints: already you have suffered
> For your loud discontents and threaten'd vengeance.
> Tis folly...
> Electra: Folly, indeed, and madness! But my griefs
> Will force their way; and while Electra breathes
> She must lament...(160-190)

In some things in life, an injustice can stay with us a long time, but sooner or later we must turn it over to fate or time, and release ourselves from the anger that takes away all the other more beautiful things in life. To vow an everlasting anger, if not self-destructive, is self-limiting for the rest of our lives. Sallust made the simple statement: "Desire and anger are very bad counselors" (The Jugurthine War 64).

Jesus taught humility as a virtue, and warned against pride in subtle ways, scolding James and John about the request of their mother to be put at his right and left hand (above the other disciples) when he came into his eternal kingdom, telling people not to sit in a seat of honor at a banquet until the guest asked them to, and blessing the meek and granting their rightful place upon the earth. Pride, especially when it is full blown arrogance, is extremely harmful to one's social life, and, in fact, is very hard to disguise. It also makes it very difficult for a person to joyfully receive that, but only that, to which he is entitled. The Greeks had many myths about inordinate pride, usually a man or woman would have the hybris (hubris = inordinate pride) to challenge the gods. Niobe was the daughter of Tantalus, the King of Phrygia, and after she had six sons and six daughters she became so proud that she claimed to be a better mother than Latona, the mother of Apollo and Diana. For her pride Apollo and Diana slew all her children (Greek gods in the myths were often quite jealous--not too much unlike Yahweh among the Hebrews). Likewise Arachne was so proud of her spinning and weaving that she claimed she could exceed the excellence of Minerva herself, which affronted Minerva who then changed her into a spider so she could play with her threads. Lucan, the Roman historian, claimed that the entire civil war, which killed many Roman soldiers and weakened the entire empire, was all caused by the pride of Pompey and Caesar. Pompey was number one in the senate's eyes because of a great history of military victories, but the younger Caesar had just defeated Gaul, a long time enemy of Rome. When he came to Rome he wanted to be treated equally, but the Senate refused. Lucan wrote, "He [Caesar] disdained to accept a subordinate position at Rome. In a word, Pompey could allow no man to be his equal, and Caesar no man to be his superior. Who am I to judge which of the two had more right on his side?"(Pharsalia 120ff). Pompey had everything, all he had to do was give Julius Caesar equal honor. He refused. Caesar chose war and defeated him, and Pompey lost everything including his life. Petronius, in portraying Trimalchio as an uncultured newborn rich of the ancient Roman society, describes Trimalchio at a banquet which he gave trying to be intellectual, and in so doing heaped much ridicule upon his very evident ignorance. That even more compounded the humiliation by showing that Trimalchio was not even aware of his splendid manifestation of the purity of his ignorance, and not being aware, thought he was overwhelming the people with brilliance. While it is humorous to read, in reality, when pride shows itself that way in a person, it is really quite tragic. Lao Tzu in his Tao The Ching (TheWay of Life) wrote that the true sage is humble and does not toot his own horn:

> Therefore the sage holds in his embrace the one thing (of humility), and manifests it to all the world. He is free from self-display, and therefore he shines; from self-assertion, and therefore he is dis-

tinguished; from self-boasting, and therefore his merit is acknowledged. (22.2)

Walter Lippmann declared:

> The delusion of men that they are gods--the pretension that they
> have a commission to act as if they were gods--is the blind arrogance
> of childish thought. It can become the very madness of a mind dis-
> eased. Yet it is not a new and recent infection, but rather the dis-
> position of our first natures, of our natural and uncivilized selves.
> Men have been barbarians, much longer than they have been civil-
> ized. They are only precariously civilized, and within us there is
> the propensity, persistent as the force of gravity, to revert under
> stress and strain, under neglect or temptation, to our first natures.
> 3.12

H. SLOTH (IRRESPONSIBILITY)

Sloth, laziness, is more than just being lazy, it is not being responsible
for one's own life and for the lives of others to which the individual is
obligated, such as children. It has always been classified as one of the
seven deadly "sins". It applies not only to those who do not achieve
anything, but those who flee from the duties which they themselves have
created. The book of Proverbs in Hebrew Scriptures heaps scorn on the
slothful person, declaring that he has neither the brains nor the energy of
an ant. He is so lowly, he can learn from an insect how to live
responsibly.

> Go to the ant, O sluggard; consider its ways, and learn from it. .
> Without having any leaders, officers or rulers,
> It saves food in the summer, and gathers a sufficient amount
>   during the harvest.
> How long will you lie there, lazy one?
> When will you get out of bed?
> A little more sleep, and a little more slumber,
>   and a bit more folded hands in restful position,
>   and poverty will be your companion (Prov. 6:6-11).

The ancient Chinese book <u>Shu</u> <u>Ching</u> (Book of History: The Documents of Chou, 15) expresses sadness that the children of hard working parents neither work hard themselves nor even give respect for their parents for what they have done. It is a trait of those who have not come to terms with life's limitations, especially the time allotted to it, that they do not want to "waste their brief time with work". "Leisure is the only way to live"--at the expense of others of course. It is an old trait, and The Shu Ching laments it.

<u>William</u> <u>James</u> criticizes those "intellectuals" who think society is obligated to pay their way in life for merely sitting around and thinking, without partaking of any social responsibility.

> Too much questioning and too little active responsibility lead,
> almost as often as too much sensualism does, to the edge of the
> slope, at the bottom of which lie pessimism and the nightmare
> or suicidal view of life.3.13

When one has difficulty accepting his mortality and chooses laziness and apathy towards life, it makes life even more meaningless and its value becomes virtually non-existent, prompting deeply implanted pessimism in the mind and heart to the point of melancholy or "Weltschmerz" which in turn can lead to the desire of suicide. So far from "getting the most out of life" by being lazy and irresponsible, one devalues even that life he had to begin with. In all the above categories of the ways in which people react to their mortality one senses the meaning of the word sin in its original Greek sense in the New Testament: "missing the mark". By reacting to the assurance of death by playing childishly with adult toys, being angry about our 'existential dilemma', by seeking a passionate and possessive romance one does not "hit the bulls-eye" of life, rather he misses and misses badly.

IV.   OTHER RELATED EVIDENCES OF HAVING LOST
CONTROL

A. CRY "VICTIM"

Of course one of the most popular "victims" of the 1990s was a former football player who has referred to his arrest, Bronco chase, and trials as his "ordeals", and how terrible it is that society has put him through such anguish just because blood evidence pointed to him as a double murderer. Perhaps when he finds the "real killers" on some golf course he will be psychologically purged from the pains of his "ordeal". But, of course, this is a trait that is too often relied upon for those who, by choice, have dug their holes of despair of their finiteness deeper with the poison options that they have selected in life. How many have been put to trial for reacting violently to a pressing situation (killing a boss who had fired them), who claimed that they were the victims because they had no job and seemed pressed into reacting the way that they did. J.S. Bonnell declared that this type of self-pity "is one of the most devastating of all human attitudes." Yes, people cry victim for virtually any kind of failure. "The legalizing of the state lotteries caused me to foolishly waste my money in hopes of avoiding work for the rest of my life." "My luck is always bad." "I never get a decent break." "I came young and talented to Hollywood, but I never got discovered, just used." "It was my lousy home-life, and my father trained me to be self-indulgent--how was I ever to learn discipline?" "I have problems that are beyond most peoples' imagination." "My pain is always greater than your pain, and my sorrow deeper than your sorrow--pity me." As long as a person can find an excuse or alibi, then he feels he does not have to face the fact that he chose to be a failure. Seneca, a Stoic who feels that manly discipline and duty give a person the strength to bear life's difficulties with grace, addresses the fact that when men play the "victim game" they are making it worse (as well as driving everyone away from themselves). In letter 78 he made these statements: "A man is as unhappy as he has convinced himself he is... 'No one had ever been in such a bad state...A man on the rack isn't torn with pain the way I was.'"3.14 Seneca said it was bad enough to complain when suffering, but after it is all past to keep on playing victim to such pain is so childish. He even becomes delusional: "What is more, doesn't everyone add a good deal to his tale of hardships, and deceive himself as well in the matter?" In general the delusional self-victim actually blames all existence and the world for his problem. "The world is so fouled up, I can not be happy or have a meaningful life." This leads us into the next attitude that makes it evident that a person is not dealing well with his mortality.

B. BLAME GAMES

This game of blaming others or circumstances for all our actions, not too unlike the "victim" games, has been around since man first had any responsibilities. The myth of Adam and Eve in the Hebrew Scriptures serves us well. Do not eat the fruit! What! you ate the fruit? It was not my fault, I was seduced and mislead by the woman that you gave me. Don't blame me! cries Eve. It was one of your slimy creatures that mislead me. The serpent evidently "lost its tongue" and was not permitted to play the blame game; he merely slithered away. In the Testaments of the Twelve Patriarchs Judah is revealed as the one who made his daughter-in-law, Tamar, pregnant--that after he had condemned her for her sexual sin. But Judah, instead of admitting that he was seeking sexual relations "to be comforted" (his wife had died some time ago--and consorting with a prostitute was never condemned, at least by law--in ancient Judaism), he relied upon Adam and Eve's blame game. First he stated that he did not recognize her as his daughter-in-law and this was true, but what follows is rather honest for a blamegamer. She was standing where the prostitutes usually do, and "the way she had adorned herself made her seem the more desirable (She looked good!), I was deceived. And I turned to her and said, Let me lie with you." But later he does fall back on the blame game: "for it was the Lord's doing". Oh, that's it, both God and the women are to blame for man's sins. In the Laws of Manu the teacher of his moral students blames women for sexual sins (at least God is spared this time):

It is the nature of women to seduce men in this world; for that
reason the wise are never unguarded in (the company of) females.
For women are able to lead astray in the world not only a fool,
but even a learned man, and make him a slave of desire and anger.

> One should not sit in a lonely place with one's mother, sister, or daughter; for the senses are powerful, and master even a learned man.(II.213-215)

Manu did not have a prejudice against women? Ha! He permitted the entire male population of the world to play the blame game. The women will destroy your virtue--beware!--even your mother and sister and daughter are dangerous, for by means of sex they desire to make you their slaves of both desire and anger. The poor weaker sex (the male) has no chance to be moral, living in this world of beautiful and sensuous amazons who will overpower their weaker victims.

Today we seem to blame biological determinism for our actions: "I get angry easily--it's in my genes." "Sure, I have raped a few women, but that is my genetic makeup, after all if males weren't aggressive the human race would have perished long ago; it's in our make up." "Heredity is a strong factor in one's anxiety." While, of course, genes and heredity must be factored in to our life's plans and our concerns for good health, and in some cases even in our emotional stability, we must beware of removing all responsibility for the person who does harm to others and emphasize choice and self-control. This is at the very crossroads of the arguments and conflicts that Logical Positivists and Existentialists have with each other. Truth in such matters is never all on one side, and therefore, in some things in life heavy judgments must come carefully and slowly. But, in reality, the blame game is alive and doing well, even taking advantage of the Positivists' position, which gives it a false sense of justification.

C. LOSS OF SPIRITUAL AND PHILOSOPHICAL GUIDES

It was mentioned in Chapter One the need that man has for the Teachers who help guide our lives, those who bring meaning and direction for the art of living. When a person is no longer concerned with seeking such a teacher, a mentor, a pastor or priest, or guru, then it is evident that he has let his finiteness end the quest for wholeness and happiness in this life. "Life is an emptiness, a series of acts without meaning or direction or responsibility." He is free, but only to wander around in his psychological vacuity. Nothing matters. Occasionally he finds a "cause" to keep him going for awhile; something as petty as being a sport's fanatic or something as viciously fanatic as a racist or nationalist, like Hitler. It is interesting to note that in Hitler's Last Will and Testament, finalized while he was in his death bunker, that he made no mention of God or any spiritual value, but wanted to be remembered for his "service to his people". Some service! Germany laid in ashes, a third of its land lost, and one fourth of its people dead. And that is not to mention what his party's cruelties inflicted upon the disabled, those born blemished, Poles, Greeks, other Slavs, Jews, and Gypsies (his liquidation of them was even more thorough than his liquidation of the Jews). The day after Hitler's death, Goebbels (his confidant) and his wife poisoned their six children before committing suicide themselves. When a person completely looses his spiritual and philosophical guides, and does not desire to have them around, he is dangerous to others and to himself destructive unto death.

Philosophia speaks to Boethius of the danger of neglecting a philosophical guide in life, for those who do fall into ignorance of the Good and step by step lose their self-control and finally their very existence: "But they lose in this way not only power, but existence altogether. For those who abandon the end common to all things which exist must in the same measure cease to exist" (Book IV, Meter II). Two of the better known atheistic modern philosophers Albert Camus and Jean-Paul Sartre themselves had lost their way to happiness. Camus is sarcastic and empty in himself and his feelings and judgments of others. In his book The Fall he states: "It always seemed to me that our fellow citizens had two passions: ideas and fornication...all Europe is in the same boat. I sometimes think of what future historians will say of us. A single sentence will suffice for modern man: he fornicated and read the papers. After that vigorous definition, the subject will be, if I may say so, exhausted." Later in the book he stated: "Fundamentally, nothing mattered."3.15 Sartre pictures his life as misery, emptiness of love, and pure hell (in his work No Exit he even concludes that "hell is other people"), he can not seem to find very many nice things to say about his family or himself. In his autobiography, The Words, he says of his grand-father: "Dr. Sartre outraged, did not speak a word to his wife for forty years. At the table, he expressed himself in signs...Yet he shared her bed and from time to time, made her pregnant"(p.9)...his father, Jean-Baptist "sought refuge in death" and Sartre said of it..."The death of Jean-Baptiste was the big event in my life: it sent my mother back to her chains and gave me freedom...Had my father lived, he would have lain on me at full length and would have crushed me. As luck had it, he died young...As for me, I was delighted: my sad situation commanded respect" (p.11)...Sartre said of his other grandfather: "He so resembled God the Father [this is sarcastic for Sartre did not believe in such] that he was often taken for Him...This God of wrath [his grandfather] gorged on his sons' blood"p.14..."our shabby end...All children are mirrors of death"(p.18)... "Our life is only a succession of ceremonies, and we spend our time showering each other with tribute. I respect the adults on condition that they idolize me" (p.20)...Sartre considered his grandfather Schweitzer a fool for thinking that he, the grandfather, was happy in life: "That Lutheran could not help thinking, very biblically, that the Eternal had blessed his house"(p.39)... "In short I had no soul"(p.55). He spoke with such emptiness:

In other words, I was condemned; the sentence could be applied at any moment. Nevertheless, I rejected it with all my might. Not that my existence was dear to me; on the contrary, because I wasn't keen on it: the more absurd the life, the less bearable the death (p.61) 3.16

Sartre's main teaching is that, since there is no god, man is "condemned to be free" and must take the responsibility of that freedom to make himself. If Sartre's own attitude is all that man can make of himself, then God help us. To say the least, neither he nor Camus adjusted well to their mortality and finiteness.

In the midst of World War II, Richard Livingstone wrote in his The Future of Education:

If you allow the spiritual basis of a civilization to perish, you first change, and finally destroy it. Christianity and Hellenism are the spiritual bases of our civilization. They are far less powerful today than fifty years ago. Therefore, we are losing that spiritual basis, and our civilization is changing and on the way to destruction, unless we can reverse the process.3.17

When man throws away the spiritual and philosophical teachers of mankind, he finds himself "lost in space" and out of control without a basis upon which he can build a meaningful life. These above evidences of not handling our limited existence well are an insufficient substitute, as are the well known evidences of drugs and alcohol, status seeking, and slavery to fear, to guilt, and to obsolete moral traditions. The next chapter presents the first step up towards a life of happiness and wholeness.

CHAPTER FOUR

STEP ONE

MEANINGFULNESS WITHIN FINITENESS

Many of mankind's great teachers believed that there could be "religion without revelation" (to use Julian Huxley's phrase) and without existence after the death of the body. For those of similar beliefs they have been very helpful in giving their followers a guide by which to enjoy that which is temporary and finite, and this is also the first step for those who believe that further steps must be taken to come to a full happiness and spiritual wholeness, as I myself believe. Some of the following steps will indeed be helpful to those also who believe in and accept their finite limitations and the termination of their existence with death, and for that reason they should read on anyway; even if the following chapters have a different point of view about man's nature and destiny. Some of these teachers do extend into the next step, but not beyond. For example, while Logical Positivists, Confucians, Julian Huxley, Herbert Spencer, and Bertrand Russell do not go into step two, such people as Aristotle, the Way of Tao (Lao Tzu), Ancient Hebrew Scriptures, some Stoics, Epicureans, Buddhists and Zen Buddhists are planted firmly in the belief that either there is a God (but no life after death for humans) or that the Universe (Heaven or The Way or Nature) is friendly to man because man is part of its whole and blends into the Cosmos after death, but without personal identity. Both for those who leap from here in Chapter Four to Chapter Seven and for those who continue on by means of Chapters Five and Six, there are certain basic precepts of wisdom that apply, and those teachings and maps given to us by the sages will be presented in this chapter, and, therefore, this chapter should serve all people of all beliefs as a foundation to a better way of enjoying life. The sections will discuss the value of unattachment to certain things which are beyond our control--the past which can not be changed, and those things that are not possible--and the things that are in our control; and, likewise, the balance of the desires and the emotions which is necessary for one's harmony of mind and body; and finally the power of choice and the will to salvage broken dreams.

I. UNATTACHMENT

A. THE PAST

Many people cannot let go of the past in the sense that it was painful in some way or other, and they can not move away from it. The dreadful things of the past seem to be attached to their minds, their souls, and personalities. The past which will always be as it was and can never be changed deadens their will to move forward and to live freely in the present and future. Understandably certain experiences will change people forever, and even cause deep fears, anxieties, and dreadful thoughts about life itself. In many ways we are the accumulation of our past experiences, at least mentally. Therefore it is impossible to act or think like that past, with its possibly frightening experiences, never happened, for it did. But a person, in order to be happy, must be the master of his fate; facing his past with power and will, and refuse to let it take over the present and the future as it has the past. The Hebrew myth of the story of Abraham, Lot, and Sodom and Gomorrah makes the point forcefully; when Lot's wife, instead of leaving her ancient home and the experiences in the past, turned to look back--instead of forward-- she turned into a pillar of stone. If we let the past solidify us in it, then our spirit gives up and dies, knowing it really has no present or future. Such depression of that spirit that is locked in the past also will damage the health of one's body. Even the ancient Greeks knew that as <u>Democritus</u> warned his students that if the mind of man were brought to trial by the body for all the evils and miseries that it had suffered in life because the mind could not get its thinking straight, the judge would side with the body and condemn the mind. The mind that will not let the body be healthy is cruel indeed: "You should therefore fix your mind upon what is possible and be content".4.1 Democritus believed that man completely ceased to exist after the death of the body, therefore he was desirous that his students would enjoy their bodily lives as much as possible, and that included letting go (being unattached to) the past and all other things which they were not able to control. A person may chose to look at past problems and turn them over and over in his mind without ever coming to a conclusion of what could have been a different choice even if he could return to the past. Some of the past that was very pleasant can also be an hindrance to the present and the future. Rabbit Run by John Updike was a popular success because it presented a sad fact of American culture: the popular high school athlete who married the popular cheer leader, and both lived in the past, and could not make a life of it together in the present. Rabbit ran away from every situation whereby he would have to come into the present and face life as an adult. He preferred to go to the park, even by himself, and shoot baskets. Each time he ran away from the present he further complicated his life.

Cicero tells of both the unhappy man, and the happy one in his Discussions At Tusculum (V.6.8-20), and tells certain characteristics of the unhappy man. One of them is his redoing in his mind the difficulties of his past, so that the unhappiness of that past time is kept alive voluntarily by the choice of the unhappy man of the present; for he relives his exile, his bereavements, his childlessness. The man complains: "How can somebody suffering from such afflictions be anything but exceptionally unhappy?" Cicero then states: "...the more he is convinced that this is so, the more desperately miserable his existence really is."

Plutarch (50AD-120AD) was traveling far from home when he received a delayed message from home that his little and only daughter had died, but despite his own great sorrow, he wrote a letter of Consolation to His Wife in which he gently consoles her with his Platonic philosophy. One can feel his own hurt in his words that are meant to lift up the spirits of his wife, such sentences as: "Above all, my dear wife, help us both preserve our customary composure in this affliction. I am of course very sensible of it and feel its force...After the birth of our four sons you yearned for a daughter, and I seized the opportunity of giving her your dear name: I know she was precious to you...The two years of her life must by no means be effaced from our memory but rathered reckoned as a pleasure, for they afforded us delight and happiness. We must never consider a small good as a large evil, nor be ungrateful for what fortune has given us because it has not filled the measure as full as we expected. Always respectfulness to the divine and a cheerful and uncomplaining attitude towards fortune produces fruit that is good and sweet."4.2   Several things are to be noted in Plutarch's Consolation to his Wife. All things are temporal in this life, some shorter in time than others, but all are to be judged by their goodness and beauty, not the length of time that they existed. This even includes a longed for and loved child. The time was small, but the blessing was great as it brought delight and happiness. Happy moments which a person can cherish are a blessing, even if those moments are not extended for as long as one might wish. "We must <u>never</u> consider a small good as a large evil." What beautiful and lovely words from this Platonic Philosopher of the First and Second Century after Christ. Both the good and the bad of the past are gone and must stay in the past; the good can be a cherished thought laden with gratitude, and the bad can be dismissed as a sometimes necessary byproduct of life itself. But it is needful that both be in the past, and that the past which was painful be unattached to the present and the future.

B. THINGS BEYOND OUR CONTROL

Many other things, occurrences and situations in life are beyond our control, not just the past. To those elements of life in which a person can have absolutely no power by which he can change them, even just a little, he must remain unattached and let them be. They are simply not in his power, and he must not let himself be in their power. In some things we can become involved, but we only make them worst and must leave the situation alone--at least for the present. Jesus told a parable about a man who had planted his crops, but while he was asleep his enemy (probably a competitor in the production of food business) planted weeds among them to dwarf their growth. The laborers asked if the man would like them to root out the weeds, but the man felt that would only further damage the crops. "Allow both the weeds and the wheat to grow together until it is time to harvest the wheat. Then I shall have the harvesters to uproot the weeds first and bind them up to be burned. Then the wheat will be harvested and brought into my granary" (Mt 13:24-30). Sometimes even happenings in our very presence must be left alone until a later time, when perhaps they can be corrected or their damage limited, and maybe, sometimes, they can never be corrected. To be attached to an unalterable past, an unchangeable present, and a future of uncertainty is to surrender our power of will over our lives. Jesus also made a significant statement about the lack of power in some of the smallest things (which today may not apply, but then it did); "You can not make one hair (on the head) black or white"(Mt 5:36). Others wanted to be much taller: the average male of that time was probably about 5'3" tall (based on the principle that the average Roman soldier was 5'4"). Stories of the past making King Saul seven feet tall and Goliath perhaps even taller assuredly filled many with the desire to be much taller than they were. Jesus even seemed to believe there was a sense of anxiety about it--perhaps because the Jews were under Roman rule. Yet for all such anxiety and hopes, and maybe even prayers, he pointed out to them that all such anxiety has not added to their heights: "But you who have been anxious about it, which of you has added one cubit (18") to his stature?" (Mt 6:27). Anxiety about things that are not in our control is psychologically defeating.

The great teacher and philosopher Epictetus said that making a distinction as to what we could change and what we could not was not always so easy, yet it had to be made if a person was going to have any peace of mind at all..

> What then is education? Education is the learning how to adapt the natural precognitions to the particular things conformably to nature; and then to distinguish that of things some are in our power, but others are not; in our power are will and all acts which depend on the will; (Discourses, Book One, Chapter 22).

To be educated is to know what you can do and what you can not do, what you can change and what you can not change. Without that distinction being made, a man has little chance of liberating himself from anxieties, fears, and ultimate dread of all life's circumstances. Epictetus added:

> ...That the things which are free from hindrance are in the power of the will; and those which are subject to hindrance are things which are not in the power of the will. And, for this reason, if he thinks that his good and his interest be in these things only which are free from hindrance and in his power, he will be free, prosper-ous, happy, free from harm, magnanimous, pious, thankful to God

for all things; in no matter finding fault with any of the things which have not been put in his power, nor blaming any of them. But if he thinks that his good and his interest are in externals and in things which are not in the power of his will, he must of necessity be hindered, be impeded, be a slave to those who have the power over things which he admires and fears; and he must of necessity be impious because he thinks that he is harmed by God, and he must be unjust because he always claims more than belongs to him; and he must of necessity be abject and mean (Discourses IV.7)

Cicero had much to say about the ability to enjoy life even after blindness set in, and encourages others to take note and courage from the examples which he gave: Antipater the Cyrenaic answered the grumblings about his blindness by his womenfolk and replied, "Don't you think one can have a good time in the night?"; Appius Claudius, who built the Appian Way (312BC), went blind but still gave counsel at the meetings of state officials; Gaius Drusus, after blindness set in, became somewhat of a guru as the multitudes came to him for advice; Gnaeus Aufidius, a former praetor, dictated his history and met with officials for their benefit, both after he was blinded; the philosopher Diodotus who lived within Cicero's household, whom Cicero thought was more mentally powerful in his blindness during philosophical discussions than he was beforehand. Cicero goes on to mention many others, who had absolutely no control over their blindness, but managed great lives over the things over which they had control. Helen Keller, who lost both hearing and vision as a child, became a respected counselor to others because of her courageous and happy life despite the lost of the two vital senses.

Boethius was "told" by Philosophia that life is divided into what can be done by the will and that which man has not the power to do. It seemed very basic, but very important:

It is agreed that there are two things upon which depends the performance of every human action: will and power. If one of these be lacking, nothing can be effected. For, if the will be lacking, a man does not even undertake that which he has no desire to perform, while, if the power be lacking, the will is exercised in vain.(IV. Prose II).

Perhaps the backbone of <u>Taoist</u> teaching is the unquestioning submission to what is beyond our knowledge and control for then one "would sleep tranquilly, and awake in contented simplicity."

C. <u>UNATTACHMENT FROM THE DESIRES OF THE MATERIAL REALM</u>

Unattachment from the past and from things not in our control must be supplemented by unattachment from the entire material realm. In the last chapter such various desires were discussed. Yet, because we are human and this is the only world we actually know and experience in a "scientific" way, the material realm seems so important to us, and is in many ways--since life is good (Chapter Two)--attachment to it seems very natural, and it is certainly in no way evil. However, it is still some-thing outside ourselves, our true being. For our true being is not in wealth, a lovely house, and how many college educated children we have. They are nice and wonderful things, but not part of our ultimate being. Therefore, because of the very beauty of their pleasantness and allure, they are all that more powerful in gaining the ultimate devotion of our life quest, and this can be quite destructive to our hoped for tranquility and happiness. It is a matter of enjoying them without being attached to them, and some people have trouble making that distinction. To two brothers arguing over the inheritance they had received, and who sought Jesus' judgment, Jesus, refusing to be such a judge, warned them both to "Beware, and withdraw yourselves from the realm of covetousness, because no one's life comes from the abundance of the things he owns" (Lk12:15). For such violent desires for one thing (in this case the inheritance) will blind the soul to all other needs and destroy the possibility of a balanced and harmonious life. <u>Epicurus</u> counseled his followers to take all into consideration, and make distinctions among our desires: "Of our desires some are natural and necessary; others are natural, but not necessary; others, again, are neither natural nor necessary, but are due to illusory opinion".4.3 <u>Boethius</u>' Philosophia reminded him: "Human spirits must be the more free the more they maintain themselves in the contemplation of the divine mind, less free when their attention is distracted towards material things, and even less free when they are tied to their earthly things." (V.ProseII).

1. ACCEPTING THE ENTIRE EARTHLY REALM AS A
    TEMPORARY LIFE: UNATTACHMENT AND RESIGNATION

The one great attachment to the one great unchangeable is the attachment to the temporal realm of which the body is a part. And, since man's temporality can not be changed, man must seek a peaceful and honest resignation to that fact, and work within it to find life meaningful. Some have great difficulty doing this as shown above with the attitudes of Camus and Sartre. But others accept it and move on to loving and happy lives. Even though Epictetus believed in a kind and loving God, he was not sure about life after death, and as most Stoics, he was resigned to whatever fate brought him during his temporal existence, and encouraged his followers to "make the best use that we can of the things which are in our power, and use the rest according to their nature". There is a Buddhist story that depicts a man who can not accept his limitations about his own life or his own possessions. It is found in Yogacara Bhumi Sutra, Ch. IV, and goes basically like this. Children were playing in the sand by the sea, and decided to built sandcastles. But the play turned to seriousness about the "ownership" of the castles, and one boy destroyed the castle of another, and the "owner" of the castle as well as his friends brutally beat the child with a stick and kicked him while he was on the ground. Each then went on "playing" and each one kept declaring "this is my castle, no one else can touch it". However, when evening approached, and the tide was coming in, no one anymore cared about "his castle", some even destroying their own castles, and went each to his own home. The evening comes to all humans, and before each one departs to his own destiny, he, only then, realizes the emptiness of being attached to his own castle, even to the point of harming others. Earth can be a playful experience and happy existence for all without such violent attachment. The story is not meant to justify the boy who prematurely destroyed another's work, but to show the evil violence in each of us over something that has a very brief life and especially if it was constructed for temporary play in the first place.

The Srimad Bhagavatam, as well as much other wisdom from the Indian Scriptures, gives man sound advice, which is summarized:

The following things have been ascertained and declared by all the Scriptures of the world to be of the greatest good to mankind:

First, to delight in the Self, which is one with God, or to love God; and
    secondly to be without attachment to anything else in the universe.
This true love and non-attachment must be developed gradually by
    these means.
By faith and reverence.
By inquiry into the Truth.
By devotion to spiritual practices.
By learning to love solitude.
By injuring no creature and by truthfulness.
By control of the senses.
By overcoming the passions.
By not speaking against other religions.
By patiently bearing the opposites of life, such as pleasure and pain,
    success and failure.
Thus will arise love for God and non-attachment to the world.
When love is firmly established in his heart, a man becomes master of
    himself and a teacher of humanity.4.4

Although God plays a central role in such moral living and happiness, still for those who do not believe in the existence of God, the striving for truth, the unattachment to things, the desire for some spirituality, the control of the senses and passions, and patience and grace under the pressures of failure and pain, and love for others are certainly avenues by which one can enrich his life and give it direction and meaning. Some men hoard their earthly wealth to the day of their deaths, and then it becomes totally out of their power anyway. The Tibetan Book of the Dead warns a departed soul which is still hovering and has not yet been assigned to a new level for its next reincarnation that if, looking down on his still earthly bound posterity, it (the soul) even then is attached to his past possessions, he is in deep spiritual trouble. It shows that he has yet to understand that he is not his possessions and must start over again at the very bottom of existence (Book II, part I).

What I like about this thought is the proposed extension that the attachment to earthly goods has into even the next phase of one's existence. For those who do not believe in the next phase, one can simply apply the idea to a dying man's thoughts who is embittered by the fact that he must leave his wealth behind for others to enjoy. Just think, a lifetime's work and thrift to accumulate what someone else will now enjoy, and that attachment enslaves a man's last thoughts before death. How sad! Was Solon actually right when he said not to call any man happy until the day of his death?

2. RESULTS: BOTH GOOD AND BAD OF "UNATTACHMENT"

This strong emphasis upon "indifference' (a word preferred by the Christian mystics) or "unattachment" has drawn criticism, especially from the West and from Christianity who, in some cases was not too pleased with some of its own mystics and monks who felt they did nothing and lived off of the work of others, and some of the criticism is just. To some it is easy to misread the intentions of those calling for indifference or unattachment, thinking that this is a way to avoid all human work and responsibilities and throw the burden of all society, including themselves, upon others. The Western critics have been quick to point out that the East, especially the areas of Indian influence, lag far behind the West in producing the necessary elements to make this world better in science and comfort of living. As I just said, this is a valid criticism. No vaccines, no excess of food for others, no artificial drugs to alleviate pain, no automobiles, no trains, no airplanes--indeed, very little has come to aid mankind's suffering or enriched mankind's earthly living standards from Central and Southern Asia; and some of these lacks may be attributed to the strong influence of unattachment to material things that is so deeply embedded in Indian religion. Having acknowledged this defect, let us give due credit to the concept of unattachment properly understood that it deserves. One element of unattachment focuses, not on being indifferent to work, but on being unattached to the results, and this lessens psychological pressure to be more excellent than one is and avoids the capitalistic dog eat dog world whereby virtue is often seen as a hindrance to "getting ahead" or being a "success"-- "success" often meaning wealth. It may mean that a person who would "get ahead" by nearly abandoning his family for the sake of work and "worldly success" is missing the mark by being too attached to work and thus his priorities are in disarray. It does no good for the West to pile up comfort after comfort and then have its citizens use a pound or two of drugs each month trying to stay operative. What unattachment means is that life is not over if you do not drive the car of your dreams or you do not have a vacation every year or if you or your children do not reach the level of "success" that you dreamed of. An artist may strive all his life to get a book published, a symphony played, a building blueprint accepted without the desired results. Unattachment means that one can enjoy the work, the quest, even if the results desired do not take place. Excellence in any activity is a virtue, indeed, but if excellence is not materially rewarded, it does not mean one ought not continue to strive after excellence, just not to strive and be attached to the results. Unattachment liberates a man from "having to have this or that", from adult toys, from keeping up with the Joneses, from being better looking than the guy down the street, from having one more bathroom in your house than your brother has, and most important, from the feeling that one's mortality makes all human activity worthless and life itself meaningless. Live life virtuously and turn its results over to Nature, to the Cosmic Spirit, or to God; for unattachment is a surrender to reality that is the necessary foundation of faith. In that sense, the East seems to be much more spiritual than the West, and we in the West can learn from their spirituality. The Bhagavad-Gita is aware of its people misreading the concept of unattachment:

But he who, with strong body serving mind,
Gives up his mortal power to worthy work,
Not seeking gain, Arjuna! such an one
Is honourable. Do thine allotted task!
Work is more excellent than idleness;
The body's life proceeds not, lacking work.
....
.........such earthly duty do
Free from desire, and thou shalt well perform
Thy heavenly purpose.(III.Virtue in Work)

And also from the Bhagavad-Gita:

But thou, want not! ask not! Find full reward
Of doing right in right! Let right deeds be

Thy motive, not the fruit which comes from them.
And live in action! Labour! Make thine acts
Thy piety, casting all self aside,
Contemning gain and merit.(II. The Book of Doctrines)

Of course, we in the West would disagree about a man having at least some attachment to the results of his work, and I agree with our thinking that we do have a right to the fruits to our work. But the above passages makes it clear that unattachment or disinterestedness does not mean avoidance of work or a life of irresponsibility. That such views of unattachment are used as excuses for laziness in India is most probable, but we also have labor slow-downs and laziness even in our own working-man's unions whereby a man seeks the fruits of his labors even when not laboring at a level that predicates such benefits.

Being unattached to the desires of the material realm, especially when we wish to make the material things the source of our pleasure, is a benefit and most helpful, in some cases in minor things, but for those who see this life as the all of reality for them, then learning unattachment to life itself helps the soul to be more at ease and simply to enjoy the benefits and happiness of the life that Nature gives to mortal humans. There is a story about Omar Khayyam from which we can learn to both desire work and excellence and at the same time be detached from wealth and other alluring status symbols. Omar and two of his friends, as youths, made a covenant with each other, that whoever would come into a great fortune would share it equally with the other two. Nizam, one of Omar's friends did come into a great fortune, and was willing to keep his covenant with Omar and Hasan, who quickly demanded his full rights to Nizam's fortune. Nizam kept his promise to Hasan as he fully intended to do all the time. Hasan later grew arrogant and tried to far surpass Nizam and even tried to overthrow the remnants of his realm. Omar came to Nizam with a detached and peaceful happiness for his friend, and although Nizam offered him his third of the fortune, Omar replied that he would be well satisfied if he could just live in Nizam's country, shadowed away in a small corner of the land, to study and spread wide the advantages of science, and to pray for Nizam's long life and prosperity. Happiness was not in money, but in the friendship and the opportunity to work for the benefit of mankind: he understood the virtue of unattachment properly.

II. TAKING CONTROL

The first section dwelt upon unattachment by which one could liberate himself from the secondary elements of one's existence to be free to take control of his life for the things that truly matter, and this section will have six parts: Burying the Past, Exercising the Control that we do have, Rising from Failures and Salvaging Broken Dreams, Lessening Desires by Rational Choice, The Balanced Life, and Gratitude.

Taking control means that each one must be personally responsible for his own life destiny; he has to make it happen for himself. Marcus Aurelius, in his Meditations (III.5) declared "Be cheerful also, and seek not external help nor the tranquillity which others give. A man then must stand erect, not be kept erect by others." We must be active (stand upright ourselves) not passive, letting outside circumstances put us in its place (not be kept up). Self-fortified and confidently we walk the path of our own choosing, then there can be inner harmony which we can use as a basis of wholeness and happiness.

A. BURY THE PAST

Anxiety about the past events is self-destructive, and the solution is simple (at least simply said): bury the past in a casket that is solid, unopenable, and airproof. Put it away once for all. Confucius, hearing a conversation about the problems of the past approached the two and said: "Things that are done, it is needless to speak about; things that have run their course, it is needless to remonstrate about; things that are past, it is needless to blame."(Analects III.21.2). Aristotle in his Nicomachean Ethics 1139b 5-10), while discussing the power and obligation of choice, told his students that choice could not apply to the past, so think about now and the future, not the past. If one is to reason about choices and decisions, he must do it about the present, for it is not possible to change the past. For, said Aristotle, not even a god can change the past.

> "It is to be noted that nothing that is past is an object of choice, e.g. no one chooses to have sacked Troy; for no one deliberates about the past, but about what is future and capable of being otherwise, while what is past is not capable of not having taken place."

While all of us have made errors of the past, and would like to be able to change them, it is not possible, and, therefore, to be heavily burdened by them is to create more obstacles for the health of our future choices. One can always laugh at one's prior stupidity. William James thought levity better for one's personality than a heavy solemnity about something we can not undo.

> Our errors are surely not such awfully solemn things. In a world
> where we are so certain to incur them in spite of all our caution,
> a certain lightness of heart seems healthier than this excessive
> nervousness on their behalf (Essays on Faith and Morals: The
> Will to Believe, VII)

Here, of course, he is not talking about a harmful and sinful act to another, which always calls for the satisfaction of justice and forgiveness. But rather the sadness we tend to have over choices of education, marriage, children, job and other important but still unchangeable things of the past. And if we are bothered by even trivial things of the past, then we are seeking depression and melancholy. Immanuel Kant once had a servant that, rather than being a help to him, was a constant source of irritation, and finally Kant fired him, and made a huge note that he hung facing himself: "Remember to forget Lumpke."

Jesus had to remind his disciples that certain traditions of the past are no longer applicable, even if they at one time had some value, and that those traditions which had become intolerable sacred laws of his people, causing great guilt in the hearts of those who broke them (Sabbath laws, divorce laws, laws of what was clean and unclean--both in personal hygiene and what one could eat, laws of justice, etc.), should be buried with other outdated laws in the past. Something new and life- giving was present in his teachings and if they were poured into the old wineskins of the past they would be lost. His way of building happiness was a new garment for mankind and if one sought to sew patches from old garments upon it, the new would be destroyed with the old. Bury the past and preach the kingdom of God was the message of Jesus, for then, and then only, could one become a new creature who was free to start with a new foundation upon which to build his life.

B. EXERCISING THE CONTROL WE HAVE

Being freed from the past, one is liberated into choice and responsibility for one's own future. Each day is a new day that is going to set forth many situations in which man must choose what he is going to do and how he is going to be responsible for it. After one excludes the past, he must then make the fine distinctions between the things he has power to change and the things he does not in the choices which are present in his life at this time. If one refuses the power to control that which is in his control, then he has surrendered any possibility for honorable dignity, wholeness, and happiness. Jesus told a story (Lk 19:11-26) in which a nobleman was to go on a long and distant trip and called together his ten servants, giving each of them a mina (unit of money), and told them to trade with the money and see what profit they could make. Perhaps this was a test for elevating certain servants to more responsible positions in the management of his realm. When he returned, he asked for an accounting of their activities: one had managed to gain ten minas more, another came and brought five minas more, but a third brought only the one mina that was given to him, because he was afraid to utilize it, fearing he would lose it and be reprimanded by his lord. The nobleman was furious, calling him a wicked person who avoided his responsibility and did not even have the courage to put it safely in a bank, for then it would have at least drawn interest. He was promptly excluded from any chance of moving to an administrative position. He was given power to control his future, and refused to take it, and lost all hope of advancement. Jesus was teaching his followers that they may seem restricted in the things that were in their power, but even if they had a single mina only, they were responsible for the way they used it or did not use it. That is man's lesson, only he can use the talent given him, no one else can use it for him. Only he who commands himself is free. Cicero reminded his friends that a wise person who stays in control of that which is in his control, need not worry about fate for "when faced with the unexpected, he will judge and decide calmly by his own established standards. There is, no possibility, that, for certain comes to my mind, that is more beatific." (Discussions at Tusculum V.28.81). A man who sets his standards by his own choice, and continues to live by them regardless of circumstances outside of himself, he is in control of his life as much as possible, and that would be man's happiest condition. In another bit of advice of Cicero, he implies the thought that "you are your body's god". Be in control! By your own choices and thoughts you can control that which is in your control, and about the rest, do not have anxiety. Mencius: "Thus it is that the superior man has a life long care, but not one morning's calamity."(4.2.7)

Marcus Aurelius stated to himself:

> If you are pained by any external thing, it is not this thing that disturbs you, but your own judgement about it. And it is in your power to wipe out this judgement now. But if anything in your own disposition gives you pain, who hinders you from correcting your opinion? (Meditations:VIII.47).

Take control! If you have the power to change it, change it. If there is a defect in your attitude that prevents you from changing a tiresome life, correct it! The Stoics did not like whiners. They bluntly said that "if there is too much smoke in the house, then leave it", meaning, if life is that tiresome or annoying, end it! For it is more noble to leave life than to stay and drag down the rest of humanity which is thankful for life and is willing to fulfill its role dutifully and cheerfully.

The Roman Satirist Juvenal in his "With an invitation to dinner" (Satire XI) tells his invited guests that the time in his house will be one of simple and happy fellowship, unencumbered by any of the guest's problems in life. For they shall not be mentioned in his house, as they tarnish and make less beautiful their mutual celebration of life and friendship.

> Far other sports our banquet boasts today,
> The tale of Ilium, or that rival lay
> Which holds in deep suspense the dubious bay!
> ...
> Forget at once, your house, your menial train,
> Forget your troubles all! Nor reckon o'er
> Friends of your youth that now be friends no more.

Be natural and enjoy the simple things that are really the backbone of pleasant times and friendship! We take control of what we can, and let the other things flow according to nature. "We must make the best use that we can of the things which are in our power, and use the rest according to their nature" (Epictetus Discourses, I.1). Aristotle, in Book Three of the Nicomachean Ethics, lets his students know that they can only logically deliberate about the things that are in their control to change, reminding them that it is a waste of time for a Spartan to question the role of govenment among the Scythians, as they have very little in their power to change it.(1112a)

Man is to deliberate about the things that are in his power, and then realize it in action. William James believed that life was worth living indeed, and that each is responsible for the value of his life.

> This life is worth living, we can say, since it is what we make it, from the moral point of view; and we are determined to make it from that point of view, so far as we have anything to do with it, a success.4.5

Carl Rogers points to the fact, a fact in his mind, that in order to change one must be honest about himself and accept what his own honesty declares him to be, and then, accepting what he is presently, he then can be in a state of mind that empowers him to change himself and his situation in life.

> ...because the curious paradox is that when I accept myself as I am, then I change. I believe that I have learned this from my clients as well as within my own experience--that we cannot change, we cannot move away from what we are, until we thoroughly accept what we are. Then change seems to come about almost unnoticed.4.6

Honesty within, about both ourselves and our circumstances in life, about both what we can do and what we do not have the power to do, is a necessity in giving us the courage and power to control our lives, enhance our lives, and give to ourselves a peaceful beauty of wholeness.

C. LESSENING OUR DESIRES BY RATIONAL CHOICES

It has been mentioned previously the damage that passions, desires, and emotions can do to destabilize a person to such a point that no harmony within can be established. Now it is necessary to lessen those desires to their proper limits and if required to destroy completely those desires that will not be harnessed and controlled by the mind. This calls for an honest deliberation as to what is necessary and what is just another stubborn "but I want it" category that is often displayed by children, an impulse that does not necessarily go away with the accumulation of years (that is why there is such profit in making "adult toys"). What makes this category of impulsive desires so dangerous is that it is not in the past and it is not out of our control, therefore, it is a real present danger to the proper development of man's maturity and growth into wisdom. Again, let us listen to our teachers, and hear them with our hearts and minds.

According to Luke 19, Jesus went into the house of a tax collector, who was "a chief tax collector, and rich", whose name was Zacchaeus, who after sharing some time with Jesus realized that he had been seeking the wrong things in life and had unjustly overtaxed people for the sake of excess profit and wealth. His mind-set was changed, and in order to fight this obsession for wealth and to do justice to those he had harmed, he declared to Jesus, "Observe me, Lord, for I am giving half of all my possessions to the poor, and if another shows that I have falsely taxed, I shall repay him fourfold of the amount of the over taxation (vs 8-9)" Evidently he started the process, and Jesus, comforted him, assuring him that such a mind-set and its subsequent actions have brought into his house the spirit of salvation. He was born again to a new perspective that will gave him inner comfort and joy. Assuredly, Zaccheus slept happily that night with a balanced soul. His desires were lessened, but his life was greatly enhanced.

Plato puts into Socrates mouth in the Phaedo (84a-b) the following words:

No, this soul [a philosopher's] secures immunity from its desires by following reason and abiding always in her company, and by contemplating the true and divine and unconjecturable, and drawing inspiration from it, because such a soul believes that this is the right way to live while life endures, and that after death it reaches a place which is kindred and similar to its own nature, and there is rid forever of human ills (trans.Hugh Tredennick).

<u>Plutarch,</u> in condemning Demetrius' avarice, wrote:

> However, he did but justify the saying of Plato, that the only certain
> way to be truly rich is not to have more property, but fewer desires.
> For whoever is always grasping at more avows that he is still in want,
> and must be poor in the midst of affluence.4.7

Of the 18 demerits (or vicious acts) of <u>Jainism,</u> five deal directly with the
desires for things: stealing (directly or indirectly), over-attachment to
one's belongings, covetousness, greed or avarice, and personal
attachment. One of the principle doctrines of <u>Epicureanism</u> is the ability
to distinguish between what is naturally necessary and what is not. "Of
our desires some are natural and necessary; others are natural, but not
necessary; others again, are neither natural nor necessary, but are due to
illusory opinion". 4.8. Luxuries and other ornamental objects, if properly
used, may actually add to the beauty or pleasure of life. But, in general,
to desire them and to spend time to earn money to buy them is
symptomatic of an emptiness and vanity within. <u>Chuang Tsu</u> (Tse)
warned his followers: "He who understands the conditions of life does
not strive after what is of no use to life."4.9 <u>Juvenal</u> lamented that the
old Roman values were gone (this was a common practice in all ancient
as well as in all modern societies: every grandfather usually says
something like "in my day"), and his day was filled with the desire for
money, excess money--wealth, and the old work ethic with its simple
pleasures forgotten or despised. From the lust of money comes crime and
even murder:

> Now the suburban garden asks for more
> than claimed the name of land in days of yore.
> Of all the fierce desires that fire the soul,
> none oftener draws the blade, or drugs the bowl
> than that of wealth! of which the impious sway.
> O'erleaps all bounds, and hears not of delay! (Satire XIV:225-230)

<u>Juvenal</u> lamented the loss of balanced thought, which man showed in his
frenzy to be rich, and to be rich quickly, even if procured by murder, and
instead encouraged his readers to live with the simple blessings of life
and work, family and house. <u>Shankara</u> warned his followers that if one

gives in to his cravings for objects, the craving will continue to grow and want more and more, and then all self-control is lost. "When craving grows stronger, self-control is lost. When self-control is lost, craving grows stronger than ever."4.10 A man's spiritual emptiness is like a vacuum, cravings keep rushing in to fill it, and that vacuum as it is fed more and more becomes something like a black-hole in space: it devours everything and can not resist anything. Man becomes a slave to his own desires. He must lessen his desires and the spiritual vacuum, unfed, will soon cease to exist. There is a short story told among the Sufis that is called "The Miser and The Angel of Death", and it shows the foolishness of spending the brief time a man has allotted in life on the pursuit of money, for it can not buy the most important things. When the Angel of Death comes to the miser and tells him he now must leave life, the miser offers first 200,000 dinars for two more days on earth. After this is rejected, the miser then offers 300,000 dinars for just one more day on earth, and this request is also rejected. The miser then realized that that for which he had worked all his life had taken his life and can offer nothing for him now, and asked for just a brief moment to write something down for those still living. This request was granted, and he wrote: "Man, make use of your life. I could buy not one hour for 300,000 dinars. Make sure that you realize the value of your time."4.11 Meister Eckhart wrote an article "About Disinterest" in which he lamented the sad fact that people had all their interests and attachments directed towards "transient goods, since they are unaware of the inner person". Yet that is precisely who a man is, his inner person, and when he ceases to care about the inner person and, instead, pursues outside objects and has a deep attachment to them, he loses himself and almost becomes the objects themselves while emptying his own soul. Goethe stated in his Faust (I):

Du bist am Ende--was du bist.
Setz dir Peruecken auf von Millionen Locken,
Setz deinen Fuss auf ellenhohe Socken,
Du bleibst doch immer, was du bist.

In the end, you are what you are.
Put on a wig with a million curls,
Put on stockings that are an ell (45 inches) high,

You always remain yet what you are.

The desires for a beautiful wig or the latest fashion of clothing will not change one's essence, but may cost a hefty fee, and soon be out of fashion; for as man himself is temporal the things for which he often lives are even more temporal. The less desires a man has, the easier it is for him to be content. Thoreau wrote the following to Blake:

> It is surprising how contented one can be with nothing definite,-- only a sense of existence...O how I laugh when I think of my vague, indefinite riches. No run on my bank can drain it, for my wealth is not possession but enjoyment.

Francis of Sales recommended attacking quickly the small desires and conquering them completely so that the larger desires are not encouraged to try to control you. Think about, meditate, and even commend yourself to God, until the desire is past or conquered:

> Do not permit your desires, however small or trivial they may be, to disquiet you. For after the little ones, those which are greater and more important may find your heart involved in trouble and disorder. When you perceive that anxiety begins to affect your mind, recommend yourself to God. Resolve to do nothing that your desire demands until it is restored to tranquillity, unless it should be something that cannot be deferred. In that case, you must with a meek and tranquil effort hold back the current of your desires, restraining and moderating them as much as possible. Whereupon, perform the action, not according to your desire, but according to reason.4.12

How much more leisurely and pleasure oriented can be a family's outing to the beach, to the woods, to the river, or up the mountain, than staying at home and nearly motionlessly play at one's video games. The health advantages of walking and climbing, running and playing, as well as the experiencing the beauty of nature, and unexpectingly seeing a little creature for the first time, are so much more delightful and soul filling, it is a wonder why people sit in front of the TV at all. Nature they have freely, and it is given up because of a desire to possess something that often is not only paralyzing but costly and empty of moral value and gratitude for the beauty of life. <u>Aristotle</u>, true enough, will remind us all that there is a golden mean to life, and that even artificially made objects can give us pleasure and add to our lives, but only when one has and exercises self-control. Yet, most of our teachers, will agree with <u>Plato</u> that the only sure way of being "rich" is not to have more things, but fewer desires. By the will and rational choice, man may enrich himself by lessening his desires.

D.   <u>RISING</u> <u>FROM</u> <u>FAILURES</u>
       <u>AND</u> <u>SALVAGING</u> <u>BROKEN</u> <u>DREAMS</u>

<u>OR</u>

<u>THE</u> <u>ART</u> <u>OF</u> <u>ADAPTABILITY</u>

Sometimes there are great changes in our lives, such as health, or in the circumstances in which we live that break our normal way of living or destroy the dreams that we are pursuing. Some quit and give up, but the wise person will "rise from the ashes" or adapt to the new situation with courage and vigor, for he knows that he still can make life meaningful and beautiful because it is in his power to do so. "All things change" were the words of <u>Heraclitus</u>, and those that can not adapt are those who voluntarily give up their "mina" or "talent" and forsake their power to change with the changing circumstances of their lives. Jesus himself went from carpenter to teacher and divine leader, Matthew from a comfortable tax collector to one who joined his spiritual cause, James and John were fishermen with a rather uncontrolled temper (they were called the sons of thunder) to disciples of Jesus, although the rough edges seemed to have stayed with them for a long time. Likewise, Simon a patriotic zealot learned there was something much greater that a nationalistic cause in the presence of Jesus, and Nathaniel went from a skeptic to a believer and a follower. Of those twelve that Jesus called only Judas had difficulties with the change he had to make from a revolutionary Sicarii to the "turn the other cheek" philosophy of Jesus, and that inability caused him a terrible end. Jesus once commended, at least the intelligence of, one called "the unjust steward", who, after learning that his master was going to fire him, quickly made some generous deals with his master's creditors to assure himself of having some friends during his jobless time (Lk 16"1-9).

Mencius saw bad circumstances as an opportunity for one who, through careful thought and by adjusting, can grow in wisdom and show that he is a wise man.

> Men who are possessed of intelligent virtue and prudence in affairs
> will generally be found to have been in sickness and troubles. They
> are the friendless minister and concubine's son, who keep their
> hearts under a sense of peril, and use deep precautions against
> calamity. On this account they become distinguished for their
> intelligence (7.1.18).

When a man is in distress, he may discover, in his problem solving, that he has a spark of wisdom of which he was previously unaware, and that realization is confidence-building for his life. He managed to separate his status of being an illegitimate child (with its accompanying shame: in English he was a bastard) with that which was in his power. To overcome the circumstances made him a wiser and more successful person.

Demosthenes was a young brilliant Athenian who desperately wanted to participate in the debates within the popular Athenian Assembly, but his voice was very weak and he was talked down or even shouted down in public debates. But he knew he could change that. He attacked his problem with a discipline and courage that few would have. He constructed a subterraneous study, strongly exercising both his body and his voice, and would practice his orations before a mirror, working on his gestures. He exercised his mouth muscles by speaking loudly with small pebbles in his mouth (perhaps to overcome a possible stuttering habit), and he ran up steep hills while speaking loudly to build up his breathing stamina and did the same while running along the seashore. He committed to memory the substance of entire speeches of others, although he condensed their length to the essential points. He became a great orator.

A brief poem from Sanskrit makes the point of bouncing back quickly instead of not meeting the challenger with one's own power, and the reaction that a man has to his challenge is indicative of the nobility of his character:

> Good noble men, after a fall
>> Bounce like a ball.
> The ignoble fall another way:
>> Like lumps of clay.4.13

Life has both blessings and difficulties, but the wise man can adjust and even learn from his difficulties teaches Meister Eckhart: "We shall never be free from such difficulties in this present life, but we do not throw away good grain just because the rats often dwell in it. For the just man, pains and difficulties can be quite fruitful" (paraphrased from his "Talks of Instruction", Section 11). What Reinhold Niebuhr, in his book Beyond Tragedy, said of Christianity can also be applied to the individual:

> Hence periods of prosperity inevitably lead to the corruption of the
> Christian faith, while periods of adversity prompt men to probe more
> deeply into the nature and meaning of human life, to move from the
> parched places and plant their tree of faith by the water, where the
> roots may reach the river and where the leaf may remain green des-
> pite the year of drought. Thus periods of adversity are the seasons
> of genuine renewal of the Christian religion.4.14

In the early Christian Church there was a blind man Didymus, blinded when he was only four years old, yet he accumulated so much knowledge with a great ability of recall and instruction, so much so, that he became a teacher. Jerome was one of his students, and always afterwards referred to him as "master" (magister).4.15

Of course, no one wants their character and depth to be tested by problems, difficulties, and tragedies, yet, if they come, one must take up the challenge by taking control, doing the necessary action, and contemplating the power within his soul and mind to effectively succeed and grow wiser with the experience. One can live well and happy "beyond tragedy". John Donne, while very devotional in his faith, does manage to complain a lot about his circumstances and his bad health: he even envied the bird; "...how much happier then are birds than men, who can change the climate and accompany and enjoy the same season ever" (Devotions XIII). But that blessing for birds is the kindness of Nature or God, and man has his own blessings, reason and will, and if he can not fly away from his problems, he can understand them and solve them where he is.

   Helen Keller was born in 1880 in Tuscumbia, Alabama and at the age of only 19 months was struck by an unknown disease that left her permanently blind and deaf. She was imprisoned, but she escaped by utter determination. She had the will and wisdom to know that her life was still under her control, and she moved forward to becoming friends with many including Mark Twain and Alexander Graham Bell. She talked with the kings and queens of Europe as well as with four American presidents: Wilson, Coolidge, F.D. Roosevelt, and Eisenhower. But she kept steady in her "calling": to serve and help the blind. She once said: "A simple, childlike faith in a Divine Friend solves all the problems that come to us by land and sea." But, even though that faith was a spark that ignited her spirit, it was her grasping control of her life and with patience, will, and discipline she fulfilled it with grace and dignity.

E.   THE BALANCED LIFE

   All the great teachers who have appealed to many peoples for many years have taught a concept of balance, avoiding extremes of any kind. Plato taught that the human soul had three parts to it: the rational, the spirited, and the emotive. The rational used the intelligence in decision making and was the basis of wisdom, which, to Plato was the chief part of the human soul, which separated it from all other animals. The spirited part brought will and courage, the motivational and power giving part of the soul. Finally the emotive part, for emotions are a necessary part of the human psyche (Plato's word for soul). But he also felt that the emotive part was the most dangerous to balanced living, because it gave in too easily to bad impulses and unnecessary and sometimes selfish desires. It was definitely the lowest part of the soul, and it was the duty of the other two parts to control it, and if it were controlled then man would enjoy the wonder and happiness of a balanced soul. The control of the emotive part was called the virtue of temperance, and when such balance was achieved a man had a "just" soul, i.e. there was justice among the three parts and each part functioned fairly and in harmony with the other parts. This then gave mankind the four cardinal virtues of Plato: wisdom, courage, self-control (temperance), and justice, which four later added to the three "Christian" virtues of faith, hope, and love represented for Western man the "seven virtues" upon which to build his life. Plato taught us to keep balanced in thought and actions if we wanted to be virtuous, which, for him, was the foundation for happiness: only the good man can be happy.

Aristotle used a concept called the golden mean to regulate both actions and desires, but it could not always apply to every act: murder was always evil and the golden mean then did not apply. But for the concept of courage, it would, for courage was, at least to Aristotle, midway between rashness and cowardice in battle. What man can learn from Aristotle is to ask himself the question, "Am I over reacting or am I under reacting, and where can I find a logical and moderate way to think and to act in this particular situation? How can I balance out each yes or no?

In almost all the philosophies and theologies of ancient India the summum bonum (the greatest good) is Moksa (liberation), which basically means that man is liberated from desires and unattached to things and events, so that he can naturally and rationally walk his path in life without outside interference.

The Sermon at Benares is attributed to Buddha in the presence of five of his students when he himself was quite old, and his "middle path" is very similar in concept to Aristotle's golden mean. Buddha declared that man is to follow the middle path and avoid both extremes. Acceptance of life in its natural form without inordinate lusts is the only way to any form of happiness and liberation from the objects of illusion.To satisfy one's natural needs of the body will not defile him, but excess of any wants or lusts will keep him in a state of slavery. For a man always concerned with his sensual passions does become a slave of them...but that to satisfy the necessities of life is not evil... And "this is the middle path". It is while on this middle path that he can recognize the difference between a "rope" and a "a snake" (as he steps upon it in the dark: a symbolic saying), and in recognizing the true nature of the rope, his fear is lost, and the tranquillity of his mind will come back to him, he will be relieved and will be joyful and happy. Aeschylus declared that possessions "must not be revered, except how men use them"(The Persians 168-169). A utilitarian possession is indeed a help to man, but its virtue (as both Plato and Aristotle explained) was in it function, and only for that is the possession to be honored. To be anxious about the possession itself, is foolish. The Gospel of Thomas attributes this statement to Jesus: "Do not be concerned from morning until evening and from evening until morning about what you will wear" (logion 36). Actually it is quite amusing to sit back and try to picture Buddha, Socrates, Plato, or Jesus concerned about what to wear, as the value of clothes was the function of cover and warmth; anything else was superfluous to them. Wear that which is natural and functional--that was it! A "white sport coat and a pink carnation" was not their "cup of tea". What then, are nice clothes evil? of course not. But be balanced, and if you dread going somewhere because you can not afford to own the "proper" and "fashionable" clothes, then you are trying to find your happiness in possessions, and that leads one away from the middle path and lets society or others dictate. Be proper, but stay in the middle of the path. "Be balanced in life" our great teachers are telling us, "and there you will find a gentle self-acceptance and a harmony within your soul".

F. GRATITUDE

The Gospel of Luke tells the story of Jesus' ministering to ten lepers in the borderland between Galilee and Samaria in which Jesus told them to go to the priests to get the final declaration that they had been healed from this terrible disease that ostracized them from the rest of society. Upon the official declaration of their cleansing, one, a Samaritan, returned to Jesus, fell upon his face before him and thanked him. Jesus was puzzled that only one of ten gave thanks. Gratitude for life and its blessings is an absolute necessity for one trying to build a life that will result in wholeness and happiness. So many blessings are taken for granted in life, and so many, instead of being thankful for all that they have and have experienced, complain about numerous other things and dwell in a bitter and ungrateful mood throughout their lives. Rudolph Bultmann lived through the brutality of Germany's two wars in which the people of Germany and others, especially those caught between Hitler's Nazis and Stalin's terrorizing forces, suffered greatly. Yet, in the midst of this, when one would think that being bitter was the only natural attitude to have, Bultmann declared that 20th Century's man's greatest sin is ingratitude. After all, Hitler and Stalin were now gone, and the West had a chance to rebuild itself into a healthy and prosperous future.

Man must leave the past, forget what is not in his control, reject bitterness, and move into the future courageously and with gratitude that a better future lies before him. Why did not the other nine lepers return to give thanks, perhaps they were still embittered for the sufferings that they had previously experienced; but one said yes to the future with gratitude. Anacreon wrote an ode (No. 11) about his aging, his hair all gone, and his appearance aged, yet he declared that he was going to enjoy the present and the future as he had the past. Aging is natural, and there was no bitterness to keep him from being happy and sportive in the present: "But this I know, that every day shall see me sportive, blithe and gay; For 'tis our wisdom so to do the nearer death appears in view." Theognis simply declared that ungrateful people were low class: "There is no gratitude in common men" (Elegies 854). Horace wrote that man should be joyful and live day by day and not be anxious about the future:

"Tomorrow with its cares despise,
  And make the present hour your own,
Be swift to catch it as it flies,
  And score it up as clearly won;
Nor let your youth disdain to prove
The joys of dancing and of love." (Odes I.9)

Marcus Aurelius starts his book on Meditations by expressing gratitude to all who have come into his life and given him what he has, starting with his mother, great-grandfather, friends like Diognetus, Tusticu, Apollonius, Sextus and many others from whom he had learned something that made his life more pleasant, and also to the gods to whom he owed gratitude and thanks because they gave him family and friends, as well as comrades and teachers. When one considers the life of Epictetus, a brilliant Greek made a slave of a brutal Roman master who beat him so badly that he limped and had a "hunched back" the rest of his life, yet, later in life put forth to humanity a most beautiful spirit in which gratitude to God for his life overflowed in joy. To those who complained about their lots in life, he had very little sympathy, except for the fact that they were choosing to deaden their own spirits.

You complaining men, you can see the benefits you have in life
with reason and senses for you to enjoy. You should confidently

say to Zeus to bring on difficulties because you can handle the challenge and make a man of yourselves. But you do not do so, instead you tremble and fear that something will happen to you, and weeping, and lamenting, and groaning everytime some difficuty arises in your lives. Yet God has given you the faculties of the senses and reason so that you could handle such problems, and He has done it like a good king and a true father, and put you in control of the way that you are going to deal with the problems of your lives. You not only do not gratefully acknowledge your Heavenly Benefactor, but, when difficulties arise, instead of praise to him for your faculties, you blame him and finding no fault with yourselves, you find fault with God (paraphrased from Discourses, I.6).

Again, this magnificent Stoic challenges our dignity by the measure of gratitude.

If we really understand our lives, should we doing anything else but singing hymns that bless the deity and tell of his benefits? Ought we not while we are digging, ploughing, and eating to sing such a hymn to God? "Great is God who gives us instruments to dig and plough to help us cultivate the earth, who has given us a body with hands, and the function of a stomach, and the power to breathe while we are sleeping." Since most of you are blind to these benefits, maybe we ought to find one to lead us in song to God. Actually singing to God is about all I can do anymore, being an old crippled man. If I were a nightingale, I would play the role of a nightingale, and if I were a swan, the part of a swan. But I am a rational creature, and that means my role is to praise God, for it is my assigned work, and I shall do it and not neglect this duty so long as I am assigned to live. I also encourage you to join me in this song of praise (paraphrased from Discourses I.16).

Plato, in describing the death of Socrates, told of his last command before he died: "Crito, we ought to offer a cock to Asclepius. Make sure it is done, and do not forget to do it." Asclepius was the god of health, and Socrates was declaring that his soul is now being liberated from the decaying body, and in so doing, the soul would regain its full health. For that reason a sacrifice was to be made to Asclepius to thank him. In death

Socrates was grateful (Phaedo 118). A poem in Sanskrit by Bhartrhari reflects the same grateful attitude of one who has enjoyed the earth but now is moving on to "the great Absolute".

> Earth, my own mother; father Air; and Fire,
> My friend; and Water, well-beloved cousin;
> And Ether, brother mine: to all of you
> For all the benefits you have conferred
> During my sojourn with you. Now my soul
> Has won clear, certain knowledge, and returns
> To the great Absolute from whence it came.4.16

Immanuel Kant teaches us also that gratitude is the natural response for mankind for the general blessings God has poured out upon all. To him it was just natural, after seeing all the blessings one has by his mere existence, to be thankful regardless of what ill might fall in one's path. For it was, in Kant's mind, enough to see the general blessings of God for all, and to understand that in the Wisdom of God man receives his blessings, that man ought never to be brought down in spirit by certain personal misfortunes. Man was not to pray for things that God had put in man's own hands to effect his own life. Be the lord of your own life, and be an autocrat for your own well being, for it is your responsibility. (Vorlesungen ueber Moralphilosophie: Von der Oberherrschaft ueber sich selbst). Later in the same Vorlesungen (lectures), he proposes that the three most hideous vices are: envy, malice, and ingratitude (Von der Eifersucht und der daraus entspringenden Misgunst und Neid).

Schiller, in his Don Carlos (IV.21) "O Gott, das Leben is doch schoen!" ("O God, life is so beautiful"). Yes, it is. Likewise, although Helen Keller was, by faith, looking forward to her next life, she expressed gratitude for the blessings of this life also.

> For three things I thank God every day of my life -- that He has vouchsafed my knowledge of His works, deep thanks that He has set in my darkness the lamp of faith, deep, deepest thanks that I have another life to look forward to -- a life joyous with light and flowers and heavenly song. 4.17

Gratitude for the very miracle of life with its many blessings and the joy of being a rational human being is a necessary foundation for building a life of wholeness and happiness, and so our many teachers, our wonderful instructors, have taught us.

The first step to wholeness and happiness is comprised of the parts presented here in this chapter. First, unattachment to the past, to things out of our control, and to the unnecessary things of the material realm. Secondly, taking control of one's life by: burying the past; exercising control over that which is in our control; lessening our desires for temporal things of the material realm; having the adaptability to rise above previous disappointments, failures, and even tragedies; living a balanced life and avoiding extremes; and being thankful for the opportunity to experience the miracle of human life.

CHAPTER FIVE

STEP TWO

A FRIENDLY UNIVERSE
AND
THE FATHERLINESS OF GOD

I. JESUS: "THE FATHER CARES FOR YOU"

After a man has taken the first step towards building his life by taking control of his own destiny and being thankful for life itself, he needs the comfort of knowing that the universe itself has a spiritual friendliness to it and that he is not battling against a fate that condemns him to misery. Our great and divine teachers have expressed this friendliness in various ways, and it is the teachings of Jesus that will be put forth first. In his Sermon on Mount he refers to God as man's Father 17 times, and this message of personalizing the universe's friendliness is evident throughout the Early Christian Canon called the New Testament, for it refers to God as man's Father 260 times. In acknowledging this, one can be led to feel that this is the main message of the New Testament, because it is found in every part of the writings contained therein. In Matthew's record of the Sermon on the Mount (Mt 5-7) one can see from selected passages that The Father in Heaven is loving, caring, and personal. The Father knows our needs (6:8), therefore, when man prays he begins "Our Father who art in heaven" (6:9), and we are welcome to come to Him even when guilty of sin for he is forgiving (6:14), and gracious (6:26), and there is no need to be anxious (6:25-31), and he is always accessible in prayer (7:11). In Jesus we see his care for everyone: lame, blind, deaf, sinful, rich, poor, one living a prosperous life or a miserable one, the humbled one, the skeptic, the foreign oppressor, man or woman, ruler or child, clean or diseased, both mystic and Pharisee, and every other station or mind-set that mankind experiences. He was a man for others. The Gospels show the loving Fatherliness of God in the life of Jesus, even claiming that God announced at his baptism that this was his son in whom is was well pleased. Jesus was criticized by his opponents as one who had a demon (in this case, an evil one) because he appeared as a glutton and a drunkard, and a friend of tax collectors and sinners" (Mt 11:18-19). People today often in their judgmentalism accuse the Father of the same things, "Can a righteous God actually love these "witches", the "drunkards" lying in the streets, and even the "brutal auditors for the IRS". Those conscious of their status image who have such a condescending attitude over against their fellowmen simply have no idea of what the Father's attitude towards his creatures is. But Jesus declared that God knows us as a good shepherd knows his individual sheep, and will go out of his way to find one who has lost his way. "You are blessed for happiness, O mankind, because the Father cares for you" cried out Jesus. "You are blessed even if you are financially poor or have a poverty stricken spirit...You are blessed even if you presently are being crushed and in a state of mourning...You are blessed even if you seem to get pushed around a lot in life...You are blessed even as you soul longs for but has not received justice...You are blessed when you offer your mercy to another, for it will come back to you...You are blessed when your heart seeks the presence of the Father in your life, for you will see Him in his workings for you now and will see him face to face in your destiny...You are blessed when you oppose conflict and even suffer as a peacemaker for in so doing you are becoming a true child of God...You are blessed even when reviled and persecuted because you seek justice for all the children of the universe, for you are then carrying in your heart the love of God, your Father" cried out Jesus in the Sermon on the Mount. "Do not be anxious and do not fear the death of the body, for your soul will reach to the very heights of heaven itself." This step of focussing on the greater world, the universe and its spiritual friendliness that Jesus so beautifully presented, causes a deep seated change of mind and attitude that lifts us up to a higher level of existence. This change of mind-set is translated in the New Testament as either "repentance" or "conversion" from the Greek word METANOIA, which was classified in this way by Plato to whom we shall refer in the next section. When one reads the Four Gospels of the Canonical New Testament, it is impossible not to hear the proclamation of Jesus that the universe is friendly and the Father in Heaven cares for and loves his creatures.

II.   THE CONCURRENCE: THE UNIVERSE IS A FRIENDLY HOME

Many during the Twentieth Century have lost contact with the universe in which they live, believing that it is either too vast or too cold for it to be man's friendly home. Carl G. Jung felt that this was a major problem for man's spiritual being, he stated:

> As scientific understanding has grown, so our world has become dehumanized. Man feels himself isolated in the cosmos, because he is no longer involved in nature and has lost his emotional "unconscious identity" with natural phenomena. These have slowly lost their symbolic implications...His (man's) contact with nature has gone, and with it has gone the profound emotional energy that this symbolic connection supplied.5.1

Many of our wise teachers of the past have taught that the universe is indeed friendly and that there is either a Spirit or Mind or God that has created it as a home for humanity. However, they are not specific nor detailed nor doctrinaire about life beyond death, for those are things also beyond what man can know as scientific fact. They are believers, but not firmly set into that which man cannot be rationally firm, and this is usually, at least among the great teachers, due to their basic humility. Nevertheless, they enjoy life as a gift and are convinced that Nature, The World Soul or Spirit, or Mind, or Consciousness, or God are in charge of man's destiny, whether they have a personal identity after death or not. In general, many do believe in some form of life after death, but they teach man, not to speculate, but to go along with their appointed existence and leave it to the Eternal Powers to take care of the rest. This is how they conquer the anxiety, fear, and dread of death. These views are reflected in much of Eastern thought and also in the thoughts of Aristotle, some Stoics, and most Epicureans: all of whom had full and spiritually satisfying lives. This optimism that gives life meaning is well expressed in the teachings of the Hebrew Canonical Scriptures: life is full and good, man's identity lives on in his male children, and the rest is left to Yahweh. While some within the Hebrew Scriptures feel that all of man's existence in terminated at death and that in itself makes life void of meaning (the Book of Eccleasiastes), most of the <u>Hebrew</u> <u>Canon</u>, while rejecting a personal life after death, still find the very fact of life in the flesh to be a wonderful gift and is to be totally enjoyed. These views were similar to the teachings of Aristotle, who believed in a perfect God, yet rejected the idea that man in anyway lived beyond his earthly years. Yet for both the Hebrew Scriptures and <u>Aristotle</u> moral rightcousncss was of the very essence of life, and happiness comes from being faithful, either to the Covenant or to a strong ethical code taught by Aristotle, for he also believed that only the good man can be happy.

Lao <u>Tzu</u>, who flourished in China 600 years before Jesus, has probably left a greater impact on philosophical thought than is generally accredited to him. He never pointed to a personal God of any kind or gave any speculation that man may possibly survive death in some form, but to many he brought a "creative quietism" that, he taught, came from a natural "instinct" or "conscience" that was planted into the psychological essence of man. He used common sense in a most uncommon way, making it irresistibly practical, reasonable, and simple. Paradoxically, some have thought his simplicity was actually mystical, because it seemed to carry a power with it that, when experienced by the hearts of men, changed them profoundly and gave them a sense of spiritual serenity. He had no use for anything speculative because he did not believe words themselves had the capacity to express existence satisfactorily, yet he made simple use of them and pointed man to "the way of life".

> The Tao that can be trodden is not the enduring and unchanging Tao.
> The name that can be named is not the enduring and unchanging
> Name.
> Having no name, it is the Originator of heaven and earth;
> Or if one gives it a name, it is the Mother of all things.
> Always without desire to understand, we must be found,
> If its deep mystery we would sound;
> But if such desire always within us be,
> Its outer fringe is all that we shall see. (I.1.1-3).

Plato acknowledged that it was wonder that caused man to think and to philosophize; Lao Tzu said it was wonder that made man experience life and to say too much more might diminish the experience of wonder. He speaks of the passing of human generations, but of the eternity of the "breath of life" that the universe freely gives, a universe that itself is deathless. Man's life is simple and natural.

> The highest excellence of man is like that of water.
> The excellence of water appears in its benefiting all things,
>   without striving to the contrary.
> It, in its service, always settles in the lowest place, which men
>   usually dislike.
> Yet it is in that low place that he finds his closeness to Tao.(I.8.1).

Intuitive awareness of the nature of life brings man the power to control his existence and blend with the way of life itself. "When we can lay hold of the Tao of old to direct the things of the present day, and are able to know it as it was of old in the beginning, this is called the unwinding the clue of Tao"(I.14.3). Man has an internal morality that brings happiness, quietism, and the gentle acceptance of reality, including his finitness. Perhaps a Westerner would call it a reference to God when he declared:

> There was something undefined and complete,
> that was in existence before Heaven and Earth.
> How still it was and formless, standing alone,
> and undergoing no change,
> reaching everywhere and yet in no danger of being exhausted!
> It may be regarded as the Mother of all things.(I.25.1)

Lao Tzu does not discuss men's fate or destiny after death in any metaphysical sense. Rather life in all its simplicity, simply happens.Man need not be anxious, he simply needs to relax and live, just live your life and do not search for eternal or ultimate purposes, and be like the sages who "accomplished their ends without any purpose in doing so"(I.47.1). For life itself is sacred and beautiful. Life is a Cathedral: "Existence is a sanctuary". Do not let the "existential dilemma of one's finite existence detour you from enjoying the beauty of life" for the sages do not fear death, for it serves no purpose at all. In a comforting thought <u>Kwang</u> <u>Tze</u> stated: "How do I know that the love of life is not a delusion? And that the dislike of death is not like a young person's losing his way, and not knowing that he is (really) going home?"(BK II.1.2) Kwang Tze (<u>often</u> <u>Chuang</u> <u>Tzu</u>) also said this of the friendly universe: "The Great (universe) gives me this form, this toil in manhood, this repose in old age, this rest in death. And surely that which is such a kind arbiter of my life is the best arbiter of my death". 5.2

<u>Confucius</u> was somewhat different in certain ways than Lao Tzu, and the main difference was that Lao Tzu spoke mainly to the individual and the Way of Life that was his personal experience of life; whereas, Confucius was very concerned about society as a whole. But likewise Confucius never taught that man lived on after death, and speaks very skeptically about the existence of any type of personal God, usually referring to Nature or to the Sky (often translated "heaven" but never in the Western conception of "heaven") that is in charge of things: like "Nature will justify the deeds of a righteous man". The rules or order of life being by nature what it is, the righteous man will have friends, prosper, and be happy; but an unrighteous man will come upon numerous difficulties in life and will not be happy. It would be well to note that most of Confucius' sayings were to those who ran the worldly order: kings, princes, and land lords. In praise of leaders who had followed the law of nature (heaven) he stated: "Sublime were Shun and Yu! All that is under Heaven was theirs, yet they remained aloof from it"...and again..."Greatest, as Lord and Ruler, was Yao. Sublime, indeed, was he. Great indeed was Yao as a sovereign! How majestic was he! It is only heaven that is grand, and Yao was proportional to it, and in that his virtue was vast. The people know no word to describe it's greatness"(Analects VIII.18-19). He was in no way either creative, speculative nor metaphysical. Rather he sought to conserve society by the laws of the ancients, which he felt gave harmony and happiness to human society in times past. "A transmitter and not a maker, a believing in and loving the ancients, I venture to compare myself with our old P'ang"(Analects VII.1). When society follows its natural course and brings harmony to the men within it, then man is happy, as nature has decreed him to be; but disobeying nature, man is in personal and societal conflict in which there can be no happiness. Man must obey the "moral force" of nature (or sky or heaven), for, if he does not, society crumbles. So Confucius, although

not believing in either a personal God or life after death, taught that "Nature" or the "Sky" (trans. "Heaven") were moral forces that blessed those who followed the natural path of life.

Into this category one may put <u>Buddhism</u>, but Buddhism is so very diverse and so many non-rational non-descript terms that it is virtually impossible for one raised in Western culture to understand it. Therefore, this section will be very short, hoping not to mislead anyone. Probably it is in Buddhism that the Russian proverb becomes most true: "As soon as a thought becomes a word, it is a lie". Intuitive experience and even emptiness of thought are seen to give a type of enlightenment which has a liberating effect upon one's attachment to the material and temporal. And when the entire system of transmigration (Sangsara) is escaped one can come to Nirvana and be liberated from existence as we know it. Nirvana is seldom described in any terms at all and it seems to be a nothingness because it is unattached to all we know by our own personal rational capacities. One thinks of the word "beyond" for it is beyond somethingness and nothingness, beyond the thought process that tries to describe it. Nevertheless, it is an escape or liberation from the life cycle of birth and death, and therefore beyond any type of sorrow or sufferings that we experience or that we can conceive of experiencing. It sort of reminds me of the Negro spiritual "we aint going to suffer war no more, no more" even if we can not describe what peace is. We are just happy to sing that there will not be any more war. The concept of a personal God who knows my name generally is absent, perhaps because it would relate to what we were in the material world of illusion and that would indicate a type of attachment which can not exist in the state of liberation in Nirvana. Despite these vague ways of thinking, Buddhism has brought great internal peace to many peoples of various nationalities and has developed perhaps the most strict moral codes of all religions: "You shall not kill (even harm) any creature". Perhaps Buddhism should not be in this section of a friendly universe, because they see Nirvana as being beyond it and beyond all visual or definable things. Yet, they do seem comforted in the hopes of the liberation that awaits them in Nirvana. W.Y. Evans-Wentz in his introduction to the Tibetan Book of the Dead states a series of 21 fundamental teachings summarizing the whole of Buddhism. His final five read this way:

17. The Goal is and can only be Emancipation from the Sangsara.

18. Such Emancipation comes from the Realization of Nirvana.
19. Nirvana is non-sangsaric, being beyond all paradises, heavens, hells, and worlds.
20. It is the ending of sorrow.
21. It is reality.

While the <u>Hindu</u> <u>Scriptures</u>, also very diverse, sometimes tend to be pantheistic, yet there is a type of joyous intimacy when thinking about the universe even though it too often sees illusion in the material world:

> By truly realizing Him (i.e. The Great God who is Lord of maya), though non-dual, dwells in prakriti, both in its primary and its secondary aspect, and in whom this whole world comes together and dissolves--by truly realizing Him who is the Lord, the bestower of blessings, the Adorable God, one attains the supreme peace...
> He, the creator of the gods and the bestower of their powers, the Support of the universe, Rudra the omniscient... 5.3

Here one sees that the Creator supports the universe, is an Adorable God, whom one can contact and from whom one can receive peace. He is also the one who is the custodian of the universe. This aspect of Hinduism brings a friendliness to the universe which is comforting for man. This despite its stress on reincarnations that can also go into the thousands of years, but here one does not find the great emphasis of the suffering that is necessitated by the material realm that one finds right from the beginning of Buddhism as legend has it that Buddha himself based his entire spiritual quest on finding out the cause of suffering.

<u>Aristotle</u>, as mentioned above, taught a very simple and plainly understood precept: the soul can not be separated from the body, and when the body dies, the soul becomes non-existent. For the soul is the living aspect or power of the body, and when it fails or ceases so does the life of the body. Aristotle believes there is no afterlife for the individual, and thus differed completely from his Divine Teacher, Plato. Yet God exists and exists in perfect virtue, the consummation of all that is good, and has even been thought to be Plato's Good beyond essence. However, this is praising Aristotle too highly, and his idea of God too highly also. For Aristotle's God is so distant and unattached to anything else (he is not even the Creator) that it is impossible to think of him as anything like

Plato's God who creates, loves, directs, and cares for man's body and especially man's eternal soul. Often people offer a blank statement that the gods of the Greeks are distant and unconcerned with humanity and in so doing reveal that they do not know the difference between a Platonist and a Peripatetic. Yet Aristotle found life to be a wonderful adventure in which he is constantly drawn to God because of God's perfection. It is in God's perfection, which is desired by all, that God moves people without himself moving towards man. Thus he is described as the Unmoved Mover. Nevertheless, this movement towards God is the movement towards virtue and virtue and wisdom plant happiness and wholeness into the lives of men. To learn, to live peacefully in a human society (one of his phrases is that man is a political animal--i.e. he needs to find his fulness in a city [polis]), to enjoy nature's beauty, to appreciate the fine arts, and to understand the plant and animal life about us, are the things that give meaning and beauty to the life of men. But death ends all: "Now death is the most terrible of all things; for it is the end, and nothing is thought to be any longer either good or bad for the dead" (Nicomachean Ethics 1115a 26-28). Yet, Aristotle and his followers find the world and the universe to be friendly, for it offers the chance to experience and find happiness in life itself: which is brief, but beautiful.

The Epicureans are not that different from Aristotle, although they do not consider a man necessarily a "political animal" who feels the need to be in a city and be part of its function on behalf of the betterment of others. They are more likely to be small groups or even individuals who take care of their body by living healthy and natural lives, avoiding pain as much as possible, and enjoying the natural pleasures that life offers. The Epicureans do not refer to "God", but rather to "the gods", but without much of a concern for them, because they feel the gods have their own existences and lives and are not concerned for mankind. Praying to the gods doesn't make any sense, that is, if you are expecting a response, but if you feel better and calmer by praying, then it may add to your pleasures in life. Epicurus, contrary to what some may think, taught a rather strict code of ethics: not that it was such a code of certain written commandments, but one that directed man to that which was rational and natural. For it was in the natural and rational approach to life that man would be a healthy person, avoiding pain, and being able to enjoy the mental and bodily pleasures associated with life. The rational life was important so that man confined himself to those pleasures that are both natural and necessary for his good. Getting drunk was not a rational pleasure because the pain of the hangover was self-defeating. The stupidity of gluttony that weakened the health and length of life of the body was also not a natural pleasure. Epicurus' ethics were one of one's independent rational thought that gave a self-controlled and moderate pleasure to man's life. He realized that men lived in fear of death and his logical answer was good enough for his followers, although for his critics it was simply abit of sophistry: "Death is nothing to us: for that which is dissolved is devoid of sensation, and that which is devoid of sensation is nothing to us." In other words, when we are alive, death is not (why fear what is not), and when we are not, death is"; so death is not relevant while we live, and after we are dead, we do not care about it. We and death never meet each other. The one logical aspect of this teaching is that many feared the wrath of the gods after death and the possible punishments and suffering they would inflict upon men, and Epicurus dismissed such fears by teaching: first that the gods have no concern for us and do not regulate us in any way, and not caring about us they are not going to set up court rooms for after death judgments, and even if they would, which they do not, we would no longer exist anyway. To us in the modern world, the fear of "hell" or any type of similar punishment after death seems childish, yet well into post Renaissance times such fear was preached even by the Western Church to, perhaps, scare people into ethical conduct, or to sell indulgences. People who still have such fears will be well served to listen to the gentle and happy lives of those who were Epicureans.

The <u>Stoics,</u> like the Gnostics and Buddhists, are so diversified that one can not classify what a "Stoic" teaching is and what it is not; except, perhaps, that there is a brotherhood to the human race and that man is to follow his natural destiny and do the duty assigned to him. In many other ways their inconsistencies are so many that they probably should be considered Eclectics. Plutarch wrote an entire work called <u>On Stoic Self-Contradictions</u>, and even Seneca, a Platonized Stoic himself, stated "Cleanthes and his pupil Chrysipus did not agree on what walking is."5.4 Because of this diversity, some of the Stoics definitely belong in this category, while others belong half in this and half in the next category. Into this category I shall place Cleanthes, Seneca and Marcus Aurelius who definitely believed the world was friendly and God was fatherly, but felt that death itself was either a finality or else a transformation into the

World Soul, and had very strong doubts that the individual would retain
his identity. In the next category I shall place Epictetus who, in addition,
expressed some hopes of personal immortality. All believed God was
fatherly and the Universe friendly, and also that life was a kind gift and
was, even though temporary, beautiful and full of meaning.
The following is from <u>Cleanthes'</u> beautiful <u>Hymn</u> <u>to</u> <u>Zeus</u>.

> O most glorious God, addressed in many ways,
> Ruler of earth, without change through endless days,
> With Power and Justice, You controll all,
> Praise to You, Zeus, for unto you
> All creatures of all lands cry out
> We are your children, we alone,
> Go throughout all earth's paths,
> Bearing your image in every place
> Everywhere we sing of your power.
> ...
> Your universal Word exists in all,
> Even in the heavens, in stars large and small
> You are the King of Kings, forever God,
> Bringing your plans into reality both
> In land and sea, as well as in the vastness of the heavens.
> ...
> Your Word....
> Is the cosmic edict,
> Which the evil do not see or understand.
> Those who honor it, by the power of rational thought,
> Experience the joyous life.
> ...
> We are your children, Zeus,
> Grant us the knowledge to know and obey your Will.
> For You yourself rule justly by reason over your creation.
> ...
> In knowledge, then, we shall honor and praise you properly,
> As befits our mortal nature, even as it is proper for the
>   Immortals to praise the Eternal and Rational way.

The universe is beautiful and friendly because God made it and put it into the hands of man, who could exert dominion over it because God also gave man the rational wisdom to control it and enjoy the life they have as a gift from God, and for that reason it is proper that many should honor God. He has also made a universal law which will help men in understanding his world by that very same reason which God gave him. This law of nature thus is for man's benefit and those who follow it will in turn be blessed by it. Here there is no complaining about death or groaning that there is no individual life after death; there is only praise to Zeus for his generous gifts that are sufficient to make men happy.

Seneca wrote many letters and from them one can see some of the same emphases: life is brief, but good; man is to rationally follow nature; he is not to be overly concerned about death, even if he has no remedy for it or idea of personal survival after it; his duty to universal and natural law is to be his concern, and in fulfilling it he finds his own goodness and the subsequent happiness that comes from being faithful to his appointed duties. Seneca stated in his Twelveth Epistle, On Old Age, that we cannot control our mortality, but can joyfully accept what God gives.

> If God is pleased to add another day, we should welcome it with glad hearts. That man is happiest, and is secure in his own posses-sion of himself, who can await the morrow without apprehension. When a man has said: "I have lived!", every morning he arises he receives a bonus. (tr. Richard M. Gummere)

About Death in Epistle Sixty Three, he said:

> Therefore, Lucilius, act as befits your own serenity of mind, and cease to put a wrong interpretation on the gifts of Fortune. Fortune has taken away, but Fortune has given. Let us greedily enjoy our friends, because we do not know how long this privilege will be ours.(tr. R.M.Gummere)

Seneca enjoyed the fulness of life as it came. At one time stationed high in the Roman government as a mentor for the young Nero, he fell from grace and eventually was forced by Nero to commit suicide. He despised evil and shallow men who whined and thought the games in which people were cruelly murdered to be healthy entertainment; for

Seneca saw such games as being far too lowly for a good man to watch. He marveled at their ugliness, especially if those men, who took such joy in seeing others slaughtered for entertainment, could not face their own deaths with dignity but mourned their destinies as mindless and self-centered children. From Stoics such as this we can learn, as their students, that if life is not all that we had hoped, then we can still rejoice in the gift of life itself and live nobly both for ourselves and for others, and with dignity accept our mortality.

Marcus Aurelius in a little book he kept for himself entitled "To Himself" but subsequently published as his "Meditations" teaches us by those thoughts he considered to be helpful in his own growth into human nobility.

But in truth they (the gods) do exist, and they do care for human things, and they have put all the means in man's power to enable him not to fall into real evils (II.11).

And reverence of the daemon (good spirit within man) consists in keeping it pure from passion and thoughtlessness, and dissatis- faction with what comes from gods and men. For the things from the gods merit veneration for their excellence; and the things from men should be dear to us by reason of kinship (II.13).

The soul of man does violence to itself, first of all, when it becomes an abscess and, as it were, a tumour on the universe, so far as it can. For to be vexed at anything which happens is a separation of our- selves from nature (II.16).

Be cheerful also, and seek not external help nor tranquillity which others give. A man then must stand erect, not be kept erect by others (III.5).

For this reason I behave towards him according to the natural law of fellowship with benevolence and justice. At the same time how- ever in things indifferent I attempt to ascertain the value of each (III.11).

...therefore in accordance with Nature's law of brotherhood I am to deal amiable and fairly with him (III.11).

Aurelius encourages himself to die with dignity and gratitude.

I go through the things which happen according to nature until I shall fall and rest, breathing out my breath into that element out of which I daily draw it in, and falling upon that earth out of which my father collected the seed, and my mother the blood, and my nurse the milk; out of which during so many years I have been supplied with food and drink; which bears me when I tread on it and abuse it for so many purposes (V.4).

There are many great teachers of humanity that, even if they did not believe in a personal life that continued after the death of the body, yet they believed in a friendly universe, most of whom felt there were gods or a God, whether or not they were concerned with men being irrelevant to their ultimate decisions about how to live and enjoy life. They too are everyone's teachers, but especially teachers to those who hold similar views of man's destiny. They teach the beauty of life on earth, the inner need and drive for goodness and virtue, the many benefits of friendship, the duty to work for justice for others as well as for themselves, the love and enjoyment of nature and its beauty. When death comes they rejoice that they have been permitted to play a part in human history and to have loved, sung, eaten, rested, and exercised reason to reach the fulness of life as much as it was possible for them to do so.

III.   THE CREATOR IS OUR FATHER AND CREATED US TO ENJOY BOTH LIFE AND HIMSELF FOREVER.

In this section a step is taken beyond the idea that the universe or nature is friendly and life is good to the idea that God is personal, that he cares for all his creatures, and, finally, that he desires that his creatures exist and enjoy his creation as well as his own presence forever. Inasmuch as it was Plato who first fully established this step of thinking in its totality, he will be presently first.

A. PLATO

Plato taught mankind that God, the Father and Maker of the Cosmos, was good and not jealous, and created the universe and all the creatures within it because he wanted to share existence with them both in their material form, which was temporal, and in their final form, the spiritual soul, which was eternal and capable of enjoying Him forever. Both states were of a good nature, but due to man's needs being in the temporal body, which was necessitated by the fact of their material substance, man often had desires to satisfy those needs even in neglect of the spiritual consciousness, and if he did not rationally control those emotions and passions he would "miss the mark" of the most healthy way to live. If his body needed food or warmth and he did not have food or clothing available, he would be tempted by his bodily needs to take from another and cause conflict. Yet, the benefits of living in the flesh made it worthwhile to God, for he knew that man could, by being in the flesh, experience wonderful, although temporary, happenings, which in no other way could be brought to him. The experience of growing from childhood to old age, the challenge of work and the pleasure of sport, the taste of food and the softness of rest were all given as wonderful gifts from God, and could only be given by putting the soul into a material body. When that experience ended by the necessary death of the body, then the soul went to the eternal, unconfined, never changing bliss for which it was initially made, and there to enjoy God and all that is forever. To keep man aware of his eternal destiny while he was in the body, God planted in him a longing for the eternal and beautiful--like a divine daemon within, gave man a consciousness of the eternal, inserted love for Him within the soul of man, and created the lower gods to be our guardians to help us through life on a spiritual path to make sure we ended at the threshold of God's heaven when we died. Christians, after the example of the Hellenised Jews, adopted these gods and their guardian functions, but called them guardian angels.

In the dialogue The Statesman, Plato spoke of God as the Creator of the Universe (269-270), the Shepherd of Mankind (271d), the Pilot of the Universe (272e), The Father and Creator of the Cosmos (273a), the Constructor of the World and Giver of All that is Good (273b), The Orderer of All according to his tender care (273d-e), and The Divine Shepherd (275b-c). In the Philibus God is the Divine Mind (NOUS) whose power causes all (30d-e), and God is called "our Savior" (66d). In the Timaeus the entire creation "comes alive" by the providence of God (30c), God is the Father and Creator of the Cosmos which He wants to be as eternal as possible (37d-e), he is a God who wants his created children to be eternal (41a-b), God gives his creatures sensation and love, and also makes the lower gods to help men (43a-b). In the Laws Plato stated that God is in an eternal state of graciousness (792b), the guardian gods given for man's benefit (907a), and that all heaven rejoices when a human honors his earthly parents (931d-e). Plato wrote at least 35 dialogues, and from the four above one can easily see that Plato presented to his students a Heavenly Father who created the entire universe to give to man every type of blessing possible, and to ordain them in their final form to an eternal life of beauty and joy in his presence. Plato saw such faith and comfort in the way Socrates died, who after declaring his faith in the next world died with honor and calmness. Plato described the feelings of Socrates' students by putting these words into the mouth of Phaedo in the dialogue by the same name:

> I had a singular feeling at being in his company. For I could hardly believe that I was present at the death of a friend, and therefore I did not pity him, Echecrates; he died so fearlessly, and his words and bearing were so noble and gracious, that to me he appeared blessed. I thought that in going to the other world he could not be without a divine call, and that he would be happy...when he arrived there; and therefore I did not pity him as might have seem natural at such an hour.(Phaedo58e).

In his defense, Socrates is given these words by Plato:

> In another world they do not put a man to death for asking questions: assuredly not. For besides being happier than we are, they will be immortal, if what is said is true. Wherefore, O judges, be of good cheer about death, and know of a certainty, that no evil can happen to a good man, either in life or after death. He and his are not neglected by the gods. (Apology 41c-d).

"God is not the author of all things, but of good only" (Republic 380c).God renders only good things to man, for he is a loving heavenly father to all, as well as having a simple and pure heart in which there is no deception: "Then is God perfectly simple and true both in word and deed; he changes not; he deceives not, either by sign or word, by dream or waking vision" (Republic 382e). God's goodness is inseparable from the creation itself:

> Let me tell you then why the creator made this world of generation. He was good, and the good can never have any jealousy of anything. And being free from jealousy, he desired that all things should be as like himself as they could be. This is in the truest sense the origin of creation and of the world, as we shall do well in believing on the testimony of wise men: God desired that all things should be good and nothing bad, so far as this was attainable (Timaeus 29e-30a).

Leaving the universe and our own fate to God, releases us from anxiety and tension that we may be free to be about the duties that are present in our earthly life: "[the wise person]...he leaves all that with God, and considers in what way he can best spend his appointed term [of life]" Gorgias 512e).

From the above one can easily understand the honor to Plato that Constantine Ritter gives to him in his work The Essence of Plato's Philosophy.

> I bring this presentation to a close with the same statement with which I closed my larger work on Plato. In this I tried briefly to characterize Plato's meaning for all time. To me, he is a philosopher second to none; an artist of first rank; a man favoured by God as few others have been; unforgettable for all time, releasing spiritual powers which have been a blessing to many and which will continue to be a blessing for all time.5.5

From Alfred Edward Taylor come these words:

> If we sometimes underestimate our debt in these matters to Plato, it is only because Platonic ideas have become so completely part and parcel of our best tradition in morals and religion. His influence,

like the pressure of the atmosphere, goes undetected because we never really get free from it (Platonism and its Influence, p.57).

And from Paul Elmer More:

It is this tradition, Platonic and Christian at the center, this realization of an immaterial life, once felt by the Greek soul and wrought into the texture of the Greek language, that lies behind all our western philosophy and religion. Without it, so far as I can see, we arc in peril of sinking back into barbarism. P.E. More, The Religion of Plato, PP.VI-VII.

When one realizes that Plato flourished 400 years before Jesus, and that the Jews, as well as Jesus, were well influenced by his thinking, one can see why the Hellenized people of Jesus' day quickly accepted his teachings and person while those not Hellenized did not. Not only in Religion, but also in Philosophy, is Plato one of the truly great thinkers and his stature prompted A.N. Whitehead to declare that "All western philosophy is but a series of footnotes to Plato".

B. CONCURRENCE FROM OTHERS

At this point I would like to point out that Plato taught that God was beyond finding out and also he was beyond essence, and that if one were to "find out" God it would be impossible to communicate him to others, and this indicates two things: the quest is personal and to express this experience with God or the personality of God's nature would be simply impossible. Yet, man must use words, and Plato as a concession to human experience called God a Father of the Cosmos, and this could relate to all people, for all have fathers. Yet, Plato insisted that the lower gods were in his image and consisted of both male and female gods and that the priesthood also should be made of both male and female priests, and the Guardian class in his Republic was to be gathered from both sexes of society. Therefore, for Plato to use the term Father was a concession, and not a teaching doctrine to make God male, for God was beyond essence itself. He was beyond gender. Plato's concession was also to the current culture of the other religions and to the historical thinking of the Greeks themselves, whose chief god was Zeus (male), as was Osiris and Aton of Egypt, Jupiter of the Romans, Odin of the Germans, and Yahweh of the Jews. The Platonic Gnostics were following Plato in giving the female element of the divinity more exposure than most, the Holy Spirit was often presented as female. Likewise, even when they were speaking of the Father God they often made "him" unisex for in The Nineteenth Ode of Solomon the Holy Spirit milked the two breasts of the Father and with it suckled mankind. In Ode 35 it is stated that God "carried me like a child by its mother. He gave me milk, his dew." In the Gospel of Philip, a Christian Gnostic work, evidence is shown that many of the Gnostics believed the Holy Spirit to be female and were wondering how a "female" God could impregnate Mary. The argument would be, of course, that after all it was a miracle. Some of this confusion arises from the fact that in Hebrew Ruach (spirit) was female, in Greek it was Pneuma which was neuter, and in Latin it was Spiritus, which was male. Even Jesus once related himself to the female gender comparing his compassion with that of a hen: "How often would I have gathered your (Jerusalem's) children together as a hen gathers her brood under her wings"(Mt23:37) and Luke (13:34) also repeated the words. The nature of God's gentleness and loving care was simply better related to a mother, even an animal mother, for the purpose of communication. Since God was beyond gender "he" could be represented with both male and female qualities. It is important that people recognize that, and also understand that it is to this same human concession that I refer to God as "He", for I have difficulties with "it" because it sound personhoodless and "he/she" is often burdensome.

The Gnostic Platonic Christian Valentinian in his Gospel of Truth expressed the happiness and joy that a person had when he knew the Father of Truth:

The gospel of truth is joy to those who have received from the
Father of Truth the gift of knowing him by the power of the
Logos, who has come from the Pleroma and who is in the thought
and the mind of the Father; he it is who is called "The Savior,"
since that is the name of the work which he must do for the redemp-
tion of those who have not known the Father. For the name of the
gospel is the manifestation of hope (1).

...proclaiming the things that are in the heart of the Father, so that
he became the wisdom of those who have received instruction (2).
...For the Father is sweet and his will is good (18).
...For this reason, God came and destroyed the division and he
brought the hot Pleroma of love, so that the cold may not return,
but the unity of the perfect thought prevail(19).

As far back as the Sumerians there was a feeling of closeness to both
nature and nature's god. In a hymn of praise to Enlil, the Sumerian God,
is seen as the Shepherd of mankind and places a king among men to
guide them:

Enlil, the worthy shepherd, ever on the move,
Of the leading herdsman of all who have breath (the king),
Brought into being his princeship,
Placed the holy crown on his head.5.6

The Rig-Veda of the Hindus also pleads to God, that as they worship
him, he would "be to us easy of approach, even as a father to his son"
(Rig-Veda 1.1). In Zoroastrianism Mazda is called the Father of the
working of Good Disposition (Yasna 45), and "the First Father of
Justice"(Yasna 44.3). In Shinto God is called the "Great Parent of your
real self" (Konko Kyo).

Among the Greeks, Zeus was known and addressed as "Father Zeus",
and even some Stoics referred to him as such. Cleanthes began a prayer
with these words "Lead me, Master of the soaring vault. Of heaven, lead
me, Father, where you will". But among the Stoics it was left to
Epictetus to fully develop the idea of God's closeness to men by his deep
felt conviction that God is for mankind an intimate Father.

If a man should be able to assent to this doctrine as he ought, that
we are all sprung from God in an especial manner, and that God is
the Father of both men and of gods, I suppose that he would never
have any ignoble or mean thoughts about himself.(Discourses Bk I,
3).

To have God for your maker and father and guardian, shall not this
release us from sorrows and fears? (Bk I, 9).

And are we not in a manner kinsmen of God, and did we not come from Him?(Bk I, 9).

Epictetus constantly made statements like "What is there to fear?" for God was always attending to the needs of men and helped to direct them in all their affairs. Epictetus was always thanking God for being the gracious Father that he was, and often rhetorically asked God in his prayers "have I ever complained?". It is also to be noted that Epictetus was alive while the Four Gospels of Christ's ministry were being written (60-138AD). The oldest of the four canonized Greek playwrights, Aeschylus (525-456BC) in his Suppliant Maidens referred to humans as the offspring of Zeus(20-25); Zeus was seen as both Father and Progenitor who watched over his children(200-215), humans in a sense were children of a heavenly birth and Zeus is our Father and we are his offspring (575-590). Plotinus referred to God as our Father and our eternal home as our Fatherland (I.6,8).

Both Hinduism and Christianity believe that the Divine, for the purpose of man's salvation, became incarnate to help man to attain eternal life; the Hindus believe in at least 10 incarnations (Avatars) of whom the best known is Sri Krishna, but the Christians believe that only Jesus of Nazareth was incarnated as the Logos of God and that he was the only one born among men in such a way. But both express the teaching that God loves humanity so much he would take such steps towards men for the sake of their salvation: a truly gracious act of a loving father.

Although Boethius in talking to Philosphia about his burdens in life, he has no trouble presenting God as loving and as a father. "O happy race of mortals, if your hearts are ruled, as is the universe, by Love." (Bk II, Meter VIII). In his quest to find answers, Philosophia said to him: "... Since divine aid must be implored in small things as well as in great (as my pupil Plato says in his Timaeus,) what do you think we must do to merit finding the place of that highest Good?" Boethius properly answered "The Father of all must be invoked". Then the companion Philosophia invoked God's guidance:

Thou who dost govern the universe with everlasting law, Founder of earth and heaven who biddest time roll on from age to age, forever firm Thyself yet giving movement unto all things,... Grant that we may behold the fount of the Good; grant that, when the

light has been discovered, we may set upon Thee the soul's un-
blinded eyes. Hurl asunder the heavy clouds of this material world,
and shine forth in Thy splendor! For Thou art to the pious a serene
and tranquil rest; to discern Thee is our aim. Thou art our beginning,
our progress, our guide, our way, our ending.(Bk III, Meter IX)
(tr. James J. Buchanan)

Thus man making his way through the cosmos to find God is given a
map by Boethius, that is to call upon the Father who will lead us on to
the ultimate goodness, even the Good Himself.

Francesco <u>Petrarch</u> (1304-1374), the "First Modern Man" was a most
beloved poet in Renaissance Italy, and brought with him a form of the
sonnet that dictated Italian poetry for centuries afterwards. Yet, he
himself looked backward to the classical antiquity, mostly of Rome, but
also to the Greek writers available to him. In fact, during his lifetime he
was a symbol of antiquity to his contemporaries for he carried on a
correspondence with the ancient writers (he himself of course was the
ghost writer for them when they answered him). It is to Petrarch's work,
the beautiful <u>Triumphs</u>, that one turns to see how he presents the soul
longing for the closeness of God in his heart now, and for the climax of
his existence in eternity. Petrarch's first Triumph is earthly love, which is
conquered or triumphed by earthly chastity (his childhood sweetheart and
love of his life, Laura, married someone else--rich bankers make more
money than struggling poets and scholars--and she always remained
faithful to her husband and stayed with him until her sudden death in the
Black Plague of 1348); thus her chastity triumphed over his love for her;
and yet, in turn, her chastity was conquered by the Third Triumph, the
Triumphant Death that conquers all earthly life. Petrarch, in honor of her
memory and to show his everlasting love for her, wrote many sonnets
and other works so that at least her fame would live on, and in that way
fame can outlast and triumph over death. But late in life, only four years
before his own death, looking at history and seeing how much had been
forgotten of antiquity, he realized that Time conquers and triumphs over
all earthly fame. Yet, time itself is finally conquered by God's eternity,
and God's eternity gives true life and beauty that will never fade. In these
Six Triumphant stages, Petrarch has taken his readers from earth and its
setting, through steps one and two of this book and touched upon step

three. One can already see the joy of the soul as it ascends the stairway upwards to the wholeness of life.

William James stated that this climb up from materialism is what gives life meaning:

> This is why materialism will always fail of universal adoption, however well it may fuse things in to an atomistic unity, however clearly it may prophesy the future eternity. For materialism denies reality to the objects of almost all the impulses which we most cherish.5.7

Jacques Maritain believed that this element of man's sonship to God is at the very core of the mystery of our being.

> A person possesses absolute dignity because he is in direct relationship with the realm of being, truth, goodness, and beauty, and with God, and it is only with these that he can arrive at his complete fulfillment. His spiritual fatherland consists of the entire order of things which have absolute value, and which reflect, in some manner, a divine Absolute superior to the world and which have a power of attraction toward this Absolute.5.8

As each person makes his own journey through this life on earth as part of the cosmos, he has to make decisions as to which teachers he wants to learn from and which paths of their maps he wants to follow through life. Some of those who have come this far may consider their journeys complete, and for them that will seem to be sufficient to give them a life of meaning, direction, joy, contentment and wholeness. It will also be sufficient to see the wonder and beauty of the universe and the joy that man has in trying to imitate it in our life and arts. This next section of man's second step upward will discuss three of our teachers about the value of the Aesthetical imitation of the beauty of the universe in the arts of men that such joy as they experienced can be shared with us.

IV THE UNIVERSE OF BEAUTY AND ITS AESTHETICAL IMITATION

Often overlooked is the great impression that the beauty of both the earth and the universe itself has had in lifting man's thoughts to the eternal and sublime levels that give such inspiration and wonder to us all. Further overlooked is the creation's beauty to teach us ethics and the basic nobility and sacredness of life itself. Beauty has such an attraction to the hearts of even the most self-centered and evil of men, that to neglect its power to change lives seems almost incomprehensible. I shall present three men who have used beauty to teach and lift up the minds and souls of men to astonishing heights and thereby enrich them deeply. Plato, Plotinus ("the second coming of Plato"), and Friedrich Schiller are our great teachers in presenting the power of beauty. While Jesus himself did not speak much of this concept, he certainly was aware of the wonder and beauty of life: the wonder of the flight of birds and their ability to find food and nourishment taught man that God cared for even them; the beauty of flowers, namely the lilies of the field, were clothed in such beauty that even a richly arrayed king like Solomon could envy them. The rainbow was seen by the Hebrews to be a sign of God's graciousness, and the heavens in general declared God's own glory. Both the Hebrews and Jesus used the beauty of the creation to teach or say something about their spiritual lives. The same is true of Plato, Plotinus, and Schiller.

In the Symposium (Banquet) Plato used man's love for beauty as a way to show that the soul longed for and would not be satisfied with anything less than coming face to face with the Absolute Beauty of the Cosmos, which, to Plato, was God himself. I have adapted and abridged his lengthy dialogue in which he led his readers from the simple beauties of everyday life up the ladder from the visible beauties to the spiritual and eternal beauties of the Cosmos. He declared that when the love which is implanted into our soul seeks to behold Absolute Beauty, it starts its ascent upwards by acknowledging the beauties bound into this world's order, but after absorbing their loveliness for awhile, the love wants to go higher for it realizes that the world's ordered beauty is not the ultimate fulfillment, and so love, while it uses the world's beauty for the foundation of thought, sets it aside, and resumes it's quest for Ultimate Goodness, and stepping upwards, from one beauty to another, one step by one, it seeks that which is the Eternal Good and Absolute Beauty, knowing that what it has left behind will never fully satisfy it. It has traveled from one beautiful body to the beautiful soul to a beautiful rainbow, to the beauty of a particular virtue, but it wants more: it wants the source of all beauty. When it finally meets Beauty itself, face to face, that Beauty that gives all creation its beauty and goodness and, as the source of all beauty, never fades, decays, or changes, is always the same and never wavers or fluctuates, then that soul knows he has become a Friend of God, beloved and uplifted by the Same to his eternal home.

Plato, in all his teachings, used beauty as a stepping stone for virtue and the desire to be with God: he used beauty to beautify the lives and souls of his followers, for such was the great power of beauty to instill love in the hearts of man. Imitate beauty in your lives and in your teachings and you will rise to a high spiritual order and fulfill the basic longing of the love within you.

> Tell me, whether there is or is not any absolute beauty or good,
> or any other absolute existence? ... Certainly, Socrates, I think so.
> ...Then let us seek the true beauty: not asking whether a face is
> fair, or anything of that sort, for all such things appear to be in a
> flux; but let us ask whether the true beauty is not always beautiful.
> (Cratylus 439d).

In the Phaedrus, Plato described the soul as a composite--a pair of winged horses and a charioteer, one horse was of noble character and the other was ignoble and hard to handle. The goal of the charioteer was to ascend to heaven where the Divine Intellect resided and the true source of knowledge existed. It is there that the soul rejoices and feels fulfilled, for there is knowledge absolute in existence absolute. But the only way the wings of the horses can be made strong enough to ascend to the abode of the Absolute Intellect is that the horses must be fed with the proper food. That proper food is the spiritual food that comes from the divine beauty, wisdom, and goodness; for without this nourishment, the ascent will be impossible.

> The divine intelligence, being nurtured upon mind and pure know-
> ledge, and the intelligence of every soul which is capable of receiv-

ing the food proper to it, rejoices at beholding reality, and once more gazing upon Truth, is replenished and made glad. (Phaedrus 246ff).

And when the soul has seen him, and bathed herself in the waters of beauty, her constraint is loosened, and she [the soul] is refreshed, and has no more pang and pains; and this is the sweetest of all pleasures at the time, and is the reason why the soul of the one who loves will never forsake the beautiful one. (Phaedrus 251e).

Their recollection clings to Him, and they become possessed of Him, and receive from Him their character and disposition, so far as man can participate in God. (Phaedrus 253a).

Let our artists rather be those who are gifted to discern the true nature of the beautiful and graceful; then will our youth dwell in a land of health, amid fair sights and sounds, and receive the good in everything; and beauty, the effluence of fair works, shall flow into the eye and ear, like a health-giving breeze from a purer region, and insensibly draw the soul from earliest years into like- ness and sympathy with the beauty of reason. (Republic 401d).

For beauty inspires wonder and philosophy begins with wonder (Theae- tetus 155d). Concerning the arts of man, Plato desired them to be works of beauty to convey the spiritual power of beauty to both those who made them and those who saw them.

True pleasures are those which are given by beauty of colour and form, and most of those which arise from smells; those of sound, again, and in general those of which the want is painless and un- conscious, and of which the fruition is palpable to sense and plea- sant and unalloyed with pain...but they (balanced lines of form) are eternally and absolutely beautiful, and they have peculiar pleasures, quite unlike the pleasures of scratching [humor here to indicate that scratching is pleasant for but a moment, for later one must scratch again]. And there are colours which are of the same character, and have similar pleasures...When sounds are smooth and clear, and have a single pure tone, then I mean to say that they are not relatively but absolutely beautiful, and have natural pleasures associated with them (Philebus 51bff).

And now the power of the good has retired into the region of the beautiful; for measure and symmetry are beauty and virtue all the world over (Philebus 64e).

In Addition, one can read from Plato's Laws (655-659) and (811c-816e) which also present Plato's view that all beauty including the fine arts of man that includes music is capable of lifting one's soul in love to the Absolute Beauty, the Absolute Intellect and Good, God himself. To Plato all the arts are concerned with immortality and virtue in order to make man as much like God as possible, for only then can man's soul feel complete and happy.

Plotinus (205-270AD), one of the greatest of the followers of Plato was known as the Second Coming of Plato, and differed from Plato in emphasis because he was adjusting Plato to the very religious age of the Roman Empire of the Third Century after Christ, and this particular adjustment came to be known as Neoplatonism and Plotinus was seen as the first of the Neoplatonists, although the process was a gradual one. He did not write works that were comparable to Plato's Republic, Statesmen, or the Laws, for his main audience called for religious answers to man's fate. One sometimes forgets that Plotinus lived 600 years after Plato, when Plato's city-state no longer existed and Christianity did. Plotinus said nothing of Christianity, but did have some strong criticism for gnostic teachings. His tractate (I.6 = First Ennead, Sixth Tractate) was the most influential of his tractates for many centuries and its topic was beauty. In it he discussed all forms of beauty: visual, conceptual, moral, audible, and geometrical. He related it all to the Source of all beauty, as did Plato himself, Absolute Beauty Itself or the very Soul of Beauty or God. He spoke of the bodily forms of beauty both of humans and the plastic arts that lured men to try to attach themselves to that very beauty in some way, and, as in Plato's Symposium, that they desired to "mount this ladder for a wider view". The climb to the source of Beauty Itself, of course, was the flight or ascent of the soul to God who was the consummation of Intellectual Beauty, the conceptual source of the idea of beauty and that in which all other beauties must partake or imitate. Balance, coloration, sound (of music), form and symmetry all were elements that lured man to the state of wonder and the desire to have or participate in such beauty; and the longing of the soul was to partake of Absolute Beauty itself. Thus all plastic and natural forms of beauty were religious in nature and were to be used to teach man about Ultimate Beauty. But the soul can not stay at the material and sensual level of beauty, for they do not ultimately satisfy the deep longing man has for the eternal and unchangabe beauty. It needs to go beyond the material level which only represents the divine. The Ultimate Beauty Itself must be reached if the soul and its love for beauty is to be satisfied and feel complete.

> And Beauty, this Beauty which is also The Good, must be posed as The First: directly deriving from this First is the Intellectual-Principle which is preeminently the manifestation of Beauty; through the Intellectual-Principle Soul is beautiful...For the Soul, a divine thing, a fragment as it were of the Primal Beauty, makes beautiful to the fullness of their capacity all things whatsoever that it grasps and moulds. (I.6,6 tr. S. MacKenna)

> This, indeed, is the mood even of those who, having witnessed the manifestation of Gods or Supernals, can never again feel the old delight in the comeliness of material forms: what then are we to think of one that contemplates Absolute Beauty in Its essential integrity--so perfect Its purity--far above all such things that are non-essential, composite, not primal but descending from This? ...For This, the Beauty supreme, the absolute, and the primal, fashions Its lovers to Beauty and makes them also worthy of love. And for This, the sternest and the uttermost combat is set before the soul; all our labor is for This, lest we be left without part in this noblest vision. (I.6,7 tr. S Mackenna)

The Authentic Intellectual Beauty Itself, the Father and Transcendent Divine Being is that from which all beauty is dispersed, and is dispersed for the purpose of being in the love in man's souls back to Himself. Thus all beautiful art is inspired from above, that both the artist and the beholder of the art will, by their innate love of beauty, be drawn up towards the Authentic Intellectual Beauty Itself, the Father of all beauty who draws all men to himself. If one sees two blocks of stone, one left in its natural and rugged state and the other that has been touched by art, well shaped, and beautified by an artist, one must remember that the grace or beauty of the stone came not from the stone itself or even from the artist, but from the idea and form of beauty which the artist apprehended by reason, and that inspiration from above accounts for the loveliness of the prepared stone. Of course, the stone's beauty will always be far inferior to Beauty itself, and is only an imitation, but even an imitation has the power to inspire.

> Art, then, creating in the image of its own nature and content, and working by the Idea or Reason-Principle of the beautiful object it is to produce, must itself be beautiful in a far higher and purer degree since it is the seat and source of that beauty, indwelling in the art, which must naturally be more complete than any comeliness of the external. In the degree in which beauty is diffused by entering into matter, it is so much the weaker that that concentrated in unity; everything that reaches outwards is the less for it, strength less strong, heat less hot, every power less potent, and so beauty less beautiful. Then again every prime cause must be, within itself, more powerful than its effect can be; the musical does not derive from an unmusical source but from music; and so the art exhibited in the material work derives from an art yet higher (V.8,1 Stephen MacKenna trans.).

Friedrich Schiller was born only ten years after the death of Johann Sebastian Bach and grew into manhood during the time of Hayden and Mozart, Kant and Goethe, and lived into the time of Beethoven, Schubert, and Hegel. When he used his earlier writings, especially his Kallias letters and other works which he remodeled for their inclusion into the newly established journal, The Graces, which he himself edited, he also included contributions by such thinkers as Goethe, Herder, Kant, Fichte, the Humbolts, the Schlegels, Klopstock, and Jacobi.5.9 Those Kallias letters he had written to a Danish Prince, Friedrich Christian of Schleswig-Holstein-Augustenburg and the basic subject of those letters was the aesthetic education of man. He desired that the beautiful arts would be used to educate men into goodness, beauty, and morality. In this he showed the strong influence that Immanuel Kant's philosophy had upon him. He believed that human civility could not be attained unless one was aware of and attracted to the beauty of life and of nature, and that the arts which in themselves had the power to express such beauty were to be used to awaken in all men, even the common men, this love within the soul for a higher morality, even a philosophical and religious purity. He was bringing the philosophy of Kant into the aethetical arts: painting, sculpture, music, architecture, poetry, and all forms of writing and human expression. He expressed his love for Kant: "my thought is completely Kantian." There likewise was a deep Platonism which was logical, for Kant himself was deeply Platonic. Reginald Snell in his introduction to the translation of Schiller's Letters, stated that the theme of Schiller's Letters was that "man must pass through the aesthetic condition, from the merely physical, in order to reach the rational or moral."5.10 For if man does not experience a great wonder at that which is beautiful, his soul cannot ever take flight to the pure and the eternal. Keat's short statement fits well: "A thing of beauty, is a joy forever." It is the artist's obligation that he himself is in this state of wonder at the eternal and the beautiful before he can produce a work that will be timeless and give a firmness of joy to his and all following generations. In a world of constant change the artist can produce something of joy that will never change or lose its power to inspire wonder of beauty. But he is not to forsake the century in which he lives. "Live with your century, but do not be its creature; render to you contemporaries what they need, not what they praise." said Schiller in his Ninth Letter. He would be the first to warn mankind to beware of the "trashy" arts and entertainment that appeals to the man not yet born of wonder and the love of beauty. For such "art" stagnates and kills any chance of producing a moral and better people. Trashy art not only loses its value for moral goodness but even fights against the possibility of spiritual growth (Letter 15). In his great poem "An Ode to Joy" he lifted the often gloomy personality of Beethoven so much so that Beethoven used it for the powerful closing choral to his Ninth Symphony. For those purists who know German the part of the poem which Beethoven used will be here presented with my English translation. The sentence in <u>Beethoven</u>'s Ninth that introduces the poem goes: "O friends, no more of these sounds! Let us sing a more cheerful song, more full of joy".

Freude, schoener Goetterfunken, Tochter aus Elysium
Wir betreten feuertrunken, Himmlische, dein Heiligtum!

Deine Zauber binden wieder, Was die Mode streng geteilt;
Alle Menschen werden Brueder, Wo dein sanfter Fluegel weilt.

Wem der grosse Wurf gelungen, Eines Freundes Freund zu sein,
Wer ein holdes Weib errungen, Mische seinedn Jubel ein!
Ja, wer auch nur eine Seele Sein nennt auf dem Erdenrund!
Und ser's nie gekonnt, der stehle Weinend sich aus diesem Bund.

Freude trinken alle Wesen An den Bruesten der Natur;
Alle Guten, alle Boesen Folgen ihrer Rosenspur.
Kusse gab sie uns und Reben, Einen Fruend, geprueft in Tod;
Wollust ward dem Wurm gegeben, Und der Cherub steht vor Gott!

Froh, wie seine Sonnen fliegen Durch des Himmels praechtgen Plan,
Laufet, Brueder, eure Bahn, Freudig, wie ein Held zum Siegen.
.

Seid umschlungen, Millionen. Diesen Kuss der ganzen Welt!
Brueder! Ueberm Sternenzeit Muss ein lieber Vater wohnen.
Ihr stuerzt nieder, Millionen? Ahnest du den Schoepher, Welt?
Such' ihn ueber'm Sternenzeit! Ueber Sternen muss er wohnen.

Joy, The sparkling beauty of God, Daughter of Elysium,
Fire-inspired, we enter, into the heavens, your sanctuary.
Your magic binds again, all that custom has harshly divided;
All men become brothers, where your tender wings linger.

Whoever has received the abundant gift of friendship,
Whoever has obtained a charming wife, unite in jubilation,
Yes, who also calls only one soul his own upon the round earth!
And he who cannot rejoice, removes himself tearfully from our circle.

All creatures drink of joy on the breasts of nature.
All who are good, all who are bad, follow her sweet smell of roses.
She gave us kisses and the grapevine, a friend proven even in death;
Even the worm was given full joy, and the cherub stands before God.
Cheerfully, as the sun flies its splendid course through the heavens,
So also brothers, run your race, happily, as a hero to victory.

You millions, you are embraced, this kiss is for the entire world!
Brothers! Above the canopy over the stars, there must dwell a loving
  Father.
Do you kneel before Him, you millions?
World, do you acknowledge your Creator?
Seek Him above the covering of the stars.
It is above the stars He is obligated to reside.

In this second step on the road to wholeness and happiness, I have discussed the teachings of Jesus, other teachings which concur with him that the universe is a friendly place in which man can find happiness, and thirdly those who also concur with Jesus that the universe has a God and a Creator who cares for the totality of the universe and each little part of it, including the human race as a whole and also as individuals. It is in this last part that one can find the spirit of Plato's love of the Absolute Beauty Himself, Plotinus' wonder and devotion to The One being beyond all, and Schiller's Creator who offers a loving kiss to all the world in his Ode to Joy. Step Three in the next chapter presents the personal relationship that can be established by the individual and his God. This step can be attained, by God's loving grace for all, in many different ways including a faithful participation in organized religions, but also directly by those who are flavored by an organized religion but desire to find their own paths despite the great variety of options within each religion: Christianity has more than three hundred organized options. The main-streamers of all religions are those who follow one nicely laid out trail through the forest of the universe in order to find God on the other side, at the end of the established trail. This is fine and if it works for them, let no other judge them. Likewise, let them judge no other either. One of the problems is that the trail, in a sense, lies outside their own experience as it is passed down from others as a sacred tradition. One of the dangers for them is that if their path or trail were obscured in someway or other, they might panic because they have relied upon it and have an often limited understanding of the goal they are seeking, having depended upon the path itself to carry them through the forest of the universe to their beloved God. Without that one trail, they cry out in fearful confusion that they may not reach the other side of the forest--unaware that other trails that have forked off of it later return to it or come out of the forest in about the same area as their initial path. Likewise there are other paths starting at other locations, sometimes even crossing their own trail a few times, and coming out near their own trail even if the other paths have never crossed. There are many paths laid out by our teachers that get us through the forest, for God in his absolute love accepts the longings of all men who desire his presence. God wants all men to enjoy his Eternal Presence and his everlasting realm, and he certainly can enlighten any path for the sake of his children's eternal destiny; even though the traditional paths may be the most secure and comforting. But even the one who makes his own path, whose knowledge of the forest and the stars is excellent, will also reach the other side: for he too will receive help from above. True, he may suffer some bruises and cuts from his loneliness and spend more time in his quest; often feeling lost and helpless. But, then again, the experience is totally his own and his journey has united his existence to his very inner self, and as a new being he arrives at the other side of the forest to meet his God. Such people are often called hermitic monks or mystics. For me, the path has been traveled and laid out, first by Plato, and then, in consummation, by Jesus as the one who "reflects the glory of God and bears the very stamp of his nature" (Heb. 1:3), who himself traveled the path as the "pioneer of my salvation" (Heb.2:10), that I might follow him into a present and future "indestructible life" (Heb. 7:16); for through him "a better hope is introduced, through which we draw near to God" (Heb.7:19).

CHAPTER SIX

STEP THREE

PRAYER AND MEDITATION

ACTUALIZING ONE'S SOUL AND FINDING ONESELF
A CHILD OF GOD

I.   PRAYER AND MEDITATION IN THE LIFE OF JESUS

A. JESUS' PRAYERS IN THE GOSPELS

A few times the Gospels simply say that Jesus went to a lonely place for it was there that he wished to pray (Mt 14:13, Mt 14:23, Mk 1:35, Mk 6:46). He went up a mountain to pray (Lk 9:28ff). He evidently believed that the temple should be a quiet and lonely place for prayer, since he overturned the money-for-sacrifices exchange table and cried out that God's "house shall be known as a house of prayer", not a cave of darkness for thieves to steal the money of the poor (Mt 21:12-13). Also in the Garden of Gethsemane he went apart from his disciples to ask help from his heavenly Father as to what he should do, for he did not want to die at that time, but was more concerned with doing the Father's will (Mt 26:36ff, Mk 14:32ff). He likewise cried out to God that he not forsake him while he was on the cross, for it seemed to him that he was very much alone (Mt 27:46). One of his prayers gave God, his Father, thanks for revealing the good news of his love to those who had no pretense of wisdom and theological understanding (Lk 10:21 ff), and indicated along with many other passages his love for the down-trodden, the broken in spirit, the outcasts, the "sinners", the "enemies", and the "tax collectors", as well as his anger at the professional holy men, lawyers, and priests who ran the temple. For God had hidden the good news from the "wise" and "understanding". Luke's Gospel relates that it was after he had prayed that one of the disciples came to him and asked him "Lord, teach us how to pray"(Lk 11:1). This was, according to Luke the setting in which Jesus taught "The Lord's Prayer". Luke's version is as follows:

Father, hallowed be your name.
Your kingdom come.
Give us today our daily bread.
And forgive our debts, as we ourselves forgive all those who are
    Indebted to us.
And do not test us with temptation.

Matthew (6:9-13) included the prayer in his version of the Sermon on the Mount, and it reads as follows:

Our Father, in heaven,
Hallowed be your name.
Your kingdom come,
Your will be done,
    On earth as it is in heaven.
Give us today our daily bread;
And forgive our debts, as we ourselves forgive all those who are
    Indebted to us;
And do not test us with temptation,
But rescue us from evil.

When Jesus celebrated the Passover, he gave a prayer of thanksgiving (Lk 22:17). And from the cross Luke stated that he prayed for those who were mocking and cheering his crucifixion: "Father, forgive them; for they are ignorant of what they are doing" (23:34). Finally, in Luke, before dying, Jesus commits his destiny to the Father: "Father, into your care I put my spirit" (24:46).

The Gospel of John is much different than the other three gospels, which, because of their similar structure, are called the "Synoptic Gospels", and also because John was written perhaps as many as seventy years after Jesus' death, most of his sayings probably should be taken, not literally word for word, but symbolically of the way he prayed. This would apply particularly to the long prayer of Jesus as it is presented in the 17th Chapter of John. For that reason, only a synopsis will be presented here. In it Jesus prays for the well being and faith of his disciples with him at the time and also for all who follow his teachings in the future. He seemed to be specifically concerned about their eternal welfare, urging his disciples to keep their focus upon God the Father, to develop their relationship with the Father by following the teachings Jesus has given them, to even become one in the spirit with the Father as he himself was, and that they would be filled with joy in their relationship with God both now and forever. It is Jesus' farewell prayer in which he pours out his loving concern for his followers both present and all those in the future.

B. WHAT JESUS SAID ABOUT PRAYER

By "prayer" I mean any way in which a person seeks to approach God: prayer (mental words or spoken words), any approach to an altar (the act of kneeling in silence or the offering of a gift), and any form of meditation whether one is standing, walking, genuflecting, or taking a unique position in order to "be silent before the Lord" even if it is entirely intuitive and completely devoid of thought, or a form of spiritual introspection which follows rational thought patterns.

To approach God, one must respect the fact that he "is on holy ground" and one must not trample such ground. Jesus said that to approach the altar to offer a gift, while one is in the state of abusing or hurting someone else with a false or corrupt dealing, is an insult to God. "First go and pay satisfaction or be reconciled with your brother, that is, cleanse your life of hurting others first, and then come to the altar and offer a gift" (Mt 5:23-25). The invitation to come "before the Lord" is always open, but wear the proper garments (virtues) or you will be cast out of the wedding (Mt 22:12). A man's soul must be cleansed of the unclean spirits before it can be swept clean and serve as an abode for the presence of God and the virtues (Mt 12:43). If a man has trouble in his prayer life, it is very possible he has some unresolved guilt for which he can make restitution, but has refused to do it. Jesus sometimes spoke in exaggerated ways often using such hyperboles to show the magnitude of the power of prayer: "...if you say to this mountain, 'Rise up and throw yourself into the sea,' it will be done"(Mt 21:21). To be in contact with the Creator was an awesome thing, yet all such prayers were to be limited to God's will, for it is most likely that God does not want to move the mountain. Jesus himself, asked in faith in the Garden of Gethsemane not to have to go to the cross, but realized the Father's will must always override our requests, for He most certainly has a greater view of reality and what is good for mankind as a whole than we do. But for such things as are needed for our spiritual health and wholeness, the The Father is most willing to hear our suggestions. Also, the very act of confronting God with our requests makes us reconsider what we think to be of great value, and usually it is the one who prays who is changed, and not his circumstances. For happiness and joy lie within us, and in coming before God in honesty and faith, we can experience the greater miracles within, where our true self and all that is eternal abides: "...how much more will the heavenly Father give the Holy Spirit to those who ask him!" (Lk 11:13). Jesus once warned about our attitude while praying, if there is no humility, there is no prayer only a self-centered exalting of ourselves thinking that God should give us a bonus of some type. "Two men went to the temple to pray, a Pharisee and a tax collector. One arrogantly boasted and 'thanked God' that we was not like the others who were tainted with sin, rather he considered himself very special because he did so many good works. But the tax collector aware of the "holy ground" on which he was standing, stood afar off with eyes lowered because of his deep feeling of inadequacy before God, and asked: 'God, be merciful to me a sinner' (Lk 18:9ff)". The tax collected went away feeling a sense of being forgiven and cleansed, the Pharisee remained in his arrogance.

C. JESUS TAUGHT HIS DISCIPLES TO SEEK THE ETERNAL

In actualizing one's soul and finding oneself a child of God it was necessary to keep one's eyes and hearts set upon the Eternal, and thus Jesus many times stressed that the "Kingdom of God" (Mark) or the "Kingdom of Heaven" (Matthew) was to be put before everything else. Throughout the Gospel of Matthew it is stated over and over again that all else is secondary to the quest of the Eternal. "Leave all and follow me." "The pure in heart shall see God". "Do not fear what can kill the body but that which can destroy the soul." "Lay up for yourselves treasures in heaven where there will be security forever." Chose either "God or mammon." "Life is more than food and clothing." "Sell all that you have for the sake of the Great Pearl, the Kingdom of Heaven." And in the other gospels similar statements like, "Mary has chosen the better thing." Earthly life is so brief, and Eternity so long, that it should not even be a contest. Yet, the necessities of the body tend to keep our soul grounded. But, it must arise and take Plato's winged chariot to heaven.

D   THE PERSONAL QUEST FOR GOODNESS WITHIN

Preparing the soul to focus on the Eternal depended much on the idea of cleansing it from the lower desires and filling it with the virtues that make one most like God, for then it is easier for the soul to be drawn to the Eternal: for like attracts like. Jesus recommended: "Be perfect as your Father in heaven is perfect." "Follow the narrow way." "Be different from those attached to the world." "A good person will produce good things." "Whoever does the will of the Father is my brother, sister, and mother." "Faith brings calmness to the soul." "Gratitude rejoices within the soul when something good happens." "You are new wine and a new fabric, do not attach yourself to the old". The story of Mary's choosing the better thing is important, because Martha was doing a kind and a necessary thing to nourish the bodies of the disciples with food and give them a place to relax. It is a warning that even the necessary things which the body needs, must be put secondary to spiritual growth. It is not always the silly and frivolous things that are the major temptations to avoid spiritual growth, but the other things that are necessary and are therefore easier for us to justify our giving our attention and time to them. Of course, they have there place, but being a good person, a thankful person, a merciful man, a generous woman, a being of faith, hope, love, courage, self-control, justice and spiritual wisdom is the foundation for wholeness and happiness, and such also helps us to focus from within on the Eternal above.

II.   CONCURRING TEACHINGS FROM THE OTHER MASTERS

A.   From the Hindu Scriptures of which the three most important are: The Upanishads, The Bhagavad-Gita (The Song of God), and The Srimad Bhagavatam (The Wisdom of God). In the Upanishads God is a Personal God and is The Ultimate Reality (according to Ramanuja), and is often presented as a Trinity: Creator (Brahma), Preserver (Vishnu), and Destroyer (Shiva) of the universe. He can be reached by prayer and can be honored by devotional hymns, and love of him (bhakti) is among the necessary ingredients that lifts the soul of man to its highest level, the attainment of Brahman of whom the Personal God is the highest manifestation (according to Sankaracharya). While there is a difference within Hinduism as to whether the Highest and Ultimate Reality is the personal God himself, or Brahman, of whom the personal God is the highest manifestation, the personhood of God is not in question. The Svetasvatara Upanishad (II.15) states:

And when the yogi beholds the real nature of Brahman
...having known the unborn and immutable Lord,
who is untouched by ignorance and its effects,
he is freed from all fetters.

...by truly realizing Him who is the Lord, the bestower of blessings,
one attains the supreme peace (Ibid. IV.ll)

Often God is called Self or I Am, that is, the non-begotten who ever is.

But those who seek the Self...
Some call Him the Father (Prasna Upanishad I.10-11).

One desires a spiritual union with God, and this, of course, is the climax of life itself. Ultimate liberation comes from knowing God. The Bhagavad-Gita states:

He who has meditated on Me alone,
And in putting off the concerns of his flesh,
Comes forth to Me, and enters into my Being.

Have Me, then, in your heart always, and fight.
You too, when heart and mind are fixed on Me,
Shall surely come to Me. All come who cleave
With never-wavering will of firmest faith. (VIII)

From the Srimad Bhagavatam:

> O revered sages, there is nothing greater or more purifying than
> to converse about God and his divine play. The highest religion
> of man is unselfish love of God. If one has this love, one attains
> to truly divine wisdom. Fruitless is that knowledge which is not
> love. Fruitless is religion itself, if it have not love. Vain indeed
> is all struggle for spiritual life if in one's heart there be not love
> ... The very truth of all religions is the Lord of Love. There is no
> other goal but he (Book I ,Chapter One. tr. Swami Prabhavananda)

This, of course, sounds much like I Corinthians 13 written by Paul of
Tarsus. The Srimad Bhagavatam (The Wisdom of God), to me, is the
most beautiful of all Hindu works, and I recommend the translation of
Swami Prabhavananda. Expressed in it is the almost magical charm that
comes upon a person who is bent down before God in meditation, if that
person comes with a holy life of virtuous actions. Even though God is far
beyond the thoughts of man, he feels the bliss of his inner self when he is
humbly before the Lord of love. It is a book that encourages a high
degree of tolerance for other religions, recognizing that there is One God,
one Absolute Truth, and one eternal existence, and, because of this, one
is not to be judgmental towards others who simply use other names by
which to call the Absolute God. The Srimad encourages all people to let
their hearts and minds be brought into harmony with this Ultimate Truth
and there find a sanctuary from all that hinders happiness.

For the Hindu teachers God is Absolute Purity and Good, and even
though his "personhood" is beyond what we can conceive "personality"
to be, yet he loves, he creates, he receives hymns of honor, and he has
mercy on the weaknesses of men, forgiving their sins and leading them
back to himself.

The Katha Upanishad presents the climb that the soul makes to the
Absolute God.

Higher than the senses are the objects of sense,
Higher than the objects of sense is the mind,
Higher than the mind is the intellect,
Higher than the Self is the Unmanifest,

Higher than the Unmanifest is the Supreme personified,
Highest is this Supreme, the Goal Ultimate.6.1

One can see from these Hindu Scriptures that God is far beyond our
thinking, yet creates, cares for, and leads mankind back to himself, for he
is bound by love and mercy for his creatures. He is accessible by prayer
and is pleased to receive the finite honors that we can possibly give him,
and it is precisely in these acts of ours, as well as a life motivated by love
for other humans, that we find liberation from our fears and anxieties and
the courage to see the beauty of life.

B.   The Platonists themselves are the source of most Western
transcendental thought, and if not the direct source then the general
backbone to philosophies and religions of the West that follow the great
spread of Platonic thought itself. Their influence upon the Stoics, the
Western Eclectics, Christianity, Gnosticism, and the Sufis is undeniable.
The enormous stature of Plato, Plutarch, Plotinus and Proclus in
themselves is overwhelming, and each represents in some way the
progression of Platonic thought in the West: Plato himself was the
source of 'The Old School', Plutarch and Philo represent 'Middle
Platonism', Plotinus of 'Neo-platonism', and Proclus of the final stage of
Platonism before it entered into the Middle Ages deprived of the
Academy, which was closed by the Christian Emperor Justinian in
529AD. Christianity was the greatest inheritor of the Platonic
philosophical-theological thought, and many of its greatest theologians
were deeply imbedded in Platonic thought before and after their
conversion to Christianity. In fact, with the exception of Tertullian,
Lactantius, and Jerome, virtually all other Church Fathers were Platonic
Christians--if judged by their views of the nature of God, and that, of
course, is what theology studies. My book Plato's Gift to Christianity:
The Gentile Preparation for and the Making of the Christian Faith is
readily available for those seeking to pursue the influence of Platonism
upon Christianity, and it is probably the most comprehensive study of the
subject in the English language. This is why I have given so much time
to Plato and the Platonists in this book, being a Platonic Christian
myself.
     Socrates, in Plato's works, is shown to be one who contemplated and
prayed many times, for it is a Platonic theme that when any undertaking

is commenced, whether great or small, one first prays for Divine help and guidance, and all life itself is the quest to meet God face to face, although it generally can be said to be beyond man's capacity, but if he ever did, then to relate such an experience to others would be totally impossible, for human language can not convey such an experience. Man's goal in life in terms of morals and ethics is to be as much like God as is possible. Man's quest and goal in life are centered upon God, The Eternal, The Good, The Beautiful that is absolute and never changes, for only there can man find true reality. While social dialogue and the meaning of words to explain the experience which they claim to project is used by Plato for all things in order to try to bring some consistent meaning to speech, prayer and meditation by oneself are the best avenues to God, for God is personal and man seeks and needs his friendship. To be a THEOPHILES (One of God's Beloved) is the great hope of all men. A friendship with God was Plato's philosophical "summum bonum", the greatest good that man can experience and the ultimate source of all other goods, like happiness and wholeness of being. Because of earlier references to Plato and Platonism, I shall just quote a few words from the Symposium (211):

"But Beauty absolute, separate, simple, and everlasting, which without diminution and without increase, or any change, is imparted to the ever-growing and perishing beauties of all other things. He who from these, ascending [in meditative thought] under the influence of true love, begins to perceive that Beauty....
This is that life above all others which man should live, in the contemplation of Beauty Absolute; a Beauty which if you once beheld [the dialogue goes on to say that all previous concepts of beauty would no longer be of value, so overwhelming is the experiencing of Absolute Beauty]...
But what if a man had eyes to see the True Beauty -- the Divine Beauty, I mean, pure and clear and unalloyed, not clogged with the pollutions of mortality and all the colours and vanities of human life -- looking, and holding converse with the True Beauty Simple and Divine? Remember how in that communion only, beholding Beauty with the eye of the mind, he will be enabled to bring forth, not images of beauty, but realities (for he has hold not of an image but of a reality), and bringing forth and

nourishing true virtue to become the friend of God [a THEOPHILES] and be immortal."

Plotinus, in discussing the power of meditation and its goal of spiritually seeing The One (Absolute God), stressed that such an experience is not one of knowledge but one of being aware of the Presence of Simple Unity. "He must renounce knowing" to obtain the vision. The burden to find God is placed upon man, for if he through contemplation does not "achieve awareness of that Life that is beyond, if the soul does not feel a rapture within it like that of the lover come to rest in love...he has no one to blame but himself and should try to become pure by detaching himself from everything". But the One can be seen by the "contemplating eyes". Plotinus assured his students that there is a Unity to the Cosmos, for it certainly did not come about by accident, and that Unity is the One who gives fulfillment to the souls who seek happiness and wholeness, and will find themselves in a state of rapture (VI.9,4-5).

Plotinus organized Plato's Cosmos as such:

THE ONE WHO IS BEYOND BEING
The Ultimate Source of Being
(Plato's Good beyond Being)

|

THE INTELLECT
THE MIND, INTELLIGENCE
(Plato's NOUS)

|

THE INTELLECTUAL REALM
(Plato's Architypes or Forms)

|

THE GENERATION OF THE MATERIAL WORLD
(Incarnation of the physical and man's body, into which the
Soul from above is implanted)
(Same as Plato)

Man's contemplation of reality will start at the bottom with the physical and material existence, but must step up through the two intellectual realms and then leave behind mind and thought in order to experience the One who is beyond mind, thought, and all being, the One Everlasting Who created all being. There is Ultimate Reality, and once experienced by mediation, the rapture will change a man forever. He will never look back, whole and unattached to the material world. Anxieties, fears, and dreads can no longer touch his soul. Plotinus' influence was indeed great as it was his Platonic philosophy that Augustine read and was through the Platonic Ambrose lifted into the arms of Christ. It was Plotinus' works that greatly influenced also Gregory of Nyssa who in turn was an influence on the Christian Mystics. Finally, the Sufis received their idea of the One and much more from Plotinus, and they themselves are more Platonic than Muslim, although they will likely deny any influence from Platonism. But in reading the Sufis one can see the softening effect of Platonism on those raised in the Islamic faith; the openness, tenderness of God, the non-judgmentalism which are all a part of Sufism comes from Platonic thought.

C.   If one were to read much of Sufi literature, it would be somewhat difficult to attach such thinking to Islam, which, in general lacks Platonic and mystical influences. Quite openly the Sufis lay claim to the wisdom in Moses, in Jesus, and in Mohammed, but I have, in my limited reading, found no references to Platonism--but when one considers the same attitude of Christianity in the modern world, i.e. its silence about the Platonic influence in the making of Christianity--then it is quite understandable. For most religions of the world trust revelation from above to certain holy men for their guidance (Judaism, Christianity, Islam, and Hinduism), rather than a God-inspired natural reason and the longing of love of the Eternal and Beautiful planted in man to drive man towards the quest of finding God. All however, who believe in a personal God, believe also that He takes the initiative in helping man to find him, whether by means of sent holy men who have a revelation or by means of planting an unrest of desire and love within man to come back to him, or in some cases a religion will believe in some, usually unbalanced, mixture of both. One thing that the Sufis have definitely to offer others is an open and gentle acceptance of wisdom or truth (as they see it) from all sources. Finding the One Himself is far more important than defending certain doctrines about Him; this can also be said of some Christian hermitics and mystics. For words are only symbols, but the experience of the One is overwhelmingly fulfilling in spirit, as was well taught, as I said, by the Platonists also.

Idries Shah has referred to this great openness of the Sufis and stated:

> The connection between the ancient practical philosophies and the present ones is seen to have been based upon the higher-level unity of knowledge, not upon appearances. This explains why the Muslim Rumi has Christian, Zoroastrian and other disciples; why the great Sufi 'invisible teacher' Khidr is said to be a Jew; why the Mogul prince Dara Shikoh identified Sufi teachings in the Hindu Vedas, yet himself remained a member of the Qadiri Order; how Pythagoras and Solomon can be said to be Sufi teachers. It also explains why Sufis will accept some alchemists to have been Sufis, as well as understanding the underlying developmental factors in Rumi's evolutionary philosophy of Hallaj's 'Christianity'; why, indeed, Jesus is said to stand, in a sense, at the head of the Sufis.6.2

From this it seems safe to think of the Sufis as eclectic mystics, who will openmindedly take in any teaching that they feel will help them in their quest to be united with The One, and this is to be to their credit. And they are not alone. Buddha was quite influenced by Hinduism, nevertheless, went his own separate way. The Jewish "Mosaic" book of Genesis borrowed from Mesopotamian literature and the book of Proverbs used many sayings from Egypt, and Christianity was formed by the presence of Platonism, in the Hellenistic Jews before Jesus, in the Septuagint translation of the Hebrew Bible into the Greek, in the person of a Hellenized Jesus himself, and by the subsequent Platonic Christian Church Fathers. The Stoics were well known Eclectics. And wherever Buddhism went it was adapted by the traditional nature of the local people: Ch'an in China, and Zen in Japan. It is to the credit of a religion that tries to focus on the main point: making people good and decent and pointing them to the Eternal and Beautiful for life more abundant, and thirdly, answering the problem, or at least the human fear, of death. This section of the book is emphasizing the concept that man is a child of God, Who Himself is accessible to man, Who takes the initiative to care for man because of his eternal state of graciousness and love, and that man becomes full and whole when he both recognizes his God and focuses his life to attain eternal friendship with God. Most of the time religions are jealous of their fundamentals and resist Light from Heaven if it does not come from one of their own believers. The 12th century philosophical Sufi, El-Ghazali's openness was rejected by the Muslim power brokers and his books were burned by the intolerant in all the Muslim lands from Spain to Syria. And even today they have little influence on traditional Islam. The Christian religion is not the only one to have burned books: doctrinaire conservatives of most all faiths seem to have an insecurity about hearing a teaching different from their own. It is to the Mystics and the Sufis and others on the edge of traditional religions that the greatest tolerance and wisdom is shone. Ghazali himself taught:

> A human being is not a human being while his tendencies include self-indulgence, covetousness, temper, and attacking other people. A student must reduce to the minimum the fixing of his attention upon customary things like his people and his environment, for attention-capacity is limited.6.3

Concerning unattachment to the material realm he stated: "You possess only whatever will not be lost in a shipwreck".6.4

Attar of Nishapur taught this about the kind character of Jesus:

> Some Israelites reviled Jesus one day as he was walking through their part of town. But he answered by repeating prayers in their name. Someone said to him: 'You prayed for these men, did you not feel the fire of anger against them?' He answered: 'I could spend only what I had in my purse.'6.5

This depiction of Jesus was in keeping with Jesus' teachings to turn the other cheek and "pray for those who persecute", for that is the very sub-stance of essence of Christ, he could act in no other way (I could spend only what I had in my purse). Jesus himself in the Christian Canonical Scriptures also lived his teachings, praying for those who ridiculed him while he was on the cross; "Father, forgive them for they do not know what they are doing." Javad Nurbakhsh wrote a book, which is now translated into English, called <u>Jesus</u> <u>in</u> <u>the</u> <u>Eyes</u> <u>of</u> <u>the</u> <u>Sufis</u> that is 125 pages long and includes numerous references to Jesus in which he is seen as a wise prophet and sometimes even as a "devotee". Nurbakhsh stated: "God has singled out amongst His Prophets only two individuals to be dubbed 'devotees': just Mohammad and Jesus" (p.32). <u>Rumi</u>, one of the most admired and influential of the Sufis, showing no concern for the judgmental doctrinal differences among the religions, puts emphasis upon his Beloved God only: from his poem "Only Breath".

Not Christian or Jew or Muslim, not Hindu,
Buddhist, sufi, or zen. Not any religion
or cultural system. I am not from the East
or the West, not out of the ocean or up
from the ground, not natural or ethereal, not
composed of elements at all. I do not exist,
am not an entity in this world or the next,
did not descend from Adam and Eve or any
origin story. My place is placeless, a trace
of the traceless. Neither body or soul.
I belong to the Beloved, have seen the two
worlds as one...6.6

Rumi, as most Christian mystics and Sufis have only one love, one concern and that is to experience God's presence, for that is the consummation of all reality: to them nothing else matters. It is the highest call, maybe somewhat like Jesus' references to those who become eunuchs for the kingdom's sake, or for others who leave all and follow him. But most Sufis live also on two levels and do not consider work, duty, family as irrelevant to life, but they too must be secondary to God. Jesus commented that he who does not hate his father and mother can not be his disciple. That, of course, is a Hebrewism which means that they must be put secondary to his call. (The Hebrew scriptures state that Jacob loved Rachel but hated Leah -- not meaning that he actually hated Leah, but that in every romantic situation Rachel was preferred). So is the quest of the soul: to put all else secondary to the love of God. Jesus said that one should call no man father, for there is only one Father. The soul is awakened and actualized when man gains his entire orientation in life by focusing upon God.

D. OTHER TEACHERS AND SAGES

Epictetus encouraged his students to be alone by themselves for introspection and meditation, for that is when man can be most honest with himself, for even Zeus sets himself apart and finds his own tranquillity within. There is much honesty the soul has to confront when man is alone before God, and not hidden among a crowd. He stated:

> As bad tragic actors cannot sing alone, but in company with many:
> so some persons cannot walk about alone. Man, if you are anything,
> both walk alone and talk to yourself, and do not hide yourself in
> the chorus. Examine a little at last, look around, stir yourself up.
> That you may know who you are (III.14).

Once a man knows who he is, he needs to relate to God:

> These things are not done, man, in a careless way, nor just as it
> may happen; but there must be a (fit) age and life and God as a
> Guide (III.21).

> But I have so much to say to you that he who without God attempts
> so great a matter is hateful to God, and has no other purpose than to
> act indecently in public (III.22).

> But wherever I go, there is the sun, there is the moon, there are the
> stars, dreams, omens, and the conversation with God (III.22).

> Reflect more carefully, know yourself, consult the Divinity, without
> God attempt nothing (III.22)

> If a man is unhappy, remember that his unhappiness is his own
> fault: for God has made all men to be happy (III.23).

Epictetus had a difficult life. For many years he was the slave of a Roman master who had beaten him so badly that he was crippled and finally set free. But his relationship with God gave to him unspeakable joy and confidence in life. He was critical of the cynics who always complained about life or their situation or the unhappy plight of man's destiny. In a defense of himself, similar in tone to Paul's defense of his being an apostle, Epictetus promotes his own life that was empty of every convenience and possession as God's example to the cynics, that one can have nothing, not even good health, but be happy and rejoice in his relationship with God:

"And how is it possible that a man who has nothing, who is naked, houseless, without a hearth, squalid, without a slave [poor cynics didn't have any slaves], without a city, can pass a life that flows easily?" See, God has sent you a man to show you that it is possible."Look at me, who am without a city, without a house, without possessions, without a slave [Epictetus' humor -- as others knew he had been a long time slave himself], I sleep on the ground; I have no wife, no children; no praetorium, but only the earth and heavens, and one poor cloak. And what do I lack? Am I not without sorrow? Am I not without fear? Am I not free? When did any of you see me failing in the object of my desire? ...did I ever blame God or man? ...Reflect more carefully, know yourself, consult the Divinity, without God attempt nothing (III.22).

Epictetus, in short, was telling the cynics, "Your real problem is that you do not know yourselves as humans in this vast cosmos, you do not meditate on your situation, and you have no Divine Friend, because you refuse His Presence."

The Hebrew Psalmist was aware that God knows us better than we know our selves and that nothing is hid from Yahweh:

> You have investigated me and known me within, O Yahweh!
> You know when I sit down and stand up,
> Even at a distance you know what I am thinking.
> You know the paths I take and when I am resting,
> And you are aware of all the ways I live.
> Even before I have spoken a word, you know exactly
>   what I am thinking.
> ...
> How you can know these things strikes wonder in me,
>   for it is far beyond my mind's capacity.
> To what place could I go where your spirit is not?
> To where could I journey and not have you present?

If I rise up to the skies, you are there.
If I go to my grave, you are there.
...
You made my inner parts,
and put me together while I was in my mother's womb.
...
You know me very well,
 Even my framework was not unknown to you. (Ps. 139)

Even though the Psalmist did not believe in life after death, he felt that Yahweh, even in death, was aware of him, at least his body. The ancient Israelites felt very close to Yahweh, even convinced that they were his chosen people among all the earth, and this closeness of feeling is found throughout all the wisdom literature and in some other books as well. Some Israelites, after their Hellenization, did come to believe in life after death as shown in the Greek Apocrypha written in the two centuries before Jesus. But even before that belief, the Israelites felt a comforting closeness to Yahweh, and that faith gave their lives meaning and morality.

The Odes of Solomon, possibly written by Gnostic Jews, probably first written in Greek, also showed this closeness to God as Father, and life after death is not ruled out, but usually not mentioned.

As the eyes of a son to his father
so my eyes turn to you, O Lord, at all times,
for with you are my consolation and joy.

Do not turn your mercy from me, O Lord,
nor your kindness,
but stretch out your right hand,
and be my guide to the end.

Care for me, and save me from evil.
Let your tenderness and love be with me. (Ode 14)

In Ancient Egypt the legend to myth of Osiris presented to the people of Egypt a god of deepest intimacy and comfort. The legend of a man who helped unify and cultivate Egypt in its prehistoric period grew to mythical proportions including betrayal, his murder, and the gathering of his mutilated body by his loving wife, his being brought back to life, and finally his ascension to heaven where he became the judge of those who died, judging whether they would enter into eternal bliss or eternal damnation based upon one's ethical life which one would have to defend first of all before the 42 gods residing in the "Hall of Double Right and Truth", in which one had to confess the "Negative Confession" of 40 to 42 negative statements, probably one before each god before he would come before Thoth and have his righteousness judged, a balancing of his good deeds against his bad deeds, and if he passed that test and was proved a righteous man, then he was presented to Osiris, who granted him eternal life. Osiris was many things to the Ancient Egyptian: the Lord of Fertility, the Lord of the Resurrection, the Lord of Law and Ethics, and the Father of the Egyptian Trinity with his wife Isis and son Horus which also presented a type of perfect family that the Egyptians were to imitate in their own lives. In Egypt the Osirian image lasted well into the Christian era and finally came to an end in the Muslim era, but for well over 3,500 years it gave purpose and comfort to the people of Egypt, and also to large segments of the Roman Empire along with a separate honoring of his wife, in the Isis legends. They certainly were the two most loved Egyptian gods by the Egyptian people themselves, and there was also a universal quality about Osiris' character that was imitated throughout the ancient world. He was seen as the Lord of Eternity as well as initially a human king who shared work, life, and death with his fellow humans. He is seen as the righteous one who, in bringing good and fertility in both land and procreation to others, is betrayed and brutally killed, even by those closest to him. Yet he overcomes evil and death as he is raised by the gods, and thus presents his people with the hope that the great barriers that hold mortals in bondage and fear are broken, for this victory over death he graciously offers to those who love him, trust him, and follow his commandments. To those taking on his name in death (a person who had died was Osiris John Doe, or the late Osiris John Doe), he gave, not only eternal life in his kingdom, but his own everlasting presence. His image simply could not die with Ancient Egypt, for he was a universal hero. In the Greek and Roman world, when not honored directly, his myth was present and flavored the other heroes of Western humanity: Tammuz, Adonis, Mithra, Cybele, Attis, and Dionysos. And, the structure of his "historical activities" were before and very similar to those of Jesus, who, especially by the Coptic Church of Northeast Africa, is seen as a fulfillment of the Osirian legend, not as a greater myth, but as an actual historical incarnation.

Among the Christian Desert Fathers and Mystics there is a strong longing and yearning to leave life quickly and be taken into paradise, although none actually considered suicide to speed up the process. Yet one can tell that their absorption with the full presence of God, in actualized reality, and not just by the eyes of faith, completely controlled their spiritual lives. These Christians unfortunately sometimes saw life in the flesh as a burden and barrier to their final and complete happiness and wholeness, and in that one can see certain similar Buddhist and Hindu features that tend to depreciate the present life to such a degree that they either insult the good gift of life God has given to them on earth or they simply avoid participation in making life better for others while they are here. Nevertheless, their powerful focus on God can be a lesson for us who are only too prone to seek our happiness in the material realm. In fact, if we listen to their thoughts and try to understand their love for God, we often feel a sense of being less spiritual than they and might even envy the fact that they are so in love with God, who as a Sun in there lives totally obscures the light of the other stars and beauties of life.

Anselm of Canterbury, very influenced by Neo-platonism, longed for the One, God, as much as Plotinus did, and also carried with him some of the diminishing of the beauty of this present life in his longing prayers. In the early part of his first chapter of the Proslogium he leads us well into the desire to set apart time for the contemplation of God, but then he falls into anguish that this life is an exile from God and is to be seen as a land of wretchedness because we do not see God face to face, at least not like he imagines it to be in heaven.

> I have written the following treatise, in the person of one who strives to lift his mind to the contemplation of God, and seeks to understand what he believes...Yield room for some little time to God; and rest for a little time in him. Enter the inner chamber of your mind; shut out all thoughts save that of God, and such as can aid you in seeking him; close your door and seek him. Speak now, my whole heart! Speak now to God, saying, I seek your face; your face, Lord, will I seek. And come now, O Lord my God, teach my

heart where and how it may seek you, where and how it may find
you. [This section is splendid, but the following section seems to
be, not so much a prayer, as a complaint because his longing has
not yet been filled]
...What, O most high Lord, shall this man do, an exile from you?
What shall your servant do, anxious in his love for you, and cast
out afar from you face? He pants to see you, and your face is too
far from him. He longs to come to you, and your dwelling place is
inaccessible...Lord, you are my God, and you are my Lord, and never
have I seen you...Finally, I was created to see you, and not yet have
I done that for which I was made. O wretched lot of man, when he
has lost that for which he was made! O hard and terrible fate!

True love and trust of God is to let him handle the stages of our lives;
when he gives us an earthly life to live and enjoy it, that is what we
should do. Of course, our focus should always be on the Eternal, but to
dismiss the blessings of the present life as a "hard and terrible fate" is
really to scorn the life God gave to us first as a loving gift. This is a
problem I have with those mystics that are excessive, and yet, I am
thankful they have spoken and taught us, for they will not let us forget
that, as Kierkegaard once said, that this world is a most beautiful place,
but it is not our final home.

Mircea Eliade in an article called "The Yearning for Paradise in
Primitive Tradition" (from the Summer 1953 issue of Diogenes printed
by U. Of Chicago Press) stated that Christian Mysticism is "dominated
by the yearning for Paradise", and that one of the thoughts of features of
paradise was to be the friendship of man and animals, for animals are
often thought to be subject to man as it was thought to be under Adam.
The prime example, of course, would be that of Francis of Assisi. This
idea perhaps ought to say something to us, namely, that the treatment of
animals based upon the loving care that any master would have for the
lives under his control is a necessity that man must learn in order to
prepare his own thoughts for paradise. Maybe in becoming as much like
God as possible requires us to learn how to treat animals, our inferiors, as
we desire God to treat us, his inferiors. Plato taught, although he was
thinking of our human society, that much can be learned about a man by
the way he treats his inferiors. Likewise, much can be learned of us as a
human race by the way we treat our inferiors. There is no doubt that

Francis of Assisi is dear to our hearts, and at least partly, by the way he shared his friendship with the animals. His closeness to nature gave us the poem Brother Sun and Sister Moon.

Most high omnipotent good Lord,
Thine are the praises, the glory, the honor, and all benediction.
To thee alone, Most High, do they belong,
And no man is worthy to mention thee.
<u>Praised be thou, my Lord, with all thy creatures,</u>
Especially the honored Brother Sun,
...
Praised be thou, my Lord, for Sister Moon
...
By which thou givest sustenance to thy creatures.
...
Praised be thou, my Lord, for our Sister Earth,
Who sustains and governs us,
And produces various fruits with colored flowers and herbage.
Praise and bless my Lord and give him thanks
And serve him with great humility.

Shankara (686-718AD), despite his brief life of 32 years, was the great reformer of Hindu philosophy, which gave it new life, logical arrangement, and a gentle and joyous spirit that reflects Shankara himself. In him one sees that same type of devotion and longing for God that was developing among the Christian Mystics of the West. There is a longing for liberation from the fetters of life and thought patterns which hinder a man's quest to experience the Divine. When this "renunciation and longing for liberation are weak, tranquility and other virtues are a mere appearance, like the mirage in the desert."6.7 One must experience his own growth into spirituality, another's experience can not help, for this longing and seeking must be personal:

A clear vision of the Reality may be obtained only through our own eyes, when they have been opened by spiritual insight--never through the eyes of some other seer. Through our own eyes we learn what the moon looks like: how could we learn this through the eyes of others?

...

A sickness is not cured by saying the word "medicine". You must take the medicine. Liberation does not come by merely saying the word "Brahman". Brahman must be actually experienced.

...

A buried treasure is not uncovered by merely uttering the words "come forth". You must follow the right directions, dig, remove the stones and earth from above it, and then make it your own.6.8

This sounds so simple, yet it is such basic teaching: spiritual growth is both personal and requires personal effort, for virtue and liberation from our fetters do not come easily. Recently I saw on TV a report about "prayer services", that is, you paid someone else to pray for you. When the person, one of those paid to pray (it was in Mexico) was asked why she offered such services, she replied that many people are good and religious people, but they simply did not have time to pray. Unbelievable! Shankara reminds us that one who is sick can not pay someone else to drink the medicine for them. The longing for spiritual liberation is both personal and hard work. Shankara stated that to experience the fullness of everlasting joy, a man must be liberated from ego within and from attachment of material objects without, and if he is fully desirous of this spiritual fulfillment he must be absorbingly devoted. Such an experience of liberation brings new insight into a man's life so that he feels a perfect union with the Divine that is "beyond words or thought, absolute bliss, incomparable and immeasurable, ever-free, boundless as the sky, indivisible and absolute."6.9 It reminds me of Martin Luther King's euphoric statement when he felt absolutely uplifted: "I have been to the Mountain top". Such experiences change people forever, and the past life is left behind.

E. TWO CHRISTIAN MYSTICS: MEISTER ECKHART AND JACOB BOEHME

Meister Eckhart in a sense was a Mystic's Mystic and perhaps only on that level can he be fully appreciated and understood, but for most he seemed to be on the far side or the edge of Christianity. For Eckhart his sole desire in life was to enjoy the presence of God as fully as possible, in soul, in mind, in feeling and in rapture. What concerned others about the form of Christianity, did not concern him at all, and things that were doctrinally important to the established church of his day he felt were so limited that the very kernel of spiritual substance was beyond it. "Wiltu den kernen haben, so muostu die schalen brechen"6.10 "If you want the kernel, you must break the shell". He lived at the highest mystical level where often one finds Neoplatonists, some of the Upanishad writers, and some Sufis. He sought a mystical unity with God that his entire life would be harmonious with Divine Reality, yet he never went so far as to lose his separateness from God. He knew there was a great gap between the Creator and the creature that would distinguish each one regardless of the unity of spirit they shared. His steps in the ascent of the soul to attain the high spiritual level upon which the Divinity Himself would become the reality of his life is likened to that of Plato's Symposium and Phaedrus as well as the writings of <u>Plotinus</u>. He introduced his Treatises with these words:

> When I preach, I usually speak of disinterest and say that a man
>   should be empty of self and all things:
> And secondly, that he should be reconstructed in the simple Good
>   that is God.
> And thirdly, that he should consider the great aristocracy which
>   God has set up in the soul, such that by means of it man may
>   wonderfully attain to God;
> And fourthly, of the purity of the Divine Nature.

Simple steps: empty yourself of all concerns and anxieties, let God do the rebuilding of your entire life and soul in the simple goodness which He himself is, show you your spiritual nobility, and be as much as possible the very purity of the Divine Nature himself. The following words he gave to help us achieve those steps.

> To be sure, this requires effort and love, a careful cultivation of the
> spiritual life, and a watchful, honest, active oversight of all one's
> mental attitudes toward things and people. It is not to be learned by
> world-flight, running away from things, turning solitary and going
> apart from the world. Rather, one must learn an inner solitude,
> wherever or with whomsoever he may be. He must learn to penetrate
> things and find God there, to get a strong impression of God firmly

fixed in his mind. It is like learning to write. To acquire this art, one must practice much, however disagreeable or difficult it may be, however impossible it may seem. [after which it becomes a part of one's being and a comfortable habit with the effect that] ...a man should shine with the Divine Presence without having to [make a special effort to] work at it.6.11

It is not surprising to me that Philipp Otto Runge, one of my favorite painters, drew great inspiration from the writings of Jacob Boehme 1575-1624AD), whose life, much like that of Meister Eckhart, drew much criticism, both during his life and afterwards. But both were very influential and had great admirers because of the personal inspiration they had received from these two mystical teachers of their quest for intimate Christian faith. Attachment to God, and God only, is the longing that drives the quest of the Mystics, as can be shown in his prayers. In prayer, Boehme is asking God to guide him on the correct path on his way to his eternal fatherland, for he knows he has much deviated from the paths of the "orthodox" who have been a "thorn at his side", for they have acted more like enemies than friends who are also seeking God's love.

One can see both Boehme's problems with "orthodoxy" and "orthodoxy's" problem in trying to give some honorable and cohesive way of presenting the truths of Christianity as each of them sees such truths. For Boehme, his path was an escape from the cold orthodoxy that, in all its rigidness, was causing hatred and wars during the 16th and 17th Centuries between the different segments of the Christian faith: Catholic and Protestant. One should note that during the 30 Year's War from 1618 to 1648, 80% of all Germans died, for the European conflict was fought in Germany, and Boehme was German. He was also Lutheran, but was more interested in fellowship with God than he was in killing other people with other views. This we can learn from all the mystics, a tolerance for those with whom we disagree, and a quest to be close enough to God so that all earthly differences seem insignificant for our own personal faith, faith that has been self-experienced and not just a repeated creed that has been handed down to us by "our own kind." We must "take the log out of our own eye, before we presume to be able to take the speck out of our brother's eye" as Jesus so well reminded us. The mystic is teaching us all that religion is personal, and that, spiritually speaking, is our main concern: our own personal relationship to God. "Seek first the Kingdom of God, and other things will be added as needed" was also voiced by Jesus. "Judge not, and you shall not be judged" again said by Jesus, and, at least at sometimes, it seems only the mystics seem to understand and follow these teachings of Jesus. Therefore, before we judge too harshly the mystics, let us read them, try to learn from and understand from them first, and we will find that they too have something to offer to improve the joy and depth of our own spiritual lives.

Using the image of the Noble Virgin Sophia as the personification of the pure wisdom sent down by God to recall us to himself, Boehme prayed that he would receive the "love-beams" from heaven as a light to guide his path in life. Finally, speaking of the incomparable and ineffable love of God in sending his Son into the flesh of humanity, Boehme declared: "We have neither pen nor words to write or to tell what the sweet grace of God in Christ's humanity is."6.12 Boehme, unlike some mystics as well as dogmatic theologians realized that, not only is God beyond human understanding and words, but also his grace and love have, beyond our imagination, miraculously expressed themselves visibly in Jesus. We can believe God and love him back, adore and follow, but not much more. Our minds and words collapse in the presence and wonder of God and the loving friendship He gracefully showers upon us.

III GRATITUDE AND JOY

Out of our actualizing of our soul and finding ourselves as children of God, two automatic responses must take place to certify our experiences within the love of the Divine Father, gratitude and joy. To me, it is impossible to reach the heights of such a spiritual state not to have gratitude for and joy in life. If we moan and groan, blame and accuse, cry "victim" throughout our lives with a "why does misfortune always happen to me" attitude, we can be assured that we have not actualized our souls as children of a Heavenly Father. Once we have had, to use a Platonic term, a METANOIA (change of mind-set brought on by the vision of the Absolute Beauty, God), we can never be the same as we were before. Our lives cannot go back. If we go back, then we have not experienced the "Awakening of the Soul", the "Beatific Vision", or the "Enlightenment", but rather we have simply misjudged a good feeling or thought to be much more than it was. When one finds his soul is a child of God, the immediate response is joy. In Luke 16 one is presented with three stories Jesus told of the response of joy when even material things which were lost are found again. A shepherd realized one of his sheep was lost, he went to search for it and found it. He is so happy that he picked up the sheep and carried it on his shoulders, mirthically laughing and rejoicing on his way. When he finally gets home, he invited everyone else to rejoice with him; for this is the way, Jesus pointed out, that things are done in the heavenly kingdom, since all heaven rejoices for one who has experienced conversion (METANOIA). A woman lost one of her ten coins and swept and sought "diligently" (she tore the house apart) to find the lost coin, and rightfully rejoiced when she found it. Again Jesus added that there is joy among the angels of heaven when one spiritually awakens to his being a child of God. The third story is the well known story of the Prodigal Son who "came to himself" i.e. found his own soul as a child of his father, and returned home to a banquet held in joy for his return. Gabriel Marcel in his work The Mystery of Being emphasized that we can only recognize such a deep feeling as this religious conversion, not as an emotional up, but by a deeper participation of our entire being.

> The argument of the last lecture led us to recognize that we can understand feeling only as a mode of participation, but that the domain of participation, on the other hand, is much more extensive than that of mere feeling as such. To feel is in some degree to participate, but to participate in a higher sense is much more than merely to feel. This point is worth emphasizing.6.13

The change of mind-set that is created by one's deep spiritual experience or conversion, enlightenment, or awakening, brings an enormous change to the person who actually experiences it. Augustine of Hippo was spiritually restless throughout his life, bouncing from one set of religious views and principles to another until he read Plotinus' works and heard the preaching of the Platonic Christian Ambrose, and, after hearing a voice telling him to pick up the New Testament and read it, he finally found his spiritual home. Augustine concluded his great work The City of God with these words: "Knowledge shall be perfected when we shall be perfectly at rest, and shall perfectly know that He is God...He shall give us rest in Himself. There with him we shall rest and see, see and love, love and praise." Earlier he had expressed the idea that he had found his rest, in God. I must state that the experience itself of being "born again" or "enlightened" or the Metanoia mind-set change, is probably never repeated, and the high experience it gives, while changing us forever, does not return because it is never forgotten in the first place. It has made such a deep mark on our souls that it cannot be forgotten. But remembrance of it can be wonderfully delightful, and the remembrance itself recreates, even if to a lesser degree, that wonderful surge of spiritual closeness to God, but even that seems too quickly to fade. Even one such as Meister Eckhart said: "Sometimes I feel such a sweetness in my soul that I forget everything else--and myself too--and dissolve in thee. But when I try to catch it perfectly, O Lord, you take it away."6.14 Jacob Boehme seemed to be quite often on a very high much of his life, and expressed in words of the delight felt with the visitation of Noble Sophia: "The soul leaps in its body for great joy in the power of virginal love".6.15 Yet even in this case, "virginal love" can only happen once, but the remembrance of it can often be repeated as it ought. Participation in gratitude and joy is the remembrance of the depth and breadth of the spiritual experience one had in the process of "being born again". It certainly was a living faith that lived and flourished in the heart of the Lutheran hymn writer, Paul Gerhardt, who lived through the 30 year war in Germany, and, most would say, experienced an utterly tragic life. His father died when he was youthful; his closest friends died in the war; he finally married at age 48, but his first child died in infancy; he had a sparse income, and was fired from his best job because his employer was of another religious conviction; he had five more children, three of whom, as children, died in a fire, and a forth died shortly after, and following a brief time after that his wife died. At his death, he left one 14 year old son, but also left 123 of Christianity's greatest hymns. One must take notice of the powerful faith, full of gratitude and joy, of the hymn "I Will Sing My Maker's Praises". Only the first and last verses are quoted:

"I will sing my Maker's praises and in him most joyful be,
For in all things I see traces of his tender love to me.

Nothing else than love could move him with such sweet and tender care
Evermore to raise and bear all who try to serve and love him.
All things else have but their day, God's great love abides always.

Since, then, neither change nor coldness in my Father's love can be,
Lo! I lift my hands with boldness, as thy child I come to thee.
Grant me grace, O God, I pray thee, that I may with all my might,
All my lifetime, day and night, love and trust thee and obey thee
And, when this brief life is Over, praise and love thee evermore.

Here is a prayer, a meditation, a humble praise of God's love and care, in
the most miserable of human conditions. Yet, Gerhardt never even thinks
of lowering his request to material benefits, but rather always focuses
upon his closeness to God, his friendship with God, and the hope of an
eternal fellowship of love within the heavenly kingdom. In short, he does
not pollute his prayer with any attachment to materialism.

IV. DETOURS THAT LEAD ASTRAY ONE'S PRAYER LIFE

I closed the last paragraph with a caution as to what can take away
from a beneficial prayer life with a "beware" of petty things and
materialism. Such materialistic prayers show God that he and his
presence are really secondary to material desires. Even praying for health
and long life are questionable, although we all do it, in part, because
Jesus encouraged us in all matters to come to our Heavenly Father and
ask, even teaching us to pray for our daily bread. But praying for daily
bread is not most peoples' problem. First of all, Jesus forbad any vows,
and "if You O God do such and such for me, then I will accept You and
love You as God" as Jacob did.

Then Jacob made a vow, saying, "If God will be with me, and will
keep me in this way that I go, and will give me bread to eat and clothing to wear, so that I come again to my father's house in peace, then
YAHWEH shall be my God." (Gen. 28:20-21).

Even though this prayer showed a lot of Chutzpah, at least Jacob asked for survival needs only. Much worse was the prayer of Jabez who prayed for wealth and deliverance from pain and misfortune.

> Jabez invoked the God of Israel, saying, "Oh, bless me, enlarge my territory, stand by me, and make me not suffer pain from misfortune" (I Chr. 4:10-11).

Much better was Socrates' prayer who was afraid that material blessings might cause him to become attached to them, and make him forget that making his soul beautiful was what a child of God should be praying for. "Dear Pan, and all you other gods that dwell in this place, grant that I may become beautiful within, and that such outward things that I have may not wage a war against the spirit within me (Phaedrus 279d).

Immanuel Kant has some sobering words to us about prayer, and while we cannot take Kant as our ultimate measure on these things, nevertheless, to heed him and his words may be beneficial for our spiritual growth. First of all, let me say that Kant believes that God is so close to us and cares so much for us, and knows our thoughts and our needs, that prayer, other than a type of silent devotion, may not be needed: for God even hears out "thought prayers". He also detests the idea that we make God our servant in our minds, requesting selfishly and arrogantly for special treatment that God does not automatically offer to all people. Material requests show either our shallowness or our human frailty and weakness of faith. Kant also teaches us that prayer is for the sake of our spiritual introspection and our growth that our soul makes by putting itself in the presence of God, our Creator; thus prayer is not for changing things but for changing our outlook by raising it up to a higher spiritual level. I quote the following from his "Ethica" from his Vorlesungen ueber Moralphilosophie: (Von Gebet).

"Concerning the matters of prayers, when they do not have the intention of negotiating a moral mind-set, but they have in view the needs of physical life, then the prayer is never validated. For example, a man is in need, yet the prayer is, objectively, not necessary, for God knows that I am in need, and in that I can have cheerfully the idea that I have no reason to have put before God such a prayer. But prayers for moral growth are necessary, when you want to strengthen your moral mind-set, but never for pragmatic earthly benefits.(202-203)."

Kant often in his pragmatic ethics sets the ideal standard, but then consents to man's natural weaknesses as a finite being and excuses such lower standards as man may find them comforting. He emphasizes that in temporal and earthly matters, prayer is simply unnecessary, and only will be answered if it was in God's plans already to do so. Nevertheless, Kant sympathizes with man's finiteness, and the fears and frailties as such can be understood both from the human point of view and from God's point of view. So, if in danger of drowning at sea, God is not going to be offended by a cry for help, for He recognizes our human frailty. But the proper and welcomed prayer before God is one in which a man seeks the strength to live as moral a life as possible. Being a good person who does good things for others to increase their value of life is the sole object of a pure prayer. This coincides with Jesus' words: "Wisdom is justified by her children (Lk 7:35), " and "You shall know them by their fruits"(Mt 7:20), as well as other sayings such "Those who do the will of my Father in Heaven are my brothers, sisters, and mother" and "Thy will be done on earth, as it is in Heaven" and many other passages in which Jesus stressed a righteous and ethical life. If your salt does not flavor and your light does not shine, of what value are you? is always prevalent in the teachings of Jesus. Kant has been criticized for over stressing morality in his theology, but he is much closer to the Jesus of the Gospels than many will admit. One critic, as I remember, called him a "Pietist in a philosopher's clothing". Much of Kant's teaching is in rejection of the "scholastic Protestants" who spend all their lives arguing over words and phrases in the doctrines which are taught variously by the different Christian groups, but often neglect a pious and righteous life of love and justice. Yet, Kant himself was attacked on two fronts, first by Hegel, and then by Schleiermacher, who also attacked those who held cold and doctrinaire teachings of a spiritual emptiness devoid of feelings. We shall look first at Schleiermacher, and then at Hegel, who later in life, switched his efforts of criticism from Kant to Schleiermacher, and eventually to the "pietists" of the new emerging age. Yes, Hegel was very busy in his 61 years of life.

Friedrich Schleiermacher became angry both at the status quo of religion within itself, being too cold and dogmatic, and at "the cultured people" who despised religion itself. He demanded, not only that religion was the natural and necessary expression of mankind, but that it was only real when one experienced the deep feelings of elevation and joy within the soul. Schleiermacher contended that he could no longer keep silent when those posing as priests showed very little joy and inspiration in their duties and in their lives. The true priest of God exhibited the Heavenly and Eternal as an object of enjoyment, and

> "strives to awaken the slumbering germ of a better humanity, to
> kindle love for higher things, to change the common life into a
> nobler, to reconcile the children of earth with the Heaven that
> bears them, and to counterbalance the deep attachment of the age
> to the baser side. This is the higher priesthood that announces the
> inner meaning of all spiritual secrets, and speaks from the kingdom
> God.6.16

Schleiermacher sought a spiritualized humanity that rejoiced in feeling the very essence of God's closeness to him. In this Schleiermacher was different from the mystics, who, although they sought the very essence of God's closeness, they were, for the greater of them, not that interested in changing man's greater culture. Schleiermacher wanted all humanity to feel the spiritual power and joy of God's immediate presence in their lives. He attacked the coldness of theology in the schools of the day. "If you regard the systems in all schools, how often are they mere habitations and nurseries of the dead letter".6.17 Hoping that men in general and especially the students of theology and the priests would become "spiritually alive" he asked them to throw out their acquired thinking and culture and start anew with the purpose of gaining a true and deeply felt spirituality. "I ask, therefore, that you turn (away) from everything usually reckoned religion, and fix your regard on the inward emotions and dispositions, as all utterance and acts of inspired men direct. Despite your acquirements, your culture, and your prejudices, I hope for good success."6.18 In the following quotations he seems to be a mystic.

"It is true that religion is essentially contemplative."
"The contemplation of the pious is the immediate consciousness of the universal existence of all finite things, in and through the Infinite, and of

all temporal things in and through the Eternal. Religion is to seek this and find it in all that lives and moves, in all growth and change, in all doing and suffering. It is to have life and to know life in the immediate feeling, only as such an existence in the Infinite and Eternal."
"Without being knowledge, it recognizes knowledge and science. In itself it is an affection, a revelation of the Infinite in the finite, God being seen in it and it in God."6.19

He believed that man must be one with the Eternal in "unity of intuition and feeling which is immediate." He defended Spinoza, one condemned by his critics as an pantheist, and claimed that he was correct:

> See in him the power of enthusiasm [being in God] and the caution of a pious spirit, and acknowledge that when the philosophers shall become religious and seek God like Spinoza, and the artists to be pious and love Christ like Novalis, the great resurrection shall be celebrated for both worlds.6.20

Speaking anthropomorphically he likened the embrace of God to the beauty of a bashful and tender kiss of a maiden and a subsequent holy and fruitful bridal embrace, as the depth of anticipation of such love and the rapid heart beat of joy and delight. In this he sounds very mythical, and he also sounds like a pietist, and also again like a pantheist. I must commend Schleiermacher on his courageous attempt to spiritualize his "cold and dogmatic" age with a Christian religion that has life and beauty and deeply felt love for God. Yet, as a Platonic Christian, I feel the criticisms leveled at him, almost immediately, not only the cold dogmaticians, but from a very rational Hegel were justified. To most Platonists he would be seen as one who let the lowest level of the soul, emotions, completely control the more substantial and religious elements of the soul, both man's spirited nature--the will, and man's rational nature. I realize that may sound strange, inasmuch as it was Schleiermacher who translated the entire Platonic corpus of writings into German for the first time, yet, in Plato also the love of God, an emotion, drives man to make such a spiritual ascent to Absolute Beauty, God, that the experience itself is above and beyond words. In this sense, Schleiermacher reflected much of what was in Plato's two dialogues: the Phaedrus and the Symposium. Likewise, the movement of Neoplatonism, beginning especially with Plotinus, was deeply religious and also quite immersed in love and the feeling of the Absolute. Indeed, Schleiermacher is a difficult person and today he has many staunch supporters and followers. But now, on to Hegel.

The first thing I wish to say about <u>Georg</u> <u>Wilhelm</u> <u>Friedrich</u> <u>Hegel</u> is that his influence has been enormous, and in this immediate context being presented now, one might think that he was important only as a critic of Schleiermacher, Kant, and Pietism. He himself established a new way of thinking that tried to incorporate all the opposing views of the past within a system of ever ongoing thought and dialogue. First one considered a thesis, and then a critical view with just the opposite view -- the antithesis, and finally to adjust the truths and exaggerations of both sides into a synthesis, which then, in turn, becomes a new thesis awaiting its own antithesis. The main thing Hegel can teach us today with this system is that things are not black and white, one thing totally correct and another abstract thought totally incorrect, and thus such a thought process causes us to temper our judgment about all abstract thought, and to consider and reconsider before we ourselves latch onto "the truth". The different "Teachers of Humanity" that I am presenting in this book all have something to say to us, and whether their views fall into a thesis category or an antithesis, or even a type of synthesis, let us hear them and learn from them rather than immediately declare that they are irrelevant to the spiritual growth and elevation of our souls, which, after all, is the very essence of religion as our souls try to ascend up, in love, to God himself.

In Hegel's response to Schleiermacher he admits that feeling is essential to true and fulfilling religion, but even though "It is true that religion is a matter of feeling, but it is also just as much a matter of representation." For feeling left alone can claim anything that is felt to be true and beneficial to the soul's growth, and that is just not the case.

> But feeling is still nothing justificatory, for everything possible is capable of being in feeling. If what is in feeling were true just for that reason, then everything would have to be true...In contrast, representation already contains more of the objective -- that which constitutes the contents or determinacy of feeling. <u>This</u> <u>content</u> <u>is</u> <u>what</u> <u>matters</u>...Regarding the necessity of representation and the path through representation into the heart, we know that religious

instruction begins with representation. By means of doctrine and teaching the feelings become aroused and purified; they are culti- vated and brought into the heart...Instruction and teaching belong to this representation, and religious formation everywhere begins from this point.6.21

These cautions of Hegel warn us also of the "detours" of being all rational or being all spirited, or being all feeling in our religious experience. For are souls need them all to be balanced in order to experience true spiritual growth, the awakening of the soul, and the joy of being the children of God. Then one can beware of those detours that have been mentioned in this chapter and also the following ones.

1. Hiding behind "busy-ness": Stop! Take time and look into your soul.
2. When praying avoid all arrogant and self-centered prayers.
3. Praying for material benefits, especially those that 90% of the world's population does not have, is a detour, a diversion, from spiritual growth, and indicates a childishness that can not elevate above the level of foolishness. This is a major detour and perhaps the most common detour among the religious today: Newsweek, 1/6/1992, quoted a "Poloma and Gallup" poll that indicated that 59% of "evangelicals" prayed for material blessings, while the average for all religious groups was only 42% (and without the evangelicals, it would be only 30some%).
4. Avoid vows especially when seeking a gain from God. Pliny the Younger ridiculed those who when they were sick, made vows to the gods, but upon regaining health forgot their vows. This destroys a person's relationship with God. As Jesus taught, never make a vow for anything.
5. Praying for wealth so that one can lead an irresponsible and unpro- dutive life is the exact opposite direction that one's path should be taking. Juvenal satirized such people in his Tenth Satire: "Yet still with ceaseless prayer the temples resound that, come what will, possessions may abound; that the kind gods may still enlarge our lands, and bags grow wider in our banker's hands." (38-43) Even Juvenal, a satirical Roman, could see how foolish a prayer like Jabez' was in seeking God's help to enlarge his land.

6. Trying to use our "meritorious" life to justify a foolish request for some benefit from God.
7. Requesting a benefit that is not readily available for all of humanity, for it is arrogant and presupposes that God should give one a special treatment: the Pharisee who thanked God that he was not like other men.
8. Using asceticism as an excuse to ask for a special privileged gift from God.
9. Prayers for the dead, for, if anything, they have met their fate and are probably praying for the living.
10. Prayers for a vision, for if one needs a vision in order to seek after God with all one's heart, he is not only asking for special treatment, he is displaying a most unfaithful and untrusting heart. "Prove to me, God, that you are worthy of my time I spend praying to you" is what such a prayer is really saying.

THREE ADDITIONAL PRAYERS

CHURCH PRAYER FOR RENEWAL OF LIFE (Adapted)
  O God, the Eternal One, You divide the day from the night,
   and turn the shadow of death into the dawn of a new day:
  Drive far from us all wrong desires,
   incline our hearts to know, do, and be in harmony with your will,
   and guide our feet upon the path of wholeness and peace;
   that while we have life, we follow your path with cheerfulness,
   and whatever comes before us, that we may give you thanks.

A SERENITY PRAYER (Attributed to Reinhold Niebuhr)
  God, grant me the serenity to accept the things I cannot change,
           the courage to change the things I can,
           and the wisdom to know the difference.

FRANCIS OF ASSISI -- THE PEACE PRAYER
   Lord, make me an instrument of your peace.
   Where there is hatred, let me sow love;
   Where there is injury, pardon;
   Where there is doubt, faith;
   Where there is despair, hope;
   Where there is darkness, light; and
   Where there is sadness, joy.

   O Divine Master, grant that I may not so much seek
   To be consoled as to console
   To be understood as to understand,
   To be loved as to love.

   For it is in giving that we receive,
   It is in pardoning that we are pardoned,
   And it is in dying that we are born to eternal life.

CHAPTER SEVEN

STEP FOUR

RATIONAL WISDOM

KNOWING ONESELF -- PLANNING ONE'S LIFE

Other than what was said in Chapter Six, the previous chapter, technical metaphysics and abstract theology will not play much of a role in these last four chapters. Rather it will be logic and ethics that will emphasize how one builds his life into wholeness and happiness. Thus the basics, logic and ethics, so essential in building anything, will be stressed. Chrysippus, the Stoic philosopher, recommended that logic be taught first to a student then ethics, after which the more technical (physics and metaphysics) and abstract (theology) be taught, and this is basically in agreement with both Plato (Do not enter unless you know geometry--were the words at the front of his Academy) and Aristotle who likewise stressed logical thinking and even wrote several works on the subject (Categories, De Interpretatione, Prior Analytics, Posterior Analytics, and Sophistical Refutations). But because the theology of Jesus, the loving care, providence, and Grace of God, is the foundation of his ethical teachings, it was necessary to lay that foundation (Chapters Five and Six), before proceeding to the specifics of his rational wisdom in which life is expressed and lived and within which one finds his wholeness and happiness, which follows the basic Platonic concept that only the ethically good man can be happy.

I. THE TEACHINGS OF JESUS ABOUT PLANNING

In Chapter One the fullness of being a carpenter was presented, that he had to plan out his job in all the specific areas of thought the construction of a building, a house, or a garden would take: the drafting and blueprinting; measuring using mathematics and geometry; cost and its economical concerns; the strength of the materials using architectural physics; the foundation whether on a rock base, soft base, or in a flood prone area, basically seeking a lasting foundation; and the capability of his partners or work force. In all these areas other actions are implied such as: choice and decision making, responsibility, commitment, perseverance and keeping the final goal in mind. All of these call for a rational base. Know yourself! Are you capable of this or that? What sort of a person are you? If you do not know that, how can you lay out before yourself a rational life plan? Do you value happiness and wholeness over greed and self-centeredness? If not, you must choose. What kind of edifice do you want your life to be? If or not you want your life to be a magnificent structure, built securely upon a rock, and surrounded by a garden of fruits, vegetables, and flowers in which happiness and wholeness roam freely and in which the spirit of love and kindness breathes upon all who enter, then listen to the great teachers of mankind, hear them well, and commit to follow them. I start with the most influential of all, Jesus the Carpenter.

In his teachings Jesus constantly referred to the task of building something or reaching a goal of some kind or other. For the man who built a house (Mt.7:24-27), he stressed first of all the foundation; and in life this means that you must know yourself, and where you want to go. A superstructure needs a different foundation than a shed, and it demands a very solid foundation. Manhattan Island is a rock, and its buildings are superstructures, they obviously are not built on a soft river bed. Man must choose for himself the value of his life, and what kind of structure he wants for himself, is he going to be a shed subject to every wind and rain, or is he going to be a sturdy rock solid building? That is his choice, but if one builds a shed in the river, and the rains keep washing it away, how dare he claim that life "victimizes" him and he never seems to get ahead because his house keeps getting washed away. Jesus also spoke of a man who might decide to build a tower (Lk 14:28-30), but if he didn't lay the proper foundation, and his ideas were greater than his logical capacities, he would not be able to finish the tower and people would look at the half-finished tower and put him up for ridicule. For after bragging about his tower, and after getting only half way done, he ran out of money, and was the object of laughter. Plan things out, and know what you are capable of doing. Jesus told also about a king who was foolish enough to put his kingdom in danger by fighting a war in which he was outnumbered two to one. What he should do, said Jesus, is to send out a greeting party with the offer of peace and goodwill, and do it when the other king is "yet a great distance away" (Lk 14:31-32). Those who sow seeds so that they may have a good harvest also must sow where the seeds have good soil, where there are not too many weeds or rocks, and away from the often used paths. The farmer must plan what kind of crop he plans to sow, how much he will need at the harvest, what he can afford, and if he will have any help, as well as the type of soil he will need. Jesus was simply emphasizing that for any venture in life, one must make decisions; plan ahead; know his capacities in skill, labor, and cost; act responsibly; be aware of what his goal is; and have the commitment to carry out the task. In building one's spiritual life the same virtues are needed. Sometimes we have to adapt, especially when we miss the mark earlier in life, but man can adapt to those failures of the past too. Jesus once commended a bad, slothful, and irresponsible servant who was acting as an accountant for his master, and when the master set the day to see his account, the unjust steward, realizing his fate, finally came to himself and recognized the need to plan ahead. He called in some of the greater debtors and made very generous deals with them to close out the debts. He recognized his situation, and for once actually planned ahead, so that after he was terminated, he would have at least a few people that were grateful for what he had done. "The Master (Jesus) congratulated the dishonest steward for his wisdom"(Lk 16: 1-9). But Jesus also said that it was a shame that such a man of the world could figure out his dilemma and provide for the future, when the "sons of light" can not seem to plan for both their material and their spiritual futures.

Two of the virtues that Jesus emphasized in this quest to build one's life, had to do with knowing oneself: honesty and introspection rather than judgment of others. The weaknesses of one's own house are not solved by destroying a neighbors house. Jesus spoke of honesty in all our actions, and not making vows: simply let your yes be yes, and your no be no. Jesus was quite aware, of course, that if a man took a vow that he was telling the truth, that would imply that the rest of the time he was probably lying. Honesty also implies that a man will be honest about his own weaknesses, and then he will focus on self-improvement rather than try to improve others by pointing out their faults, often a little self

-rightously. It is all too easy to be honest about the other person's faults and a little dishonest about the ugliness of our own.

Other applicable passages declare Jesus' advice to: rank your responsibilities (Lk 20:24-25), judge things and make decisions when you are in light and not in the darkness (see the issues clearly before a decision is made) (J 8:12-15); do not use materials or ideals or goals that do not work together (new wine & old wineskins) (Mk 2:21-22); know the values of rules and laws and how they are to be applied rationally (Mk 2:23-27); it takes effort to achieve success (Mk 4:24-25); learn from the wise and let them lead you (Lk 6:39), so choose wisely whom you follow (Mt 9:9); if you have a log in your eye, do not think that you will be able to remove the speck in your brother's eye -- see things clearly before calling a brother shortsighted in life -- good vision is good judgment (Lk 6:41); in fact, do not judge at all, that you yourself not be judged (Mt 7:1); do not think that you can be evil and produce good -- an evil man, cannot be happy (Lk 6:43-45); one must make a rational use of talents (Lk 19:11-27); and be prepared daily for your ultimate fate (Mt 24: 40-42).

II. CONCURRENCE FROM THE OTHER SAGES FOR A RATIONAL LIFE PLAN

A. CHOICE AND RATIONAL DECISIONS

Hesiod in his basic Works and Days, a type of manual for basic values and common sense, warns man not to spend his time idly gossiping all the time but to plan ahead, at least for the next winter: "Each labor, Perses! let the seasons guide."(350). Do in the summer what must be done in the summer, for winter will be very long if not prepared for. A man has a choice not to plan and not to work, then he will steal and say "I had no choice, for I was hungry". Success and security are hard work: those who are idle and only hope will end up with hardship and often turn to crime. This requires the most simple logic, but the decisions still often are not rational. Then one can have a complete breakdown of character, for the man becomes aimless without any rational planning for his life. Aristotle stated: "Character is that which reveals moral purpose, showing what kind of things a man chooses or avoids" (Poetics VI.17).

<u>Democritus</u> put it bluntly when he stated that even "Beauty of body is merely animal unless intelligence is present" (DK 'Diels/Kranz' 68 B 105). <u>Epicurus</u> declared:

> It is impossible to live a pleasant life without living wisely and well and justly, and it is impossible to live wisely and well and justly without living pleasantly. Whenever any one of these is lacking, when, for instance, the man is not able to live wisely, though he lives well and justly, it is impossible for his to live a pleasant life.7.1

> If you do not on every separate occasion refer each of your actions to the end prescribed by nature, but instead of this in the act of choice or avoidance swerve aside to some other end, your acts will not be consistent with your theories.7.2

Rational choice is the key in building a life that is free of most problems that normally confront those who live with "neither rhyme nor reason". <u>Epictetus,</u> a Stoic who had little sympathy for whiners, constantly pointed out the fact that the one who whines is the very one who made the choice to be in the situation that he is whining about: "For remember this general truth, that it is we who squeeze ourselves, who put ourselves in straits" (I.25). It takes labor to build a man of excellence, Epictetus declared: "What then makes a man beautiful? Is it not the possession of the excellence of a man? And do you, then, if you wish to be beautiful, young man, labour at this, the acquisition of human excellence" (III.1). He encouraged men to examine themselves, even referring to the Socratic saying that an unexamined life is not worth living: "Examine a little at last, look around, stir yourself up, that you may know who you are" (III.14).

A man's destiny is the outcome of what kind of sense he has in his head, so stated the <u>Viking</u> <u>poem</u> in which Odin acquired wisdom. Wisdom is part of the theme of the entire poem ("Sayings of the High One"), for the man who has little wisdom has little to look forward to in life. "It takes wits to travel the world...in the flicker of an eye the fool is found who wanders among the wise...a man won't find a better friend than his own head full of sense...lucky the man who can look to himself to provide his praise and wisdom...If a man takes with him a mind full of sense he can carry nothing better; riches like this on a stranger's road will do more good than gold."7.3 Know yourself, and know your mental capacities, for they are the basis of success in the world. Lao Tzu put it quite simply, that a man who rationally and successful achieves it, will stop there: he will not overextend himself in effort or arrogance. "He will be on his guard against being vain or boastful or arrogant in consequence of it."(29.3). Solid and simple advice: set proper goals that accord with your abilities and nature, keep the costs in money and time within reason, and do not overrate yourself, that is, remember the material you are working with, and what are its possibilities. The Dhammapada teaches that man must control his rambling mind and set it in order, for a mind that does not settle its thoughts and organize them can never "escape the realm of Mara (the tempter)". "A wise man makes straight his trembling and unsteady thought."(III) This is a call to stop everything, sit down, and think out your life! But many go from one flighty thought to another with no rational connection or goal binding them together. "By rousing himself, by earnestness, by restraint and control, the wise man may make for himself an island which no flood can overwhelm"(II). In the Ramayana there is a discussion in which one party, Swallow (who is actually Sita), is unhappy, feeling that her fate has been unjust, but doesn't know why it is. But Uncle Ho forces her to think by stating to her: "Only if you knew who you are could you answer that question."7.4 For any rational decision about one's life he must know who he is in his relationship to himself as well as his greater circumstances in life, and what path he is currently taking to find happiness in this universe. One needs a "philosophy" of life, a life devoted to the love of wisdom, and a life that will listen to, learn from, and follow the wise ways of the great philosophers. Cicero declared with joy: "O Philosophia, the leader of men's lives, you find out virtue and and expel evil. Without your presence among us, what could have been possible in the lives of men? and, what, indeed, would have become of all human life?...[you enabled humans] to communicate with one another by speaking and writing. You are the inventor of laws, and you have been the teacher and enforcer of morality. You have given us tranquillity of life and taken care of the terror of death." 7.5

In his work The Nature of the Gods, Cicero stated that wisdom, simply put, "is knowing the difference between good and evil, and of the things which are neither" (III.38). For it is by choosing the good that we attain to happiness, likewise, it is by choosing the evil that we lose our way and wonder from the path laid out by the gods for one's happiness. Wisdom is also that which decides if some things are neither good nor bad. Aristotle called those things in the borderland between the good and bad, Adiaphoria, which concept was also much used by Philip Melanchthon, the leader of the Lutheran Church after Luther's death. The ability to know what is good, what is evil, and what is neither is important, not only for our own growth, but to keep us from falsely judging others. This responsibility is ours, and not to take the time to think about such choices is self-destructive. We have the mental power and the rational responsibility within ourselves: "We may consecrate shrines to Reason, Faith and Virtue, but we know that it is only in ourselves that they are to be found" Cicero declared (The Nature of the Gods III.88). In every culture and every age there are the teachers who call us to practice rational thought in order to understand ourselves, our hopes, our capacities, our loves and our longings in life. But such ability, the art of thinking, must be used, and when knowledge is used well it becomes wisdom.

B. HONEST SELF-CRITICISM

Jesus used the illustration of not trying to clear another's vision of the world, by taking away the "speck" that is in his eye (that is the wrong way in which he is looking at the world), when you have a log stuck in your own eye, thereby making your own view of the world much worse that the other person's. First, said Jesus, take out the log from your own eye and then you will see clearly enough to be of help in clearing the vision of your brother. After all, those that are blinded to their own faults can not lead others blinded to theirs. Honest self-criticism is a wonderful but rare virtue, which is a shame because it is so valuable in setting straight one's life and then setting goals appropriate for one's capabilities. "Face one's weaknesses", "learn to say Mea Culpa", and "cleanse oneself first" are heard often, but seldom applied in honesty. To make excuses for rude thoughts and damaging actions is not to face them, and to transfer blame for one's failures to another "crying victim" is even more detrimental to spiritual growth.

The Dhammapada stated very clearly that responsibility for our-selves is in our own hands:

> Make yourself an island, work hard and be wise!
> When your impurities are blown away and you are free
> from their guilt, you will enter into the heavenly world of the elect...
> The fault of others is easily perceived, but that of one's self is
> difficult to perceive; a man winnows his neighbors' faults
> like chaft, but his own fault he hides, as the cheat hides
> the bad die from the (other) player.
> If a man looks after the faults of others
> and is always inclined to be offended,
> his own passions will grow,
> and he remains far from the destruction of his passions. (XVIII)

When we refuse to look inward honestly, we prepare for our own destruction, and yet proudly talk about the faults of others. Such blindness that hides us from our own reality! Mencius said, "The respectful do not despise others,"(4.1.16) for he is too busy making sure he does not damage himself, for "When Heaven (fate) sends down calamities, it is still possible to escape them. When we occasion the calamities ourselves, it is not possible any longer to live"(4.1.8). Aesop in his fabulous way of explaining such behavior told this story:

> Once upon a time when Prometheus fashioned men he hung two
> bags from their necks, one in front of them, filled with other peo-
> ple's defects, and one behind their backs containing their own de-
> fects. Thus men can see their fellows' faults a mile away, but can
> never perceive their own.

Epictetus criticized the Cynics because they themselves dwelt in vices of all sorts, yet had the audacity to parade around and reprove others: "a cunning knave and fellow of no principle, since while he himself is entangled in some vice he will reprove others" (III.22).

An Indian poet wrote in Sanskrit that if a man can perceive his own faults, has personal benefits from it, but he cautions that very few are honest in this respect:

Most men can see another's faults;
Another's virtues some can see;
And there are those who see their own
Shortcomings. Yes? - Well - two are three.7.6

Seneca likewise emphasized that self-examination must be prior to all other actions, and in this he strongly followed Socrates and Jesus: "...Therefore, as far as possible, prove yourself guilty, hunt up charges against yourself; play the part, first of accuser, then of judge, lastly of intercessor. At times be harsh with yourself. (Letter 28). Another Stoic, Marcus Aurelius, had similar instructions to himself in his "Meditations": "How much trouble he avoids who does not look to see what his neighbour says or does or thinks, but only to what he does himself, that it may be just and pure; or as Agathon says, look not round at the depraved morals of others, but yourself run straight along the line without deviating from it"(IV.18).

Bernard of Clairvaux spoke likewise in his work The Steps of Humility, only with a little more "preachy" spiritual force:

But observe what you are, that you are wretched indeed, and so
learn to be merciful, a thing you cannot know in any other way.
For if you regard your neighbor's faults but do not observe your
own, you are likely to be moved not to truth but to wrath, not to
condole but to condemn, not to restore in the spirit of meekness
but to destroy in the spirit of anger...The great thick beam in the eye
is pride in the mind. By its great size, although empty, not sound,
swollen, not solid, it dims the mind's eye and overshadows truth
in such a way that, when pride fills your mind, you can no longer
see yourself, you can no longer feel yourself such as you are actually
or potentially (IV.13-14).7.7

Such a way of thinking -- to seek out the faults or others, instead of looking hard for our own -- is truly harmful and destructive to our own growth, and harms both our actuality of soul and our potentiality of virtue. In the "ever present battle of the sexes" it is common for men to blame it on the women and women to blame the men. Goethe, addressing men, in his Entschuldigung stated:

"Du verklagest das Weib, sie schwanke von einem zum andern!
Tadle sie nicht: sie sucht einen bestaendigen Mann."

"You accuse the woman, she changes from one man to another!
Do not find fault with her: she is only looking for a reliable man."

The common self-destructive attitude is that it is always the other person's fault that my life is so unhappy. In personal goals, relationships, vocational advancement, or whatever, one must find his destiny within himself, and cease complaining that life is difficult or others are the problem. One must see this clearly -- get the log out of one's eye, and look within first and look not outward until all the "business at home" is taken care of. This is what all our teachers tell us. We simply cannot discard them all. Anton J. Boisen, a founder of clinical pastor training, in his work Religion in Crisis and Custom, made this very simple but powerful statement, drawn from years of counseling: "As a rule, the patient who blames himself has a good chance to recover. At least, he has a far better chance than the man who dwells on his grievances, blames others, and finds alibis for his mistakes".7.8

C.   FOCUSING ON AND PLANNING THE FUTURE

After a man rationally finds himself and recognizes who he is, cleans up his own life and faces his strengths and weaknesses, then, as a personally responsible being, he can focus upon his future and set his goals. As mentioned in Chapter Four he must bury the past and focus upon the future, and this is not always so easy. For example, in burying the past and directing oneself towards the future, a person must know the age he presently is in and accommodate his plans accordingly, for an outmoded concept of life or success will be a big hindrance; one can not personally bring back the "good old days", for they too are the past. "Future Shock" caused by the rapidly moving age in which we live, can be frightening for the timid, but one must "jump on board" and move with the rest of society into the future. I personally took a lot of ribbing from friends for staying with my typewriter long after all my friends were smoothly functioning with the computer. Finally, fate dragged me to the computer, and after two months of civil war within me, I realized that the future was so very much better than the past, and am grateful to those who ridiculed me enough to finally move me out of my barbarian comfort zone into the modern world, which, of course, will change every decade at the present rate. Focussing upon the future will entail some adaptability, and goals must be kept clearly in the mind, for it is also necessary to know when you reach a goal that you stop and take pleasure in the fact that you have succeeded. There is the story of Bronko Nagurski, the hard running football player who hit the line like a battering ram. When his team came close to the opponents' (Washington's) goal line, as his coach, George Hallas, told it, Bronko got the ball and hit the line with all the speed and power he could muster, and with tacklers hanging on him he plowed on head down and bounced off of the goal post, which was then at the front of the end zone, but because the tacklers were still hanging on, he shook free of them and still with head down ran through the end zone and with full force ran head first into the stadium wall. Knocked semiconscious, he was helped to the side lines and looked up and said, "Coach, that last guy hit me awfully hard."(LAT, 10/31/1999). It is important to stop once in awhile in life, and see where we are in respect to our goals: sometimes we reach them and never stop and enjoy our conquest, but plowing recklessly on harm ourselves.

Besides focusing on the future, the rational planning of how to get there is, of course, vital. Here too one must be honest as to his talents, his commitment, his patience and his power of will to succeed. Likewise, since happiness always depends upon goodness, goodness can never be compromised in the quest for wholeness and happiness of life. Other things may be achieved, but without goodness there will not be a happy ending. Unanticipated difficulties will come, and one must have the moral fortitude to face them, and preparation in moral integrity will help to overcome grave detours and disappointments. Seneca stated:

> Among these comrades (grief and sickness etc.), life is degener-
> ate. You are not able to flee them, but you can hold them in con-
> tempt. And you will scorn them, if you repeatedly think about
> and prepare for the future. No one is stronger to face such
> difficulties, as he who has prepared for them. But the unprepared
> are exceedingly terrified about even the trifles of life. (Letter CVII.3)

Epictetus was quick to remind those who had the high dreams of winning an event at the Greek Olympic games that they must rationally prepare for such and count the cost. He stated:

> In every act consider what precedes and what follows, and then proceed to the act. If you do not consider, you will at first begin with spirit, since you have not thought at all of the things which follow; but afterward, when some consequences have shown themselves, you will basely desist. "I wish to conquer at the Olympic games." "And I too, by the gods: for it is a fine thing." But consider here what precedes and what follows; and then, if it is for your good, undertake the thing. You must act according to all the rules, follow a strict diet, abstain from delicacies, exercise yourself by compulsion at fixed times, in heat, in cold; drink no cold water, nor wine, when there is opportunity of drinking it. In a word you must surrender yourself to the trainer as you do to a physician (III.15).

This is an illustration from sports, and it is certainly true that those who listen to their trainers, work constantly on strength and conditioning, year in and year out, do not cheat their self-discipline, and learn the art and limits of their talents, can have long and prosperous careers. In the quest for moral goodness and spiritual wholeness, one must also pay the price, avoid cheating the rules, be daily committed, keep out self-centered and evil impulses, shun the lure of materialism, and constantly keep the game plan. For any goal in life, such are the rules. The teachers of every age, in their wisdom, have laid it before us, and if we cheat, we cheat only ourselves. This, unfortunately, has not been taught to our young in the USA. Time Magazine, 11/01/1993, referred to a survey of 2000 "high-achieving" 16 and 17 year-olds, and found that 78% of them admitted to cheating and 67% to copying another person's homework. It also hasn't been learned very well by many "high achieving" adults who exaggerate, as CEOs, a company's earnings in order to receive a greater annual bonus, and others who falsify their resumes when applying for a job. They are later found out, discredited (even if they did a good job in their new position), fired and shamed. Cheating is cheating oneself, and also making it impossible for virtue to exist within and be a source of wholeness or happiness. A fragment of Polycrates reads: "Above all, happiness depends upon wisdom." Knowledge applied properly for the desired results is wisdom. If a man seeks the conveniences of life for himself and his family, he has reason which empowers him to carry out his plans, and turn his thoughts into realities by effecting the things dear to him, then he might reach his goals. But he must work to have a loving family in which extraordinary affection is shown by all for each other. To be successful in one's vocation all the above requirements are needed, and then they are needed again in making of a family, and again in one's quest for philosophical and spiritual wholeness and happiness, and make of himself a beautiful person who also beautifies the lives of those with whom he is in contact.

Vance Packard put forth six things a person must consider when choosing his vocation:
1. The social importance of the task performed.
2. The authority and responsibility inherent in the job.
3. The knowledge required.
4. The brains required.
5. The dignity of the job.
6. The financial rewards of the occupation.7.9

Too often people think of number six and want it to come first, which, of course, is a mistake, for the other five are properly put ahead of the desire for wealth. A job with a social service, a personal dignity, and in harmony with one's talents is far more important than how much excess money above a person's basic needs can be made. There is a need in one's life plan to consider priorities, and how much happiness and wholeness count. Man is a rational creature, but when he gives up his power of reason, his end will be no better than that of a beast.

III. APPLICABLE VIRTUES AND COMMENTS BY OUR
TEACHERS AND SAGES

A. PERSONAL RESPONSIBILITY

One of the strengths of the modern existential school of philosophy is its stress on the responsibility of mankind, both as individuals and as a human society. Man will make of himself what he chooses to make of himself, and he alone is responsible for the results. This, of course, has been taught by all the great teachers of human history. As early as Theognis the dilemma of not knowing when a man would die affected the way he spent his savings after his working days were over. It never was an easy decision: for there was always a chance of dying too rich or too poor. One died too rich, if during his last years he deprived himself of many things in fear of being without money in the future, and then left his money to perhaps an unworthy heir. But, on the other hand, if he thoroughly enjoyed himself, but lived years beyond his expectations, he would suffer poverty at his most helpless age. Theognis (902-928). Self responsibility is first, that is, always to take care of oneself and then be a blessing to others, but never risk self-sufficiency for immediate pleasures or charity that one cannot afford. This was also the teachings of the Dhammapada:

Bad deeds and deeds hurtful to ourselves are easy to do;
What is beneficial and good, that is very difficult to do.
The foolish man who scorns the rule of the venerable, of the elect,
    of the virtuous,
And follows a false doctrine, he bears fruit to his own destruction,
    like the fruits of the Katthaka reed.
By one's self the evil is done, by one's self one suffers.
By one's self evil is left undone, and by one's self one is purified.
The pure and the impure stand and fall by themselves,
No one can purify another.
Let no one forget his own duty for the sake of another's, however great;
Let a man, after he has discerned his own duty,
    be always attentive to his own duty.(XII.163-166).

Again, if a man's virtue is seen through an eye hindered by a log in it, and yet presumes to help another, he is foolish. A man drowning can not save another. Be first responsible for oneself. In Chapter XVIII the Dhammapada states: "Make yourself an island, work hard, be wise!" and there alone cleanse yourself.

The Khaggavisana Sutta (The Rhinoceros Discourse) was, according to legend given by Buddha to his favorite disciple, Ananda, and emphasized that he had to learn to live on his own behalf, and each statement ended with the phrase: "Let one walk alone like a rhinoceros". The purpose of the teachings was two-fold, avoiding materialistic and earthly attachments and self sufficiency and responsibility. It was also specifically directed to Ananda and monks who were in training. While it was not meant for the populace in general, yet it stimulates the individual to be on his own, think on his own, and walk self sufficiently and proudly on his own, just as a rhinoceros does. In the discourse there are 41 teachings, each ending with the directive: "let one walk alone like a rhinoceros." If one visualizes the power of a rhino and how it walks the fields with its heavy natural armor, then one can experience the power of the discourse. Below I have presented four of the 41 statements.

As a beast of the forest prowls, free, withersoever he will for pasture, even so let a wise man, observing solitude, walk alone like a rhinoceros. (No.5)

Divested of greediness, deceit, longings, not disparaging others unjustly, in the whole world; released from evil affections and ignorance; desireless, let one walk alone like a rhinoceros. (No.22)

Not being greedy of savory things, not being unsteady, nor maintained by others, begging from house to house without any distinction, not having a mind attached to this or that family, let one walk alone like a rhinoceros. (No.31)

In fit time, observe kindness, impartiality, mercy, freedom from sin, and delight at the prosperity of others: unopposed to the whole world, let one walk alone like a rhinoceros. (No.39)7.10

After reading all 41 of the sentences, one actually has his chest pumped up and thrust forth with the pride of his individuality and almost feels like a rhinoceros: so strong, independent, and self-sufficient. It is when one reaches that state of independent and personal responsibility that he can then "observe kindness" et cetera and focus on being beneficial to others.

In the Laws of Manu one finds similar teachings, for success starts and ends with one's own efforts, and not that of someone else.

"Let him carefully avoid all undertakings which depend upon others; but let him eagerly pursue that which depends on himself (IV.159).

Everything that depends on others (gives) pain, everything that depends on oneself (gives) pleasure; know that this is the short definition of pleasure and pain"(IV.160 from the Rules for a Snataka).

Langland in his work Piers the Ploughman speaking of the deadly sin of greed, declared that there is not forgiveness for the business man who has robbed others if he does not repent and make restitution to those he has robbed. One may think here of the conversion of Zaccheus while Jesus was visiting him. Only the man who has committed the crime is responsible both for what pain it has caused and also for making restitution for the crime itself. Langland stated that an honest Friar, refusing a bribe for forgiveness, ought to say thus to the business thief:

> You are a vile wretch, and I cannot give you absolution. You must
> first settle accounts with all the people you have robbed. I have no
> power to pardon you till all their losses are made good, and Reason
> has entered it in the register of Heaven. For it is written, "The sin is
> not remitted unless restitution be made." And all who have received
> any part of your (fraudulently acquired) wealth are bound before God
> to help you pay it back...For no man who uses your ill-gotten gains
> can ever prosper.7.11

Martin Luther in his Small Catechism took the second table of the law (i.e. the 4th to the 10th Commandments), which, with the exception of the Fourth Commandment, are stated in the negative "You shall not...", and, in his explanation, restated them all with a positive responsibility. To "You shall not kill", he added "but help and befriend him in every bodily need". To "You shall not commit adultery", he added that "each love and honor his spouse". To "You shall not steal", he added "but help him to improve his property and business". To "You shall not bear false witness against you neighbor", he added "but defend him, speak well of him, and put the best construction on everything." And to the final commandments concerning one's coveting anything that belongs to another, he added "but be of service to him in keeping it" and to wife and servants, he added "but urge them to stay and do their duty." So the personal responsibility is not only in not doing evil but is also, if one seeks goodness and happiness, in helping the other. It is not only, not to knock a man down, but to help him up when he falls. If man is seeking wholeness and happiness, there is no other way, except through human goodness to oneself and to others.

Wilhelm Reich's theme of his work Listen, Little Man is that man is responsible for himself, his goals, the paths he walks to attain his goals, and his happiness. But because a man refuses to take such responsibilities upon himself, he remains a "little man" who cannot experience the wholeness of life. Reich unleashes a truck load of sarcasm upon the irresponsible who then complain because their lives are empty. They are full of desires, but refuse to make the effort. Reich declared that Truth told him:

> The Little Man does not want to hear the truth about himself. He does not want the great responsibility which is his. He wants to remain a Little Man, or wants to become a little great man. He wants to become rich, or a party leader, or a commander of the legion, or secretary of the society for the abolition of vice. But he does not want to assume the responsibility for his works, for food provision, housing, traffic, education, research, administration, or whatever it may be.
>
> Did your 'liberator' tell you that? No, He called you the 'Proletarian of the World,' but he did not tell you that you, and only you, are responsible for your life.
>
> Do you understand now why happiness escapes you? It wants to be worked for and wants to be earned. But you only want to devour happiness; that's why it escapes you; it does not want to be devoured by you.
>
> You think the goal justifies the means, even the vile means. You are wrong: The goal is the path on which you arrive at it. Every step of today is your life of tomorrow. No great goal can be reached by vile means....Your Christian love, your socialism, your American constitution lie in what you do every day, what you think every hour, in how you embrace your mate and how you experience your child, in how you look at your work as your social responsibility, in how you avoid becoming like the suppresser of your life.7.12

Sometimes our quest for goodness and wholeness requires an ultimate sacrifice, and in such situations each must ask himself what his ultimate goals are. During WWII there was a humble German clergyman, <u>Paul Schneider</u>, who was torn between love of life with his beloved family and speaking out against the tyranny of Hitler. His wife cautioned him to be more discreet, because his words were too forcefully directed against the Nazis. She begged him to quit lest he be executed for treason and leave his family without a father and unprovided for. Paul Schneider replied, "My wife, shall I care for our children's bodies and fail their souls? Shall I feed them, clothe them, educate them, and yet not show them what is the truth, and the courage to live for it? No, my wife, maybe if you and they are to be kept faithful, I shall have to die." Paul Schneider was taken and executed by the Nazis. But, despite all circumstances, he reached his goal to live courageously for the truth. Responsibility is always a complex issue, yet one must be responsible for oneself first, and in the most difficult situations, he must walk alone like a rhinoceros.

B. COMMITMENT, PERSEVERANCE, AND DISCIPLINE

These three words are often seen as quite scary or painful and are generally avoided. "He's afraid of a commitment." "He just cannot persevere." "He has no discipline." Now someone comes and asks for all three, ugh! Yet, as Reich mentioned, happiness has to be worked for, and a full life of beauty and wholeness must be pursued by commitment, perseverance, and discipline, as has been well noted above. Likewise, in such matters intentions are easy but actualization is difficult, and the spirit is willing but the flesh is weak. It almost seems natural that there are so few people who actually feel whole and happy, for most are so empty they spend most of their excess money on being entertained in order to have a memory of something which they consider pleasant, regardless of how shallow the activity or thought happened to be. America is filled with complaining, whining, and bored people who avoid, at any cost, any process that demands commitment, perseverance, and discipline. Which is such a tragedy, seeing that America is a country in which so very many opportunities in all fields of study exist. One wonders how the average middle class American would respond to Jesus' request to be his disciple: for the Son of Man has nowhere to lay his head, and even the foxes and birds have more than that. Even when families go camping, they take their televisions, so that they can be entertained! Unbelievable!

In the fragments of <u>Democritus</u> are short sayings that point us in the correct direction:

One must learn to have any skill or wisdom.
Time itself does not teach us wisdom, it comes by training and nature.
And more men become good by training than by nature.
The training of children does not need to be costly.
A man's temperance will show his children the best way.
Knowledge and hard work produce life's good benefits.
Once a man receives the benefits of his labor, the labor becomes much
    more satisfying than laziness.
If one's attitude towards work is positive, it is easier to preform than that
    which is done against the will.
Once a man is accustomed to working, it is lighter to bear.
Children who are spoiled and kept from working, will not learn to read or
    write, be able to utilize their musical or gymnastic abilities, or even
    to understand the virtue of work or the shame of laziness.7.13

In other words, learning the hardness and disciplines of life begin when we are young, and if blessed with a parent who gives a good example of such, the idea of discipline and the work ethic become ingrained in us and such an attitude is then habitual. Wisdom does not come without some difficult reading and thinking. Playing the piano at concert level comes only with long daily practices. Edison's idea that genius is 98% perspiration and 2% inspiration, is quite valid. Likewise, in building a life of virtue, wholeness, and happiness, all the above steps and the following steps are necessary. <u>Cicero</u> declared that for man to be good he must learn philosophically what it is, and then after he has disciplined himself rationally to see the truth that virtue is the basis of happiness, he must then be virtuous both within himself and in his duties to others. This is a common theme of his work on <u>Offices</u>, especially in Book One.

<u>Immanuel Kant</u> hoped that man's mind would grow to such a virtuous extent that he would be disgusted at the thought of any vice: lying, cheating, harming another or any such thought or action. From early

childhood such a character ought to be built into the mind of the child.He stated in his <u>Vorlesungen</u> <u>ueber</u> <u>Moralphilosophie</u> (<u>Moralphilosophie</u> <u>Collins</u>: <u>Vom</u> <u>obersten</u> <u>Principio</u> <u>der</u> <u>Moralitaet</u>:65):

> We should already from a child's youth instill a direct abhorrence against such [evil] actions, not an indirect abhorrence which has only a practical use. We must not present the [evil] action as forbidden or as self damaging, but as in its very self worthy of only abomination.

A well nourished mind set on virtue and beauty will be repulsed at the idea of doing anything else. What dishonesty and cheating offer can not move a truly good man to do evil. No amount of money, better grades, advantages at work, a better chance to win an election, none of them can even tempt a good person because immediately he will find such dishonesty utterly detestable. However, such dishonestly is, not only harmful to virtue itself, but also a hindrance to wholeness and happiness which are themselves built upon and in need of those very virtues.

<u>Jimmy</u> <u>Carter</u>, after the Nixon scandal, won an election for the Presidency of the United States by stating that he would never lie to the American people. He did not claim to have reached Christian excellence, but lying simply was detestable to him. In a speech in Detroit to a Christian Businessmen's Committee on May 11th, 1974 he declared: "I am, as best, a mediocre Christian. It is obvious that in these present times, as Christians we need to recognize frankly our own inadequacies and failures, ask for God's forgiveness, and commit ourselves to a standard of perfection." But despite those admitted weaknesses, he deplored lying, both in his personal and political lives.

C. MODERATION, INTEGRITY, AND SELF-HARMONY

Unless our impulses are under rational control there can be no moderation or temperance, and this, according to Plato, is one of the four basic virtues, and it is absolutely necessary before one can have, in Plato's terminology, justice within the soul, or what we would call self-harmony. To live within a rational life plan, it is necessary that our emotions are in concurrence with our mental thinking before we can be self-harmonized, and put away the common struggle that many have within themselves. A balanced soul, a harmony of the mind and spirit, and a moderately conformed thought process are all bound together in the concept of what Plato called SOPHROSYNE. Such a state of being breeds wholeness, and without it, neither wholeness nor happiness is possible. In the <u>Republic</u> <u>Plato</u> stated:

And suppose injustice abiding in a single person, would your wisdom say
   that she loses or that she retains her natural power?
Let us assume that she retains her power.
Yet is not the power which injustice exercises of such a nature that wherever she takes up her abode, whether in a city, in an army, in a family,
   or in any other body, that body is, to begin with, rendered incapable of
   united action by reason of sedition and distraction; and does it not become its own worst enemy and at variance with all that opposes it,
   with the just? Is not this the case?
Yes, certainly.
And is not injustice equally fatal when existing in a single person; in the
   first place rendering him incapable of action because he is not at unity
   with himself, and in the second place making him an enemy to himself and to the just? Is not that true, Thrasymachus?
Yes. (I.352).

<u>Plato</u> divided the soul into three parts: reason which gives wisdom and knowledge; the spirited part which gives will and courage; and the emotive part which gives emotions such as joy and anger. The four necessary virtues of the soul (one's central and real being) to Plato then were: <u>wisdom, courage, moderation</u> (of the emotions), and when each played its proper role, then that state of harmony was, by Plato, called <u>justice</u>. A person could not experience harmony within unless each played its proper role. A man could be wise and self-controlled, but if he were a coward and feared everything, he could not be whole. Likewise, he could not be just if he were courageous and wise but could not control his emotions. Often people refer to only one of them, for example, "Control yourself!" or "Think about it!" or "Have a little courage!" but sometimes they request inner justice itself: "Until you put yourself together, do not come back to work!" The well balanced, harmonious, or just soul is that foundation upon goodness, morality, happiness, and wholeness depend. These four virtues appear many times in the writings

of Plato, in the Republic they are the central theme, and in other writings often one of the four will be the theme: Charmides (self-control or temperance), Laches (courage), Gorgias, Protagoras, Theaetetus, and the Philebus (wisdom or knowledge), and in the Republic and the Laws (justice). Many other of our teachers speak of them individually.

Wise people show moderation, says the <u>Dhammapada</u>, in all states during their life times and "purge themselves of all the troubles of the mind". Putting all the virtues together so that man has an inner harmony is called the "conquering of self",

> If one man conquer in battle a thousand times a thousand men,
> and if another conquer himself, he is the greatest of conquerors.
> One's own self conquered is better than all other people; not even
> a god, A Gandhava, not Mara, could change into defeat the victory
> of a man who has vanquished himself, and always lives under self-
> restraint.(Dhammapada VIII.)

> Mules are good if tamed, and noble Sindhu horses, and elephants
> with large tusks; but he who tames himself is better still (XXIII).

<u>Democritus</u> likewise claimed that moderation is most necessary: "If one oversteps due measure, the most pleasant things become the most unpleasant" and "Moderation increases enjoyment, and makes pleasure even greater" and again "It is childish, not manly, to have immoderate desires". It is up to reason to control desires and harness them with moderation: "It is hard to fight with desire; but to overcome it is the mark of a rational man."7.14

<u>Horace</u> taught (Odes II.2):

> If avarice you can still subdue,
> To you more glory will accrue
>   Than had you power to bring
> Libya to Gades, or to sway
> Each Carthage, should they both obey
>   You as their rightful king.

And

> When dangers press, a mind sustain
>   Unshaken by the storms of Fate;
> And when delight follows pain,
>   With no glad insolence elate.(Odes II.3).

The Srimad Bhagavatam teaches that a man who cannot control himself is slave to his passions, for he cannot move away from them like a man fleeing danger brought on by others.(V.1).

D. KNOWLEDGE, WISDOM, EDUCATION

Aristotle made the point that a person does not have knowledge unless he knows four things about his subject or statement: that it is in actuality, why it is, how it is, and that it cannot be otherwise. If one does not know all four elements of the subject in question, he does not have knowledge, but rather opinion: and opining is not knowing. There is the story of Jesus in the second chapter of the Gospel of Mark in which Jesus' disciples began to pluck ears of grain which was forbidden by the Jewish Sabbath law. Jesus reminded the Pharisees, who had been quick to question their actions, that although they were correct in knowing that the law existed, they did not know why it existed, which was to give the body the restful nourishment it needed from six days of labor. And, Jesus concluded that since a hungry body needed nourishment of food as much as it needed rest from work, what they were doing in collecting food to satisfy their hunger was in keeping with the main purpose of the law. To know a law without knowing the why, the how, and that it cannot be otherwise, was not true knowledge of the law. This can be applied to doctrines, customs, cultic rituals, social manners, and a host of other things which, obeyed, can be a curb to harmful or uncouth actions, yet it cannot be a knowledge of the making and purpose of the law. A church ritual, without knowing the why of the ritual, can be totally empty, as can a doctrine or any other such teaching. Therefore, without knowledge, a person could be, in judging others by a law, actually be the one who is breaking it, as the story of the plucking of grain on the Sabbath showed. Likewise in Mark's Seventh Chapter the disciples did not wash their hands before eating and were criticized for eating with defiled hands. But the hands were not dripping with blood or stained by having done some evil, they simply may have had some dust or dirt upon them, and therefore, no moral law was violated. Mark goes on to say that the Pharisees have many such customs. Of course, if water is available, washing hands before eating makes sense, but there is no morality involved. It is knowledge of the laws and customs that is the source of making a man good. This was one of Plato's main teachings -- that knowledge was the basis of goodness, for without knowledge man can not make a rational decision as to whether an act is right or wrong in its natural state. Therefore, in Plato, that is the purpose of an education, to teach men to know, and in knowing, being empowered to choose that which is good, and in so choosing, they become good themselves. In Plato's Laws he stated it very clearly: "But if you ask what is the good of education in general, the answer is easy -- that education makes good men, and that good men act nobly"(I.641c). It is by man's ability to reason about life that gives him the chance to establish a sense of nobility.

And can he who misses the truth of anything, have a knowledge of that
   thing?
He cannot.
Then knowledge does not consist in impressions of sense, but in
   reasoning about them; in that only, and not in the mere impression,
   truth and being can be attained?
Clearly (Theaetetus 185c).

   Hesiod offered this advice to one looking for a wife -- make a careful and rational choice so that your neighbors do not mock you for the choice you have made! "Look circumspect and long; lest you be found the merry mock of all the dwellers round."(424-425) A rational choice in such a situation was certainly important for one's happiness, for a bad choice is one of the worse things that can befall a man.
   Full knowledge of something, and Kant, following Plato -- Aristotle's teacher, would add to Aristotle, the absolute moral goodness of the act, and how that can be used within the universal imperative of moral goodness, is prudence (wisdom) and by that wisdom man becomes good, noble, and inwardly happy. "Prudence is the ability to use the means

towards the universal goal of man, happiness...wisdom requires us to clearly realize both the end and the means to be used in acquiring it." No end can ever justify an immoral act, for the end of man, happiness, cannot ever be attained by an evil act or thought. For an end cannot remove the absoluteness of an attribute necessary for goodness, like honesty and kindness. Unconditional moral imperatives are actually ends in themselves because they are of the essence of goodness and happiness, and the joy of inner worthiness. Kant stated <u>Vorlesungen</u> <u>ueber</u> <u>Moralphilosophie</u>: <u>Moralphilosophie</u> <u>Collins, Prooemium</u>:

> The moral imperative demands an absolute, without the seeing of the goal. Our doing freely with self-permission has an inner good-ness, which gives to one an immediate inner and absolute worth of morality.

This is what is meant by having inner justice or harmony of the soul, the joy of being in one's very nature as a light whose automatic beams going out towards others are good and beautiful and moral at the highest level. This is according to Plato, Jesus, and Kant the only way a man can be good and whole, and enjoy, as Jesus called it, the life more abundant. This also is wisdom at its highest level, thus only those who have such knowledge can be good. Learning and knowing are naturally related and as such I should like to quote <u>Carl R. Rogers</u> from his book <u>On Becoming a Person</u>:

> By significant learning I mean learning which is more than an accumulation of facts. It is learning which makes a difference -- in the individual's behavior, in the course of action he chooses in the future, in his attitudes and in his personality. It is pervasive learning which is not just an accretion of knowledge, but which interpenetrates with every portion of his existence.7.15

I hope the teachings of Jesus and the other great sages of humanity that I have presented in this book lead to such a life changing and building learning process, indeed, that life may be more abundant.

IV. DETOURS TO RATIONAL LIVING

On occasion the detours to rational learning that come in this section have been referred to before in this book, but because they do present such barriers and obstacles to personal growth, I have listed them separately with a few comments from our teachers about such dangers that these "detours" present.

A. PLAYING 'VICTIM' OR THE 'BLAME GAME'

This is not a new game, for it goes back to Adam blaming Eve, and Eve blaming the Serpent, in the Hebrew creation story. Aesop told this story in which a common trait of blaming fate for all their problems is presented:

> A man who was tired after a long journey threw himself down on the edge of a well and went to sleep. He was in imminent danger of tumbling in, when Fortune appeared and woke him. 'If you had fallen in, my friend,' she said, 'instead of blaming your own lack prudence you would have blamed me.'7.16

It was not unusual for the ancient world to blame the gods, as Adam did by stating that it was the woman Yahweh gave him that led him astray. You, O Yahweh, started my problems. Theognis taught:

It's easy to blame your neighbour and to praise
Yourself; the masses do a lot of this;
Gossiping, slandering, they won't shut up
But gentlemen keep measure in all things. (Elegies 611-614).7.17

Aristotle too was confronted by the defensive pleas that "I didn't know what I was doing" or "I was drunk" or "I was in an angry rage, not really myself" when I did it. People and defense lawyers today use the same arguments to lessen the atrocity of the crime, as if the damage done to the true victim is any less because he was murdered by a drunk. Ignorance, inebriation, and anger do not make the act "involuntary".

In his <u>Nicomachean</u> <u>Ethics</u> Aristotle stated:

> Indeed, we punish a man for his very ignorance, if he is thought
> responsible for the ignorance, as when penalties are doubled in
> the case of drunkenness; for the moving principle is in the man
> himself, since he had the power of not getting drunk and his
> getting drunk was the cause of his ignorance.(1113b 30-35)

In his Table Talk, <u>Martin</u> <u>Luther</u>, who taught Aristotle at Wittenburg, repeated this thought. Germans drank a lot of beer then (then?), and drunkenness was quite common, and therefore drunkenness was often used as an excuse for some stupid but damaging action. Luther, like Aristotle, replied "O if you were drunk too, well that increasing the crime." The blame game that the alcohol made me do it makes a person more to be shamed and punished, because he gave up his human reason to become an irrational beast.

Anger is usually blamed on the other person also. "You made me angry!" Again, man is claiming that he has given up his rational state and permitted another to manipulate his thinking and acting by planting anger into his persona. And this, of course, he claimed, he was powerless to stop.

A man may kill or steal because he freely gives up his rational manhood to circumstances that do not please him. He kills his wife, because she asked for a divorce -- "she made me do it". He robs a store because he lost his job, "hard times forced me into crime". Even media uses such irresponsible statements like "Driven desperate by his circumstances, he committed suicide -- after he had killed his wife and three children". His lawyer will say that he was depressed. Legally people who play "victim" seem to be of impression that this qualifies them for a legal special privilege. This playing of the victim is now an epidemic in the USA causing people to completely lose their sense of responsibility. Below I present many articles of this plague that must be stopped by tough love and honesty so that people realize that this playing of "victim" is a flight from reality into an illusionary existence in which there can be no "self-esteem", no love of virtue, and no hope of wholeness or happiness. It is totally self-destructive.

A college student claims that his book "Cheating 101" is helpful to other students, and is justified by the inadequacy of the faculty. "Cheating", he says, "is a natural defense mechanism triggered by irrelevant courses and professors who look forward to their paychecks more than they do teaching." (Newsweek 1/06/1992).

A college teacher was fired for several sexually aggressive acts with his female students in his office. His plea was that he was "sexually obsessive", and his lawyer presented a psychiatrist in his behalf who testified that the teacher "suffered from an 'impulse control disorder'". The state's lawyers 'scoffed at the claim', and the man did not get his job back. (LAT 5/03/1994).

A man who had been unemployed for two years (did he try McDonald's?), shot mortally both his father and mother, and seriously injured his brother with a gun shot. He was 'despondent', yes, but how in the world would it in his own crazy mind justify killing his adult family? (LAT 5/12/1994).

Often the burden is put upon the American Nation because there are millions of poor people. Sometimes leaders do make harmful decisions, but it wasn't the nation that dropped out of high school, had three babies by age 18, and did not seek some type of industrial education. As long as these people find someone else to blame, they will never solve their problems and never find a life of wholeness and happiness.

A newspaper article reported that parents blamed the public schools for their children's lack of educational progress. But they never blamed themselves who are really the first in line for the responsibility of their children's future. Some parents even prefer home-school with very little help from "the system", for they recognize their responsibility as parents. (LAT 5/17/1998).

Adultery, the breaking of a personal trust with one's life mate, has been blamed on an irresistible inner pain suffered by the adulterer, who was "simply crying out for help", as if a personal decision was never involved.

On a TV program, 11/09/1994, a woman appeared who had suffocated her 15 month old child. During the program she looked up to God and asked, "Why did <u>you</u> let me do something like that?" Yes, it was God's fault for neglecting his duties again.

Many other articles and programs present this sad state of affairs within the minds of unhappy people. "I am not responsible, I was a middle child". "My medication caused me to shoot that 14 year old boy in the head". "I was addicted to the power of my credit card which is really responsible for my debts that I cannot pay." "My genes forced me to drink that alcohol" (I am not trying to belittle the chemical makeup of certain people -- a study which is certainly valid, but it is simply used too often to cry "victim"). A man in Bangladesh filed a suit against the World Soccer powers for banning his idol Diego Maradona from World Cup play because it "caused him so much anguish that he had a mental breakdown" and could no longer meet his responsibilities (LAT 7/13/1994) -- (I felt I had to note the source on this one so that the reader would not think I was kidding). People who have both molested and killed children have pleaded innocent because of a certain mental disorder. But enough of this "victim" and "blame" and of all other games that are played: entitlement games ("I am entitled to welfare payments that make my life and my four children respectable", and "I just finished college and society owes me a high paying job"), the whining and all other ways in which people over 12 years old avoid life, avoid honesty, and avoid ever becoming whole. Please! You are killing your opportunity for happiness! Listen to the great and wonderful teachers of mankind here presented, as well as many others.

With a sense of humor a <u>Sanskrit poem</u> declared; "A girl who's less than perfect always blames the dress." <u>Marcus Aurelius</u> told himself to face up with courage to his own faults in his Meditations to himself: "Abstain then from all thoughts of blame." <u>Nero</u>, of course, played the blame game when he accused the Christians of starting the devastating fire that decimated Rome; and accordingly they were executed without mercy. The blame game not only hurts the person playing the game, but it can be devastating to others who are truly innocent. It is most certainly a wandering far off the path of spiritual growth.

B. CHOOSING THE WRONG ROLE MODELS

In the United States, unfortunately, "celebrities" of all sorts are pursued as if their "contributions" to society were actually so significant that their mere appearance somewhere was to be "celebrated". It is the common worker, like the garbage man who puts himself through much unpleasant smell but keeps our cities from plagues and our streets free from rats, that one must honor. September 11, 2001 was a tragedy, and it is likewise a tragedy, that only at times like that do we honor the firemen and the police the way that they ought to be honored. In the first chapter of this book, I tried to honor teachers at all levels in America, for they do more for the average American than the entire entertainment industry. Jesus, who tried to keep us from being backwards in our honoring people, reminded us that in true reality, often the first will be last and the last first. The farmer will be told to sit up higher and closer to the place of honor, and others will be moved downward. Decent people of quality who live a happy and charitable life towards others, regardless of what they own or their social status, should be imitated and used as role models, and they are the ones who should be "celebrated". The common man and his decency is the "celebrity", even if he lives in a very humble setting. Seneca stated: "Anyone entering our homes should admire us rather than our furnishing" (Letter V). Juvenal in his Eighth Satire stated the same thing, that one honors his home more effectively with virtue than with statues, usually of ancestors who were considered part of Rome's nobility of the past.

"Let modelled clay and marbel do their best,
Virtue alone can generous blood attest.
Live then, as Paulus, Drusus, lived before;
Bear thou a people's love, as Cossus bore,
And let the brave, the just, the generous deed
That marks thy worth, thy lictor's rods precede!
Claim we as debt from the illustrious few,
That, graced by birth, they shine in merit too."

Epictetus used coins as an illustration; for a man leaves imprint upon coins and he likewise leaves his imprint or image upon society by the quality of his life. He stated:

> ...but I mean the things which belong to him as a man, the marks in his mind with which he came into the world, such as we seek also on coins, and if we find them, we approve of the coins, and if we do not find the marks, we reject them. What is the stamp on this Sestertius? "The stamp of Trajan." Present it. "It is the stamp of Nero." Throw it away: it cannot be accepted, it is a counterfeit. So also in this case. What is the stamp of his opinions? "It is gentleness, a sociable disposition, a tolerant temper, a disposition to mutual affection." Produce these qualities. I accept them: I consider this man a citizen, I accept him as a neighbor, a companion in my voyages. Only see that he has not Nero's stamp.

Give your love and your honor and your imitation to noble role models; and to those not noble, throw away their stamps and images and statues. As Jesus said, "Do not give to dogs what is holy; and do not throw your pearls before swine" (Mt 7:6). To the honorable, give honor, and use such only as role models. The teachers presented in this book, to me, are my friends and my role models, even if it means taking up a cross to follow them. Likewise, one must be careful in choosing his leaders or gurus or role models. Remember: Jonestown in Guyana, Southwestern Uganda where a doomsday sect massacre killed more than 924 (more than Jonestown) (LAT 4/01/2000), Oregon's Bhagwan Shree Rajneesh--whose followers game him all, and he purchased 93 customized Rolls-Royces and later left the country (LAT 1/20/1990), preaching gurus that promise you your "entitlement" to miracles and wealth--for "affluence is your divine right"(LAT 2/10/1985), gurus to tell you to commit suicide and catch the comet (San Diego), gurus who claim their land is "holy ground" and later end up in jail for not supporting their two children (LAT 4/25/1994), "hippie" gurus who murder their ex-girl friends (LAT 10/18/2002). Again, the words of Jesus: "Do not give to dogs what is holy; and do not throw your pearls before swine". One's life is holy and his wealth is to be used wisely, both for himself and for others -- one's life and wealth are precious and to be handled wisely. One must chose leaders, teachers and role models wisely. I have tried to present those of human history that I believe are the most trustworthy and, by historical standards of judgment, the most loved and successful.

C. LEGAL VENGEANCE

Sometimes there is a fine line between justice and vengeance, often simply the anger and attitude that it is shown. But what I am speaking of is an excess of retribution that causes unfair damage to the other person, usually caused by a hateful attitude between the two fighting in court. Unfortunately lawyers are not always helpful, depending on how they are paid. Direct vengeance is forbidden by law and by Jesus, and is much more harmful to both parties than the harm that is done through our legal system, which itself is always more concerned with what is legal than what is just. It probably has always been that way. Even in ancient Athens where lawyers were forbidden, there were speakers or orators that would present a certain side of the argument to the court. <u>Plato</u> presented them as individuals who were enslaved by the desire to win and would avoid justice at any cost to win, and in comparison to the virtue of a philosopher their corruption and slavery looked so pitiful to the philosopher's honesty and freedom. He stated:

"I mean to say, that those who have been trained in philosophy and liberal pursuits are as unlike those who from their youth upwards have been knocking about in the courts and such places, as a freeman is in breeding unlike a slave.
In what is the difference seen?
In the leisure spoken of by you, which a freeman can always command: he has his talk out in peace...--if fancy takes him, he begins again, as we are doing now, caring not whether his words are many or few; <u>his only aim is to attain the truth</u>....But the court orator is always in a hurry; there is the water of the clepsydra [a water clock] driving him on, and not allowing him to expatiate at will: and there is his adversary standing over him, enforcing his rights; the indictment...is recited at the time: and from this he must not deviate. He is a slave, and is continually disputing about a fellow-slave before his master [the court of law], who is seated and has the cause in his hands...The consequence has been, that he has become keen and shrewd; he has learned how to flatter his master in word and

indulge him in deed; but his soul is small and unrighteous. His condition, which has been that of a slave from his youth upwards, has deprived him of growth and uprightness and independence; dangers and fears, which were simply too much for his truth and honesty, came upon him in early years, when the tenderness of youth was unequal to them, and he has been driven into crooked ways; from the first he has practiced deception and retaliation, and has become stunted and warped. And so he has passed out of youth into manhood, having no soundness in him (although he now thinks he has a hold on wisdom). Such is the court orator" (Thcactetus 172c-173a).

Plato continued on declaring that the court orator has a limited mind that has been fenced in by his legal system so that he is virtually incapable of asking what justice or prudence or anything else of value really is. It is in such discussions that the philosopher has his revenge.

"When that narrow, keen, little legal mind is called to account about all this, he gives the philosopher his revenge; for dizzied by the height at which he is hanging, whence he looks down into space, which is a strange experience for him, he being dismayed and lost, and stammering broken words, is laught at...by every man who has not been brought up a slave" (Theaetetus 175d).

There are those who use such courts to extract revenge upon another to the limit permitted by law, and yet they think that such an attitude can actually help them to become whole and happy persons. Justice, yes, of course. Vindictive punishment and destruction because of unsatisfied anger, never. They cannot be compatible. In the second great Indian Epic, the Ramayana, Ravan seems to get himself into situations in which he demands the death of his adversary. War breaks out and many die, for Ravan demands a slaughter for the sake of his son who was killed. "Arm each chief and gallant Raksha! Be our sacred duty done. Ravan seeks a fitting vengeance for his brave and noble son." For this, Ravan went into war for the third time, and this time he himself was killed. Justice never entered his mind, for he was driven by what he considered a "sacred duty". His mind was limited by a concept of sacred duty, just as the court orators above were limited of mind by their legal training. Such thinking is a major detour in one's quest to live in harmony within his soul. In

February 2003 a woman was judged guilty for killing her husband by running over him several times with the family car, for he had had an affair. The prosecutor, a woman lawyer, was, of course, correct in seeking a charge of murder, and in this she was successful. But in stating that the defendant went beyond justice in murdering her husband, she said that the woman, implying that such and such would be justice, ought to do what other women do. As the Los Angeles Times (2-13-03 A23) recorded her words:

...........(the Prosecutor) argued that Harris (the defendant) had a right to be angry but "she didn't have the right to kill." "The solution is to get a divorce," she said. "You do what every other wife would do, you take him to the cleaners. You take his car, his children, his respect in the community. You can make him wish he were dead but you don't get to kill him."

If that is what every other wife would do, I personally feel quite happy about being single. When Jesus stipulated that divorce was not to be easily granted, his disciples said "If such is the case of a man with his wife, it is not expedient to marry." But Jesus said to them, "Not all men can receive this precept, but only those to whom it is given" (Mt 19:9-11). Divorce and adultery are usually quite painful for at least one of the partners in a marriage, but to be so vindictive and seek such legal vengeance is a detour to happiness. Other situations also apply, e.g. seeking huge, completely out of proportion, settlements that would equal most state lotteries, for the sake of greed and vengeance, are not ways to stay on the path that leads to a spiritually enriched life. "Where your treasure is, there is your heart also" (Mt 5:21). If a person's heart is set on wealth or vengeance through the legal system, virtue and goodness have no chance to find a place within.

D. EMOTIONALISM --FINDING ONESELF IN EMOTIONALLY ALTERED STATES OF MIND

The way I am defining an emotionally altered state of mind, is that state of mind in which a particular emotion has completely taken over the ability to process thought rationally. A person becomes possessed by a passion and cannot free himself or his thinking from that particular passion. Usually it is said something like this "driven by anger" a man commits a crime. But in reality, the man has chosen to permit himself to be angry, for he is not passive in his life, and he cannot morally ever claim that he had no power to stop the process of being possessed. Giving oneself over to emotions in order to plead 'not guilty by momentary insanity' is a legal, but immoral excuse. Legally, one may be cleared, but his life has suffered an enormous setback in his quest to happiness. A person must simply stop and ask himself for a rational answer to his tendency towards any passion: "Why am I choosing to let this other person and his idiotic acts control my emotions?" "Why do I give up my own rational powers because someone else is acting crazy?" It is so very easy to be swayed emotionally and find oneself being taken over by an impulse that is contrary to reason. To lead a harmonious life of goodness, one must be the rational master of his emotions, not a powerless slave to them. If you suffer "road rage" then you have let yourself be infected. If you have been betrayed, handle it rationally, and do not let the betrayer also infect you with wild and raging emotions, for then he hurts you twice as much. Lao Tzu knew that one must control his words and his senses:

"Let him keep his mouth closed,
and shut up the portals of his nostrils (signifying anger),
and all his life he will be exempt from laborious exertion.
Let him keep his mouth open,
and spending his breath in self promotion,
and in all his life there will be no safety for him. (Chapter 52).

The Dhammapada likewise urges man to be master of himself and his emotions, for they are so destructive, especially anger which infiltrates the mind, body, and soul.

Let a man leave anger, let him forsake pride, let him overcome all bondage!...He who holds back rising anger like a rolling chariot, him I call a real driver; other people are but holding the reins. Let a man overcome anger by love, let him overcome evil by good...let him overcome the liar by truth.

...

Beware of bodily anger, and control thy body! Leave the sins of the body,
and with thy body practise virtue!
Beware of the anger of the tongue, and control thy tongue! Leave the sins
of the tongue, and practise virtue with thy tongue!
Beware of the anger of the mind, and control thy mind!
The wise who control their body, who control their tongue, the wise who
control mind, are indeed well-controlled. (XVII - On Anger).

Aristotle, in his Nicomachean Ethics, taught that actions of the emotions,
even out of control, are not involuntary and therefore man is responsible
for them.

"Again, what is the difference in respect of involuntariness between
errors committed upon calculation and those committed in anger? Both
are to be avoided, but the irrational passions are thought not less human
than reason is, and therefore also the actions which proceed from anger
or appetite are the man's actions. It would be odd, then, to treat them as
involuntary" (1111a.34-1111b.4).

Aristotle's views here coincide with his earlier views on drunkenness,
that being drunk or, here, emotionally upset does not lessen the crime
and it remains at least equal to one rationally planned. For just as the man
chose to become drunk, he likewise chose to be controlled by the
emotive passions, and thereby put himself into a state of mind that he
would have difficulty controlling. Guilty twice! Indeed, it would be
absurd to count such crimes as being involuntary.

Occasionally a story appears that tells of a man or woman who killed
someone but pleads that he did it out of love. Most often such a person is
equating love with a jealous obsession, and fearing that "the beloved"
would leave him and have to settle for a "lesser love" elsewhere, so he
kills her -- because he "loved" her. In such cases the mind is so altered by
emotionalism that he may actually believe such. From a Sufi Notebook
the following is given for contemplation.

"On Love:

What is generally called love can be harmful to the lover and the object of the love. If this is the result, the cause cannot be called love by a Sufi, but must be called 'attachment' in which the attached is incapable of any other conduct. Love not only has different intensities, but it also has different levels. If man thinks that love only signifies what he has so far felt, he will veil himself thereby from an experience of real love. If, however, he has actually felt real love, he will not make the mistake of generalizing about it so as to identify it only with physical love or the love of attraction". 7.18

Softly said, and gently true. Both the lover and the beloved are harmed by such possessive "love" or "attachment" of the one for the other. I do disagree with the phase above "is incapable of any other conduct", but the point is well taken that the passion has become the master, and the man the slave. However, slaves can free themselves.

The idea of "falling in love" reflects the same lack of reason, as does one who claims instant "chemistry" with another. It is simply emotion running wild with no rational thought implied. M. Scott Peck in his popular book The Road Less Traveled warned of this feeble minded emotion:

"Falling in love is not real love for several reasons...
Falling in love is not an act of will. It is not a conscious choice.
...
Falling in love is not an extension of one's limits or boundaries; it is a partial and temporary collapse of them. The extension of one's limits requires effort; falling in love is effortless. Lazy and undisciplined individuals are as likely to fall in love as energetic and dedicated ones.
...
Real love is a permanently self-enlarging experience. Falling in love is not. Falling in love has little to do with purposively nurturing one's spiritual development." (p.89).

Emotions are a wonderful human experience, but they must not become ever the master of the human soul, that is for the mind, for that rational power we possess is what makes us human, the power to think, plan, control ourselves, and limited the effect of our emotions upon our mental state of being.

E. OTHER TEMPTATIONS TO FORSAKE REASON

There are other emotional states of mind that try to push reason aside, because sometimes thinking out a situation is difficult, and to adopt an irrational emotion seems so much easier. One chooses to be morbidly gloomy (melancholy) because thinking about one's situation and trying to improve it would simply take too much mental disciple. "I am so sad and distraught, please feel sorry for me" is the cry of those who choose to avoid a rational discipline, like knowing themselves and their status in life, and choosing a plan to change it. Another complains that life is not fair, and emphasizes that he wants a little pity because everyone else has had more breaks in their lives than he: this is the "why me" plea, which seeks consolation and affection, sometimes just as an attention getter or an excuse for some failure. Living through others is a plague visited upon our children by unfulfilled parents. Little leagues of the different sports often are disrupted by fights among the macho male parents, whose kid was "unjustly" treated by the referees or the members of the opposing team. Girls, five to twelve years old, are dressed up in adult makeup, loaded down with all sorts of cosmetics, taught stiff and artificial movements and paraded across stages by vanity possessed mothers who want in some way to participate in "beauty", living again through their daughters, poor children! Each year as many as three millions little girls are used by their mothers this way. Many of our young college graduates suffer from the entitlement complex thinking that because they studied a few extra years the world owes them a good and high paying job, and this is just as bad as the third generation welfare family that thinks it is entitled to other people's money by forced and legal charity. Finally, there are those who refuse the rational discipline of working out a life plan for economics, spiritual needs, and bodily comfort by turning to tortoise shell readings (ancient China in the I Ching and the Shu Chung), consulting the sacred chickens (ancient Rome), and magic (universal). There is the story of a ship's captain, a Roman who was fighting against Carthage in one of the Punic wars, who when the wind was right to attack the Carthaginian fleet asked the on-board priest to check the sacred chickens for an omen. If the chickens drank water, that was a positive and an approval to attack the Carthaginian fleet. Water was brought to the chickens, and they would not drink, frustrating the Captain. They tried again, the chickens still wouldn't drink the water. Finally, the Captain, fearing he was going to lose his good wind advantage, grabbed the chickens and threw them overboard into the sea, and then declared, "Now they're drinking water." Reason prevailed over superstition.

Thinking is not always easy, and the more academic the book or the more difficult a life situation, the harder thinking becomes. But it is precisely thinking through the difficult concepts of a philosopher or great teacher or working through mentally the hard and confusing times of one's life, that one grows into wisdom. It is the graduate school of life in which one must confront the ultimate meaning of our brief lives, and to turn such lives over to emotional and superstitious ways, is far beyond reason. If we had no place to go, one could understand. But when mankind has set before us the wisdom of all the great sages and holy men of the past, whose loving advice for their disciples is given to all humanity, then let us feast on such nourishment that our lives will be built sturdy and strong, so that when the winds blow and the rains come, we shall stand, knowing who we are as we trod our paths through the cosmos walking alone and powerfully like a rhinoceros.

CHAPTER EIGHT

STEP FIVE

FRIENDSHIP
THE
FLOWER OF HUMAN LIFE

The first four steps to wholeness and happiness have emphasized the growth into fulness by the individual himself: his unattachment to the temporal and material, his acceptance of the universe in which he lives as a friendly cosmos, the actualization of his soul as a child of the loving and caring Creator, and, understanding himself to be such, the rational planning of his life and goal as he steps towards his own destiny. Now that he has "come to himself" and has "known himself" and all that is about him in his life setting, he has the base of goodness within and can reach out to others. He has become salt or light by which he now has the ability to flavor and enlighten others. He in his fulness can enter friendships, and fellowship in justice and joy with his human brothers and sisters. He is now one of many and is obligated to make human society work, and bring the most good to the most people that he is able to. In this obligation, by means of functioning justice and loving friendships his life is enriched and his joy reaches the highest levels. For what else but a functioning and mutual friendship with another is the flower of human existence? He can bring a blooming and beautiful element into the lives of others, because he himself is good and happy. Likewise, as the old saying goes, "the farther a light shines, the stronger it is at its source", he can cast his glowing life upon many. To put himself in the midst of human society he has put himself where his light can shine the farthest.

I. JESUS ON FRIENDSHIP AND LOVE

Jesus himself had what Henri Bergson in his book The Two Sources of Morality and Religion called an "open soul", that is, he automatically loved and accepted everyone and was open to all humans and in that respect reflected the love of God for the entire world. However, that did not mean that he did not show his disappointment and even wrath towards certain ones. Jesus attacked those of five categories: (1) those who tried to control other's lives, (2) those who used peoples' piety in order to rob them (the den of thieves scene at the temple), (3) the arrogant and haughty who suppressed those they opposed and then classified them as "sinners", (4) the hypocritically religious, and (5) those who harmed others economically or physically. His friends seemed to be everyone else, with some much closer to him than others. He helped the deaf, the lame, the blind, the widowed, and, not only associated with the poor, but refused to own anything himself. Those considered the "lawless", i.e. those living outside the law of Moses were not attacked by him, and he himself seemed to trample upon some of the more customary traditions which the "good" people kept. He liked the children, blessed them, and warned others not to hurt them in any way, for their guardian angels came before the face of God daily -- yes, the children have friends in very high places, and one who harms them is bound to be punished. Bluntly put, he was saying, "Don't mess with the kids!" He often ate with tax-collectors, "sinners", women who had to make their living in various ways, and even did not shy away from the lepers. Besides his family and disciples, his other friends included Mark, Mary, Martha, Lazarus, and, it seems, Joseph of Arimathea, and Nicodemus, as well as soldiers of the enemy army, and numerous others, such as Mary Magdalene, who, in fact, if the Gospel of Philip is to be trusted, was indeed his closest friend even to the whispered criticism of the disciples. The Gospel of Philip stated:

"There were three who always walked with the Lord: Mary, his mother (1), and his sister (2), and Magdalene (3), the one who was called his 'companion'. His sister and his mother and his companion were each a Mary."

...

"And the companion of the Savior is Mary Magdalene. But Christ loved her more than all the disciples and used to kiss her often on her mouth. The rest of the disciples were offended by it and expressed disapproval. They said to him, 'Why do you love her more than all of us?'"

There are legends, started quite early in the church, that Mary Magdalene had formerly been a prostitute, however, none of the Four Canonized Gospels make such a reference. However, there is no doubt that she was among the very most intimate friends and companions of Jesus. She was at the foot of the cross and watched him suffer and die, and Matthew stated that on that first Easter morning: "Mary Magdalene and the other Mary went to see the sepulchre." Whether the "other" Mary was Jesus' mother or his sister, she was surely put secondary to Mary Magdalene, and simply referred to as the "other" Mary. Again in Luke of those who mentioned the resurrection to the disciples, Mary Magdalene is mentioned first, before a Joanna and Jesus' mother. Also in Gospel of John it is Mary Magdalene who was the first to see the resurrected Jesus and firmly embraced him. However, Jesus was to move on, and asked her to release him: "You must cease holding me, for I have not yet ascended to the Father; but go to my brethren and say tell them that I am ascending to my Father and your Father, to my God and your God" (J 20:16-17). Mary Magdalene then went to the disciples and told her story. She probably was the first human to proclaim the resurrection. Perhaps "companion" meant much more than the church has ever admitted.

One thing I should like to point out in the above quotation from John's Gospel, Jesus' words to Mary: "go to my brothers and say to them". Just think about it. The last time Jesus saw his "brethren", that is, his disciples, was from the cross, and the last acts of them that he would remember were that one betrayed him, one who was appointed to led the others denied him, and the others fled the scene, and left it to Joseph of Armathea to bury him. Cowardly and disgracefully they disowned his friendship. But the first thing that Jesus did was to refer to them as his brothers. That was grace and love beyond the power of most of us. Jesus' power to love and forgive was absolutely divine, and he had told his disciples that "as I have loved you, you shall love one another." If one can make that kind of love incarnate in his own life, he will have no problem being surrounded by deeply grateful friends. To see God's love for humanity in Jesus is not a very difficult task. A friendship filled with love is indeed the flower of humanity, and it blossomed to its greatest beauty in the life of Jesus.

II. CONCURRENT TEACHINGS OF OTHER SAGES

One might ask himself upfront, "Who hasn't written about love and friendship?" My purpose here, of course, can not be a comprehensive elucidation of all that has been written on the topic, but rather to present some thoughts from throughout the entire world and throughout all the ages of man about love and friendship. It does occupy much literature simply because it is within the hearts of the universal being to experience them, to have them, and to live within them. Life without love and friendship is a life among the weeds and ugliness, for love and friendship are the flowers and beauty of the human experience. It is the man or woman who is good that can be a friend to another, and upon goodness only can such love and friendship be planted and nourished. The first four chapters stressed the birth and growth of the individual into goodness, so that he now can share it with others.

Plato said, like the rest of humanity, so very much about love and friendship, and most certainly it was a reality among his 22 students at the Academy. The love of his students for him was so great that they and the following generations of Platonists referred to him as the "Divine Plato", and Aristotle said that only the truly good were worthy to praise him. In Plato's Symposium, which is a long and lovely dialogue on the essence of love, he said many things which have been admired and followed throughout human history.

"For the principle which ought to be the guide of men who would live nobly--that principle, I say, neither kindred, nor honour, nor wealth, nor any other motive is able to implant so well as love"(178c-d).

"Love will make men dare to die for their beloved--love alone; and women as well as men. Of this, Alcestis, the daughter of Pelias, is a monument to all Hellas; for she was willing to lay down her life on behalf of her husband, when no one else would...and so noble did this action of hers appear to the gods, as well as to men, that among the many who have done virtuously she is one of the very few..."(179b-c).

"Evil is the vulgar lover who loves the body rather than the soul, inasmuch as he is not even stable, because he loves a thing [the beauty of the body] which in itself is only temporary, and therefore when the bloom of youth which he was desiring is over, he takes wing and flies away, in spite of all his words and promises: whereas the love of the noble disposition is life-long, for it becomes one with the everlasting [the soul of the other person].(183e)

In speaking of the love of the Beautiful, i.e. God who is the Essence of love, Plato declared:

"...from the love of the beautiful, has sprung every good in heaven and earth. Therefore, Phaedrus, I say of Love that He is the fairest and best in himself, and the cause of what is fairest and best in all other things." (197c)

Plato emphasized that only the good and those whose goodness functions can be a friend.

"And therefore, my boy, if you are wise, all men will be your friends and kindred, for you will be useful and good; but if you are not wise, neither father, nor mother, nor kindred, nor any one else, will be your friends" (Lysis 210c).

Simply put, a person who is not wise as to who he is, is not good at heart, and is useless in all matters, can not be a friend to another. This is why the first four steps all led the reader through those very topics before it was possible to have him step into either a friendship or a society and to "find" happiness. For if one is not good, not wise, and not happy, he can hang around a different group every night and travel to every "corner" of the world and will not find happiness. No one else can make him happy. That also is why playing the victim and avoiding personal introspection makes it impossible ever to be good and experience friendship. Plato continued his dialogue on friendship, Lysis, by stating that friendship, the loving harmony of two good people, is an end in itself. For if one used "friendship" for the purpose of gaining something else beside the friendship itself, then there is no friendship, for it can never be used as a means to another thing.

Aristotle, Plato's student for 20 years, reflected much of Plato in his teachings on friendship. He stated: "For without friends no one would choose to live, though he had all other goods" (Nicomachean Ethics 1155a 5). "...with friends men are more able both to think and to act" (NE 1155a 16). "Perfect friendship is the friendship of men who are good, and alike in virtue; for these wish well alike to each other *qua* good, and they are good in themselves" (NE 1156b 6-10).

Euripides in his work Electra tells of the friendship that never wavers when those who are involved are good. "Ah! Pylades, I put thee first amongst men for thy love, thy loyalty and fiendliness to me, for thou alone of my friends wouldst still honor poor Orestes, in spite of the grievous plight whereto I am reduced." (Electra 166-170).

A Mahayana Buddhist text reads:

> Friendliness means to have hopes for the welfare of others, to long for it, to crave for it, to delight in it. It is affection unsullied by motives of sense-desire, passion, or hope of a return.8.1

Here again one can see that friendship seeks nothing except the friendship itself, except the welfare of the friend. Nothing more is desired by the lover of the friend. This is loving another as one loves oneself. Envy or jealousy or any such emotion can not exist between true friends.

A Sanskrit poem speaks of the growth of friendship through the years:

Slender at first, they quickly gather force,
Growing in richness as they run their course;
Once started, they do not turn back again:
Rivers, and years, and friendships with good men. 8.2

Cicero, in his essay Laelius: On Friendship, which is truly one of the great essays on the subject, stated:

"...at the same time I lay it down as a fundamental axiom, that true friendship can only subsist between those who are animated by the strictest principles of honor and virtue...

"When friendship therefore is contracted between men, who possess a degree of virtue not inferior to that which adorned those approved personages I have just named, it is productive of unspeakable advantages. 'Life would be utterly lifeless,' as old Ennius expresses it, without a friend on whose kindness and fidelity one might confidently repose."

III.   TWO MORE ESSENTIAL ELEMENTS OF FRIENDSHIP

A.   FRIENDSHIP AS AN ACTUALIZATION OF LOVE AND CARE

Probably in no other situation is love and care more activated than in a friendship, for each knows that if something would happen to diminish or kill the other person, he himself would be diminished or partly die. It is therefore, natural that friends act with loving care to aid each other that they would both have good health, financial security, high morals, and a deep spiritual life. In the Ancient Greek battle formation, the phalanz, which was a marching and striking order, with close ranks and files, with shields and spears overlapping, that is, partly covering the soldier next to one's left. For the spears were held by the right hand, and therefore, the right side of the soldier was less protected than the left side for he carried his shield on the left. The problems occurred when individuals would instead of walking straight ahead would start walking to their left, directly behind their shield, but this caused an opening in the line and created a weak spot in the line of attack or defense. To correct this, the soldier to the right would have to give up a little of his protection to shield the vulnerable spot for the soldier to his left. Therefore, the leaders of the phalanz encouraged friends to fight next to each other, because he knew that friends would make that sacrifice for each other, and that in turn, would keep them all marching straight on. The phalanz under Alexander the Great was nearly indestructible, for friendship was a most highly honored virtue among those Greeks.

The most beautiful thing about being good is that it makes the person himself happy, and, of course, of secondary, but of great value also, is that it helps the other to confirm the joy of the friendship shared between them. For without caring, a man greatly diminishes himself. In a simple, lovely, and delightful poem, Lao Tzu said it so very well:

All the world says that, while my Tao is great,
It yet appears to be inferior [not a fully developed system].
Now it is just its greatness that makes it seem to be "inferior".
But if it were like any other system,
Then it would be small in influence.
I have three precious things which I prize and hold fast.
The first is gentleness;
The second is economy;
And the third is shrinking from taking precedence before others.
With that gentleness I can be bold;
With that economy I can be liberal;
Shrinking from taking precedence of others,
I can become a vessel of highest honour.
Now-a-days they give up gentleness
And are all for being bold;
They give up economy,
And try to be liberal;
They give up the lower place,
And seek only to be foremost.(67).

Cicero pointed out the fact that a false friendship is quickly exposed when the one runs into serious difficulties through loss of stature, fame, or money, and the other one leaves and seeks another "friend", rather than "stepping down and joining him in his trouble." Few indeed, are such friends. Then Cicero referred to Ennius' statement that "...it is in the hour of adversity that friendship must principally prove her truth and strength". Cicero continued:

In short, the deserting of a friend in his distress, and the neglecting of him in one's own prosperity, are the two tests which discover the weakness and instability of most connexions of this nature. To preserve, therefore, in those seasons of probation an immovable and unshaken fidelity, is a virtue so exceedingly rare, that I almost called it more than human (Laelius: An Essay on Friendship).

If one says he has no friends, then let him listen to a very succinct statement by <u>Kant</u>: "If men complain of the lack of friendship, it comes about, because they themselves have a mind-sent and heart that are not friendly to others." Kant goes on to say that similarities in morals, intellect, and basic understandings about life also play a factor in making friendships. But an innate ethical goodness is always required to be a friend.

> They must have similar principles and a similar understanding of morality itself, so that they can completely understand each other. ...then they can have a unified and correct thinking of goodness and each other. By right thinking, openheartedness, trustworthiness, by means of a conduct that is free from evil and falsehood, but with cheerfulness, loving kindness, a happy spirit, by these friendship is formed.(<u>Vorlesungen ueber Moralphilosophie:</u> <u>Moralphilosophie Collins--Ethica, Von der Freundshaft, 498</u>).

B. LOVE AND FORGIVENESS BIND FRIENDSHIPS

There are no perfect people, and sometimes a beloved friend disappoints a person either in act or attitude, and there is a natural hardening of the gentle feelings between them. Love however is not simply a weak feeling, it is a committed force that drives people towards a mutual goodness in which the care, mentioned above, is possible. True love does not exist if it can not forgive certain acts, and only the individuals involved can make the separation between what is forgivable and what is not. Jesus himself made no personal limits. Likewise, the guilty one, to show his love, must make some kind of penance or satisfaction to show that his goodness upon which the relationship is based is still intact. In the previous chapter, after the Resurrection, when Jesus still called his disciples his "brothers", despite their spineless forsaking of him, and reaccepted them, the love was so powerful that they never failed to recognize him again, and legend has it that most of them even died rather to deny their faith in him. Forgiveness can be so overwhelmingly powerful that love is miraculously enhanced and the relationship made stronger. Goodness can constantly recreate itself on a higher and higher level, and loving forgiveness often is the force that makes it and the friendship born of it greater.

    Theognis knew that Zeus, in order to keep his relationship with men alive, had to be the one who did the forgiving, because men are not perfect.

"If Zeus took mortal actions seriously,
Since he knows the inward thoughts of every man
And all the deeds of just and unjust men
It would be devastating for mankind."(Elegies 897-900. tr.D.Wender).

Every religion that believes in a personal and loving God, teaches, for it must, that the relationship depends upon the mercy of God to forgive. It is always grace and nothing else that can ease the pain of guilt and give a rebirth to one who has fallen away from the path that leads to goodness and to God. A God who cannot be called "Merciful" will not be worshipped. Every loving relationship depends upon mercy and forgiveness at one time or other of the relationship.

Even a loose and axe wielding Viking can be redeemed, and such is recorded in the Saga of Hrafnkel. Early in the Saga, Hrafnkel's accuser stated the obvious truth: "It's nothing new that Hrafnkel's killing men," said Sam,"He's always been free with his axe." Later in the Saga it is stated: "Hrafnkel was a changed man now, and much better liked than he used to be. He could still be as helpful and generous as before, but he'd become gentler and quieter in every way." In another Icelandic Saga, Ale Hood, a reconciliation took place: repentance and satisfaction and a true desire for friendship were all present.

> Next day Broddi walked over to Thorkel Geitisson's booth, went in and spoke to Thorkel, who was in a bad mood and made no reply. Broddi said, 'The reason I've come to see you, kinsman, is that I realize how ill-chosen my words to you were. Please, blame that on the silliness of my age, and don't let our kinship suffer because of it. Here's an ornamented sword I want to give you, and I'd like you to accept an invitation to come and visit me in the summer. I promise you I've no treasures in my hands finer than the ones I'm proposing to give you.'

Thorkel accepted this gladly and said he would very much like them to observe their kinship properly. Then Broddi went back to his booth.

Another Viking poem called "Sayings of the High One" speaks much of the need, value, courtesies and substance of friendship. Some of the statements are as the following:

"Don't stay forever   when you visit friends,
   know when it's time to leave;
Love turns to loathing   if you sit too long
   On someone else's bench.
.....
A man should be faithful   to a friend
   and to the friends of a friend;
It is unwise to   offer friendship
   to a foe's friend.
.....
Always as a young man   I traveled alone,
   and I would lose my way;
I felt I was rich   if I made a friend --
   no man by himself is happy.
.....
Always be faithful,   never be the first
   to fail a friendship;
.....
True bonds are formed   where men keep faith
   and don't hide their hearts.
Anything is better   than a breach of friendship --
   a real friend will say   what you'd rather not hear.8.3

IV. FRIENDSHIP EXTENDED

In the preceding sections of this chapter, friendship in its basis, essence and benefits has been presented, and in this section it will discussed in its specific forms: friendship between two individuals, within a family, and within various groups of like-minded people. All of which can be tremendously rewarding to those who are morally and lovingly bound to others in friendship.

A.   FRIENDSHIP BETWEEN INDIVIDUALS

Robert Graves in his book Goodbye to All That, described his participation in the British army in World War One and his friendship with Siegfried Sassoon who also fought with him on the British side. However, the fact that Graves himself was of German Lutheran extraction, that his favorite uncle was Uncle Siegfried, that his relatives continued to write to their German relatives in Germany during the hostilities, made life as an Englishman unbearable. When he went to Charterhouse School he was listed as Robert von Ranke Graves, so that all the other schoolmates would know about his German connections, this instead of his usual Robert R. Graves. And as the war went on, and his fellow British soldiers were saying that only dead Germans are good Germans, and when his friend fighting with him in the British army risked his life to save some allies (he was shot through the throat but stayed at his position until he collapsed), and was recommended for a "Victoria Cross" of honor, and the recommendation was refused by a higher command because his first name, Siegfried, was a German name, Graves stood by his friend, but began doubting his government. He went to Egypt after the war and sympathized with the Egyptians who were occupied by the British, and that was about it for him. He left England as a young man and never returned to live there again. He said, "Goodbye to All That". Frankly, friendship and loved ones are closer to our hearts than the government by which we are ruled, because friendship between good people is the flower of human life. It excels every other human relationship.

There is also the well known story of Jesse Owens and Hans Lutz a fellow Olympian at the 1936 Olympic Games held in Berlin while Hitler was the Chancellor of Germany. They both were broad-jumpers, and Owens was probably quite nervous -- considering the circumstances. He was the best broad jumper there, but had faulted his first two qualifying jumps and had only one jump left. Lutz went to him, calmed him down, encouraged him by telling that he can easily qualify even if he jumps from a foot behind the jumping mark. Owens jumped as Lutz had recommended on his last chance to qualify and did easily qualify, as Lutz had told him he would. Owens went on to win the broad jump, but more important, he and Lutz, who finished second, formed a friendship that lasted until Lutz was killed in WWII. An American Black athlete, who was segregated and could not even vote in many states in America and a German athlete who did not buy into the Nazi propaganda of the super-race, before the world at the Berlin Games, made a true and lasting friendship ended only by death. Such a friendship is indeed priceless.

Other wonderful friendships were Basil and Libanius, Luther and Melanchthon, F. Schleiermacher and F. Schlegel, Socrates and Plato, Aristotle and Theophrastus, Ruth and Naomi (legendary), Siddhartha and Ananda (legendary), Enkidu and Gilgamesh (mythical), Achilles and Patroclus (legendary), Alexander and Apelles and, of course, many others. Alexander the mighty warrior was not "camera shy", and his favorite painter was Apelles, and when Alexander asked him to paint a portrait of his most beautiful concubine, Pancaste, undraped, Apelles consented. Apelles however while he was engaged in the process, and getting to know her, became very much enamored with her. Alexander noticed this and saw that the attraction was not unappreciated by Pancaste, released her to him, and thus Alexander, known well for his military victories, showed even a greater spirit in self-command and generosity. Dietrich Bonhoeffer wrote a book called "Life Together" on the eve of World War II, and he wrote it to encourage the "Confessing Church" to stand together against Hilter, and not let fear break their resolve. He knew that each one had to have a friend close at hand that they might mutually encourage each other. "...the Christian needs another Christian...He needs him again and again when he becomes uncertain and discouraged, for by himself he cannot help himself without belying the truth...He needs his brother."8.4 Especially in times like those is it important to have another good person who is deeply concerned about your care and welfare, both physically and spiritually. Helen Keller, a truly remarkable woman, who at the age of 19 months, because of an unknown disease, became totally blind and deaf, yet went on to be a great lecturer and helper of the handicapped, and paid her own bills during her lifetime. She spoke this way of her personal friendships:

My life is a chronicle of friendship. My friends -- all those about
me -- create my world anew each day. Without their loving care
all the courage I could summon would not suffice to keep my heart

strong for life. But, like Robert Louis Stevenson, I know it is better to do things than to imagine them.8.5

To have a friend is light to the blind,
a symphony to the deaf,
an atomic power to the weak,
an angel of courage to those in fear,
and a warm embrace to the rejected.
Within it all personalities become flowers in fresh blossom,
giving off a fragrance of joy and love.
It is the most precious of all human interactions(JDE).

B.   FRIENDSHIP IN MARRIAGE, AND FAMILY, AND AN INNER-GROUP

This section is by far the most difficult of all friendships because some of the rules stated above to qualify a person for friendship, such as basic goodness, similar views, and, at least to a degree, a form of equality are not automatic within marriage and family. Also, the Church has debated the quality of such friendships, but usually, at least historically, put its beauty and virtue below that of abstinence for men, like clergy and monks, and for women, virginity ranked higher than marriage. The reason for this is that the Church has had a very narrow and slanted attitude about man's sexual function. Sexual function of any degree of pleasure was seen as a participation in sin, even within marriage and even for the sole purpose of having children. This distorted view must be looked at in more depth to see the sadness of the Church teachings which have caused untold damage to man's third most powerful physical drive; only hunger and sleep are more naturally imperative to the human, and most any animal, than sex and procreation. Added to this confusion among the teachers of the Church has been the hypocrisy of its leaders at the very highest level, who easily exercised their natural sexual desires, while, at the same time, declared such to be sinful for the lower clergy and the laymen. In Chapter Two I made some reference to this contemptible teaching and hypocrisy of the Church, but unfortunately there are many more instances of the anti-natural teachings that, in themselves alone, caused many of the so-called "heretical" movements away from the Church throughout history, and, unfortunately some of them were even more extreme. Tertullian, in seeking absolute sexual virtue, ended up first a Montantist, and then also an extreme Gnostic group (known as Encratites) that considered everything material as evil, even being alive in the flesh as a participation of the cosmic evil that plagues the souls of men. In this move, he followed Tatian. One wonders about the sincerity of the Church in Italy where throughout the Middle Ages divorce was forbidden, but female prostitution was not. To show how absolutely evil the Church's teachings were and how confused the "degree of guilt" was for the priests in determining penance and satisfaction, manuals were actually written for that purpose. One manual included 16 levels or degrees of guilt corresponding to the various sexual sins in each category. This manual ranged from "sensual kisses" (the "French kiss" was always a sin) to having sex with animals (which was evidently the worst kind for the author of this particular manual). To me bestiality would be a lesser sin than having sex with another man's wife secretly and against the man's will. But the Church thought this way: whenever the release of sperm takes place it must be planted where it can give birth. So if a man destroys another person's marriage or even rapes some one, he is less guilty than utilizing his favorite ewe. That is why, in this very manual, it is a lesser sin to rape one's daughter than to masturbate, for at least the sperm has a chance to impregnate and grow and give life in an act of incestuous rape.8.6 Yet, even in the Early 20th Century in England, young unmarried women who gave birth were excluded from society by imprisonment, sometimes for the rest of their lives. Even in procreation sin must be punished. Even if a man had intercourse with his willing and married wife, and if he was so "defiled" that he enjoyed it, he was guilty of sin. Francis Bacon, in rebelling against the authority of Aristotle in all the scientific studies, stated that man needed a new way of thinking, a New Organon, A New Instrument of the inductive method by which man can reclassify and reorder scientific knowledge (one of the most obvious was to rid oneself of Aristotle's geocentric system for the revived solar system first presented by Aristarchus and his followers even before Jesus, and to listen to Copernicus who had revived the idea). For as surely as the Papacy was guilty of condemning people for believing the reality of the solar system and condemned Galileo, Bacon's contemporary, we and the entire Western Church and Eastern Church (Catholics, Protestants, & Orthodox) need at this time in history a Novum Organum (Latin) to rethink and revaluate the entire matter of sex and the form of marriage. Some passages of Jesus here will be discussed in view of the Jewish background and the age in which he lived. Mark who was the earliest extant written Gospel will be presented first, then the two by Matthew, and finally the one by Luke. Those differences from Mark's words will be underlined to show that the writers of the Gospels are not quite on agreement on what Jesus actually said, and Matthew itself has two different statements. The Pharisees who brought the question to Jesus, had a tendency to test his knowledge, and to do so with such an unsettled doctrine was a direct challenge to him, even more so because they probably suspected he would disagree with the sacred Law of Moses which would be their position.

"The Pharisees approached Jesus for the purpose of testing him, and asked, 'Is it in keeping with the law for a man to divorce his wife?' Jesus answered, 'What command did Moses give?' They replied, 'Moses permitted a man to release himself from his wife, by writing a certificate of divorce.' To them Jesus said, 'Because of man's hard heartedness, he gave such a commandment. But from the very beginning at the time of creation, God made them male and female as a unit, and that is why a man departs from the house of his father and mother, and joins together with his wife, forming a new unity. The two become one in the flesh. What then God put together, let man not put apart.' Later when they were in the house, the disciples asked again the same question. He answered, 'Whoever dismisses his wife and marries another commits adultery against her; and if the wife dismisses her husband and marries another, then she commits adultery.'(Mk 10:1-10)

"And it was said, 'Whoever releases his wife, let him give her a bill of release.' But I say to you, whoever releases his wife, apart from her having unlawful sex (PORNEIAS), makes her commit adultery; and whoever marries a released woman commits adultery'". (Mt 5:31-32).

In Mt 19:3-10 the same thought as in Mt 5 is repeated, but this is added: "The disciples said to him (Jesus), 'If such is the case of man and wife, there is no gain in being married.' But he said to them,'Not all have the capacity to fulfill this declaration, but only those to whom such capacity is given...to the one who has been enabled to receive this saying, let him receive it.'"

"Everyone who releases his wife and marries another commits adultery, and everyone who marries a woman released by her husband, commits adultery." (Lk 16:18).

Mark and Luke give no justification at all for a divorce, and both emphatically reject the idea that a man can do such and then marry another without committing adultery. They also firmly declare that a man, whether previously married or not, who marries a divorced woman is also guilty of adultery. Both of them imply that once a marriage takes place, the two are married forever: neither being able to marry another, and a single man who marries a once married person is still committing adultery against her previous husband. These are ultimate statements, and are uncompromising. Matthew, however, adds two thoughts to the subject: one that enables a man to divorce his wife if she has sexually broken the law against him with another man; and, two, a most interesting insight into human nature, is the thought that such a marriage, or maybe even marriage in general, is not beneficial for most men, for the precept is beyond the average man's capacity. This is particularly interesting inasmuch as neither the Hebrew Canon (Tanak: Law, Prophets, and Sacred Writings) nor in the New Testament Greek Scriptures is prostitution forbidden -- PORNEIA is not to be used for that inasmuch as it means committing a sexually unlawful act, and prostitution of an unmarried person was not legally forbidden in the Hebrew Canon: however, it is well to remember that a promised (i.e. engaged) woman or a virgin living at her father's house was not considered unmarried. She was, in the case of the engaged already "claimed" by the future husband, and the virgin at the father's house was still his "property" and sexual activity with her would be considered an act of against her father (and he would thereby be deprived of an offered dowry and here at least some financial considerations or compensation could keep the man from receiving a more severe penalty for his sexual sin). I would like here to present a couple of quotations, and the reader will find more references in the notes, as this is an often touchy subject. From the Encyclopaedia Judaica:

The extramarital intercourse of a married man is not per se a crime in biblical or later Jewish law. This distinction stems from the economic aspect of possession, and adultery constituted a violation of the husband's exclusive right to her; the wife being the husband's possession, had no such right to him.8.7

Johann J. Stamm concurred:

The man can only commit adultery against a marriage other than his own, the woman only against her own...Intercourse of a man outside the marriage with unmarried and unbetrothed women gives no offence (Gen. 38 & Jud.16), and the seduction of an unbetrothed daughter of a family is an offense against property (Ex. 22:15f).8.8

And Elliot Binns added:

The Israelite Law worked very unfairly against the woman in regard to sexual offenses; since she was regarded merely as the property of the husband he had rights against her, but she had none against him; a man, for example, could not commit adultery against his wife, but only against another man.8.9

In Genesis 38 it is also well to note that Judah sought out a harlot, which was acceptable, but was misled by Tamar who had disguised herself as a harlot. Judah's sin was that he never permitted Tamar to bear a son for her deceased husband by means of another son of Judah, which was prescribed by law. She then, in order to have such a blood related son, played the harlot when she knew her father-in-law, Judah, who, after his wife had died, was seeking out a harlot to be comforted. Likewise in the story of Judges 16 Samson started a relationship with the harlot Delilah, and for this there was no condemnation. Prostitution, seeing a harlot, and any other sex outside marriage were not unlawful and therefore not considered sinful, as long as a man did not violate another man's wife or an engaged woman, or a virgin living under her father's roof and care. A man could also easily get a divorce from his wife, but not the other way around. A man's divorcing a woman could put her into great survival difficulties, as she seldom owned anything (she was actually property herself), and if her parents were dead or poverty stricken, she had to beg, live off of the "Peah" tax (3% of a man's harvest must be left unharvested for the poor to glean: this was what Ruth was doing when she was fortunate enough to meet Boaz), or perhaps become a concubine or a harlot. It was against this historical background that Jesus rebelled, for its unfairness was repulsive to him. The unfairness was reemphasized when a double standard of punishment was actually brought before him. A woman was caught in the act of adultery, thrown before him, and was about to be stoned. 'She was caught in the act of adultery', well, then where was the man? If she sinned against her husband, so did the man for having sexual intercourse with another man's wife. Yet, only she was brought forth for condemnation. Jesus wrote some notes in the sand and told the men who had brought her forth that the one who himself had not committed sin (probably meaning "this sin") could cast the first stone. None did. Those notes in the sand must have been quite revealing. It is now more understandable why Jesus was so much against divorce, and exactly what he said we do not know. Although Mark and Luke agree, most Biblical scholars would say that Luke simply copied Mark, as he did use him for his own outline. I agree with that. Now suddenly those "two witnesses" become just one, Mark. Matthew's notes and the final redactor of the Gospel of Matthew used two sayings: one with the PORNEIA exception and the other stating that not all men are capable of living an entire life without a divorce, even if he was not by Jewish law sexually confined to his wife. Jesus set forth an ideal, as he saw it in the beginning of mankind, and it is most probable that he did compromise because of either a sexual act against the husband or because some men could not receive his teaching in its fulness. In the Gospel of Matthew there is another unexpected curiosity: the genealogy of Jesus back to Abraham. In this genealogy from Abraham to Joseph, there are only four women mentioned: Tamar who had played the harlot to have sexual intercourse with her father-in-law; Rahab (wife of Salmon) accepted by the early church fathers to be Rahab the Harlot (only two other mentions of a "Rahab" occur in the New Testament and both are of Rahab the Harlot, who was also a Canaanite (Heb. 11:31, Jas. 2:25)); Ruth, a widow, who tried to seduce Boaz; and the wife of Uriah, the Hittite (Bathsheba) who was forced into adultery by David, who, after he had Uriah sacrificed on the battlefield, carried out his evil plans by marrying Bathsheba. So the author of Matthew presents only four females in Jesus' genealogy: a woman who played the harlot to participate in incest, a Canaanite prostitute, a sexually aggressive widow, and an unfortunate woman of an Hittite soldier forced into adultery. In this Matthew was being very honest -- that's the way it was, folks.

Unfortunately the church learned little from Jesus in relation to the fairness that should be shown between men and women -- he always stressed that justice was far better than man's traditions and the various sacrifices they presented. Justice! legal and interpersonal fairness was one of the stronger elements of Jesus' teachings, and this included relations between male and female. As mentioned above, he certainly had love and special feelings for Mary and Martha, and likewise a special relationship with Mary Magdalene. But eventually the Church followed not Plato and Jesus, but Aristotle (who taught that a woman was an incomplete male, physically and mentally), and in following Aristotle even defiled him. Whereas Aristotle taught men to have special care for women during menstruation, the Church classified her as an untouchable who was not permitted to take the sacrament during the time of menstruation 'less she defile the altar area', and in the Eastern Church she was not even permitted in church during her time of "defilement". Everything related to sex, even childbirth, was defiled by the sexual act itself. Just to use one of Carolly Erickson's many poignant passages to show the sad way in which sex and women were treated during the Middle Ages:

> As she neared her full term a pregnant woman was encouraged to
> take communion, both because the likelihood of death was high
> and because from the onset of labor until her churching [that is,
> rechurching after the forty or eighty days after the childbirth, in
> which time she was defiled], passed, she would bear the double
> stigma of unclean blood and the "filth of sin" (sordes peccati) with-
> out the consolations of the church. (The filth or "bodily uncleanness"
> -- immunditia corporis -- was the sinful residue of the lust of con-
> ception) 8.10

When one adds that if there were difficulties during childbirth, the value of the child was greater than that of the mother, and if one were to be sacrificed, it would have to be the mother. Think of that! The woman is considered in a state of defilement, caused by her sexual lust by which act she became pregnant, was excluded by virtue of her uncleanness of entering the church for the sacrament, and in this "filth of sin" she faced death. This unbelievably sordid attitude was so different than that of Jesus, that one often wonders if the Medieval Church ever heard of Him. The Historical Christian Church, both East and West, Protestant, Catholic, and Orthodox must find a new instrument, a Novum Organum, upon which to build the healthy and happy life of wholeness which Jesus envisioned for his followers as the "life more abundant". Now it is possible to go on and discuss real love and friendship within marriage and family and an inner circle, and time to leave behind much of the past, but not that of our great teachers.

There have been numerous forms of marriage through out the history of mankind, all of which had varying degrees of love and friendship. This is to be considered right at the outset because today when one thinks of marriage, he generally thinks of a monogamous and sexually exclusive legalized marriage. But it is probably only one of twenty some different forms that humanity has tried and experienced, some not so successful, but in most there were less divorces than there is today in an average American marriage. Most of us are aware of the Mormon experiment (condemned by American law), and the Islamic law that prescribes no more than four wives for the believer; lately, the world has been introduced to Osamah Bin Laden's father who had 20 wives and 50 children. So there still exists various forms in the world today, despite government regulations and strict laws of punishment against those not conforming to the laws of a particular state or religion. Looking at the Hebrew Scriptures one can designate seven different forms of marriage that were practiced within the early Hebrew community: matriarchal marriage, patriarchal marriage, polygamy, monogamy, exogamy, endogamy, and the Levirate marriage. And if one adds to those the variations of including concubines, maids, and slaves, one can see a very far different world than our own in the very Hebrew Scriptures of what is unfortunately called by Christians the Old Testament, which is still part of the Judeo-Christian Bible. Five of the focal figures in Ancient Israel: Abraham, Jacob, Moses, David, and Solomon were polygamous. Abraham had a wife, Sarah, and she had an Egyptian maid, and Abraham bore children by both of them. After Sarah died, Abraham took Keturah to be his wife and she bore him six male children (only males were counted). Abraham also had concubines, but their number and names are not mentioned. So he certainly had an extended family. Jacob had two wives Leah and Rachel, and showed favoritism towards Rachel, but Leah was more fertile, so Rachel asked Jacob to plant the seed of life in her maid Bildah, and Leah, not to be equaled, gave her maid Zilpah also to Jacob for child bearing. Twelve boys, and one girl, Dinah (we know of her only because she was a point of contention that led to the slaughter of Hamor's family by the sons of Jacob). Moses was known to have married Jethro's daughter, Zipporah, and the Cushite woman. David seemed much more desirous of women than his predecessors. He seemed to have women everywhere: Michal, Abigail, Ahin'oam, Ma'acah, Haggith, Abital, Eglah, and let 2 Sam. 5:13 suffice for the rest: "And David took more concubines and wives from Jerusalem, after he came from Hebron." Yet, in his lust he committed adultery with Bathsheba and had her husband murdered. And, finally, Solomon who "had seven hundred wives, princesses, and three hundred concubines" (I Kings 11:3), although the writer of Chronicles felt this was not one of his 'wiser' moves. However, it was admitted that there was friction within most of those marriages. Yet, in neither the Hebrew Scriptures nor the Greek Christian Scriptures is polygamy forbidden. Although monogamy is not mentioned in the New Testament, but existed at least in actual practice for the average person (but certainly not for Herod the Great who had 10 wives, and 8 of their names are known). Yet, even with the knowledge of Herod's polygamy, Jesus no where condemns it as such.

In Ancient India polygamy was common, at least among the more wealthy, and for the poor man who had a sterile wife, he was encouraged to marry another woman, but rather than divorce the first wife, he kept her also. If the new wife bore a child, then she became the preferred wife. The famous verse in Kalidasa's Shakuntala gave this advice to a newly married woman:

Obey your elders; and be very kind to rivals;
Never be perversely blind and angry with your husband,
Even though he should prove less faithful than a man might be;
Be as courteous to servants as you may,
Not puffed with pride in this your happy day;
Thus does a maiden grow into a wife;
But self-willed women are the curse of life.8.11

The young maiden, probably between 10 and 13 years of age, was to grow into being a wife by not being jealous of her rivals, that is, her husbands other wives, and she was to be obedient to him always and not to have a mind of her own. One can understand this advise to a preteen bride, but for modern woman, both the age of the bride and the advice are a bit too much to stomach. The only point I mean to make is that marriage has taken on many forms in the past: even polyandry such as practiced by the Toda tribe of the Himalayas, and that we must rethink our present situation. Throughout this work I have been strongly critical of the Christian Church through the ages in the way that sex, women, and marriage have been dictated. Yet, sadly enough, things for young women in some other countries, non-Christian, have been even worse. In India, women in general have been greatly depreciated, and polygamy has not helped their cause. Added to this is the history of marrying child brides. A study done in 1927 by Katherine Mayo provided these disheartening facts: one tenth of all girls between the ages of 5 and 10 were married in 1921, and 40% were married between the ages of 10 and 15 for the same year. One half of all the young women in India were married by the age of 15. And many suffered not only from lack of care, because of polygamy, but also brutal abuse. The medical records of 1891 showed such things as a 9 year old girl, the day after her marriage admitted to the hospital because her left femur was dislocated, her pelvis crushed out of shape, and her outer flesh virtually shredded. Case after case showed the abuse these child brides suffered, one, a 7 year old died in great agony after three days of marriage.8.12 Additionally, by Hindu custom, although forbidden today, was the practice of suttee, when the devout Indian wife was expected to throw her body on the funeral pyre of her deceased husband. When one considers the youthful age of some of these women, it was, without much thought at all, an evil custom. Even today life in India for a woman, at least among the commoners, is difficult.

In the ancient Inca society man and woman were pushed into marriage by the time the man was twenty, and if they could not find a mate that was to their liking, the marriage was arranged for them. The commoner was basically monogamous, because of economic conditions. But the upper classes were all polygamous, and the Incas often had a great array of wives and concubines, as many as 700. If this were not so self-serving for the Inca man in itself, the brutality of the system was shown at the time of the Inca's death, for all of his wives were forced to follow him into the next world. This was similar to ancient Egypt, and was even much worse than Indian Suttee simply because the number of wives involved. The Inca's widows were first made drunk, they danced, and then they were strangled, and then buried with their "beloved Inca lord".8.13 In such cultures, it seems to me, that it was only the poorer classes where man and woman shared some type of mutual need and affection, and there perhaps it was possible, if not for love and friendship between them, at least a sense of common respect for each other. These societies and their failures ought to serve today as teachers to us about what man can be at his worst. They may also be a reminder of the fact that Judeo-Christian and Greco-Roman cultures, despite all of their inexcusable faults, were not the worst when it came to loving one's wife and family. Likewise, while strict monogamy presents us with bitter divorces, murder-suicides, one parent families -- all deplorable in themselves, yet culture has developed some great loving and thoughtful husbands and teachers for us, at least as a stepping stone to something that can be better and offer to more people a greater participation of a sexual, loving, binding of friendship between the sexes. The greatest good for the greatest amount of people is to be sought, and the binding concepts of the past, whether based on religion or not, if they are a hindrance should at least be removed as the only legal way that man and woman can live together. There are so many options, that it is a crime against humanity for both the church and the state to permit mankind only one form of marriage or inner-circle type of family involving sexual relations. Here I want to quote Bertrand Russell's remarks in 1929 in his "Marriage and Morals". He is very much in disagreement with the imposed morality of the English Government and the English Church at what it was doing against the right of humans to have a full and abundant life. His feelings were expressed in the statement that follows:

"In this connection there is one respect in which our existing moral code might be altered with advantage. There are in England some two million more women than men [the WWI losses and the cost of the English Navy to" Rule the World"], and these are condemned by law and custom to remain childless, which is undoubtedly to many of them a great deprivation. If custom tolerated the unmarried mother, and made her economic situation tolerable, it cannot be doubted that a great many of the women at present condemned to celibacy would have children. Strict monogamy is based upon the assumption that the numbers of the sexes will be approximately equal. Where this is not the case, it involves considerable cruelty to those whom arithmetic compels to remain single."p.170.

It would be well to remember that unmarried women who had children at this time in England were put into a women's prison, often for life. But it is not only the lack of opportunity for such women to have had children, they could not even engage in any type of intimacy, not even a lesbian affair, in which another's marriage was not effected in any way, for it also was not approved. This vicious stranglehold legally enforced upon Western Society by both Church and State cannot in any way be called moral, much less kind or loving. Human society is always changing, and, if the correct teachers are followed, the change can be ever upward to a more loving and humane "pursuit of happiness" which some states proclaim, falsely of course, is the right of their citizens.

In the Viking myths of the Valkyries, the extraordinary women warriors of Viking folklore, marriage was tolerated for only seven years by these women, and then they went off to become what they were, warriors. This was concept of temporal marriage for a certain time in life when it was profitable. Plato in his Republic which he called the best possible city recommended that the ruling guardians, who had to make all the necessary decisions and fight the wars of defense for the city, should be formed of a group that could own absolutely nothing, not even spouses or children, that every decision they made would be freed from any personal attachment for self or for family. The entire group was the family and sexual activities were by free choice, using only wisdom as a guide. It was tried at Syracuse, with less than hoped for results, and Plato was put on the block to be sold as a slave. Fortunately someone recognized him and purchased him and then immediately set him free. So he wrote a "second best city" called the LAWS and in it, all three levels of society were based upon the family unit of a monogamous marriage. But he felt it wasn't the best man can do, but 2350 years ago it was obvious that man was not yet ready for anything better. Jessie Bernard in her 1972 book The Future of Marriage discussed at length various forms of marriage, and their appropriateness according, in one chapter, to men, and in another, to women. On the cover she presented the two paradoxical thoughts about marriage by men and by women. "His --

traditionally, men consider marriage a trap for themselves and a prize for their wives. Statistically, marriage is good for men -- physically, socially, and psychologically. Hers -- traditionally, all women want to marry, and most want to become mothers. Statistically, childless marriages are happier; and marriage, literally, makes thousands of women sick."8.14 This book does not have the time to go into such detail, but what I am trying to say is that man and woman ought to open up, along with Church and State, to more flexible and more variable forms of relationships between them. If the Church would be less judgmental when someone does not agree with their dictates, and the State would permit "legally" various forms of marriage, mankind overall, may have a chance to become much happier that it is now. One of the only significant theologians of the last 500 years to show some flexibility on the subject was Martin Luther. When Philip of Hesse wanted a divorce, Luther said no to the divorce but offered to bless his marriage to a second wife. Luther also stated: "I confess, for my part that if a man wishes to marry two or more wives, I cannot forbid him, nor is his conduct repugnant to the Holy Scriptures". In some of his ups and downs with Katie, his beloved wife, Luther was not beyond playing with her emotions, although Katie did not have trouble fighting back. One time when Luther had his usual students and guests at his house for food, fellowship, and discussion, Luther was talking about man's natural tendency towards polygamy. When Luther said that "We shall yet see the day when a man will take several wives." Katie, now irritated, stepped into the conversation by blurting out, "The devil thinks so...Paul says, 'Let each man have his own wife.'" Luther scholastically replied: "Yes, his own wife, but not only one: that is not in Paul." Katie stood her ground, "Before I would stand for that I would go back to the convent and leave you and all your children." Yet, despite his honest openness towards the concept of polygamy, Luther himself never entertained the thought of another wife, and deeply loved and appreciated Katie. They had three boys and three girls, and to Luther they were God's gracious miracles of creation. Once, away from home, he became very ill, and it was thought by some that he was going to die, and Luther himself felt so. He later stated that the most horrifying thought about dying at that time was that he would never see his wife and children again. To Spalatin he wrote in 1526, "I have received, by the blessings of God, a little son, Hans Luther, and by God's wonderful grace, I have become a father."8.15 Luther wrote many hymns and he led his family in their singing, as he himself had a good voice and played both the lute and the flute. For his children to sing a new Christmas hymn he "From Heaven Above" with tender words such as these:

"To you this night is born a child
Of Mary, chosen mother mild;
This little child, of lowly birth,
Shall be a joy to all the earth.

Ah, dearest Jesus, Holy Child,
Make thee a bed, soft undefiled,
Within my heart, that it may be
A quiet chamber kept for thee."

One of the saddest, if not the saddest, times of Luther's life was the death of his 13 year old daughter, Magdalene, who was in some ways his favorite because she had the prettiest voice in the family: her voice lifted the family's singing into a state of beauty. In her last moments, when it was obvious she was going to die, Katie left the room in tears, while Martin was holding "Lenichen" ("little Lena") in his arms while she lay in bed. His lasts communication with her went: "Magdalenchen, my little girl, you would like to stay with your father here and you would be glad to go to your Father in heaven?" And her reply was, "Yes, dear father, as God wills." When she was buried Luther said, "Du liebes Lenichen, you will rise and shine like the stars and the sun. How strange it is to know that she is at peace and all is well, and yet to be so sorrowful!" 8.16 Even a man of great faith, who was willing to give his own life for his faith, could not but be crushed with pain at the death of a young loving child, such as Magdalene. For life is good, and the friendship and love that can be experienced in a family is that goodness that is seldom excelled in happiness and wholeness. The openness of Luther's views about marriage can never be said to be as such destructive of the goodness of the family.

Yes, the family is the beginning of the individual man's greater outreach towards society in his love of humanity. Loving one individual is the first movement outward, the extended family the second, and the third, to be handled in the next chapter, is comprised of larger non-relationed groups, and also in the next chapter, the fourth outward movement is an extension of love to all humanity, expressed in the society in which one lives. A final reach of love, which has been mentioned before, is the loving kindness one can show to all creatures. The last two outreaches are, unfortunately, seldom taken, and all of humanity and each one of us within it, then suffer this lack of the love which Jesus and Siddhartha showed to all. Nevertheless, love within the family is an early and helpful step in the process. One who eventually embraces all mankind in love, is the most whole and happiest of living beings. Cicero's house was always an extended family for those whose ultimate desire was to find truth, goodness, and human happiness. He loved having close friendships, especially with his world's great thinkers and philosophers, who were often housed with him for long periods of time, including Diodotus, Philo, Antiochus and Posidonius. Like Luther his love for philosophy was deeped with the death of a daughter; Cicero's daughter Tullia died in 45BC. He in his anguish over her death turned himself completely to philosophy because he felt there was no other cure than the study of truth and virtue. Love of and within the family is a great joy, and unfortunately when that is lost, one must spiritually confront himself and journey down deeper into the very soul of one's being. It, sometimes, is only when we have lost something that is very precious, that we realize just how precious it was to us. Therefore, in this section it is well to think of the love and friendship that is now present in one's life and to acknowledge just how much happiness one already has.

Tu Fu (712-770 AD) wrote a beautiful poem about his own life experience. He was taken into the military for a distant campaign leaving his young wife and young boy child and two infant daughters. During the battle he was captured and imprisoned for a year, and naturally in those days, no communication was possible. When he was released, he had to make the long journey back home by foot, and all the way home he asked every possible question about his family: "Are they still alive?" "Did my wife marry another out of necessity?" "Where are the children and are they in good health?" "Do they still live in the same place or have they moved far away?" "Did my wife leave because she thought I was killed in battle?" It was a long walk back and there was much time to build fear and anxiety about his beloved wife and three young children. The poem tells of his leaving the battle scene and the camp, leaving those who suffered many wounds and were still in shock and groaning and bleeding. The distant camp faded into the background as he walked along the path towards home. He listened to the tiger's roar and passed through the mountain ridges, and he found joy in the mountain berries and scattered nuts which he found, and took heart that he would reach home. Finally, nearing home, and then recognizing it, he begin to go faster in his haste, and spotting his wife, he rejoiced even though she was dressed in old rags that still served for clothing. He embraced her, and they both wept. Soon after the children in even worse and uneven clothes make their appearance. He beholds his family and weeps for joy. While he rests from his journey, too tired to even play with the children, he watches with joy as they go about their normal activities. All the horrors of the past years he is now slowly putting aside, and he rejoices that he is alive and at home with his family. How wonderful it was to be family again.8.17

Family love and friendship are incomparable blessings which deposit happiness and wholeness into the hearts of those so united. Li Po (701-762 AD) while away from his family on business for too long of an extended time (three years), sent a letter to his two small children so that they would know just how much he missed them. The poem was in the form of a "spirit-journey" in which he describes his thoughts as though they became alive in actions. He had planted a tree before he left, and in his poem he projects both the growth of the tree as well as his two children, and the tree is the scene of his spirit-journey and letter.8.18

These three examples of family love from lives of Luther, Tu Fu, and Li Po emphasize the wondrous joy that can be experienced in the loving friendship that is created within a family. It also, however, is a reminder of how sad a divorce can be for children and for loving parents of those children, for it too can cause a deep sadness of separation. With small one unit monogamous families experiencing such a high rate of divorce, and often a subsequent move away even to a distant state by one of the parents after the divorce, it seems to me that, indeed, a Novum Organum is needed or at least should be considered so that there can be some type of stable extended family for the children. Let us not be so harsh on the parents who do get divorced that we avoid finding a new concept of family for the sake of the children. Self-righteous judgment against divorced parents does not help the children, and legal and church sponsored inflexibility certainly do not help children find this very first of the extended love and friendship that people have to offer. Perhaps one needs to reread some of the writings of Margaret Mead ("Sex and Temperament in Three Primitive Societies"), Jessie Bernard ("The Future of Marriage"), Bertand Russell ("Marriage and Morals"), Bronislaw Malinowski ("Sex and Repression in Savage Society"), and even Wilhelm Reich ("The Invasion of Compulsory Sex-Morality"). Perhaps a better way can be found to relieve adults of the sexual obsession they experience in America and children of the fear of being left by a beloved parent. The present situation does not make people more pious or happier, it only makes divorce lawyers richer, the only group being benefited by this. It likewise may do away from some of the situations in which clerics are forced into a unnatural state of "celibacy", and as a result altar boys and loved-starved women are abused by those most trusted to help them. The monogamous family can certainly work and has blessed millions of couples and their children, yet, not all fit that mold, and they must be given a chance to form their own "family" structure without the State or the Church condemning them. As Malinowski reminded us:

> "The family has changed enormously during the development
> of humanity, passing from its first promiscuous form, based on
> sexual and economic communism, through 'group-family' based
> on 'group marriage,' 'consanguineous family,' based on 'Punalua
> marriage,' through the *Grossfamilie* and clan kindred to its present-
> day society form -- the individual family based on monogamous
> marriage and *patria potestas*."8.19

As to the monogamous family without divorce, as Jesus said, that precept is not for all men (Mt 19:11). Perhaps it is time to let history continue to develop new forms of family and marriage. Below I have gathered numerous references to articles and studies that must tell us that changes in our concept of family and the states' restrictions on the forms of marriage allowable must be reconsidered. There is simply too much frustration and misery caused by the present laws and limitations.

An ex-wife kills newly weds -- she felt despised and alone after the man divorced her. She had no greater family to help her. (OCR 11/07/1989).

"The Marriage Experiments" a Life Magazine article discussing 1. An unmarried couple with a child. 2. "Frontier partners" in Idaho. 3. "Collective Marriage". 4. The troubled marriage. 5. A contracted work marriage for household and vocational obligations. (Life Magazine 4/28/1972).

"Marital woes cited in slaying of wife and child". A husband, jealous, because his wife was going to leave him, murdered wife and daughter. (LAT 2002).

"Strange Days in Utah". Story of Rulon Jeffs who had between 19 and 60 wives. Article said that between 20,000 and 50,000 in the USA lived in polygamous families. (Newsweek ll/13/2000).

"Seven women claim to be wife of Texas man who died Friday" by the Dallas Morning News (date lost).

"Mail Order Brides". Article of American men seeking Asian women for marriage". More evidence that not all is well on the Western Front (OCR 6/27/1985).

On the front cover of BUNTE "Scheidungskrieg: Wer is schlimmer: Maenner order frauen?" Yes, Germans have divorce wars also. BUNTE 22/3/1990 (March 20, 1990).

"Wives Just Wanna Have Fun" about a book that "suggests that an affair to remember can revive a trouble marriage". (Newsweek: 6/29/1992).

"Can a Marriage Be Saved by Adultery?" Article discussing female unfaithfulness which is present in somewhere between 20% and 70% of all marriages. (LAT 12/18/1992).

"Facing Up to the Ethical and Moral Issues of Marriage" is an article about the frustration of one person meeting all the other person's needs within the monogamous marriage. (LAT 4/08/1988).

Cato lent Hortensius his wife so that she might bear him a child: Life of Cato by Plutarch.

"Divorce Rise in Soviet" but not to fear, USA is still No. I. (Kansas City Star 5/17/1972).

"Help Me I'm Alone" name of an organization founded in Palo Alto, CA. In 1963 and subsequently known as SOS to help people who were divorced cope with being alone.

"How long will it last" an article on the fact that 7 of 10 high school age marriages end in divorce.

"Terrible Violence in Our Homes" discussed the brutality that takes place in homes in which the couple is unhappy about the marriage. (Kansas City Star 5/22/1978).

In 1975 in the USA there were 1,036,000 divorces and 2,126,000 marriages. There were 20.3 divorces for every 1,000 marriages per year, which, after 40 years would amount to 812 divorces for every 1,000 marriages.

"Republic Stirs Debate By Allowing for Multiple Wives" in Russia. (LAT 8/15/1999)

David Koresh was reported to have said that all the women followers belonged to him. It is known that he had 17 wives. A Waco wacko, true enough, but also a reality. (San Gabriel Valley Tribune 3/02/1993).

Thousands of priests have left the Roman Catholic priesthood.

Hundreds of priests have been charged with molestation and of other sexual misconduct.

LA-NBC reported that 1/8 of all homicides are husband and wife killings. (2/02/1990)

"7 States Still Classify Cohabitation as Illegal" (LAT 8/20/2001).

"A Split Verdict on America's Marital Future" article in Newsweek (1/13/1992).

"More Europeans opting not to Marry: New Social Order Lacks Old Stigmas" San Diego Union-Tribune 3/24/2002.

"Divorce, Republican Style". A presentation of the leading Republican candidates for presidency of USA, while supporting Republican Platform of "Family Values": "Gramm's first wife filed for divorce in 1969, citing "excesses and cruel treatment". Wilson (Pete) "split with his first spouse in 1981 and married the ex-wife of another San Diego lawyer". Bob Dole "left a teenage daughter and the wife who had nursed him through his grievous war wounds." [He then married E. Dole, his current wife who had a better political aptitude -- bracket comment is mine] Newt Gingrich "dumped his first wife in 1980 -- showing up to discuss the terms of divorce in her hospital room as she recovered from cancer surgery." (Newsweek 9/04/1995)

The French Mitterrand's wife and mistress both were at his funeral. (Newsweek 1/22/1996).

"Defendant Says He Has Right to Sex With Wife" but she said no and he was on trial for "attempted spousal rape", and he was convicted. (LAT 1/29/1996).

In 1993 Aid to Dependent Children cost Los Angeles County more than Two Billion dollars.

"Crushed by Burdens of Age, Men Choose Suicide" -- alone and not self-sufficient. (Kansas City Times 2/01/1979).

Hindu widows gather at the Ganges to die for there is no hope for them.

"Self-Immolations on Rise in Afghanistan: The Women are apparently trying to escape arranged or unhappy marriages" so the douse themselves with fuel and set themselves afire. (LAT 11/17/2002).

"Leisure World Couple Die in Murder-Suicide". A not uncommon happening when two very old people can not take care of either themselves or the other person -- and with no "extended family" for their monogamy had excluded such, they die. (LAT 2/08/2003).

These situations and facts certainly must be enough for people to rethink the role of family and marriage in the USA, and in the world as a whole. Some of the very difficult positions that individuals have experienced by being divorced, by having a mate die, by having financial difficulties, by having other options for sex without feeling a man must rape his one and only wife, by having a wider concept of family help a pregnant teenager, by providing for children when either the man or the woman has vacated his or her responsibility for raising the child, and from the fear of older women who fear becoming bag ladies because they do not personally have enough money to survive and are alone since their husband has died. The new expanded family could be more of a clan or tribal type group. Monogamy is not for everyone, and good governments will seek out that which brings happiness and wholeness to its people. For a country made up of many different religions, cultures, races, and "old country" customs and traditions, it is imperative that it continues the quest of history to find the best forms of family, and to permit them and to support them. Taxes could simply be based on an individual basis with no deductions or penalties for whatever form of family they live in or whatever form of marriage they take unto themselves. I say this because, let's face it, government is usually more concerned with taxes and the economy in general than it is with the personal happiness of individuals.

C. LOVE AND FRIENDSHIP IN EXTRA-MARITAL GROUPS

1. Worship Groups

The value of a worship group is that it brings together people of similar social and spiritual values into a setting in which one is humbled before God, where prayer, honest introspection, confession, singing, a unified ritual, and a social hour before or after the worship service takes place. It is also often a center to plan other social activities and discussions about political and neighborhood concerns during the following week or month, depending upon the frequency of the worship service. In the United States the many denominations of the Christian Church have been by historical foundation and by numbers the leading example of this category. For many, such united meetings have been life changing, life supporting, spiritually refreshing, and socially enhancing even to the extent that if one weekly service is missed participants often feel unfulfilled until they can again join the rest of the worshipping group. Such life building experiences to some are absolutely necessary to their well being and are irreplaceable. Such services without a doubt increase the capacity for love and friendship to a much larger circle of people, and that spiritual growth deepens the goodness of those who experience such love and friendship. The quality of love and friendship does not lessen, rather the person is enhanced with greater power to love and make friends. William James stated in his Essays on Faith and Morals: "I point out to you that, as a matter of fact, certain persons do exist with an enormous capacity for friendship and for taking delight in other people's lives; and that such persons know more of truth than if their hearts were not so big"(p.286). The worship service gives people that opportunity to expand their capacity for love and friendship. The Srimad Bhagavatam tells of Navi and his priests who, during a sacrificial rite at the temple, felt strongly the presence of God. They were overwhelmed with joy and bowed down and sang a hymn according to their heart's worship. Together, in worship, their mutual singing to the Lord of the Universe gave the entire group a sense of being delivered from any evil that was a threat to them: their service became a charm against evil itself.8.20 In the verse it made it clear that worship is not for the growth or enhancement of God in any way, rather it is the privilege for finite mortals to say "thank you" to their God, to feel his presence, and in that atmosphere, to feel the evil leaving their presence. This, to them, "is following the way of the wise." While it is mainly Jews and Christians that practice a weekly worship service, there are holy days in virtually all other religions or festivals or pilgrimages where groups gather to encourage each other. Some of those religions that have moved into the West have also established more frequent worship services for their community, for it helps them to bind together and encourage each other in faith and morals. During World War Two, Dietrich Bonhoeffer was taken away from his Confessing Church and thrown into prison by the Nazis, yet he worked within the prison so that fellow prisoners could feel the power of their own community even within a Nazi prison. In his book

"Life Together", which he wrote before he was cast into prison, he encouraged such small groups to bind together in encouragement and not be polluted or broken down by the treatment they received from the Nazi party..

"Therefore, the Christian needs another Christian who speaks God's Word to him. He needs him again and again when he becomes uncertain and discouraged"(p.13).

"Every Christian community must realize that not only do the weak need the strong, but also that the strong cannot exist without the weak. The elimination of the weak is the death of the fellowship"(p.84).

"The second service that one should perform for another in a Christian community is that of active helpfulness. This means, initially, simple assistance in trifling, external matters. There is a multitude of these things wherever people live together. Nobody is too good for the meanest service. One who worries about the loss of time that such petty, outward acts of helpfulness entails is usually taking the importance of his own career too solemnly. We must be ready to allow ourselves to be interrupted by God"(p.89).8.21

2.   Interest and Action Groups

These groups are usually formed for some type of social action or political campaigning or demonstration activities. They are powerful, and one would be well encouraged to use them for the purpose of extending love and friendship. A caveat that is always with us is that some of these groups have such a special interest that their action is only for themselves or their "kind", and these often are formed for the forceful action of a partiality, that shows favors and concern for one group against another "kind" of people. They sometimes even foster anger and hate, and, needless to say, they work against one's own goodness and happiness and often harm society much more than they bring wholeness and peace to it. If the purpose of the group is to enhance the expansion of love and friendship, and in actuality does it, then it will also help the individual grow into goodness, love, and friendship. For any group activity often does to each individual within it that which it does as a unit. Beware of the fellowship's nature and activity before you become part of it! Seek those good groups with love in hearts and nonviolence as a means for they can and do exist, and do have enormous power in changing and beautifying society at large. They are not only encouraged, but are necessary for one's growth outward to the greater world, where one can make a difference. Asoka changed himself and his military group to one that sought peace and happiness for all his subjects and promised them no more war. The Srimad Bhagavatam speaks highly of King Rishava who used his power base to bring goodness and happiness to his subjects. But, of course, he could only do so because he was good within himself. Even though the account may be a little exaggerated, he probably deserved such praise: for the Srimad calls him a "free soul" and one who was "pure in heart". He was a friend to the entire world, including animals. His virtues included: sympathy, temperance, and working for peoples' success and freedom. And his life was so admired that his subjects experienced a type of contentedness.8.22

Sometimes our activities within an action group raise us to the level of leader, as was the case of Rishava and Asoka, and then we have reached a level where we can not only profess love and friendship for a great number of people, but can actually exercise it. But, as in the case of both Asoka and Rishava, it can only be done well, if the person himself has been lifted to this love for others within and had become good. In the next chapter such expanding of love and friendship will be the topic. But first, a brief summary of detours to love and friendship about which one must beware.

V. DETOURS TO LOVE AND FRIENDSHIP

Friendship love is not a possession of another nor does it insist on claiming a right upon another. It gives and shares, but does not grasp and demand.

Friendship love is not a romantic obsession that seeks another for the purpose of fulfilling oneself.

There are some who are not capable of sharing friendship love on the personal and individual level, and one must be suspicious of them from the beginning. Perhaps they will change, but do not cast your happiness into their hands, they may "crush the sweetest rose", and begone. The following are such people.

1. Self-centered people.
2. Whiners. "Why me?" syndrome.
3. Leeches: they never say "could you give me a buck", they say, "could you loan me a buck". They are dishonest from the beginning.
4. People so obsessed with their own goals, that they consider personal friendship a waste of time, unless it can be used to get to their goal.
5. The superior attitude: "I am better, smarter etc. than you. But I condescend to let you enjoy my friendship."
6. The "friend" hopper. A friend in need is a friend indeed. The hopper is totally self-centered and unreliable.
7. The competitor who must always win and be number one between the two of you, or number one within your small group.
8. Bad or evil people. Friendship, as stated many times in this work, is only possible between two genuinely good people. "There are people who are a plague upon others and damage the virtue of their associates" (Seneca Letter CXXII.9).
9. The controller. The person who wants to control your life wants to be a small tyrant and uses you as his imprisoned subject. He will not leave you alone. Lao Tzu (57) stated that people will get along just fine, even without someone else trying to control their lives.
10. Those who use "love and friendship" for other benefits they derive from their "friends". Ulterior motives usually show up quickly. After Wagner took his conversion to Christianity seriously and showed it in his "Parsival", Nietzsche could no more use him for his own views and disowned their "friendship".
11. Those who think it unmanly or unworthy of themselves to compromise with their "beloved".
12. Those who "take offense" constantly, claiming discourtesy or racism or snobbishness. Loosen up, people, and quit jumping on every spoken word says William James: "To what is the fact, if fact it be, due unless to the over-active conscience of the people, afraid of either saying something too trivial and obvious, or some-

thing insincere, or something in some way or other not adequate to the occasion? On the other hand, conversation does flourish and society is refreshing, and neither dull on the one hand nor exhausting from its effort on the other, wherever people forget their scruples and let their tongues wag as automatically and irresponsibly as they will"(Essays on Faith and Morals, p.254).

13. Those who do not want one's friendship. Aristotle,"We must never treat a man as our friend against his will."

14. The gossip. Do not be so naive that your secrets will be safe with a gossip as a "friend", for he seeks gossip, not friendship.

CHAPTER NINE

STEP SIX

THE VIRTUES OF SOCIAL HARMONY
JUSTICE, DUTY, COURAGE

Beginning with the Sumerians man started to establish cities and to share each other's talents in a form of social harmony, each contributing the fruits of his own calling to the whole of society, and in turn receiving the benefits of the work of others. Instead of each man, with the aid of his family only, building his own shelter, growing his own food, fetching his own water, and providing security to both his family and property, each family had the shared benefits of the other families; theoretically, each providing what each best did. Men provided defense against others and animals, women bore children, children spread seeds, man hunted for meat, men and women were in charge of the vegetation growth and both taught the young, most often, women prepared the food, and man built the shelter. When the arts and crafts were developed then a form of specialization was needed and each then found a new vocation. Together the many families formed small societies called, at least today, cities, but were initially more like small villages. When the needs became greater, for the cause of defense or population growth, the city was born. A man who had no city, was totally on his own, and his survival rate was poor. Man needed his city. Aristotle stated that man was a ZOON POLITIKON (a political animal), and since POLIS in Greek meant "city", Aristotle was saying that no man was an island; he needed the social harmony and shared work and benefits of other men which he could find only in the city. Love of one's city was considered a great virtue, and devotion to it was highly praised. Socrates chose to drink the hemlock rather than to leave his city and escape, for the city was the nourishing mother to all its inhabitants. Ezekiel, in exile, lamented greatly his not being in his beloved Jerusalem. A man without a city, CIVIS in Latin was uncivilized, that is, he had no city and was destined to be a vagabond, barbarian, or even a savage living off of the natural fruits of the land with no friends, no or little shelter, and no defense against the roaming wolves, dogs, and lions. Today the city has lost its overwhelming power in forming mankind, and has yielded to the greater force of the nation, for much the same reasons that caused the city to be needed in the first place, but on a much greater scale.

If, however, man is to relate in "civility" and under a "political" form that molds him together with many others, then some order or rules must be established to give men guidelines for exercising and protecting the harmony among them. Plato tried to build the best city possible in his "Republic" which, to him, presented man with a format for building the ideal city which would function well and bring the greatest goodness and happiness to the greatest amount of people, and if properly executed all could be happy. But its idealism was far beyond man's ability to be selfless and wise at that time, and therefore he wrote his "second best city" in the work, "The Laws", which if not followed, in Plato's mind, man would return to being a beast among other beasts surrounded by walls. But in both he hoped man would function in the area of capability in which nature had best blessed him, and he, a least theoretically in the Republic, divided the city into three parts: 1) the thinkers, the wisest of men who had the greatest rational abilities (LOGOS & LOGIKOS) who in their wisdom would make the major decisions for the functioning of the city, 2) the protectors, the most courageous and spirited among them would serve as army against an enemy and a police force to protect the physcially weak within the city, and 3) the artisans and laborers, the common people, who did the necessary work to provide food, shelter, and all life's necessary commodities for the whole of the city. When all three functioned properly and for the benefit of the whole, then the city was a just city, and justice prevailed. In all forms of modern societies that are somewhat democratic this basic structure of Plato's appears in one form or another. In the USA the three are the Thinkers as the President, Congress and Supreme court (unfortunately, unlike Plato's Republic, not made up of the wisest but of those with the most power, money, and popularity): the courageous as the military: and the common man who does all the other necessary work including paying the cost of the other two parts of the nation.

Now the role of the average man of goodness in a world which he can only partly control is to be discussed. As is mentioned many times above, each individual, even regardless of the way his city or nation is governed, must be responsible for his own life and the way he relates to others within his city, nation, and now even the way he relates to the rest of the world. Even Jesus, facing his own limitations, had to do this, for as he looked upon the rebelliousness of his own people towards the Romans, he wept and lamented that he tried to gather his people under his guidelines and attitude towards enemies for the sake of their salvation, as a hen gathers her chicks in time of danger under her wings, but he could not (Lk 13:34, 19:41 & Mt 23:37-38).

I.   JESUS' WORDS AND LIFE

Jesus' Sermon on the Mount, as presented by Matthew, is undoubtedly the most quoted three chapters of the New Testament in reference to one's duties towards others. While it is also full of thoughts for one's personal growth, the outreach obligations of his followers to the world cannot be overlooked, although they always point back to or assume the individual's goodness and wholeness as the source of his ability to be the functioning of the Spirit of Goodness among others. Such passages bring forward the following thoughts:

Happy in wholeness are those who serve as peacemakers, for they shall be known as the sons of God.

Happy in wholeness are those who, in bringing righteousness into society, are persecuted for their efforts.

You are the salt of the earth, but if you do not flavor and preserve society, then of what value are you?

You are the light of the cosmos, so set yourself upon a hill and by your righteous deeds show what you are before men, that they may see the glory of God in your efforts to better the cosmos.

Live your lives by the heavenly law of perfection, not only not killing another, but do not even curse him or resort to "fool" calling.

Do not think that running to church or to court brings you release from the obligation you have of creating harmony between yourself and others, and if you owe satisfaction to another, pay him, and thus restore your peaceful relations with him (Salvation came into Zaccheus' house after he stated that he would repay four-fold those he had cheated as a tax collector).

Honor the marriages of others, not only in not committing adultery, but do not even think about it, for coveting will destroy both you and your attitude towards your neighbor.

Be honest at all times; for swearing is not only not necessary, and swearing by anything is evidence that you need to swear before God or a court before people will believe that what you say is true. Simple honesty will do: yes for yes and no for no.

Learn how to forgive, even the most painful and harmful acts, for there is great power in nonresistence to evil personally done to you. [This passage, Mt 5:38-42, has often been used to unfairly judge the laws of the Torah found in Ex. 21:24, Lev. 24:20, Deut. 19:21 which are passages that demand justice for those abused by the rich and powerful of antiquity, and such laws are necessary for the well-being of society as a whole, for they promoted equality of among men: if a king kills or puts out the eye of a poor man, he cannot give satisfaction with money, he must give up his life or his eye, for the weaker man's life is as valuable as the more powerful man's life. Actually such laws initiated the concept of democratizing all men's lives. However, what is different about Jesus' handling of these passages is that he does encourage that other satifactions can be made, and none are to be demanded -- a form of taking up the cross for other men's sins. Also, in an incorrect way, this passage is misquoted by those against capital punishment, for Jesus repeats only eye for eye and tooth for tooth, for the man is still alive and can forgive the one who acted against him. But there is no personal forgiveness available when the potential forgiver is killed, and no one else can give a murderer a murdered man's forgiveness. No man can forgive a sin that hurts another and not himself: he can forgive only the acts against himself. Even a father cannot forgive a man who murders his daughter, unless the father really believes that his daughter was no more than simply his own property. For a father to "forgive" someone who murders his daughter is an insult to the value and dignity of his daughter's humanity.]

Try to be as completely good as your Father in heaven is completely good.

Do not put on public displays of your goodness for it betrays a type of childishness and self-centeredness. Frankly, tooting your own horn does not go over well in heaven.

The more gracious you are to others, the more gracious your Father in heaven will be with you.

Beware of money-lust for it takes away from you the ability to help others by means of the very money you have, and such deeds to others are treasures laid up in heaven. The choice is simple, you cannot be held by both the joy of money possession and the joy of using it wisely in helping mankind in the name of God.

Judge not others, and you will not be judged. Get yourself a pure soul and a habit of exercising goodness to all, and this will take up much of your effort, and with this self-introspection you will notice the sins of others diminish and your own sins as much more of a danger to your happiness that anything others do.

How you would like others to treat you, treat them likewise.

There is a great effort needed in being good, it is really a narrow gate that you must enter to be good to yourself and beneficial to others.

In all these teachings Jesus presupposed a divine help from above, for only God is good, and he, as man's Heavenly Father, is only too willing to give whatever we ask for the sake of purifying and beautifying our lives and our souls. When our lower emotions flare up and are confronted with social injustice towards ourselves, Divine Aid is available. For the gate is narrow. Immanuel Kant described it this way:

> Only since the time of the Evangelical Gospel is now the greatest purity and holiness of the moral law fully evident, although it lies similarly in our own reason. The law must not be leniently held, but be demonstrated in its greatest purity and holiness, and we must in our weakness wait upon Godly help, that He might provide us with enough that we might be capable of, even in our frailty, being pure and holy.9.1

After Leo Tolstoy was converted and chose to be a follower of Jesus, he wrote the book "The Kingdom of God is Within You", using the teachings of Jesus, especially those on the Sermon on the Mount (Mt 5-7) as the basis of "being a Christian". In general he was opposed to the organized churches of Christianity because of their disunity and their eagerness to join the local nation in the European slaughterhouse of war, one "Christian nation" destroying and killing the people of another "Christian nation". He also disliked all the traditional elements added which diminished in value the very teachings of Jesus himself. These feelings between him and the organized churches were mutual, they condemned each other as being heretical. Yet Tolstoy is an important figure and his courageous quest to present Jesus and his teachings to others at any cost makes him an honorable man, and a teacher from whom all men in the West can learn. He wanted the followers of Jesus, not only to love themselves, family, nation, but the entire world that the growth of love in the hearts of the followers of Jesus would actually reach their potential and in some worthy way represent the love of Jesus. He speaks first of man seeking a path to travel and then declares that path is love as presented by Jesus. Each idea is presented in the three following quotations:

"The essence of religion lies in the property of men prophetically to foresee and point out the path of life, over which humanity must travel, in a new definition of the meaning of life, from which also results a new, the whole future activity of humanity...and establish a new comprehension of life"9.2

"By a natural progression, from love of self to the love of family, of the race, of the nation, of the state, the social conception of life has brought men to the consciousness of the necessity for a love of humanity, which has no limits and blends with everything in existence...(The teachings of Jesus) recognize the love of self, family, nation, and of humanity, -- not only of humanity, but of everything living, of everything in existence; it recognizes the necessity for an endless widening of the sphere of love."9.3

"The teachings of Christ consist in pointing out to man that the essence of his soul is love, that his good is derived not from the fact that he will love this or that man, but from the fact that he will love the beginning of everything, God, whom he recognizes in himself through love, and so will love everybody and everything."9.4

II. CONCURRENCE FROM OTHER SAGES AND TEACHERS

That one's personal goodness by nature will reach out to others and try to improve one's society and enhance the beauty of life for others is a precept taught by most all of the great teachers of humanity who have tried to set a path for man to walk and therein find happiness. The very earliest laws of the priests of ancient religions emphasized the social obligations of individuals within society, and "sanctified" those obligations by law codes.

The pre-Hammurabi laws of the Mesopotamian Eshnunna established basic and fair laws of commerce, wages, property, marriage (which was a form of commerce), sexual laws, murder, assault, and divorce. The laws helped to settle and harmonize the society in which men lived together, but they were not democratic at this point. I pointed out earlier that the Jewish Torah in teaching an eye for an eye was a democratizing law, and such can be seen by the Jewish demand for a life for life, eye for eye, tooth for tooth as it is compared with the Laws of Eshnunna:

"If a man has no claim against another man, but kidnaps another man's slave girl...and causes her death...he shall give two slave-girls to the owner of the slave-girl as a replacement" (23), but

"If a man takes another man's wife or child...and causes their death...he shall die." (24) Also,

"If a man bites the nose of another man and severs it, he shall pay 1 mina of silver: an eye...1 mina of silver...a tooth ½ mina of silver...an ear ½ mina of silver...a slap in the face 10 shekels of silver" (42).

While these laws may seem fair because of the strong monetary fine, they are not fair if a rich person knocks out the eye of another, the fine is easily taken care of out of his abundance of wealth. But for a poor person, it seems fair, but is not democratizing. The rich would think twice before knocking out a poor man's eye, if he knew that he likewise had to give up his own eye. Against this background the Torah of the Jews is definitely a step forward in honoring the dignity of all men. Nevertheless, the Laws of Eshnunna do offer a stabilizing effect on group living, whether hamlet or city. They are strictly legal in nature, but love, honor, or graciousness are not incorporated. The <u>Laws of Hammurabi</u>, c. 1700 BC, extend the scope of social order and in greater detail. People have, unfortunately, the idea that if it is not illegal, they can operate unjustly for gain, and therefore, as societies grew, so did the law codes to control those who had no cares about others. Merchants, soldiers, laws of irrigation, purity of wine, more extensive divorce and dowry laws, nuns, the lex talionis between equals (a half-way step towards the Jewish Torah), false charges in court, building codes and punishments in case of injury, ox gorings, and shepherd and livestock laws were enhanced. In India the <u>Laws of Manu</u> were put into writing (Sanskrit) in the Second Century AD, but reflect codes from the distant past and are attributed by tradition to Manu. In the Laws of Manu as well as the Jewish Torah the strong religious element is present to give them added force, and likewise are much more extensive. One of the unfortunate aspects of these Laws of Manu is the sanctifying of the Caste system of Hindu India, which, while it may have given stability to society (i.e. "Each person knew his place"), it was contrary to the democratizing element which had been established in Greece five centuries earlier and had spread to many other countries from there, although it was not well utilized and in most cases disappeared in the West also by the time of the "Middle Ages". In the Far East, China, Confucius took a great step forward by teaching the political rulers of his day that, not only laws are important, but the goodness of the leaders must be evident in their rule. For rule is to be more than social order, it must be an exercise in goodness. <u>Confucius</u> taught:

"It is virtuous manners which constitute the excellence of a neighborhood".(IV.1).

"If the will be set on virtue, there will be no practice of wickedness". (IV.4).

The Master said, "I have not yet seen a person who loved virtue above all, or one who hated what was not virtuous".(IV.6).

For Confucius believed there to be a "moral force" in the universe that promoted goodness in society, and that those charged with the duty of running society were obligated to bring such goodness into reality among the people commited to them. None were perfect, but for perfection of virtue all must strive.

<u>Mo</u> <u>Tzu</u> (Fifth Century BC) was certainly one of the most idealistic men of ancient China, a man I personally admire and try to reflect his teachings in my own life. He felt that Confucius was too limited in his concept of Goodness and taught that love for every person could be as lively as love for one's own relatives. The incorporation of this love into society was the duty of the honorable and worthy men who governed the peoples, for this, he thought, would be the only way to keep them from attacking each other for sake of land or wealth. He believed that Heaven made no distiction among men as to giving blessings, and men, likewise, following the example of Heaven, should be indiscriminate with charitable deeds, at lest to the honorable and the worthy. One of his sayings is:

"It is the business of the benevolent man to try to promote what is beneficial to the world and to eliminate what is harmful. Now at the present time, what brings the greatest harm to the world? Great states attacking small ones, great families overthrowing small ones, the strong oppressing the weak, the many harrying the few, the cunning deceiving the stupid, the eminent lording it over the humble -- these are harmful to the world. So too are rulers who are not generous, ministers who are not loyal, fathers who are without kindness, and sons who are unfilial, as well as those mean men who, with weapons, knives, poison, fire, and water, seek to injure and undo each other. When we inquire into the cause of these various harms, what do we find has produced them? Do they come about from loving others and trying to benefit them? Surely not! They come rather from hating others and trying to injure them." (III. 16). (tr. Burton Watson).

Mo Tzu went on to ask the nature of these evil actions, and concluded that it was partiality, that is, a lack of universality in the care and love which men have in their hearts. Give this love to all, and such evil will cease. He then went on to apply the Golden Rule to all humanity and to cities and states as well. "If men were to regard the families of others as they regard their own, then who would raise up his family to overhrow that of another?" He repeats this for one's attitude towards cities, states, individuals and all other groups -- regard them as you would regard your own. Love them as you would love your own. Only love motivated by universality can bring peaceful benefits to all people.

"The universal-minded man will say, 'I have heard that the truly superior man of the world regards his friend the same as himself, and his friend's father the same as his own. Only if he does this can he be considered a truly superior man.' Because he views his friend in this way, he will feed him when he is hungry, clothe him when he is cold, nourish him when he is sick, and bury him when he dies. Such are the words and actions of the universal-minded man." (III.16).(tr.Burton Watson).

These last words remind most Christians of the words of Jesus spoken some 400 years later:

"I was hungry and you gave me food to eat, I was thirsty and you gave me water to drink. You welcomed me when I was a stranger. I was naked and you clothed me. I was ill and you came to visit me. I was imprisoned and you visited me there also." Then the righteous will him, "Lord, when did we feed your hunger, and give water to you when you were thirsty? And when did we welcome you as a foreigner, or give you clothes when you had none? And when you were sick and imprisoned, when did we visit you?" And responding to them, the King will say, "Most surely I declare to you, as you did these things to the least of these my brothers, you did them to me."(Mt 25:31-40).

Unfortunately Moism was eventually crushed by Confucianism, which the people felt was being much more realistic in demanding a more "closed soul" approach. Mo Tzu came after Confucius, and the great Confucian, Mencius came after Mo Tzu. Mencius was a practical man of goodness and good ethics, but he could not rise to the level of Mo's universal idealism. In the works of Mencius the story is told of one who had visited the Moists and said to Mencius that E Che, a Moist, stated: "To me it sounds that we are to love all without difference of degree; but the manifestation of love must begin with our parents" (implying that it then would spread out in equal measure to all the world). Mencius' reply was, "Now, does E really think that a man's affection for the child of his brother is like his affection for the infant of a neighbor?"(3.1.5). Yet, Mencius had a high regard for social love and justice, but it must be, in his mind, limited to our natural capacities. He also realized that only the good man could be of benefit to others, but even the good man by his proper nature can be broken down by the evils inflicted upon him. "And so also of what properly belongs to man; -- shall it be said that the mind of any man was without benevolence and righteousness? The way in which a man loses his proper goodness of mind is like the way in which the trees are denuded by axes and bills. Hewn down day after day, can the mind retain its beauty?"(6.1.8). In the global village the modern man today lives in, perhaps Mo Tzu should be allowed to teach us more than he has been permitted in the past. For since the world has become so small, it is necessary that our hearts become bigger and our capacity to love more open and be more far reaching. Mo Tzu and Jesus certainly have taught us that this is the way of Heaven (Mo Tzu) and the way of our Father in Heaven (Jesus).

Buddhism has brought us the wonderful world of the teachings of the Dhammapada that speaks to this subject with the following words:

"The virtuous man delights in this world, and he delights in the next; he delights in both. He delights and rejoices, when he sees the purity of his own work".(I.).

"But, like a beautiful flower, full of color and full os scent, are the fine and fruitful words of him who acts accordingly...and the odor of good people travels even against the wind; a good man's (influence) pervades every place."(IV).

"Good people shine from afar, like the snowy mountains." (XXI).

Buddhism, in general, has an open soul and a universal flavor of goodness to it. Four principles are stated as some of the many "white actions" to be taken to cast out "black deeds".

1. Not to consciously tell a lie, even to save one's life;
2. To encourage others to engage in virtuous pursuits and, in particular, to follow the Universal Way.
3. To see every bodhisattva as the Buddha, and to proclaim his or her virtues; and
4. To maintain a noble attitude towards others.9.5

After his coversion to Buddhism, King Priyadarsi (Asoka) posted edicts of Dharma throughout his kingdom for the purpose of revealing to all the path of goodness and happiness that all may participate in the joy he had found. One Edict reads this way:

King Priyadarsi says:
    Twelve years after my coronation I ordered edicts on Dharma to be inscribed for the welfare and happiness of the people, in order that they might give up their former ways of life and grow in Dharma in the particular respects set forth.
    Since I am convinced that the welfare and happiness of the people will be achieved only in this way, I consider how I may bring happiness to the people, not only to relatives of mine or residents of my capital city, but also to those who are far removed from me. I act in the same manner with respect to all.
    I am concerned similarly with all classes.
    Moreover, I have honored all religious sects with various offerings. I consider it my principal duty to visit the people personally.(Pillar Edict VI).(tr. N.A. Nikam & R. McKeon).

One can see here the "open soul" of universality that Mo Tzu and Jesus have also presented to us. The farther the light shines, the stronger it is at its source.

Plato and Aristotle have been mentioned above, but I would like to quote an early Greek, Persius, who realized that a sacrifice to the city's gods must be accompanied by a man who respected the duties of required of him by the city:

"To the just gods let me present a mind,
Which civil and religious duties bind,
A guileless heart, which no dark secrets knows,
But with the generous love of virtue glows,
Such be the presents, such the gifts I make,
With them I sacrifice a wheaten cake.(Satire II.133-138).

The Golden Rule, popularized by Jesus, was well spread throughout the world even before his ministry. Lao Tzu even implied that what one did to another, he did to himself, since all are in a way connected: "With the knowledge that one is unified with the entire body of humanity, one will properly take care of others." Confucius presented the words of Tsze-kung: "What I do not wish men to do to me, I also wish not to do to men".(Analects V.11). And again in the Analects (XII.2), "It is, when you go abroad, to behave to every one as if you were receiving a great guest; to employ the people as if you were assisting at a great sacrifice; not to do to others as you would not wish done to yourself." Again, for a third time, the Confucian Analects state: "Tsze-kung asked, saying,'Is there one word which may serve as a rule of practice for all one's life?' The Master said, 'Is not reciprocity such a word? What you do not want done to yourself, do not do to others." (XV.23).

Plato does likewise refer four times to the concept, but long before Plato, Hesiod, among the Greeks, laid down a principle that very same "Golden Rule" principle.

"Get good measure from you neighbor;
Give good measure back.
Return as much, or better, if you can,
So that when you are yourself in need
You will find him able to supply it."9.6

The Jewish story of Tobit, Second Century BC, Tobit gives Tobias this advice, along with much more, "And the things you hate, do not do to anyone else" (4:15). The Roman Stoic, Seneca, a contemporary of Jesus, stated, "But the essence of my teaching is this, treat your inferiors in the way in which you would like to be treated by your own superiors," Which was borrowed directly from Plato (Letter XLVII).

As was Seneca above, so was Marcus Aurelius a Stoic, and one of the principle teachings among the Stoics was the universal brotherhood of men, and in this sense a completely open soul, such as Mo Tzu taught, was called upon. Aurelius taught: "Adorn thyself with simplicity and modesty, and with indifference towards the things which lie between virtue and vice. Love mankind. Follow God." (Meditations: VII.31). William James claimed that our call to improve the world came from a "moral energy born of faith", and while it was not stated as love, it was directed towards the benefit of the world: "This world is good, we must say, since it is what we make it, -- and we shall make it good."9.7 The person born of the moral energy of faith, in order to find his own completeness, must extend his care and benefits to the world. Jacques Maritain reminded us once again that the extension of good works and love can be effected only by one who is strong within his own soul and motivated by the good within and who stands upon his own strength in meeting his personal vocational responsibilities and choices. In remembrance, he still has the power to walk like a rhinoceros.

> Yet in order to reach completion such a necessary reform must understand, too, that to be a good citizen and a man of civilization what matters above all is the inner center, the living source of personal conscience in which originate idealism and generosity, the sense of law and the sense of friendship, respect for others, but at the same time deep-rooted independence with regard to common opinion.9.8

For the person who wants to make a difference in his world by being involved in politics, it would do him well to read his Plato and Aristotle, whose works have been mentioned in this book, but it would also be well for him to read Petrarch's "Treatise on Princely Government" in which he stated that a ruler is to love his people as truly as he loves his own son, as well as reading <u>Erasmus'</u> work <u>"The Education of a Christian Prince"</u>.

III. <u>JUSTICE, THE BACKBONE OF HUMAN HARMONY</u>

"...with liberty and justice for all" is a well known and much repeated and respected phrase in the USA, and for good reason. Social harmony and tranquility are built upon justice for all, and, just as an individual seeks internal harmony and tranquility because wholeness and happiness cannot exist without them, a society likewise needs people to live in harmony with one another if the society is to have wholeness. Loving one's fellow citizen as one loves oneself, means that one is to seek to build the foundation of a society with the same effort and excitement with which one builds his own personal foundation capable of supporting and giving growth to his own happiness. As a mother rejoices when she gives life to a child, so also the just man rejoices when he is instrumental in giving others a foundation that gives birth to a life of happiness. A coach rejoices when his team plays well and plays to together in enjoyment and harmony. A teacher rejoices to see her students prospering in their adult lives. A good man is not complete until he makes life more beautiful for others, and in society, that possibility starts with justice for all. Plato called justice the harmony of the virtues, both within a man's soul and within the citizenry of a city. Such harmony is symphonic music that balances life and brings a soothing to mankinds' soul. Seek justice that man can have a foundation upon which to build his life and the life of his society! The first two sections of this chapter dealt with the general aspects of love's reaching out to others in order to bring them the enriched life which one feels in his own heart. This section and the following sections will present specific virtues to be established within society so that the people will be capable of being enriched in their own personal lives: justice, duty, courage, and other virtues that are the bricks and mortar needed to build society.

So much has been written about the idea of justice that it seems impossible to justify more words on the subject. Yet, I have put justice forth as a moral element that unites itself to a man's goodness and gives that man a personal wholeness and happiness to his own character. For the love in man necessitates by its very nature the drive to create better lives for those he can reach, see, and with whom he can form relations. Otherwise that love dies, or turns to selfishness in which there is no ultimate goodness and happiness. The religious man sees his God as Love itself, and as his God has created, reached out, blessed, and covered with grace his creatures, so man also, made in the same image, must do the same or disown his own personal nature as a child of God. Justice, in fact, is the fulness and harmonization of all social virtues, including love. Therefore, in speaking of justice, other virtues will be spoken of as being naturally a part of justice itself.

In the Vedas, some of the oldest philosophical writings in the world, there is the concept of RITA which is the basis of truth and the source of moral harmony both metaphysically and within the world of mankind. It gives to mankind the sense of just order in which man within wisdom's power can bring into being in human society that men can live in harmony with each other. I.C. Sharma stated this about RITA:

It represents the sublime moral order, which is inviolable. The inviolability of Rita makes it superior to gods and cosmic ethics on the one hand, and individual human beings on the other, because Rita works throughout the cosmos inevitably and justly.9.9

A Zoroastrian prayer asks help from Ahuras Mazda to come to the worshippers and bring justice with him that the worshipers may be among those of the earth that make life fulfilling and meaningful and thus advance mankind towards a more beautiful future. The prayer is hopeful that the group together can advance their individual thoughts to form the virtue of wisdom within, and by thus attaining such wisdom they and others may live in harmony with justice (Yasna 30-31).

All forms of Greek literature presented the problem of creating a society in which justice ruled: the dramatists -- both tragic and comedic --, the epic writers, the philosophers and both the moralists and novelists. Stobaeus stated: "The cheerful man because he is always impelled to just and lawful deeds is happy, vigorous, and free from care, whether waking or dreaming".9.10 So very early the Greeks proclaimed this essential link between goodness and happiness, and justice was a form of social goodness whose function made men happy. Anacreon, in his Ode "On the Lyre" speaks of his conversion from singing heroic hymns to war heroes to singing only about love. For war represented to him a breakdown of social justice, whereas love was that which binds men together in harmony.

"While I sweep the sounding string,
While the Atridae's praise I sing,
Victors on the Trojan plain,
Or to Cadmus raise the strain,
Hark! In soft and whispered sighs,
Love's sweet notes the shell replies,
Late I strung my harp anew,
Changed the strings -- the subject too--
Loud I sung Alcides' toils,
Still the lyre my labor foils;
Still with love's sweet silver sounds
Every martial theme confounds.
Farewell! Heroes, chiefs and kings,
Nought but love will suit my strings." (trans. Thomas Bourne)

Persius acknowledged that it was not in the praise of others that the reward of virtue was to be found, but the feeling within that one had been just and beneficial to another.

"I feel from praise no genuine delight:
But praise ought not to be the only end
For which our morals or our lives we mend;
For which our virtue struggles to excel,
And seeks pre-eminence in doing well." (Satire I, trans. W. Drummond)

The deed of justice has its own reward: wholeness within. The dramatist Aeschylus in his "Suppliant Maidens" has the chorus singing a constant plea for justice and encouraging his audience to seek the same:

"Yet Justice champions those that fight for her"(340), and

"Be thou the ally of Justice and not law; judge thou as judge the Gods and stand of them in awe"(395), and

"Search deep and then rise up more strong for Justice,

Be the minister that reverentially protects from wrong
The stranger and the sojourner"(419), and

"Submit not to the sight
Of divine Justice set at naught by might"(428).(trans. G.M.Cookson)

In Plato's Crito, the "Laws" within Socrates are presented to show that Socrates could not in his own mind ever consider leaving Athens or breaking the laws of his city by avoiding his declared punishment, the taking of hemlock. Better to die in good conscience than to live unjustly by avoiding the call to duty. The "Laws" are making their demands upon Socrates and Plato recorded it thus:

"Listen, then, Socrates, to us who have brought you up. Think not of life and children first, and of justice afterwards, but of justice first, that you may be justified before the princes of the next world. For neither will you nor any that belongs to you be happier or holier or juster in this life, or happier in another, if you do as Crito bids [Crito had encouraged him to flee Athens in a waiting ship]. Now you depart in innocence, a sufferer and not a doer of evil; a victim, not of the laws but of men. But if you go forth, returning evil for evil, and injury for injury, breaking the covenants and agreements which you have made with us [the laws of his conscience], ...we shall be angry with you while you live, and our brethren, the laws in the next world, will receive you as an enemy"(54).

The man who avoids doing justice or right when his life is at stake, will not save the life that he had when he was just, and his welcome into the next world greatly diminished. This reminds Christians of Peter's suggestion that Jesus not go to Jerusalem, avoid his call and mission, and avoid the cross. Jesus replied to Peter that he was very wrong in suggesting that Jesus was a coward: "You accused me of being a coward, and a rebel against the call of my Father in Heaven". The Biblical recording is "Get behind me, Satan", but one must remember that "satan" meant "the accuser", and just what was Peter accusing Jesus of if he actually thought Jesus would avoid his mission other than a rebellious coward against his own Heavenly Father. Socrates was hearing the cry of Justice, and that it demanded to be put before life and his beloved little children. Without Justice the harmony of the city would be lost, and then Socrates would be aiding in that destruction of all that he loved.

Only the good man can be just, and Aristotle reminded his students that when a drama is written it is important to establish the good character of a man who in an existential dilemma will have the fortitude to chose justice or the right thing to do: "Character is that which reveals moral purpose, showing what kind of things a man chooses or avoids". (Poetics VI.9) Sallust in his Conspiracy of Cataline laments the fact that kings spend so much time in preparing war and so little time in seeking peace, which is far better for their subjects:

> And if kings and rulers, would exert their abilities in peace, as they do in war, the condition of human affairs wuld be much more steady and uniform; nor should we see so frequent revolutions and con-vulsions in states, and such universal confusion.(I.2).

Yes, it is the peacemakers who will be called the sons of God. Epictetus stated that if a man is making progress towards virtue, he is also making progress towards good fortune, tranquillity and happiness for both himself and society: "Now if virtue pormises good fortune and tranquillity and happiness, certainly also the progress toward virtue is progress toward each of these things."(I.4) The virtue a man attains makes life better for himself and also for the society which surrounds him. The Viking poem "The Insolence of Loki" presented the wiser Frigg telling Loki that in minor matters, forgive and forget is both the wiser and more just way to settle such problems. But Loki, now entering his decline from a very likable god to a self-centered trouble maker told Frigg to shut up, to which Frigg replied that Loki was acting childish and really needed a good beating (in politically correct language a "spanking", but it must be remembered that the subjects are Vikings and therefore 'beating' is a preferable translation). Loki continues his rejection of good advice throughout his growth and ends up being about as evil as Viking gods could get, losing the respect and love of all the other gods: in ruining himself he infected his society, which in turn rejected him. Lack of virtue leads to lack of justice which leads to a dis-gruntled society that will fight back against the unjust individual. For one to fulfill his own happiness a just man must reach out to flavor and enlighten and change his society: as salt he must flavor others or be put on the dung heap, and as light he must shine to the world around him. Another <u>Viking</u> <u>poem</u> presents a wise <u>Angantyr</u> counselling Hervor that she should not seek justice by means of a personal revenge by the sword for that would start a system of each side trying to "get the last kill", and the fighting would never stop:

"Listen to me, Hervor, let me tell you,
Daughter of princes, what will come to pass:
Maiden, you will doom all your descendants;
If you trust Tyrfing [her sword], all will be destroyed."
(The Waking of Angantyr, 18)

An impulsive person who cannot control his passions and emotions can have neither justice within himself or justice within his society: he brings personal breakdown to himself and death to his society, even his own descendants. Man's personal virtue and unity are so tied into his own society that even without thinking about it, his fate affects that of his community. <u>John</u> <u>Donne</u> said it very well:

"Who bends not his ear to any bell which upon any occasions rings? But who can remove it from that bell which is passing a piece of himself out of this world? No man is an island, entire of itself; every man is a piece of the continent, a part of the main. If a clod be washed away by the sea, Europe is the less, as well as if a promontory were, as well as if a manor of they friend's or of thine own were: any man's death diminishes me, because I am involved in mankind, and therefore never send to know for whom the bell tolls; it tolls for thee."9.11

   <u>Martin</u> <u>Luther</u> believed that once a person was made good by faith in Christ, he no longer was totally tied into his own quest of salvation, but rather was born a new and good tree that naturally bore good fruits (deeds) for the benefit of his fellowman and the community in which he lived. The nature of a good man, a virtuous being, is to automatically reach out to others in order to do them well and enhance the goodness of their lives also. In his <u>Preface</u> <u>to</u> <u>the</u> <u>Epistle</u> <u>of</u> <u>St.</u> <u>Paul</u> <u>to</u> <u>the</u> <u>Romans</u>, Luther stated:

"Faith is a divine work in us that transforms us and begets us anew from God, kills the Old Adam, makes us entirely different people in heart, spirit, mind, and all our powers, and brings the Holy Spirit with it. Oh, faith is a living, busy, active, mighty thing, so that it is impossible for it not to be constantly doing what is good. Likewise, faith does not ask if good works are to be done, but before one can ask, faith has already done them and is constantly active...This [action] the Holy Spirit works by faith, and therefore without any coercion, a man is willing and desirous to do good to everyone, to serve everyone, to suffer everything for the love of God and to his glory, who has been so gracious to him. It is therefore as impossible to separate works from faith as it is to separate heat and light from fire."9.12

A good man, a man of virtue, automatically reaches out to others, for it is part of his goodness, and for the sake of his own wholeness he must let this love for others exercise itself in order to retain his own spiritual harmony. Fire can not be fire unless it gives off both light and heat. From the time of Plato the West has known that virtues must function for that is their very soul, just as the virtue of an axe is in the cutting, so the man of just harmony within will bring that just harmony to society. Jesus warned that if a man is given talents and he does not utilize them, he shall lose them. For a man to retain happiness and wholeness he must bring the same to others, not just to his small group of beloved ones, but to society at large.

   Henri Bergson in his book The Two Sources of Morality and Religion speaks of two different kinds of people: ones with a closed soul and ones with an open soul. The closed soul individual is always turned inward, but the opened soul person, while not diminishing his care and love of self, learns step by step to bring his love to those outside of himself and when his soul is completely open, then to all humanity. While the closed soul goes about in circles around the self, the open soul "embraces all humanity" and even this is not too far, but not far enough, for "its love may extend to animals, to plants, to all nature". Step by step the open soul is associated with "love for one's family, love for one's country, love of mankind," and in these three inclinations there is "one single feeling, growing ever larger, to embrace an increasing number of persons." Whereas the closed soul brings about strife and hatred, the opened soul brings justice and love.9.13 Bergson's concept of the opened

soul is the same as Plato's God and Father of Creation who desires not
one person to be neglected, Mo Tzu's universal love, and Jesus'
teachings to love and pray for even those who are a threat to you and
bring about a peace among men by non-violent means. The next section
speaks about this opened soul's love for all, not only as a natural
reaction, but as a divine duty. "Be ye perfect, as your Heavenly Father is
perfect" said Jesus. What a man needs to form a deep basis upon which
to build a true and inner happiness, is a powerful infused and nourished
sense of fairness and justice in his dealings with other people: so much
so that he would feel a deep sense of shame if he were to prosper in any
way by means of an injustice, however small or big. I fear that as a nation
we are very far from that ideal, because of attachment to self and
self-glory. In 1999 the USA Women's Soccer team "won" the World
Cup by "defeating" China, and it was celebrated to an unlimited
narcissism: this despite that the Chinese women had scored a goal that
was not credited during the match that would have given them the
victory in the game's regularly allotted time, and would not have gone
into an "overtime" shoot-out. The Chinese women did not complain.
Then in the overtime shoot-out, our goal keeper cheated on each kick to
defend the goal. The Chinese women did not complain. Consequently,
the American team scored the "victory" and throughout the country they
were were celebrated as our wonderful women bringing home the
victory. I couldn't believe it and thought "was nobody feeling any shame
for this?" To lose one's soul for a soccer game! Our men of today are no
better. In 1940 a confused referee in a college football game gave Cornell
a fifth down with three seconds left to play, and Cornell scored a
touchdown on that fifth play, winning 7-3. Cornell, at that time, was on
an 18 game unbeaten streak and was ranked number one in the nation.
But, as soon at it was discovered that they were given a fifth down by
mistake, they, without any outside requests, surrendered the victory and it
was awarded to Dartmouth. Yet in the Fall of 1990 a similar confusion
gave Colorado University a fifth down on the Missouri team's goal line.
They likewise scored to win the game at the last moment. But, unlike
Cornell, Colorado relished the win and celebrated to their own glory. It
will be on their record forever as a dirty little football injustice that they
took advantage of, and showed the 80 players on the team that winning a
football game was more important than fair play. If we teach our young
to shame their sense of honor for the sake of the final score of a football

game, then how can university leadership ever complain about their students' cheating later in the business world?

IV. <u>DUTY</u>

From the examples of the lives of Socrates and Jesus one can get a sense of the power of duty, yet in probably no other philosophy is duty stressed more than in Stoicism, where nature sets the table of life and it is your duty to follow it. This "duty" concept of the Stoics appealed to the Roman's feeling of duty towards their city, then country, then empire, and as a result Stoicism and/or some eclectic form of it was seen to the Romans as an inforcing way of life that made it's call to even the highest order of the Empire: Seneca, counselor to Emperor, and Marcus Aurelius, himself an Emperor. In modern times it was Kant who emphasized the need to follow dutifully the divine and categorial imperatives of goodness. One of the more delightful ways in which duty was expressed was the work by <u>Aristophanes, Lysistrata</u>, where women take it upon themselves to pursue peace and stop the civil war between Athens and Sparta. It is fiction and comedy, but it was a desperate attempt by Aristophanes to show the men of Athens and Sparta the folly of the war. In the play, an Athenian magistrate mocks Lysistrata, for war is a man's business, not for someone who wears a veil in public, i.e. a woman. But she stands firm and adamant declaring that if he wants the veil, he can have it, and throws it at him and tells him to wrap it around his own head, for she has made this war a woman's business. The business of war was carried out by the women who refused to have sexual intercourse or participate in any form of sexual climax for their husbands, and probably for any soldier. "Stop the war and you can return to the glories of sexuality!" was her cry. She then told the women they had a duty to be the peacemakers among the Greeks. One must remember that this war went on sporatically over thirty years. Some women complained that by the time they won their men over to peace they would be old and not desirous anymore. Lysistrata told them to empower themselves to the maximum, because it was their duty to stop this war. She prayed that the God of Love and the sweet Cyprian Queen would give them an abundance of seductive charms and sensuality that the men would be so stirred by sensual desires that they would "stand as firm as sticks". This was their task to inflame and torture him with seductions, caresses, provocations, and every form of igniting desire, every favor -- except the final and deepest pleasure, for that would be forbidden by their mutual oath. Finally the men give up war and were restored to the "forbidden pleasure", got drunk with the enemy and embrace each other, and an Athenian then declared that when our envoys go to Sparta they "should always be drunk". Peace seemed to come easier when men were enjoying their wives and were drunk.

Civic duty by the rich in Aristophanes' city, ancient Athens, was made imperative by the LEITOURGIA (a service to one's city) during the prospects or the reality of war. The trierarchs were responsible for building a warship, called a trireme (three banks of oars on each side of the ship), and to pay for the crew and other expenditures for one full year. He could pay for it himself or form a group of his friends that would be willing to help in the cost. Obviously the cost was tremendous, and when one was nominated to become a trierarch, he could nominate another for the tax by declaring the other to be more wealthy than himself. But he had to back his finger pointing at another's wealth by offerring to make an exchange: his wealth for the other's. He then would not foolishly point to anyone, unless he honestly thought the other to be of great wealth, at least close to his own, but hopefully more than his own. Nevertheless, the one so "honored" to become a trierarch faced a hugh social duty, but if one were to enjoy the wonders of Athens, and one who prospered greatly because of Athens, he had a duty to pay for the defence of Athens. If one loved Athens the way Socrates did, and one had the means to pay for the building and function of a trireme, it was his loving duty to separate himself from much of his wealth. Today, in the USA, there are people who are just the opposite. They grow up in or make their money in one state, but keep a legal residence in another state that has lower or maybe no state taxes at all. These people have never let their love become full for the benefits they have received, and do not have a very deep idea of what duty to one's community is. There even have been people in the highest offices of the nation who have done the same thing, and yet talk about their patriotism. It is always sad when a nation is led by such selfish people. Yet, the person who is just and dutiful to his "homeland" is the person who is good and is the person that feels the joy of extending his love to others in his state or country.

The great Stoic Epictetus scorned the cynics of his day because they fled from every duty possible, and prided themselves in being liberated from the common duties of mankind and the ordinary relations of life. They simply do not maintain a character that can be classified as one of honor and goodness. The cynic cares nothing for his wife and children or his parents or inlaws. He will not wash a child, even his own, nor be there to care for and comfort his wife when she bears a child. He scorns duty as a distraction to his free way of life. "How can he have time for this [personal quest of freedom] who is tied to the duties of common life? Is it not his duty to supply clothing to his children, and to send them to the school-master with writing tablets, and styles. Besides, must he not supply them with beds?...(how can he)...kill them in this way?" (III.22). Actually, claimed Epictetus, the Cynic knows nothing "about happiness and unhappiness, about good fortune and bad fortune, about slavery and freedom".

Immanuel Kant taught that it is our duty to conform our will and actions that they are brought into harmony with the validity of universal moral law. Once there, and well praticed, our will shall be moulded into the moral righteousness of universal law so well that our voluntary actions automatically conform to it, and thus man gains his true freedom, for he no longer has the moral law outside of himself compelling him through conscience and society to do what is just and dutiful. Man will also experience peace with the Supreme being and have an additional happiness and wholeness within. One who becomes perfectly good, like God, will find no obligations from the outside, for he will naturally do the good and the dutiful. When he arrives at that state, man has fulfilled his moral duties to himself, for when a man respects his inner most value, that every thing that makes him a good man, he will see that his total value is no more than his ethical value, to himself and to others. Kant makes it very clear that one who fulfills the universal moral law towards others increase his own moral worth and happiness. Reaching out in duty to the rest of mankind, makes oneself worthy of one's own happiness. In so making oneself worthy of happiness, based upon his goodness, he verifies to himself, by his actions, that he is truly a good man. This also is a greater piety than one who never misses his prayers, for the very purpose of praying is to enhance our own goodness, both to self and to others. He likewise experiences a freedom, for he is not pressed by an external force or law to be good, but he is good by his very nature and thus he is not only good for others, but liberates himself.

In his book, The Valley of the Shadow, Hanns Lilje enumerated the many of the Resistance Movement against Hilter who died, many in the last days of Nazi rule "when liberation was at the door". The vindictive Nazis, knowing their cause was lost, instead of being finally abit humane, they executed as many as possible who had resisted them and their rule. Likewise the many of the Berlin Confessional Church were slaughtered at the last moment. Not only these, "But there were others also, outstanding Trades Union leaders, politicians on the left; Count Moltke, the leader of the Kreisauer circle...as well as some leading Roman Catholics...Almost every old Prussian faimily was represented, and, finally ...(those who) were related to one or another of the conspirators."9.14 Indeed, when there is a great evil power trying to control our lives, then duty is often very hard, yet Lilje looks back not in pity but in love and honor to those who died fighting against the doctrine, that according to Lilje, was "such absolutely pagan doctrines like those of the worthlessness of human life." Lilje stated about those executed by the Nazis:

> ...but even in memory we must not let bitterness have the last word,
> but only the conviction that God's holy purpose was fulfilled in their
> lives, and thankfulness for the fact that He granted them strength to
> face death with faith and confidence. We who were privileged to see
> and accompany these brethren on the last part of the way that they
> had to tread on earth, are glad to bear our witness to their victory,
> in gratitude and reverence. In the sight of the unwise they seemed to
> die, and their departure is taken for misery...but they are in peace.9.15

Dietrich Bonhoeffer, one who was executed just days before the Nazi surrender, stated in one of his essays:

> We will not and must not be either outraged critics or opportunists,
> but must take our share of responsibility for the moulding of history
> in every situation and at every moment, whether we are the victors or
> the vanquished. One who will not allow any occurrence whatever to
> deprive him of his responsibility for the course of history -- because

he knows that it has been laid on him by God -- will thereafter
achieve a more fruitful relation to the events of history than that of
barren criticism and equally barren opportunism.9.16

One of the areas of personal responsibility that is almost discarded by
present day America, is that of finances. In this area, Americans are far
from either mature, rational, or good. They cave in to silly commercials
that tell them they must have some material benefit to be happy, whether
or not they can afford it or ever will be able to afford it. "Go ahead and
buy it, you deserve it" is the idiotic cry that one hears quite often. At least
half of all divorces come from financial problems created by childish and
unrealists passions for things. Often, more than a million a year, families
or individuals declare bankruptcy, one of the more popular ways to
legally steal from others: some even hide assests fraudulantly to increase
their guilt of theft. One systematic, ongoing and legal way to steal from
others which is by far the most popular and is passed on from one
generation to another is that of receiving welfare paid for by the work of
others. Paul in his Second Letter to the Thessalonians stated that "If any
one will not work, let him not eat," and "Now such persons we command
and exhort...to do their work in quietness and to earn their own living."
Mahatma Gandhi, was furious with his fellow citizens of India, because
so many did nothing but collect welfare while India's economy was
devastated. "To a people famishing and idle the only acceptable form in
which God can dare appear is work and promise of food as wages. God
created man to work for his food and said that those who ate without
work were thieves. Eighty percent of India are compulsorily thieves half
the year. Is it any wonder India has become one vast prison?"9.17 While
it certainly is not 80% in the USA, especially since the crackdown and
life limitations brought some rational thought into the system during the
1990s, yet in 1995 both the welfare and its evil companion of selling
food stamps for money (1995 sales of food stamps for money reached the
one billion dollar mark) were still well and thriving: in 1993 it was stated
that 60% of child-welfare cases involved fraud. In 1999 the Los Angeles
Times reported that $16,000 were paid to a foster mother for the sole
purpose of giving two girls quinceaneras, a type of "debutante coming
out" social event for 15 year olds (LAT 6/29/1999). Also it was stated in
1997 that 60% of the people on welfare at that time never had a job that
lasted six months. In the USA theft is also rampant among those who

took out college loans and never repaid them. This was a game of theft by the young and irresponsible, feeling that to steal in such a way was a type of entitlement (many immediately upon graduating, declared bankruptcy). In 1992, 558 colleges and universitis had default rates so high that they were about to lose their eligibility to remain in the federal program

Aristophanes ridiculed people who went to law court to steal from others. Strepsiades wants a sophist teacher to teach him the tricks of the law court so that he can avoid paying all of his debts, which were many, "do let me learn the unjust logic that can shrink debts: now do just let me learn it" (The Clouds 245-250). It almost sounds like a bankruptcy lawyer today in his commercials: of course, in avoiding his debts to others, the man must pay the sophist or the lawyer. Likewise people like to steal by means of "deep pockets" law suits that ask for, not just retribution, but enormous sums of money. The lawyers excuse such greed as simply "sending a message to the big corporations", but everyone knows that it is simple greed and that they are trying to take money from those who have invested in the company. Stealing in any form is the defeat of personal duty, society's harmony, and personal growth towards goodness. It cheapens each man's dignity for the sake of material benefits. Ruthless CEOs who protect by legal means their ill gotten estates, are truly sad people who have no sense of honor or duty for the country's people in which they live. A man who was on welfare still can redeem himself by paying back what he received -- but, realistically, how many will? It would surprise me if one in a thousand actually did. Zaccheus the tax collector, who stole legally, in the presence of Jesus promised to restore up to four-fold what he had unjustly taken from others. With that statement, Jesus announced that salvation had now come into his house. I will close this section on duty with a quotation from Anton Boisen:

"Our recognitionof the social nature of man enables us to understand the significance of that fact. A teaching, a philosophy, an ethical code must be incarnated in some personality before it can become religiously vital. Ethical standards and religious value do not exist in and of themselves. They are functions of the social relationships. It is therefore a fact of cardinal importance that Christianity had in the person of its founder an object of loyalty who represented so beautifully the loftiest potentialities of mankind."9.18

V. COURAGE TO BE JUST AND DUTIFUL

Courage can be displayed in many different ways, but the way in which I want to present it is the courage to do that which is just and dutiful to one's one character according to his perceptions of reality and the depth of his love for others. Such courage has been referred to already in the lives of Socrates, Jesus, and several of the people who opposed Hitler within Germany during his reign of irrational terror. Now it is time to look at what humanity's great teachers said about courage. Plato made courage one of the four cardinal virtues that both man and society needed in order to become whole and happy; his living illustration was the life and death of Socrates, whom he called the most righteous man of his generation. He also wrote a dialogue discussing its many forms and the essence of the concept of courage itself: the Laches. Confucius stated: "...to see what is right and not do it is want of courage" (II.24). Mencius talked about the balance of loving life and the courage to put justice ahead of even one's life:

> I like life, and I also like righteousness. If I cannot keep the two
> together, I will let life go and choose righteousness. I like life very
> much, but there is that which I like more than life, and therefore,
> I will not seek to possess it by any improper ways.(6.1.10).

Persius in his First Satire scorns those court poets who write nothing but insincere, dead, depraved poems for the sake of flattering the powerful, and avoid any type of honest criticism of the evil that they do to others. Gone from their poetry are spirit, virtue, and genius. Their works trample the sacred ground of honest poetry. They have neglected the duty of poetry, and yet they pride their pusillanimous selves. They have not the courage to even speak the truth, let alone carry the message straight to the evil ruler. In Ovid's poem "Cadmus" he tells of the foolish slaughter among relatives, which in reality was a criticism of Rome's civil war in which Romans killed in battle their fellow Romans, their city's brothers:

The dire example ran through all the field,
Till heaps of brothers were by brothers kill'd;
The furrows swam in blood, and only five
Of all the vast increase were left alive.
Echion one, at Pallas's command
Let fall the guiltless weapon from his hand,
And with the rest a peaceful treaty makes,
Whom Cadmus as his friends and partners takes.
So founds a city on the promised earth,
And gives his new Boeotian empire birth.(Bk III: Cadmus 170-179)

Finally one had the courage and wisdom to risk his life by dropping his weapon and asked for peace, and wisdom prevailed. Pliny the Younger made mention of the danger of dissent during the 15 year reign of terror by the Roman Emperor Domitian (81-96AD). But the philosophers stood strong against him and suffered greatly for it, either by death or by banishment. In 89AD they were first proscribed for banishment, and again in 93AD they were severely punished. Pliny felt helpless, but did continue his dissent. He stated in a letter to Julius Genitor: "This I did though I had before my eyes the sufferings of seven of my friends; Senecio, Rusticus, and Helvidius being just then put to death, at the same time that Mauricus, Gratilla, Arria, and Fannia were sent into exile. And scorched as I was with the lightning of the State, which thus flashed around me, I had great reason to expect it would not be long before it destroyed me too." 9.19 Courage is indeed a serious and hard virtue, but cowardice is so defeating to one's image that it makes self-love impossible. The good man does hate death, but he hates cowardice more. Philostratus stated: "To be blamed by a friend for appearing cowardly is something more than all your enemies' deeds put together. You cannot fail to be detested for your show of cowardice."9.20 Philostratus also told of a beautiful Arcadian boy that was desired by the Emperor Domitian, but had the courage to say no, and was so respected the the court of public opinion that even Domitian granted him release from his desires: "...he won admiration for his firmness, and so sailed back to Malea. He was more of a hero in Arcadia than those who win the endurance test of the whips at Sparta" [Spartan training of young soldiers included contests as to who could stand the most strikes in a flogging, sometimes the contest turned fatal].9.21   Karl Jaspers in his book <u>Way to Wisdom</u> referred to courage as a way to be in command of one's authentic self, and offered the examples of the courageous men of the past which were to serve as our teachers: Socrates, Tomas More, Seneca, Boethius and Bruno. They were men who knew, despite normal human frailties and failures, how to die, for they understood the idea of unconditional imperative that proves their true value: "The unconditional imperative comes to me as the command of my authentic self to my mere empirical existence. I become aware of myself as of that which I myself am, because it is what I ought to be".9.22 Martin Luther stood before the Diet at Worms, knowing that if he did not recant he would be classified as a heretic and his life in all probability would soon be ended by force, yet he did not recant, and stated: "Hie stehe ich, ich kan nicht anders, Got helffe mir. Amen" ("Here I stand. I cannot do otherwise. God help me. Amen.") He was authenticating his true self by means of courage, and as such, he could not possibly recant. Life had to be secondary to his self authentification, for without such he could not love himself, let alone others. To go against the grain for the sake of justice takes courage. The Baptist preacher who was named after Martin Luther, <u>Martin Luther King, Jr.</u>, also made a statement in word and life of the value of courage in which men validated their virtue and exercised their love for others. He stated:

> Courage is an inner resolution to go forward in spite of obsticles and frightening situations; cowardice is a submissive surrender to circum-stance. Courage breeds creative self-affirmation; cowardice produces destrutive self-abnigation. Courage faces fear and thereby masters it; cowardice represses fear and is thereby mastered by it.9.23

All people are aware of the horror of Nazi power in Germany from 1933-1945, but the Confessional Church of Germany by their courage and suffering made a bold stand against the Nazis, and I have alluded to their sufferings earlier this chapter. The Jewish and Gipsy populations were utterly devastated, so the words of the the Jewish Albert Einstein are much to be listed to, especially for those who think that the members of the Confessional Church of Germany died in vain. They did not die in vain. From Time Magazine, December 23, 1940, p.38 the words of <u>Albert Einstein</u> were reported as:

Being a lover of freedom, when the revolution came in Germany, I looked to the universities to defend it, knowing that they had always boasted of their devotion to the cause of truth; but, no, the universities immediately were silenced. Then I looked to the great editors of the newspapers whose flaming editorials in days gone by had proclaimed their love of freedom; but they, like the universities, were silenced in a few short weeks...Only the church [i.e. The Confessional Church of Germany] stood squarely across the path of Hitler's campaign for suppressing truth. I never had any special interest in the church before, but now I feel a great affection and admiration because the Church alone has had the courage and persistence to stand for intellectual truth and moral freedom. I am forced thus to confess that what I once despised I now praise unreservedly.

The Confessional Church of Germany suffered many deaths, but saved its own soul, and verified its own value and wholeness.

Paul Tillich in his book The Courage to Be made these statements about courage:

"Courage is strength of mind, capable of conquering whatever threatens the attainment of the highest good."

"Courage listens to reason and carries out the intention of the mind. It is the strength of the soul to win victory in ultimate danger."9.24

There are, of course, many other social virtues that extends man's love from himself to his society: sharing with those in need, giving physcial care to the elderly, rational teaching that shows the way to those lost and have no path to follow, being peacemakers and counsellors of encouragement to those in conflict and depression, and helping others to learn the self value of forgiving another for his human frailties. In all such activities man makes himself complete in letting his love stretch far from himself to the furtherest reaches of mankind, and also to the animal kingdom whose companionship has added immersurably to mankind's happiness. One is to beware of those things that hinder his growth in love and service to the social community in which he lives. They can be called sins (missing the mark), detours from the path of righteousness, or spiritual building infractions that weaken the structure of society. Some of them are listed blow that one can beware of them infecting one's life goals.

Prayers and thoughts of revenge.
Forgetting justice and stating: "If its legal and I can prosper from it, I'll do it."
Thinking popular customs make happiness.
Rashness in actions or of "settling accounts".
Demanding social "entitlements" like welfare or some other legal advantage over another.
Self-centered grandiosity.
Making foolish oaths or vows, or making oaths and then treating them lightly.
Glorifying nationalism and war: an open soul does not have national bounderies or limits to its love.
Being judgmental towards others to make oneself feel superior.
Any form of racism.
Breaking trusts which destroy marriages and relationships.
Status and class arrogance: for they are truly shameful.
All acts of discourtesy.
Interpersonal rudeness.
Harming another in any way.

This chapter has presented so very many of the world's great teachers and sages that encourage an open soul, at least to each one's capacity, that our love and care would reach to every living being, for of this creation we ourselves are a part, none being an island. And, in so reaching out in care, justice, courage, and duty we find our own enrichment in happiness and wholeness. The farther one's light shines the more powerful it is at its source.

Each person can be a river,
   who wanders far and brings his blessings to many.
Who, while on his way to his final destination,
   brings refreshment and life to those he touches.
His water gives life to those fish within,

and to those he passes by.
When others come to him,
   He is generous with his nourishing presence.
He is loved when he is steady and dependable,
   but he is hated when he superimposes himself upon others.
In quiet calmness he gives joy,
   but in a rage he destroys all of that he has given.

Dear Creator, give to me a deep sense of temporate care,
   that others might prosper in my presence.
And subdue my raging passions that shame my beauty,
   And bring destruction and sorrow into the lives of others.
May the substance of my power and essence,
   Make beautiful all the hearts and minds I touch.
So that as I flow on to the Eternal Sea,
   I can look back and see the happiness
   that has been planted and nourished by my passing by.

CHAPTER TEN

STEP SEVEN

LEAVING BEHIND SIN AND JUDGMENTALISM

I. WHAT IS SIN?

A. THE TEACHINGS OF JESUS

Jesus never gave a specified list of things that would be classified by him as sin. He did give us some commands that are helpful in our quest to understand what he considered those attitudes and actions that were in keeping with the Father in Heaven and in harmony with our own growth into wholeness and happiness. Some were simple repetitions of past commandments or thoughts. From Deuteronomy (Dt 6:4-5) he repeated "You shall love the Lord your God with all your heart, and with all your soul, and with all your mind, and with all your might", although it should be noted that Jesus added "and with all your mind" to the verse in Deuteronomy, which was a significant addition that stressed man's rational capacities. He added in the same verse in Mark 12:30-31, the second part of his own answer, the words of Leviticus 19:18: "You shall love your neighbor as yourself." However, there was a much more open soul flavor to this than in Leviticus, for in Matthew 5:44 he stated that a man should love his enemies and thus one's neighbor became the whole of the living race. One can assume that when he used the proverbial "Golden rule" which was world wide in use, he also meant it in a cosmic sense, therefore, "Treat others as you would have them to treat you." would mean to open up your actions of love and concern to the world. Also from the Beatitudes of Matthew's Sermon on the Mount, Jesus instructed his followers to be humble, meek, to desire justice, to be forgiving and merciful, to be pure in heart, be peacemakers, and also to be salt that gives a good and lasting flavor to humanity, to be a light that shines forth goodness and lightens the path to righteousness, to be respectful even to the fool, not to leave your wife in poverty and distress, not to lust for that which is not properly yours, be so honest that vows become unnecessary, in some cases suffer for the sins against yourself by turning the other cheek, even love your enemies and those who persecute you, do not be hypocritical about your piety, do not judge others -- rather clean up your own act, talk to your Heavenly Father especially when things are difficult, build your lives solidly upon the rock of goodness, forgive as you would have God forgive you, keep focused on your eternal fate and do not take comfort in worldly treasures, be trusting in the Heavenly Father and let not anxiety control you, and seek above all else the righteousness which is in heaven and is eternal, and, in short, be "completely righteous as your Father in Heaven is perfect". These are the thoughts which comprised the path which Jesus desired for man to walk, and in walking this path, he would become full with a life more abundant and filled with human wholeness as a child of God. The Gospel of Philip said Jesus was perfect because he was never a burden to anyone else. "Blessed is the one who on no occasion caused a soul distress. That person is Jesus Christ. He came to the whole place and did not burden anyone. Therefore, blessed is the one who is like this, because he is a perfect man. This indeed is the Word." I would like to add my take on the concept of sin in the mind of Jesus. To him it was certainly not ever proper to burden anyone else, but more than that. I would put it this way, sin is an act or a thought that makes either my own life or someone else's less beautiful, and also a conscious neglect of an act which could make my life or another's more beautiful. That is being the salt and the light of the world.

B. SIN AS UNDERSTOOD BY THE OTHER SAGES

The Greek word used in the New Testament for sin was HAMARTEMA, and the cognate word for "to sin" was HAMARTANO. In Greek literature the word is used primarily for one who misses the mark, as in throwing a spear (symbolizing a defect in excellence of function) and thus also signifies failure to achieve one's purpose or to go wrong. It can also mean a failure of capacity, a human frailty, or deprivation of function (e.g. one who loses his sight or hearing). It also can mean, but is rarely used this way, to neglect or err. In no sense is it inherently attached to evil. It is more a falling short because of lack of excellence or lack of one's capacity. All the meanings fall well into Platonic philosophy which often speaks of man's deprivation of excellence or incapacity because of human frailty to achieve the most noble and most knowledgeable lives. Not knowing something or having a wrong perception of a thing is missing the mark. In the Theaetetus, Socrates says that there are difficulties in acquiring the proper perception of something seen or said: "...like a bad archer, I miss and fall wide of the mark -- and this is called falsehood [or error]"(194a). For example, one can not know God, for God is beyond finding out, and even if one were to know God, to communicate this knowledge to another would be impossible. One can believe and have faith in God, but to know him has not been given to man's capacity, and man's quest falls short and his thoughts can not hit the mark directly. Likewise in life, no man at all times can live perfectly, for all have missed the mark and have fallen short of the glory of God, as Paul would say. Therefore, the need to forgive others as God has forgiven us plays a huge role in Jesus' script for our building our own lives. Plato could find no perfect man, Diogenes' lamp shined upon no totally honest face, and Jesus said to call only one Good, the Father in Heaven. Therefore, as men fall short of their own expectations and the expectations of others, they are to be forgiven and taught a better way. Of course, as mentioned before, murder can not be forgiven, for the victim, the only one who can forgive, is no longer alive to do so. The Heavenly Realm may forgive, but in human society he must pay life for life.

Bad and wrong thinking are usually involved in crime when one lets his desires override his temperance and rational thought. Thus one may naturally think of the crime, which is evil, as the product of wrong thinking and doing, which is true. This wrong doing, sin, hurts both the victim and the criminal. The harm to the victim is self-evident, but the harm to the criminal is not well taught to the people, and as a result their wrong thinking forgets about the harm done to themselves in such actions against others. Juvenal in using the concept of the Greek dramatists' use of the Furies (who haunt a guilty man until there is satisfaction for the evil deed done), stated in his Thirteenth Satire:

"If such his fate, who yet but darkly dares,
whose guilty purpose yet no act declares,
What, were it done! ah! Now farewell to peace!
Ne'er on this earth his soul's alarms shall cease!
Held in the mouth that languid fever burns,
His tasteless food he indolently turns.(274-279).

Doing wrong to another is doing wrong to oneself. A man of crime, of sin, is never a good or a happy man. Retribution must take place, but with a sense of pity, and, hopefully be educated into the joy of becoming a good person. Confucius taught that participation in rituals and traditional festivals taught man to feel a unity with his fellow man and thus paved the way for moral goodness, creating a "moral force" and loyalty among the people. As a result, he taught, a good leader of the people will see to it that such honorable rituals and festivals are kept and practiced with necessary frequency. In ancient China, as with the Greek word HAMARTANO, it was taught that archery was actually used as a test of character. It was thought that unworthy men would not hit the mark frequently.10.1 The Buddhists teach that man "misses the mark" because he is unenlightened and as such his spiritual and mental capacities are frail because he is living in a mind-set of illusion. Mencius taught that all men have innately four essential feelings (the heart of) for social righteousness, but men themselves are responsible for developing them. Mencius said:

"From the feelings proper to it, it is constituted for the practice of what is good. This is what I mean in saying that the nature [of man] is good. If men do what is not good, the blame cannot be imputed to their natural powers. The feeling of commiseration belongs to all men; so does that of shame and dislike; and that of reverence and respect; and that of approving and disapproving. The feeling of commiseration implies the principle of benevolence; that of shame and dislike, the principle of righteousness; that of reverence and respect, the principle of propriety; and that of approving and disapproving, the principle of knowledge. Benevolence, righteousness, propriety, and knowledge are not infused into us from without. We are certainly furnished with them. And a different view is simply from want of reflection. Hence it is said: 'Seek and you will find them. Neglect and your will lose them.'" (6.1.6).

It is often debated about the nature of man as to his native gifts at birth: (1) he is born in sin and concupiscence; (2) he is born blank -- tabula rasa -- neither good nor bad; (3) he is born frail and weak and needs enlightenment or education or a spiritual experience to grow into goodness; (4) he is born with the native qualities needed, but must find them or recollect them in order to become good; (5) or he is born good but ruined and polluted by society. All but the last one require that man is ultimately responsible for what he becomes, for the search, quest, effort, and knowledge needed are all within his grasp to be in conformity to his own well being and to the needs of his society: not to be perfect, but to be in conformity. The last one is a view held by the Positivists, which I feel have definitely made a contribution to our knowledge about the maturing of a child, yet I must reject the main thrust of their argument because it gives those who do not want to be responsible for their actions a platform from which to plead, "I am a victim and my responsibility for my actions should be dismissed, because I am what society has made me, and thus society is guilty for what I have done" or "I am not responsible for my actions, because my genes long ago determined that I should respond with anger and violence when I do not get my way". While the Positivists have given man an additional insight to our human behavior, the logical progression of their basic thought, because it can lead to irresponsibility, must be taken in quite critically. To be happy and whole, each man must decide to leave behind sin, to stay on a proper path, to follow nature, to obey the decrees of Heaven, to start hitting the mark, to think wisely and to act as a good being, and to let love lead him to the far reaches of all humanity bearing the gifts of wisdom, justice, courage, and duty that others might live the good life and thereby enjoy personal wholeness and live in a community of harmony and kindness..

II. LEAVING BEHIND JUDGMENTALISM

It is sadly interesting to observe how many things that the Church condemns in Jesus' name that Jesus never condemned at all. This type of judgmentalism is both bad for the spiritual soul of the Church as well as offensive and harmful for those so judged as immoral. This book takes the stance that what Jesus did not condemn or judge as evil, the Church likewise ought not to condemn or judge as evil.The individual also must be aware that his judgmentalism and condemnation of others that reach beyond the teachings of Jesus are neither good for the internal happiness of his own soul and also reaps far too much harm upon those whom he judges in, not only his own name, but in Jesus' name. The history of the Church's arrogance in speaking in Christ's name, what Christ himself did not teach, in order to control the lives of its members and inflict painful guilt upon them, often for the purpose of financial profit through the sale of indulgences and the cost of seeing the "holy relics", is truly an abomination of cruelty. I shall now speak of some of the atrocities committed by both the organized church of all ages as well as by narrow minded and intellectually shallow individuals who have used this arrogant judgment to prop up their own self-proclaimed dignity and virtue.

For years the Church consigned to hell those who committed suicide, following Augustine but disregarding the nonjudgmental earlier fathers of the Church, who even in some cases praised it, as well as the simple fact that not only Jesus, but the entire "Bible", i.e. both the Hebrew and Christian canons never condemned it. Because of the condemnation of the Church, the grief and pain it brought to the families of the suicide was great, and certainly drove a wedge between a God of love and those survivors who could not even have a Church burial for their tragically lost loved one. People have the right to choose to live or to die at all times, but especially during the painful and irreversible breaking down of the body.

Marriage and sex revolved so much around the idea that both were for the purpose of having children, that those who could not or desired not to have children were always pitied or in some cases condemned as being under God's punishment. Much worse was said about those who used birth control of any kind, even when the doctor told the woman that another birth might kill her (before Caesarians were popular). Childlessness made both men and women to be somewhat cursed or inferior to others who were "blessed by God with children".

The ancient and medieval mind-set that lasted well into the age of the Enlightenment was that there were witches who were agents of Satan and their presence among us was a danger to the morality and salvation of every person within their community. "They must be sought out and destroyed" was the cry both in Europe and New England. Built upon ignorance, hatred, and fear, they were hunted down, tortured, and burned to death. After one witch hunt in Trier only four women in the entire community were left alive, as those accused were tortured until they gave the <u>witch-hunters</u> more names of "other witches", and then they could mercifully be killed; for with new names the hunt could go on for new victims. The Church led this drive for the "purification" of the community from the hands of Satan. Since witches were almost always women, witch hunters built upon certain both taught and implied doctrines that women were the cause of much sin and are to be suspiciously and critically viewed at all times. There are many books that speak of this terrible situation in the church, but three that are available and helpful to understanding the depth of the evilness of witch hunting can be found in <u>H.R.</u> <u>Trevor-Roper's</u> book <u>The</u> <u>European</u> <u>Witch-Craze:</u> <u>of</u> <u>the</u> <u>Sixteenth</u> <u>and</u> <u>Seventeenth</u> <u>Centuries;</u> <u>Daniel</u> <u>P.</u> <u>Mannix's</u> <u>The</u> <u>History</u> <u>of</u> <u>Torture;</u> and <u>Uta</u> <u>Ranke-Heinemann's</u> <u>Eunuchs</u> <u>For</u> <u>the</u> <u>Kingdom</u> <u>of</u> <u>Heaven:</u> <u>The</u> <u>Catholic</u> <u>Church</u> <u>and</u> <u>Sexuality.</u> The main forces that motivated the vicious witch hunts were from Roman Catholicism and Calvinism, and the main opposition came from the Platonic Christians: Erasmus, Johann Weyer, William V.--Duke of Cleves-Juelich-Berg-Mark, Cornelius Agrippa of Nettesheim, the 'Platonic' Court of Catherine de Medici, Reginald Scot, and some of the Cambridge Platonists.

There were the notorious "<u>heresy</u>" hunts that killed off not only individuals but large communities, who had a different view of Christianity than the controlling Church. The <u>Inquisition</u> lasted for centuries, the last "heretic" being executed in 1806. Their theology was condemned and often their alternative lifestyles were condemned. The ominous power and control of the Church upon so many people, simply because they thought differently or asked sincere questions about the faith, came down so viciously that it is hard to believe that any of the Church leaders had ever read the Sermon on the Mount. Power and not Jesus was their lord. For close to 2000 years the scorn, persecution, condemnation, and death went on. The list is unbelievable: Gnostics, "pagans", modalists, Eutychians, Nestorians, Arrians, Waldensians, Cathars, Martin Luther, Copernicans and followers of Galileo, Evolutionists, and many others. The church, of course, had every right to reject certain teachings and life styles, but to criminally enforce them and execute those who chose in some way to be different was without doubt, a rejection of Jesus as Lord by the very church itself that vocally proclaimed him as such. As early as the Fourth Century the Church upon receiving its legitimacy from Constantine, before its power became so widespread, condemned those who did not "buy the whole package of the latest Church Council". "Heretics" chose what to believe and not to believe ["heresy" is taken is the Greek word HAIRESIS, which means election or choice], and those heretics "had the disrespect to chose for themselves what the tenants of their religion should be". Church edicts demanded, "Conform or die!" These were the followers of Jesus?? Philip Schaff in his history of the Christian Church stated:

"The ancient heresiologists -- mostly uncritical, credulous, and bigoted, ... zealots for a narrow orthodoxy -- unreasonably multiplied the heresies by extending themselves beyond the limits of Christianity, and counting all modifications and variations separately. Piloastrius or Pilastrus, bishop of Brescia or Briozia (d.387), in his Liber de Hoeresibus, numbered ... 128 Christian heresies; Epiphanius of Cyprus (d.403), in his PANARION, 80 heresies in all, 20 before and 60 after Christ; Augustin (d.430), 88 Christian heresies, including Pelagianism; Proedestinatus, 90, including Pelagianism and Nestorianism. (Pope Pius IX condemned 80 modern heresies, in his Syllabus of Errors, 1864).

It is my contention that no creedal statements should be extended beyond the teachings of Jesus as they are found in the Four Gospels, unless they are acknowledged to be symbolic and not absolute in character. Early in the history of the Church they were by many taken to be just that: statements of belief that were, in themselves inadequate, to what was something of spiritual truth that was far beyond the actual words or creeds themselves. And instead of creedism, such a study was called "symbolics" because of the very nature of the inadequacy of human words and logic to express the ultimate truth. The creeds were not knowledge, but symbols of a truth that lay far beyond the very words which were used: the worded creeds were symbolic. I myself, in my theological training, had two courses called "Symbolics". The Church has forgotten the humble position that some of the Early Fathers took in naming their statements of faith as symbols, and this, in itself, should have led to a more flexible attitude towards others that did not symbolize their faith with those very exact words. Ask Michael Servetus, who being burned at the stake for "heresy", cried out "Jesus, the Son of the Eternal

God, have mercy upon me." One of the bystanders arrogantly stated that it was a shame, for had he said, "Jesus, the Eternal Son of God, have mercy upon me", he would not have been executed. Actually, Servetus' statement was much closer to Peter's confession, "You are the Christ, the Son of the Living God", which Jesus fully accepted and proclaimed that Peter could only proclaim such truth by being guided by heaven. But Jesus' statement and his opinion did not seem to matter much to John Calvin, whose Geneva Church ordered the execution. For Calvin the symbolic creed became a straight-jacket for his thinking so much so that the words of Jesus could not function in his thinking. To demand perfect compliance to the words of creeds made up by men, often even politically motivated, in the distant past, instead of using them for helpful symbols to reach out to God, is heresy hunting at its worst. Such judgments of others harm them and harm those who judge by making their minds slaves to the human words which inadequately symbolized the conceived idea of truth.

Divorced people still have a stigma attached to their character by the Church, and it is even worse if they have remarried. Despite the fact that the divorce was of a kindly nature and all children were provided for by both the parents. Even a couple without children, were condemned for divorce (a double whammy for they were also pitied for not having children in the first place). This process of condemning divorce did have passages to support such condemnation, but as I mentioned above, Jesus said such precepts were not for all men. Therefore, not all are to be under the binding of Jesus' ideal statement, as well as taking into consideration the different and more difficult life setting for women in Jesus' day than in today's circumstances for the divorced women. A caution here is needful: if a person is in the process of divorcing his mate, then let him obey all the rules of kindness, fairness, and treat his mate as he himself would like to be treated, and, if necessary, make provisions for her future welfare, that the marriage may be remembered in a healthy way and the good benefits that they once shared not be forgotten. One can certainly have a divorce in a "Christian" way. Also the hypocrisy of denying a marriage that has been existent for several years and produced children by the clerical "loophole" of annulment, is a childish game which is used to deny reality and protect the "purity of the church's teachings".

People were once condemned for their Race or Caste because God is punishing these people according to some misinterpretation of the love that reveals itself from above. White Christians in the West used the "curse of Ham" to avoid the loving ethics and gracious fellowship which Jesus commanded to his disciples. In John the only command is to love each other as Jesus himself has loved them. The Caste system of India, when seen outside its doctrine of reincarnation and dharma, is just as evil and inflicts just as much painful experiences upon those discriminated against, and even punished by or deprived of certain benefits by law. Judging another by race or caste shows that one has never looked at the Gospels and noticed with whom Jesus associated: fishermen, tax collectors, zealots, Canaanites, lepers, Roman centurions, demoniacs, paralytics (one of whom Jesus addressed as "my son"), the "unclean" women, blind men, harlots, the deaf and dumb, those who did not keep the Law of Moses -- "sinners" and "lawless", and many others. He mingled among the harassed and helpless crowds, and he also talked with scribes, Pharisees, Sadducees, and Herodians. He cared about honesty, humility, gentleness, justice, hope, and love. He simply made no distinction at all in terms of social status, education, race or caste. He, as the Father's Son, so loved the world. A good person makes no distinction at all whether he works with a different kind of person or marries a woman or man of a different race. He opens up his soul completely, and leaves racial and all other judgmentalism behind, that his soul may be free to enjoy the love of God and find its wholeness and happiness in being saturated by such love.

It is well also to acknowledge the fact that Jesus never condemned -- he never even mentioned -- abortion, nor did the rest of the New Testament Canon. Yet today, thousands will block clinics and some will even kill a physician who helps a woman have a safe abortion. While I can understand the deep feelings on both sides, it is necessary to be honest that neither the Hebrew Scriptures nor the Christian Scriptures equate the fetus with a living being. Abortion and exposure were widely practiced in the world in which Jesus lived, yet not one of the Four Gospel writers ever referred to the subject. It was not considered an important teaching of Jesus, if he even said anything about it. If a person is against abortion, fine, let him demonstrate, but never in the name of Jesus, for that is either ignorance or hypocrisy. Most Greek philosophers approved of abortion. In Plato's Theaetetus the role of midwives and the skill of their profession mentions one of their abilities, especially if the woman is having difficulty bearing the child, was to smother the child while still in womb (149d), and this would be evidence that in time of trouble the living mother's life was preferred to that of the embryo or fetus. Plato made his views very clear when he recommended in his Republic (V.461c) that a woman over 40 should have an abortion due to the fact that the child may be less than healthy. Aristotle in his Politics (VII.1335b25), when he is discussing overpopulation, stated: "...and if couples have children in excess, let abortion be procured before sense and life have begun" -- basically a reference to the first tri-semester. The ancient Semitic laws, do not say much about abortion, but they do in fact treat the fetus, in case of crime or accident, as property, not as a human life. The Law Code of Hammurabi (209-210) stated that if a "seignoir" struck another seignoir's daughter and caused a miscarriage, he would have to pay 10 silver shekels for the destruction of her fetus: but, if the daughter herself, whom he struck, died, then his own daughter would be put to death -- life for life. The Torah (Law of Moses) took the same position (Ex. 21:22-25): payment for the destroyed fetus, but if the woman herself was hurt or killed, then eye for eye, life for life, etc. The Catholic Church until 1869 tended to accept a form of Aristotles' teaching that the soul was added to the fetus after 40 days for a male and after 80 days for the female, but since then has tended to teach that the soul may enter the body as early as conception.10.2   With the great teachers of humanity at variance with one another, and the Church not consistent through the ages, although the first 1800 years tended to follow Aristotle, and with Jesus' making no reference at all about abortion, it is certainly wrong to claim that Jesus forbad abortion or that it is wrong in the sight of God, when the Word made flesh did not seem to think the issue worth discussing. One may honestly believe and live his strong convictions for himself, but when he or she judges another on this issue, he is putting himself in a situation that not even Jesus did. A Christian's goal and duty is to obey what Jesus actually taught, and not add thereto in his name. To make such a judgment against a person who is already suffering from the ordeal and having to make a decision about her circumstances, is quite cruel and to try to keep her from her physician is not in the spirit of any form of love. One might erroneously claim that natural law is opposed to abortions because it seems so repulsive to so many people. But that is hardly the case. An extensive study of approximately 350 primitives societies by George Devereux (A Study of Abortion in Primitive Societies) shows that customs, traditions, taboos, moral codes, priests, and economic circumstances had tremendous variations in the different societies' view of abortion. He even has a chapter on "Compulsory Abortion" that was dictated by individuals, tribes, and customs. He discussed six well documented circumstances for compulsory abortion: 1. Children fathered by a suspected "demon", 2. The offspring of incest, 3. The children of old, ailing, or weak fathers, 4. The children inseminated by some male outside the tribe, 5. Children planted by an act of adultery, 6. Legitimate children, tainted by an act of adultery by pregnant mother. Other abortions were prompted by economic matters, i.e., the inability of the family to feed more children. Three women of the Chukchee tribe volunteered personal information: one had 5 living children, 2 dead, and 5 were aborted; the second had 7 children living, 3 dead, and 3 aborted; and the third had 6 living, 2 dead, and 2 aborted. There is, then, no natural law against abortion and likewise no teaching of Jesus, for those who follow him, that condemns abortion. Therefore, let each believe as he will, but, also, let not one judge another.

People are also strongly and wrongly judged who do not jump on the band wagon of nationalism in the time of a possible war crisis. Most people are patriots and care about the country of their births and the benefits they have received from it. But nationalism is really a quasi-religion (as Paul Tillich called it), and unfortunately becomes an idol to many, to be worshipped and unquestionably obeyed in every circumstance. "My country, right or wrong!" is one of the most destructive attitudes for human righteousness that appeared in the 20th Century: in Germany, in Russia, in England, in Japan, in France, and, yes, in the United States. I know, for I had to counsel some objectors to the Vietnam tragedy, who were judged and even disowned by their parents and despised by former "friends". Judging others can be so easy and so shallow, yet clothed in some form of self-righteousness. Jesus, Buddha, Asoka, Plato and Mo Tzu had bigger hearts and widely opened souls whose love went far beyond one's citizenship of city, state, or nation.

The last three areas in which judgmentalism has gone rampant all relate to sexual relationships "outside the box" of "traditional" propriety, but none of which were condemned by Jesus: sex among the unmarried, homosexuality, and prostitution.

Among some of my older friends I heard often, when I was younger and they were married, that those who were living together outside of marriage, were "trash people" who were "shacking up together". Later in life when these same friends were either divorced or widowed, they would live with their sweethearts without getting married, for marriage was now "too binding at their time of life", or they were worried about losing some Social Security benefits, or did not want each other to be attached to the upcoming medical debts that were in the near future, or they wanted their inheritance to go to their children and a legal marriage might complicate that. Now, in their circumstances, "shacking up together" was suddenly the appropriate and wise thing to do, and they went to Church together and, in turn, were now also scorned by others for "shacking up together." Life situations throughout history change, from polygamy with additional slaves and concubines to shacking up together. The monogamous, sexually-exclusive marriage scene can still be idealized and workable for some, but for many others, variations of marriage or no marriage at all seem to work better. Why must the State and the Church impose themselves legally upon a couple or group who chose to live differently? As to the state or national government, it was not even in the business of marriage until 1580AD, when the first civil marriage was conducted in the Netherlands. It is a "Johnny come lately" to the marriage process, and now flexes its muscles like it is the sole arbiter of how people can form families, and with the power to imprison those who do not comply. What arrogance! Who is being hurt? And if someone were being hurt in the relationship, would being legally married according to the state's sole form of marriage really help in someway? Probably it would actually complicate the relationship with a stress that might even magnify the hurt between the two. Sadly, Paul's recommendation was that instead of lusting as a burning fire for sex, a man should get married. Ugh! Men are inclined constantly towards sexual pleasure, as it is an inbuilt thing for him, and to offer marriage to another simply because he wants a sexual release, is far too simple, and also greatly insulting to the woman. Marriage is for great romantic love and the desire of both to share their all with only each other, or for procreation and the building of a family. Since people can be faithful to each other without marriage, the only reason for marriage today is that it legally assures the children being born to have parental and economic support and nourishment growing up, and even then such can take place without the marriage certificate. I, of course, am, in no way, against marriages that are legalized and the couples are faithful to each other so long as they both shall live. But to say that that is the only way people can share their love and their lives with another or others is not true, and to judge those who choose to go a different way, simply because they go a different way, is not kind and is not proper.

Another situation in life that has sparked much controversy and equally as much judgmentalism is the case of homosexual relations as well as the quest for some to change sexual gender as much as possible so that they may feel more attuned to their psychological being. At this point I feel a historical review is needed to understand why certain laws both secular and religious condemned homosexuality in the past, and in this way it can be more readily decided as to whether such laws are relevant today. In antiquity most societies feared that due to famine, pestilence, war, weather extremes, difficulties of child birth and other dangers to human life, it would be possible for a society to be so weakened that it could not survive. As a result the priests and the kings of such societies would prohibit any sexual activity that would "waste the sperm". Childlessness was shamed and if a wife could not bear a child she was expected to find another woman, if she did not have a slave or maid, to bear children for her husband. Polygamy was also a safeguard that protected a man from not producing children. Priests helped the King by making the laws "sacred" to conform to the greater production of children: bestiality, of course, was prohibited; but so were certain forms of heterosexual penetration (oral or anal) and also homosexuality which would necessitate those very forms of sex. Such forbidden forms of sex then became "sinful" because the priest said the laws came from the tribal or the city's god or gods. Those now "sacred laws" from "above" were implemented, often brutally, to encourage high birth rates as well as encouraging polygamy. Forbidden then were: homosexuality (at least among the males -- the Hebrew Canon does not forbid female homosexuality for no sperm is lost), no withdrawal of penis at point of ejaculation (called Onanism -- Gen.38), no castrations (except for the male guardian of the rich man's or king's harem), masturbation (condemned by Church), and, in addition, the shame of barrenness caused women to give their husband's another mate with whom to procreate. Some societies even provided female partners in the shrines of certain fertility goddess, and these women were called sacred prostitutes.

Strabo, the Greek historian, said the cult of Aphrodite early in the first century of the Christian era had a thousand priestess-prostitutes attached to its Corinthian temple. It was even taught in the Hebrew Scriptures that man's "soul" lived into the future in the bodies of his male children. It became an absolute necessity for man to reproduce male children for the sake of his own destiny and for the sake of his people's destiny, and it was commanded by the people's god to do so.

Concerning Jesus: no known early writing of the Church implied that Jesus had children. Yet, he is presented as the complete and perfect man. Also no writing claimed his virginity (as it did Jephthah's daughter -- Judges 11) and some Gnostic writings implied a sexual relation with Mary Magdalene (see Gospel of Philip). All Four Canonical Gospels do not consider Jesus' sexual or non sexual activities a subject important enough to discuss, as such would have no bearing on the excellence of his virtue. For Jesus focused on man's personal virtues, the righteousness and justice of his deeds, and his acts of love for both those close and far away, that man might meet his God in the expectation of eternal salvation. Likewise, the reproduction of children for a man was made irrelevant, because the man himself had an eternal soul, and he would live on in heaven with or without children. Jesus dismissed the questions of the Sadducees about family, reproduction, and who would be one's mate in heaven, by simply stating that men become like angels, and they never die, and therefore no reproduction of themselves is necessary. In heaven, since no one any longer died, replacing oneself with a child for the next generation was ridiculously illogical. And since one lived on in one's own soul in eternity, there was no longer any theological validity for laws against homosexuality, other ways of wasting the sperm, and even general castration. However, societies still had the king's problem to worry about, even though Jesus purged man from the priestly dictates to control man's sexual activities. The King and society in general still worried in the time of Jesus about population loss and avoiding the production of children was still scorned by many leaders of the nations and their lawgivers. Caesar Augustus' wanting more Romans to be born to defend the ever expanding Roman Empire was repeated among every tribal group, city-nations, and other vast empires. King David of Ancient Israel was so satisfied with his peoples' reproductive efforts, he arrogantly had a census made of "his" kingdom to see how many people "he" ruled: but in the eyes of the priests and the prophets, Israel was still

Yahweh's people, not David's, and David came in for some strong criticism. Today, 2003, the world is vastly different than 2000 years ago and in the 20th Century the world's population multiplied rapidly, going from 1.2 billion in 1900 to over six billion in the year 2000. All forms of industrial, nuclear, and non-dissolvable waste pollutes mother earth beyond imagination. Forty to fifty thousand children die each day in the world because of malnutrition, despite the world's record production of food. The earth's natural resources are being quickly depleted, the atmosphere is changing, and thousands of species are now extinct which were alive at the time of Jesus. Population negative-growth (to result in the lessening of the world's population) is now, not only not to be scorned, but is one of the great virtues that thinking and moral people can render to the beauty of God's earth for future generations. Unfortunately there are still three general motives for an expanded population: nationalism, racism, and religions -- each being more concerned about the growth in numbers of their "own kind" than they are concerned about the pleasantness and goodness of the life quality for the very children they are producing.

In view of both the theology of Jesus and most religions who believe in a life for the individual after death, and not in his children, and the already overpopulated world of this third millennium after Jesus, all reasons to judge or condemn people who choose -- for any reason -- not to have children or to perform sexual acts by which there cannot be fertilization, are irrelevant and discredited. I, personally, have no children and one vasectomy. 2000 years ago I would have been condemned for wasting the "seed" of life, as women, by some, are still condemned today for taking birth-control pills or using other devices for the same reason. For myself, I usually tell others who ask why I do not have children, that I "cut off my children at the 'vas'". Judgments against those not having children based on pre-Platonic theology or upon the need for the survival of the human race are simply childishly ignorant. Likewise, to be rejected as pompous and non-loving, are the judgments against life styles that do not produce children, such as man and wife who choose to be non-fertile by use of vasectomy or birth-control pills, the castrated eunuchs, the practice of masturbation or withdrawal before ejaculation, and homosexuality (both male and female). There is left no logical or theological reason for a follower of Jesus, who believes in man's eternal soul, or a governing body, who has plenty of people, to forbid or scorn the choices of non-propagation.

Most people, however, will consider such choices of non-repro-duction as being unnatural or unromantic (in a once popular song, the woman sings, "I want to have your baby"). I have now been single (divorced) again for more than 20 years, and I have accepted the fact that some women do not find an infertile man to be what she wants -- that's fine, and I accept it, even if she does not accept my reasons for the vasec-tomy. It's her choice and she has that right. It is also a person's choice not to consider a barren woman or a homosexual man as their future mates -- no problem. However, to scorn, condemn, and declare an anathema upon another's choice does not coincide with either the flow of history or the unqualified love of Jesus. Not everything that does not appeal to one unit of thought is necessarily an evil that is to be blamed, like some religionists, for all the problems of our society or the world. Even if such a unit of thinking were to be correct, if they were followers of Jesus, they would be wise to let both the wheat and chaff grow together until the final harvest, lest they act in ignorance and find out that they themselves are the ones with the log in their own eyes and have tried arrogantly to clear another's vision. Galileo, ruthlessly and arrogantly condemned by his Church, stated in his great work "...Plato himself admired the human understanding and believed it to partake of divinity simply because it understood the nature of numbers". He, besides this precept that numbers do not lie in the measuring of the solar system, also warns the "theologians not to cry heresy when a major change of mind is required because the old way of thinking is, at least, inadequate today and is most likely to be itself a heresy in the future". Already man is making many inroads to knowledge as to why we choose different ways of thinking and how we choose our sexual gender. Even into the very recent past the new born babies who were born "inter-sex" (partial or even full development of both male and female genitalia) were, even without the knowledge of the parents, surgically "corrected" as the doctor made the decision which sex the child was to be. There are many born not completely male or female, and for some one else, like the physician, to decided for them what gender they would be, and then for society to judge them unmercifully for their future adjustments to their own personal desires, is so very unkind. Even over and above this, as has just been discussed, no judgment should ever be against a person striving to be themselves and understand themselves when there is absolutely no harm done to others, and where both the Church and the State have no business, except to vainly exercise the power to control the lives of their subjects. In 1967 <u>Brock Chrisholm</u>, the Director-General of the World Health Organization, stated:

> Man's method of dealing with difficulties in the past has always been to tell everyone else how they should behave. We have all been doing that for centuries. It should be clear by now that this no longer does any good. Everybody has by now been told by everybody else how he should behave...the criticism is not effective; it never has been, and it never is going to be.

<u>Prostitution</u> is ever with us, and our basic nature wants to hide the truth as to why it has always existed among all peoples at one time or other, usually most times, and why there is such a strong demand for it. The Kinsey report of 1948, written well before the "sexual revolution" of the 1960s, reported that 70% of the men had had sexual intercourse with a prostitute (not to mention other forms of sex with prostitutes), and this despite its being illegal. He also reported that 97% of men engaged in forms of sexual activity, at some time of their lives, that are punishable as crimes under the law (at least in 1948). Also, that is -- in addition to wanting to hide the truth, some traditional thinkers and believers who were raised in pietism, Puritanism, or "Queen Victorianism" cannot feel comfortable with prostitution in their midst, and have done their utmost to legally suppress it. It hasn't worked and never will. California's historic legal brothels, due to the pressure exerted upon government officials by the "invading" "pious Puritans" of the Midwest moving into Southern California , were shut down and made illegal in 1909 in Los Angeles and by 1917 in San Francisco when the "Red Light Abatement Act" destroyed all the pleasure parlors. Did it stop prostitution? No, but gave rise to unmonitored street walkers who spread disease, stole what they could, and often ended being a dope addicts. It also made Tijuana a booming city and Nevada a tourist attraction. Other than in English speaking countries and the countries of Islam, prostitution is legal. Islam has its own form of variety by providing polygamy to society and some men, those quite wealthy by oil, have accumulated great harems, numbering far more than the four approved of by Mohammed. The

"Biblical" societies, the Ancient Hebrews and the ancient Greeks, never legally forbad prostitution, even though it was probably true that no Hebrew or Greek fathers ever wanted their own girls or boys (among the Greeks) to become prostitutes. Nevertheless, it was legal. In the case of Jesus one can see that he in no way apologized for socializing with prostitutes, and they seemed to number among his friends. He even stated that they were closer to the kingdom of God than the educated and holy ones of his own people. Of course the use of prostitutes by married men against the will or knowledge of their spouses is harmful because of the fraudulent character of the act, the betrayal of the spouse's trust, the use of family funds, the possibility of being a carrier of disease he could then give to his spouse, and the damage done to their social image. All such are very harmful, and are contrary to the way in which any moral teacher, especially Jesus, would teach as a path to happiness and wholeness. In the somewhat recent past, two "evangelical" preachers, very popular, used women they paid for sexual activity against the will and knowledge of their spouses: one ended up in jail and the other weeping "I have sinned". My contention is however, that it was in the hypocrisy, the betrayals of vows, the inconsideration these men, and others, had towards their wives, and the clandestine use of family funds that constituted the "sinfulness" of the acts. For a man or woman to seek out sexual relations, with payment or without payment, against the will or without the knowledge of one's spouse is a betrayal of trust and an act of selfishness which destroys one's own sense of dignity and weakens, if not annihilates, the trust of one's married mate. But it is no more possible to legally destroy prostitution than it is to eliminate sex itself. For myself, I would recommend that prostitutes be legalized for the sake of eliminating diseases, theft, drugs, and so many other things harmful to society that always accompany illegal prostitution. Likewise, since I do not personally feel it is in the best interest of the prostitute herself to remain a prostitute, I would encourage them, if possible, to quickly find a new vocation and restore the personal sense of self-dignity that I am sure many of them have lost. But to classify them as evil people upon whom the wrath of the preacher and the punishment of the courts is warranted is not in keeping with redemptive love and kindness. And judging them harshly keeps one from learning how to love those who have not chosen, at least in the minds of those judging, the most beautiful way to share their most intimate selves with others. Also, one must ultimately ask if using one's body and the pleasures it can give to another person is in itself wrong, even for the sake of money. Perhaps not, but perhaps so. Either way it is imperative that others do not judge the choices people make when there is no harm or fraud inflicted.

It behooves followers of Jesus to move to more self-examination and personal cleansing as well as a greater love and acceptance of all those for whom the Gospel was given. The happiness and wholeness of an individual can never be fully effected if one does not let its loving power reach out to all within its reach, and to treat everyone the way one wants everyone to treat him. Love is so much more nourishing than hate, acceptance so much more refreshing and joyous than rejection, and kind courtesies so much more human than rudeness and scorn. Likewise, on the more cautionary side, it is those who judge the most harshly now who themselves will receive the wrath of future judgment. Today Galileo looks good and the Church looks bad; the ones who quoted "Holy Scriptures" to support slavery look bad, and those who promoted true secular democracy look good. Jesus, in his kindness, warned us "Judge not, and you will not be judged."

For ourselves then, to take the final step to complete happiness and wholeness, it is necessary to open up our soul to the world to give the love within ourselves the avenue by which it can find its fullest expression, reaching out so very far from its home base that it brings a new reality of light and salt into the world, whereby others are blessed, and we ourselves can feel the joy which God himself has in loving all the people of the earth and seeing that not the least of them is neglected. In love then we leave behind sin and judgment as a final step to our spiritual liberation from the cares of the world. When we exercise such love, we ourselves take on a type of divinity whereby we can reach the greatest possible good that is available to humanity. In Jesus' prayer to his Righteous Father, he prayed that "the love with which You have loved me may be in them, and I in them".

III. VARIOUS SOCIAL CODES OF HUMANITY

For the sake of human harmony and mutually advantageous living, certain groups have established rules, laws, codes, or guidelines for those within the group to follow so that all could receive the best of benefits of belonging to that group. The following are selected passages and thoughts of various codes of some of the civilizations of the past. They, in no wise, are a complete summary of the feelings and laws of those societies, but are glimpses of what they considered necessary and proper conduct of a good and caring society.

A. THE CODE OF HAMMURABI

The code of Hammurabi, about 1700 BC, contained 282 statutes or statements, each as a rule or law. But I have taken the most basic eight of them and presented them below. Forbidden are:
1. Murder
2. Sorcery
3. False Testimony (during legal proceedings)
4. Theft
5. Limits on Loan Interest
6. Adultery

And the two most general forms of justice
7. The Punishment of the Lex Talionis (eye for eye, life for life) for physical injury
8. The Punishment of the Lex Talionis for death or injury due to building infractions [e.g. If a man build a house for another and, because it was poorly built, it collapsed and killed someone in the family, then the same person (daughter or son) in the builder's family was to be killed]

B. THE EGYPTIAN BOOK OF THE DEAD

In the Egyptian "Book of the Dead", so named because it was found in a tomb, but probably the heading means "The Breaking Forth of Dawn" which emphasizes rebirth in eternity rather than death, included a "Negative Confession" of (usually) about 40 declarations of innocence by the one being judged after death. The confession and the bulk of the entire book is probably much older, but the manuscript that is the basis of modern study dates from about 1500 BC. The eight following "I have nots" are symbolic of the code in general.
1. I have not robbed with violence.

2. I have not stolen.
3. I have done no murder, nor harm.
4. I have not defiled another man's wife.
5. I have not worked grief.
6. I have not stirred up strife.
7. I have never fouled the water.
8. (in general, in many different ways "I have not been Sacrilegious")

C. THE JEWISH TORAH

In the "Ten Commandments" there is generally a division between, first Yahweh, and secondly, the rest of Jewish society. I shall just present those towards society, and keep the Sabbath law as a societal law, not a religious one, for I believe the Sabbath law was for the purpose of human health and a ban against working servants or slaves every day of the week (Man is not made for the Sabbath, but the Sabbath for man).

1. You shall remember the Sabbath and keep it separate (from the working days).
2. Treat your parents with honor and respect.
3. Do not murder another.
4. Do not commit adultery.
5. Do not steal.
6. Do not bear false witness against another.
7. Do not covet what is not yours.

D. HINDU SOCIAL DUTIES

From Vaisesika's classification of 13 universal duties, I have chosen to present those that have social connotations.

1. Nonviolence
2. Kindness to all living creatures
3. Truthfulness
4. Non-stealing
5. Mental purity
6. Freedom from anger
7. Alertness in performing one's duties.10.3

E. CONFUCIUS

Going through the Analects of Confucius I found 9 duties that seemed to be in constant theme.
1. Keep a pure heart, let no evil thoughts within.
2. Be trustworthy.
3. Cowardice does not excuse you from your duties.
4. The Golden Rule (repeated 3 times in the Analects)
        Treat others as you would have them treat you.
5. Harm no one.
6. Beware of lust.
7. Beware of strife.
8. Beware of avarice.
9. Properly mourn the death of parents.

F. MAHAYANA BUDDHISM

The Brahmajala Sutra (406 AD) lists the "ten grave rules".
1. Not to kill
2. Not to steal
3. Not to be unchaste
4. Not to lie
5. Not to drink alcohol
6. Not to speak of the faults of others
7. Not to praise oneself
8. Not to envy
9. To show gratitude to others
10. To praise the Three treasures (Buddha, His Order, His teaching) 10.4

G. THE EDICTS OF ASOKA

Asoka was a warrior king who thoroughly defeated his enemy, but at great human cost, by which he himself was repulsed. He then adopted the Buddhist faith, and vowed to create a kingdom of harmony, justice, and tolerance that never again would he see such a human slaughter. He then had pillars erected on the major highways of his kingdom declaring his code of ethics for the general good of all his subjects. I have put together

12 statutes from the edicts which I feel best represent the flavor of his intentions, and have somewhat paraphrased them.

1. Consider your own moral conquest (to be good within) as the only true conquest.
2. Promote noble deeds (compassion, generosity, truthfulness, purity, gentleness, and goodness).
3. Be courteous to everyone, even your slaves.
4. Honor all religious sects.
5. Practice Dharma (that is, do good deeds).
6. Practice Self-examination.
7. Obey your father and mother.
8. Control your passions, do not be destroyed by them.
9. All faiths are to be practiced freely everywhere.
10. You are all my children: treat each other as brothers and seek each other's happiness.
11. No living creature is to be slaughter in the Capital City (Asoka had hopes of eliminating all animal sacrifice).
12. Make available medical treatment for all men and animals.

From these it is very easy to see that there does seem to be a "Natural Law" that all men by nature agree to, for the above codes have many commendations and condemnations in common. But there are also some differences in priorities and they too help us today to understand the intentions of the good men of the past, and their desire that man's goodness within would reach out as far as possible to all men everywhere and also to the other living creatures as much as possible. One will also notice that those things listed above in which men have been so judgmental towards others [suicide, childlessness, heresies (in most cases), divorce and remarriage, race or caste, abortion, nationalism (in most cases), homosexuality, and prostitution] are not part of the universal law system. Deep down, if man desires his own purity and goodness, and then tries in a loving way to bring true goodness to all people, he will leave his judgmentalism concerning the things not mentioned in the common agreement of universal law far behind. He will say, "Goodbye to all that" and move on instead, by the power of his caring love and goodness for all men everywhere, and also, I personally hope, to the animal kingdom likewise. I personally believe that Jesus of Nazareth has well established by his life and teachings that path to be followed that I have recommended in this book, and far from being alone, the rest of mankind's greatest teachers, both divine and secular, have been in agreement with the basic teachings of Jesus, and many of them preceded him on the stage of human history to show us such a path to personal happiness and wholeness and the serenity of societal harmony that one can have from being a good and noble person.

CONCLUSION

This book has not been a short one, simply because the road to wholeness is not short and easy, but rather long and difficult. Likewise, the greater the work of art, the more difficulty is involved in making it. The greater, higher, stronger, and more beautiful the edifice, the more cost, endurance, rational planning, and effort are needed. Each person chooses the type of life he wants to build, if he desires any building of it at all. He may choose to live in a cave or dilapidated shed that is at the mercy of the storms of life, or he may want to build rationally and carefully upon a rock so that he may be well sheltered from the difficulties and tragedies he will experience during the course of his life time. A house that is utilitarian and good in structure can offer great joy and comfort to those who dwell within. Building a life, of course, parallels the laws of strong "building codes" that are established by communities to ensure their citizens of comfort and protection. Those lives that blossom into great joy and goodness are based on goodness, a strong ethical code, and a rational plan to use the "materials" they have been given in life. Those lives of happiness and wholeness are not built overnight, but each day the process continues in which man refines his goodness and his value to himself as well as to others that he himself can feel the wholeness of his being within and utilize his love and justice for those outside himself.

Like any other task in life, one needs a teacher, a mentor, a guru, a master or a leader to show the better way to build a life, or how to navigate a ship, or find one's way through the cosmic forest in which we find our existence. The great teachers of humanity have been presented in order that the reader can follow the seven steps to wholeness in the best way possible, and also to avoid those self-inflicted detours that we are all prone, accidentally or foolishly, to follow once in awhile in life's journey. I have presented the teachings of Jesus of Nazareth first in each chapter because his ministry is so well known to us in the Western World, and also because of all the great teachers of the world he has become, at least in numbers, the most beloved teacher in man's short history on earth. There likewise are many of the wise sayings of Plato, because, in my mind, he has been the most influential philosopher in the Western Word, and equally as important, if not more important, he first established the path that Jesus later walked and consummated. I personally agree with the following statement made early in the Twentieth Century by Paul Elmer More:

"It is this tradition, Platonic and Christian at the centre, this realization of an immaterial life, once felt by the Greek soul and wrought into the texture of the Greek language, that lies behind all our western philosophy and religion. Without it, so far as I can see, we should have remained barbarians; and, losing it, so far as I can see, we are in peril of sinking back into barbarism." (P.E. More, The Religion of Plato, pp. VI-VII)

Despite my very strong affection for Plato and Jesus, I realize that throughout the history of the entire world, peoples have been blessed with holy men who have taught, enlightened, lifted, and given hope to the souls of men that there are ways of building their lives into meaningful, happy, and whole ones. To neglect their wisdom in such an important process of building one's life, would be not only irresponsible, but absolutely foolish. One can see from the "Contents" section at the beginning of the book that eastern thought offers much wisdom in certain of the following seven steps. They are particularly helpful in teaching us how not to become slaves of the material world order, but rather they give us the wisdom how to detach ourselves from this ephemeral materialism to which much of the West is enslaved. There is an enlightenment that comes from the East that offers much liberation from the many anxieties that we create from our wants. While such detachment to the temporal and the material was also deplored by Plato and many others in the West, the whole of existence can be more completely understood when seen by as many different wise view points as possible. One may say that if he has Johann Sebastian Bach and Ludwig van Beethoven his soul needs no more than this to lift itself to the highest of musical pleasure. But to refuse to listen to Mozart, Wagner, Verdi, and Brahms because one is already satisfied with his level of musical joy, is to deprive that joy of so much more available nourishment that will even recreate that joy itself into a new and deeper form.

Not only is the individual's wholeness greatly increased by being taught by the many teachers and masters rather than by the few, he also becomes rationally and spiritually aware of his closeness to all his human brothers who are likewise reaching out to that which is eternally good and beautiful, and even to God himself. There are certain groups of people who teach us much about this common human quest for physical and spiritual wholeness: the Sufis and the mystics being the foremost among them. They help us to go beyond the "symbolics" that teach us much, and are necessary, but still are limited when trying to discuss all abstract concepts: love, justice, hope, courage, wisdom, faith, temperance, friendship, happiness, wholeness, and even God himself. In each of the seven steps I have presented, one can see the contributions that every culture has made to the mixing bowl of mankind's wisdom. It is easy to accept a television made in Japan, a silk scarf made in India, a sports shoe made in China, a automobile from Germany, and wonder at the pyramids of Egypt; but, at the same time, to reject their wisdom and soul-building teachings that make a far greater contribution to the happiness and wholeness of our lives. Perhaps, in that, we can see our own attachment to the physical and material realm, in that we are more open to reach out farther for material benefits than we are for spiritual blessings and wholeness-building wisdom. "Seek first the kingdom of God." is something that, if we listen to what it means, can be a tremendous foundation for all our thinking and planning in life.

The first three chapters spoke to the importance of teachers, the goodness of the temporal life in our material form, and the problems man has in adjusting to his situation as a human being in this absolutely vast and majestic universe. Chapter Four presented the first step, encouraging the reader to use his wisdom to understand why unattachment to the non-essential things of our existence is necessary, what he can change and what he cannot, and how he can take control of those things that he can change. Chapter Five presented the universe as a beautiful place in which to live and is to be enjoyed, not feared. It is friendly and there is a moral force that can sustain our spiritual quest for wholeness and meaningfulness in life. Chapter Six, sought to encourage the individual to join the cosmos as its child, for whom the Creator has a loving kindness. In this realization the soul is activated and can communicate with the Creator God, sometimes in words, sometimes in thought, and sometimes in a blank, but receptive, form of meditation: just "being there". Chapter Seven put demands upon man's rational wisdom to plan logically his life in every form: material benefits, vocation, family, personal goals, and spiritual reach. The burden for doing so rests totally upon the individual, and there are no excuses: it is all personal responsibility. In an age of excuses and mental laziness, personal responsibility succumbs to playing "victim", or playing the "blame" game, choosing childish role models, seeking legal vengeance, emotionalism, and whining because one does not hit the lottery. If man cannot think and grow up, then he cannot move on to Steps Five to Seven. Any type of meaningful friendship will not be possible, he will not fit well into the social structure--especially with those who are working hard to meet their own responsibilities, and he will not leave sin and judgmentalism behind. Rather he will thrive on judging others and will miss the mark in every endeavor he undertakes.

Throughout the book the virtues are stressed, because I believe that Plato was absolutely correct when he taught that only good men can be happy. Likewise, rational wisdom, since it taught man what is good, is the primary basis of stepping towards wholeness. Honest thinking about oneself and choices and moral values is not easy, it is hard. This book is not short or easy, because the path to wholeness is not short or easy. Many other books make the journey to happiness all too simple and often they require a minimum of thought and discipline, and the results will be parallel in value, which will be minimum. Once these Seven Steps are taken, they must be revisited over and over again, for each new day man recreates his being, but hopefully on a higher level each day, so that he will never want to return to the emptiness of value that lies at the bottom of the steps.

GLOSSARY

Agora.　　　　(Gk) The market place where shopping, fellowship, and political and philosophical discussions took place in Athens.

Bhakti.　　　　(Hindu) Devotion to or the love for God.

Cosmos　　　　(Gk KOSMOS) The created material universe.

Dhamma.　　　　(Pali) or DHARMA (Sanskrit). Good conduct that follows moral instruction.

Didaskalos　　　(Gk) Teacher.

Dosa.　　　　(Buddhist) Hatred.

Hamartema.　　(Gk) The missing of a mark, sin.

TRINITY.　　　(Hindu): Brahma, the Creator; Vishnu, the Preserver; Shiva (Siva) or Rudra, the Destroyer.

Judeo-Christian.　　A Christian who believes that the Hebrew Scriptures (Canon) were an inspired preparation for the coming of Jesus, and also prophesied his coming.

Kathegetes.　　(Gk) Teacher or Master.

Leitourgia.　　(Gk) A public service rendered to one's city, often at great cost.

Lobha.　　　　(Buddhist) Greed.

Logos.　　　　(Gk) Word, Reason, or Rational Pattern or Expression.

Merimna.　　　(Gk) Anxiety.

Metanoia.　　　(Gk) Change of mind-set. Conversion, and sometimes Repentance.

Moha.　　　　(Buddhist) Illusion.

Moksa.　　　　(Hindu) Liberation by means of a balanced life.

Novum Organun.　(L) A new "instrument" by which to think scientifically.

Phobeo.　　　（Gk) To cause to fear or to terrify.

Platonic-Christian.　A Christian who believes the nature of God as taught by Jesus was foreshadowed in the teachings of Plato.

Pornea.　　　　(Gk) Unlawful sexual relations, adultery.

Rita.　　　　(Vedic) The Sublime Moral Order.

Samsara. (Hindu) Transmigration of the soul: a succession of births (sometimes sangsara).

Theophiles. (Gk) A friend of God or "beloved by God".

Torah. (Heb) The Canonized Jewish Law Code known as the Law of Moses.

CHAPTER ONE

1.1   Alex Osborn. Wake Up Your Mind. P.66.
1.2   Jacques Maritain. Education at the Crossroads. P.10.
1.3   C.H.Dodd. The Founder of Christianity. P.53.
1.4   Maurice Goguel. Jesus and the Origins of Christianity: Vol. II. P. 281.
1.5   AntonT. Boisen. The Exploration of the Inner World. P.296.
1.6   World of Buddha, ed. Lucien Stryk. Pp.318-322.
1.7   Dhammapada, tr. Max Mueller .(VI).
1.8   ibid. (I).
1.9   The Tibetan Book of the Dead, tr. W.Y. Evans-Wentz. P.199.
1.10   Buddhist Texts Through the Ages,ed. Edward Conze et al. Pp. 120-123.
1.11   The Four Books: Analects of Confucius, tr. James Legge. (IX.7).
1.12   ibid. (XVII.8).
1.13   The Four Books: Mencius, tr. James Legge. (VII.2.40).
1.14   ibid. (VI.1.7).
1.15   H.I. Marrow. A History of Education in Antiquity. P.368.
1.16   M. Grant. Jesus: An Historian's Review of the Gospels. P.69.
1.17   Pliny's Natural History, ed.Loyd Haberly. P.125.
1.18   Wilhelm Reich. Listen, Little Man! P.93.
1.19   John Sutherland Bonnell. No Escape from Life. P.46.
1.20   Mencius. Op. Cit., (VII.1.41).
1.21   J.S. Bonnell. Op. Cit. P.56.

CHAPTER TWO

2.1   Meditations fromWorld Religions, ed. Quinter M. Lyon. P.187.
2.2   Jacob Grimm. Teutonic Mythology, Vol. I. P.390.
2.3   Pliny's Natural History, ed. Loyd Havberly. P.102.
2.4   ibid. P.123.
2.5   Pliny's Letters, Vol. II. LCL. Pp. 255-257.
2.6   Kant's Vorlesungen. Ethica 579-582 (Pp.459-460).
2.7   Wilhelm Reich. Listen, Little Man. P.107.

2.8   Paul Tillich. <u>Theology of Culture</u>. P.41.
2.9   Bede. <u>A History of the English Church and People</u>. I.27.
2.10   Paul Tabori. <u>Secret and Forbidden</u>. Pp.18-19.
2.11   <u>The Philokalia, Vol. I.</u>, tr. Palmer, et al., P.76.
2.12   <u>The Essential Gandhi</u>, ed. Louis Fischer. P.242.
2.13   Carl Rogers. <u>On Becoming a Person</u>. P.174.
2.14   <u>Myth and Mythmaking</u>, ed. Henry A. Murray. P.44.

CHAPTER THREE

3.1   Paul Tillich. <u>The Courage to Be</u>. P.35.
3.2   Albert Camus. <u>The Plague</u>. Pp.137, 165.
3.3   <u>Poems from the Sanskit</u>, tr. John Brough. P.78.
3.4   <u>Poems of the Vikings</u>, tr. Patricia Terry. P.16.
3.5   <u>The Wisdom of China and India</u>, ed. Lin Yutang. P.634.
3.6   <u>Li Po and Tu Fu</u>, ed. Robert Baldrick, et al. P.188.
3.7   C.S. Lewis. <u>The Discarded Image</u>. Pp.83-84.
3.8   <u>Hsun Tzu: Basic Writings</u>, tr. Burton Watson. Pp.122-123.
3.9   <u>Cicero: On the Good Life</u>, tr. Michael Grant. P.69.
3.10   <u>India's Love Lyrics</u>. Laurence Hope. Pp.15-16.
3.11   <u>The Poems of Sappho</u>, tr. Susy Q. Groden. P.10.
3.12   Walter Lippmann. <u>The Public Philosophy</u>. Pp.70-71.
3.13   William James. <u>Essays on Faith and Morals</u>. P.8.
3.14   <u>Seneca: Letters from a Stoic</u>, tr. Robin Campbell. P.134.
3.15   Albert Camus. <u>The Fall</u>. Tr. Justin O'Brien. Pp.6-7, 49.
3.16   Jean-Paul Sartre. <u>The Words</u>. Tr. Bernard Frectman. P.61.
3.17   Elton Trueblood. <u>The Predicament of Modern Man</u>. Pp.19-20.

CHAPTER FOUR

4.1   <u>Early Greek Philosophy</u>, ed. Milton C. Nahm. Pp.216-218.
4.2   <u>On Love, The Family, and the Good Life: Selected Essays
       of Plutarch,</u> tr. Moses Hadas. Pp.93ff.
4.3   <u>Greek and Roman Philosophy after Aristotle</u>, ed. Jason L.
       Saunders. P.54.

4.4   Srimad Bhagavatam: The Wisdom of God, tr. Swami
        Prabhavananda. P.76.
4.5   William James. Essays on Faith and Morals. P.30.
4.6   Carl R. Rogers. On Becoming a Person. P.17.
4.7   Plutarch. The Lives of the Noble Grecians and Romans:
        Demetrius.
4.8   Greek and Roman Philosophy after Aristotle, ed. Jason L.
        Saunders. P.56.
4.9   Chuang Tzu, tr. James Legge. (XIX.2.1).
4.10   Shankara. Crest-Jewel of Discrimination. P.79.
4.11   Idries Shah. The Way of Sufi. P.70.
4.12   Francis of Sales. Introduction to the Devout Life. P.247.
4.13   Poems from Sanskrit, tr. John Brough. P.97.
4.14   Reinhold Niebuhr. Beyond Tragedy. Pp.114-115.
4.15   Barrows Dunham. Heroes and Heretics. P.96.
4.16   Poems from Sanskrit, tr. John Brough. P.131.
4.17   Helen Keller. The Faith of Helen Keller. P.21.

CHAPTER FIVE

5.1   C.G. Jung. Man and His Symbols. P.85.
5.2   The Wisdom of China and India, ed. Lin Yutang. P.659.
5.3   The Upanishads. Swami Nikhilananda. P.135.
5.4   A.A. Long and D.N. Sedley. The Hellenistic Philosophers. P.316.
5.5   Constantin Ritter. The Essence of Plato's Philosophy. P.308.
5.6   Samuel Noah Kramer. History Begins at Sumer. P.93.
5.7   William James. Essays on Faith and Morals. P.83.
5.8   Jacques Maritain. Education at the Crossroads. P.8.
5.9   Friedrich Schiller. On the Aesthetic Education of Man. P.3.
5.10   ibid. P.12.

CHAPTER SIX

6.1   Sri Chinmoy. Commentary on the Bhagavad Gita. Pp.18-19.
6.2   Idries Shah. The Way of Sufi. P.114.
6.3   ibid. P.53.
6.4   ibid. P.57.
6.5   ibid. P.63.
6.6   The Essential Rumi, tr. Coleman Barks. P.32.
6.7   Shankara. Crest-Jewel of Discrimination. P.39.
6.8   ibid. Pp.42-43.
6.9   ibid. Pp.93
6.10 Meister Eckhart, tr. Raymond B. Blakney. P.XIV.
6.11 ibid. P.9.
6.12 Jacob Boehme. The Way to Christ. P.70.
6.13 Gabriel Marcel. Mystery of Being, Vol. I. P.54.
6.14 Meister Eckhart, tr. Raymond Bl Blakney. P.145.
6.15 Jacob Boehme. The Way to Christ. P.57.
6.16 Friedrich Schleiermacher. On Religion p.7.
6.17 ibid. P.16.
6.18 ibid. P.18.
6.19 ibid. P.36.
6.20 ibid. P.41.
6.21 G.W.F. Hegel. Lectures on the Philosophy of Religion (1827). Pp.151-152.

CHAPTER SEVEN

7.1   J.L. Saunders. Greek and Roman Philosophy after Aristotle. P.53.
7.2   ibid. P.55.
7.3   Poems of the Vikings, tr. Patricia Terry. P.14.
7.4   Quest for Sita. Maurice Collins. P.25.
7.5   Cicero. Disputations. V.2.5-6.
7.6   Poems from Sanskit, tr. John Brough. P.68.
7.7   Bernard of Clairvaux. The Steps of Humility. IV.13-14.
7.8   Anton T. Boisen. Religion in Crisis and Custom. P.104.
7.9   Vance Packard. The Status Seekers. Pp.82-85.
7.10 World of Buddha, ed. Lucien Stryk. Pp.220-223.

7.11 William Langland. Piers the Ploughman. P.69.
7.12 Wilhelm Reich. Listen, Little Man. Pp. 17-18, 23, 50, 78.
7.13 John Mansley Robinson. An Introduction to Early Greek
    Philosophy. Pp.225-226.
7.14 ibid. Pp.223-225.
7.15 Carl R. Rogers. On Becoming a Person. P.280.
7.16 Fables of Aesop, tr. S.A. Handford. P.161.

CHAPTER EIGHT

8.1 Buddhist Texts Through the Ages, ed. Edward Conze, et alii.
    P.180.
8.2 Poems from the Sanskrit, op. cit. P.69.
8.3 Poems of the Vikings, tr. Patricia Terry. Pp.19-31.
8.4 Dietrich Bonhoeffer. Life Together. P.13.
8.5 The Faith of Helen Keller, ed. Jack Belck. P.18.
8.6 Steven Ozment. The Age of Reform: 1250-1550. P.218.
8.7 Encyclopaedia Judaica, 1971 ed., s.v. "Adultery," by Jeffrey
    Howard Tigay. P.314.
8.8 Johann J. Stamm. The Ten Commandments in Recent Research.
    P.100.
8.9 Westminster Commentaries: The Book of Numbers, ed. Walter
    Lock and D.C. Simpson. The Book of Numbers. L. Elliot
    Binns. P.31.
8.10 Carolly Erickson. The Medieval Vision. P.196.
8.11 Kalidasa. Shakuntala. P.48.
8.12 David & Vera Mace. Marriage East and West. Pp.190-191.
8.13 Victor Wolfgang von Hagen. Realm of the Incas. Pp.48-49, 120.
8.14 Jessie Bernard. The Future of Marriage. Pp.111-112.
8.15 William H. Lazareth: Luther on the Christian Home. P.31.
8.16 Roland Bainton. Here I Stand. P.304.
8.17 Li Po and Tu Fu, tr. Arthur Cooper. Pp.183-185.
8.18 ibid. P.118.
8.19 Bronislaw Malinowski. Sex and Repression in Savage Society.
    P.19.
8.20 Srimad Bhagavatam, tr. Swami Prabhavananda. Pp..99-100.
8.21 Dietrich Bonhoeffer. Life Together.

8.22   Srimad Bhagavatam. op.cit. P.102.

CHAPTER NINE

9.1   Immanuel Kant. Vorlesungen ueber Moralphilosophie: Collins
         Philosophiae: practicae universalis; Grade der Imputation.
         117-119.
9.2   Leo Tolstoy. The Kingdom of God is Within You. P.90.
9.3   ibid. P.110.
9.4   ibid. P.111.
9.5   Jamgon Kongtrul Lodro Taye. Buddhist Ethics. P.195.
9.6   John Manley Robinson. An Introduction to Early Greek
         Philosophy. P.21.
9.7   William James. Essays on Faith and Morals. P.102.
9.8   Jacque Maritain. Education at the Crossroads. P.16.
9.9   I.C. Sharma. Ethical Philosophies of India. P.72.
9.10   Selections from Early Greek Philosophy, ed. Milton C. Nahm.
         P.218.
9.11   John Donne. Devotions. Pp.108-109.
9.12   Die Bekenntnisschriften: Solida Declaratio, IV. Von guten
         Werken: 11-12.
9.13   Henri Bergson. The Two Sources of Morality and Religion.
         Pp.38-39.
9.14   Hanns Lilje. The Valley of the Shadow. P.59.
9.15   ibid. Pp.71-71.
9.16   Dietrich Bonhoeffer. The Martyred Christian. P.122.
9.17   The Essential Gandhi, ed. Louis Fischer. Pp.160-161.
9.18   Anton J. Boisen. Religion in Crisis and Custom. P.204.
9.19   Letters of the Younger Pliny. Vol.I. Book III.XI. Loeb. P.235.
9.20   Philosratus. Life of Apollonius. P.181.
9.21   ibid. P.200.
9.22   Karl Jaspers. Way to Wisdom. Pp.53-55.
9.23   "I Have a Dream" (Martin Luther King, Jr.), ed. Lotte Hoskins.
         P.31.
9.24   Paul Tillich. The Courage to Be. Pp.4-5.

CHAPTER TEN

10.1   Clae Waltham. Shu Ching: Book of History. P.33.
10.2   Who Shall Live? American Friends Service Committee.
          Pp.36-37.
10.3   I.C. Sharma. Ethical Philosophies of India. P.182.
10.4   B.L. Suzuki. Mahayana Buddhism. p.112.

The Plays of Aeschylus. Tr. G.M. Cookson. GBWW, 1952.

Fables of Aesop. Tr. S.A. Handford. N.Y: Penquin Books, 1983.

The Ancient Near East, ed. James B. Pritchard. Princeton: Princeton U. Press, 1958.

St. Anselm.Tr.Sidney Norton Deane. La Salle, IL: Open Court Publishing Co., (orig.1903) 1951.

The Plays of Aristophanes. Tr. B.B. Rogers. GBWW, 1952.

Aristotle's Theory of Poetry and Fine Art. Tr. S.H. Butcher. N.Y: Dover, 1951 (orig. 1897).

The Works of Aristotle. Vol. IX. Tr. W.D. Ross. London: Oxford U. Press, 1915.

The Edicts of Asoka. Tr. N.A. Nikam & Richard McKeon. Chicago: U. of Chicago Press. Phoenix Books, 1966.

The Meditations of Marcus Aurelius. Tr. George Long. GBWW, 1952.

Francis Bacon. Ed. Sidney Warhaft. N.Y: Odyssey Press, 1965.

Bhagavadgita. Tr. Edwin Arnold. N.Y: Dover, 1993 (orig. 1885).

Roland Bainton. Here I Stand: A Life of Martin Luther. N.Y: Abindgon Press, 1940.

The Other Bible. Ed. Willis Barnstone. San Francisco, CA.: Harper & Row, 1984.

Bede. A history of the English Church and People. Baltimore: Penguin Books.

Die Bekenntinisschriften der evangelish-lutherischen Kirke. Goettingen: Dandenhoeck & Ruprecht, 1956.

Bergson, Henri. The Two Sources of Morality and Religion. Tr. R.A Audra, C. Brereton, & W.H. Carter. Garden City, N.Y: Doubleday, 1954.

Bernard, Abbot of Clairvaux. The Steps of Humility. Tr. G.B. Burch. Notre Dame, Indiana: Notre Dame Press, 1963.

Bernard, Jessie. The Future of Marriage. N.Y: World Publishing Co., 1973.

Boehme, Jacob. The Way to Christ. Tr. Peter Erb. NY: Paulist Press, 1978.

The Consolation of Philosophy. Boethius. Tr. W.J. Oates. U.S.A: F. Ungar, 1957.

Boisen, Anton T. The Exploration of the Inner World. N.Y: Harper & Brothers - Torchbooks, 1962.

Religion in Crisis and Custom. N.Y: Harper Brothers, 1955.

Bonhoeffer, Dietrich. Life Together. Tr. J.W. Doberstein. London: SCM Press, 1960.

Ethics. Tr, N.H. Smith. N.Y: MacMillian Co. 1965.

The Cost of Discipleship. Tr. R.H. Fuller. N.Y: Macmillian Co., 1963.

Bonnell, John Sutherland. No Escape From Life. N.Y: Harper & Row, 1958.

The Egyptian Book of the Dead. Tr. E.A.Wallis Budge. N.Y: Dover, 1965 (Orig. 1895).

Bultman, Rudolf. Jesus and the Word. Tr. L.P. Smith & E.H. Lantero. N.Y: Charles Scribner's Sons, 1958.

Buddhist Ethics. J.K.L. Taye. Ithaca, N.Y.: 1998.

Buddhist Mahayana Texts. Ed. E.B. Cowell et.al.N.Y.: Dover, 1969.

Buddhist Texts Through The Ages. Ed. Conze, Horner, et al. N.Y: Harper & Row, 1954.

A Dictionary of Buddhism. T.O. Ling. N.Y: Charles Scribner's Sons, 1972.

Camus, Albert. The Fall. Tr. Justin O'Brien. N.Y: Alfred A. Knopf, 1960.

The Plague. Tr. Stuart Gilbert. N.Y: Modern Library, 1948.

Carnegie, Dale. How to Stop Worrying and Start Living. N.Y: Pocket Books, 1948.

Carter, Jimmy. I'll Never Lie to You. Ed. Robert L. Turner. N.Y: Ballantine Books, 1976.

Cassirer, Ernst. The Myth of the State. New Haven: Yale U. Press, 1963.

Language and Myth. Tr .S.K.Langer. N.Y: Dover, 1946.

Cawthorne, Nigel. Sex Lives of the Pope. London: Prion, 1997.

A Celtic Miscellany. Tr. Kenneth Hurlstone Jackson. Baltimore: Penguin Books, 1971.

Chaucer, Geoffrey. Troilus and Cressida. Adapted by G.P. Krapp. N.Y: Vintage Books, 1959.

The Writings of Chuang Tzu. Tr. James Legge. From The Sacred Books
of China, Vols.1-2. N.Y: Dover, 1962 (orig. 1891).

Cicero. Vols. 1 & 3 Tr. Duncan, Cockman, Melmoth. London: A.J.
Valpy, 1833. FCL.

Cicero: Letters to His Friends, Vols. 1 & 2. Tr. W.G. Williams.
Cambridge: Harvard U. Press. 1958 (orig. 1927 & 1929). Loeb.

Cicero: Tusculan Disputations. Tr. J.E. King. Cambridge: Harvard U.
Press, 1968 (orig. 1927). Loeb.

Cicero: Nature of the Gods. Tr. C.P. McGregor. N.Y: Penguin Books,
1984.

Cicero: On The Good Life. Tr. Micchael Grant. Baltimore. Penguin
Books, 1971.

Confucian Analects. Tr. James Legge. N.Y: Paragon Book Reprint Corp.
1966 (orig. 1923).

Demosthenes: Orations Vols.1-2. Tr. Thomas Leland. London: FCL,
1832.

Devereux, George. A Study of Abortion in Primitive Societies. N.Y:
The Julian Press, 1955.

Dhammapada. Tr. F. Max Mueller (1870). From The Wisdom of China
and India. Ed. Lin Yutang. N.Y: Modern Library, 1955.

Dodd, C.H. The Founder of Christianity. N.Y: Macmillan , 1976.
The Parables of the Kingdom. N.Y: Scribner's Sons, 1961
(orig. 1935).

Donne, John. Devotions. Ann Arbor: U. of Michigan Press, 1960 (text
1624).

Dunham, Barrows. Heroes and Heretics. N.Y: Dell, 1963.

Meister Eckhart. Tr. Raymond B. Blakney. N.Y: Harper Brothers, 1941.

Ehrlich, Jerry Dell. Plato's Gift to Christianity. San Diego: Academic
Christian Press, 2001.

Encylopaedia Judaica, 1971 ed. S.V. "Adultery," by Jeffrey H. Tigay.

The Discourses of Epictetus. Tr. George Long. Chicago: GBWW. 1952.

Erickson, Carolly. The Records of Medieval Europe. Garden City, N.Y:
Anchor, 1971.
The Medieval Vision. N.Y. Oxford U. Press, 1976.

Frager, Robert. Heart, Self, & Soul. Wheaton, IL: Quest Books, 1999.

The Little Flowers of St. Francis and Other Franciscan Writings. Tr.
Serge Hughes. N.Y: New American Library, 1964.

Words of St. Francis. Ed. James Meyer. Chicago: Franciscan Herald
    Press, 1952.
Francis of Sales. Introduction to the Devout Life. Tr. John K.Ryan.
    Garden City, N.Y: 1962.
Galileo. Dialogue Concerning the Two Chief World Systems. Tr.
    Stillman Drake. Berkeley: U. of California Press, 1967.
The Essential Gandhi. Ed. Louis Fischer. N.Y: Vintage Books, 1963.
Goethe Saemtliche Werke (40 Baenden). Berlin: J.G. Gotta'sche
    Buchhandlung Nachfolger, 1902.
Goguel, Maurice. Jesus and the Origins of Christianity, Vol.1. N.Y:
    Harper Bros., 1960.
Grant, Michael. Jesus: An Historian's Review of the Gospels. N.Y:
    Charles Scribner's Sons, 1977.
Graves, Robert. Goodbye to All That. Garden City, NY: Doubleday
    Anchor, 1957 (orig. 1929).
Greek and Roman Philosophy after Aristotle. Ed. J.L. Saunders. N.Y:
    Free Press, 1966.
Grimm, Jacob. Teutonic Mythology. Vol. 1. Tr. J.S. Stallybrass. N.Y:
    Dover, 1883.
Hagen, Victor W. Von. The Aztec: Man and Tribe. N.Y: New American
            Library, 1958.
                    Realm of the Incas. N.Y: New American
            Library, 1963.
                    The World of the Maya. N.Y: New American
            Library, 1960.
Long, A.A. and Sedley, D.N. The Hellenistic Philosophers. N.Y:
    Cambridge U. Press, 1987.
Hesiod. Tr. C.A. Elton. London: FCL. 1832.
Hillerbrand, Hans J. A Fellowship of Discontent. N.Y: Harper & Row,
    1967.
Hope, Laurence. India's Love Lyrics. N.Y: Triangle Books, 1902.
Horace. Tr. Philip Francis. London: FCL. 1831.
Hegel, G.W.F. Lectures on the Philosophy of Religion (1827). Tr. P.C.
    Hodgson, Berkeley: U. Of California Press, 1987.
Hrafnkel's Saga and Other Stories. Tr. Hermann Palsson. Baltimore:
    Penguin Books, 1972.
Huxley, Julian. Knowledge, Morality, & Destiny (Orig. New Bottles for
            New Wine). N.Y: New American Lib., 1960.

Religion Without Revelation. N.Y: New American Lib., 1961.

James, William. The Varieties of Religious Experience. N.Y: New American Lib., 1958 (Lectures of 1901-1902).
Essays on Faith and Morals. N.Y: World Pub. Co., 1961 (Orig. 1910).

Jaspers, Karl. Way to Wisdom. Tr. Ralph Manheim. New Haven: Yale U. Press, 1962.

Jowett, B. The Dialogues of Plato. Vols. 1-2. New York: Random House, 1937 (orig. 1892).

Joergensen, Johannes. St. Francis of Assisi. Tr. T.O'Conor Sloane. Garden City, N.Y: Image Books, 1955.

Jung, Carl G. Man and His Symbols. N.Y: Dell, 1977.

Juvenal. Tr. Charles Badham, 1831. FCL.

Kalidasa. Shakuntala. Tr. A.W. Ryder. N.Y: Dutton, 1959.

Kaltenmark, Max. Lao Tzu and Taoism. Tr. Roger Greaves. Stanford, Stanford U. Press, 1965.

Kant, Immanuel. Gesammelte Schriften: Vorlesungen, Band IV. Berlin: Walter de Grunter, 1974.

The Faith of Helen Keller. Ed. Jack Belck. Kansas City, MO: Hallmark, 1967.

King, Martin Luther, Jr. Strength to Love. N.Y: Pocket Books, 1964.
I Have a Dream. Ed. Lotte Hoskins. N.Y: Grosset & Dunlap, 1968.

An Analysis of the Kinsey Reports. Ed. D.P. Geddes. N.Y: New American Lib.,1954.

Kramer, Samuel Noah. History Begins at Sumer. Garden City, N.Y: Doubleday Anchor, 1959.

Langland, William. Piers the Ploughman. Baltimore: Penguin Books, 1966.

The Tao Te Ching of Lao Tzu. Tr. James Legge. N.Y: Dover, 1962 (orig. 1891).

Leibniz. Ed. PhilipP. Wiener. N.Y: Scribner's Sons, 1951.

C.S. Lewis. The Discarded Image. Cambridge: Cambridge U. Press, 1976.

Lilje, Hanns. The Valley of the Shadow. Tr. Olive Wyon. Philadelphia: Muhlenberg Press, (no date).

Li Po and Tu Fu. Tr, Arthur Cooper. Baltimore: Penguin, 1973.

Lippmann, Walter. The Public Philosophy. N.Y: New American Lib.
    1955.

The Table Talk of Martin Luther. Ed. Thomas S. Kepler. N.Y: World
    Publishing Co., 1952

Lyon, Quinter Marcellus. Meditation From World Religions .Nashville:
    Abingdon Press, 1960.

Malinowski, Bronislaw. Sex and Repression in Savage Society.
    Cleveland: World Publishing Co., 1963.

Mannix, Daniel P. The History of Torture. N.Y: Dell, 1964.

The Laws of Manu. Tr. Georg Buehler. N.Y: Dover, 1969 (orig.1886).

Marcel, Gabriel. The Mystery of Being, Vols.1-2. Chicago: Henry
                Regnery Co., 1960.
                Homo Viator. N.Y: Harper Bros., 1962.

Maritain, Jacques. Education at the Crossroads. New Haven: Yale U.
    Press, 1963.

Marrou, H.I. A History of Education in Antiquity. Tr. George Lamb.
    N.Y: New American Lib., 1964.

Maslow, Abraham H. Religions, Values, and Peak-Experiences. U.S.A.
    Viking Press, 1983

Mead, Margaret. Sex and Temperament in Three Primitive Societies.
    N.Y: New American Lib., 1962

The Portable Medieval Reader. Ed. J.B.Ross and M.M. McLaughlin.
    N.Y: The Viking Press, 1968.

Menander. Dyskolos. Tr. W.G. Arnott. London: U. of London, Athlone
    Press, 1960.

The Works of Mencius. Tr. James Legge. N.Y: Paragon Book Reprint,
    1966 (orig. 1923).

More, Paul Elmer. The Religion of Plato. Princeton U. Press. Reprint
    From New York: Kraus Reprint Co., 1970 (orig. 1921).

Mo Tzu. Tr. Burton Watson. N.Y: Columbia U. Press,1966.

Myth and Mythmaking. Ed. Henry A. Murray. Boston: Beacon Press,
    1968.

The Myths of the Hindus and Buddhists. Ananda K. Coomaraswamy and
    The Sister Nivedita. N.Y: Dover, 1967 (orig. 1913).

Selections from Early Greek Philosophy. Ed.Nahm, Milton. C F.S. Crofts
    & Co., 1934.

The Nag Hammadi Library. Ed. James M. Robinson. San Francisco;
    Harper & Row. 1981.

Niebuhr, Reinhold. Beyond Tragedy. N.Y: Scribner's Sons, 1937.

Nurbakhsh, Javad. Jesus in the Eyes of the Sufis. Tr. T. Graham, L. Lewisohn, H. Mashkuri. London: Khaniqahi-Nimatullahi,1992.

Rubaiyat of Omar Khayyam. Tr. Edward Fitzgerald. Garden City, N.Y: Dolphin Books, (no date).

The Oriental Philosophers. Ed. E.W.F. Tomlin. N.Y: Harper & Row, 1963.

Osborn, Alex. Wake Up Your Mind. N.Y: Dell, 1952.

Ovid. Tr. Dryden, Pope, Congreve, Addison. London: 1833. FCL.

Ozment, Steven. The Age of Reform:1250-1550. New Haven: Yale U. Press, 1980.

Packard, Vance. The Status Seekers. N.Y: Pocket Books, 1959.

Peck, M. Scott. The Road Less Traveled. N.Y: Simon & Schuster, 1978.

Pike, E. Royston. The Strange Ways of Man. N.Y: Pocket Books, 1970.

Petronius: The Satyricon and Fragments. Tr. J.P. Sullivan. Baltimore: Penguin Books, 1972.

The Philokalia: Nikodimos and Makarios. Tr. Palmer,Sherrard, & Ware. London: Faber & Faber, 1979.

The Philosophy of the Upanishads. Paul Deussen. Tr. A.S. Geden. N.Y: Dover, 1966 (orig. 1906).

Philostratus, Flavius. Life of Apollonius. Tr. C.P. Jones. Baltimore: Penguin Books, 1970.

Pliny's Natural History. Ed. Loyd Haberly (based on Bohn edition,1855). N.Y: Frederick Ungar, 1957.

Pliny's Letters. Vols. 1-2. Tr. William Melmoth. Cambridge: Harvard U. Press, 1918. Loeb.

Plotinus: The Enneads. Tr. S. MacKenna. N.Y: Penguin Books, 1991 (orig. 1917-1930).

The Essential Plotinus. Tr. Elmer O'Brien. N.Y: New American Lib., 1964.

Plutarch. The Lives of the Noble Grecians and Romans. Tr. Dryden. GBWW.

On Love, the Family, and the Good Life: Selected Essays of Plutarch. Tr. Moses Hadas. N.Y: New American Lib., 1957.

Prabhavananda, Swami. The Spiritual Heritage of India. Hollywood, CA: Vedanta Press, 1969.

The Sermon on the Mount according to Vedanta. N.Y: New American Lib., 1972.

The Ramayana and the Mahabharata. Tr. Romesh C. Dutt (1910).
    London: Dent (Everyman's Lib.), 1969.
Quest for Sita: The Ramayana. Retold by Maurice Collis. N.Y:
    Capricorn, 1965.
Ranke-Heinemann, Uta. Eunuchs for the Kingdom of Heaven. Tr. P.
    Heinegg. N.Y: Penguin, 1990.
Rawls, John. A Theory of Justice. Cambridge: Harvard U. Press, 1971.
Reich, Wilhelm. The Murder of Christ. N.Y: Noonday Press, 1972.
            The Invasion of Compulsory Sex-Morality. N.Y:
        Farrar, Straus and Giroux, 1971.
                Listen, Little Man. Tr. T.P. Wolfe. N.Y: Noonday
                Press, 1972.
The Rig Veda. From Sacred Writings, Ed. Jaroslav Pelikan, Vol. 5. Tr.
    Ralph T.H. Griffith (1896). N.Y: Book-of-the-Month Club, 1992.
Robinson, John Mansley. An Introduction to Early Greek Philosophy.
    Boston: Houghton Mifflin Co., 1968.
Rogers, Carl R. On Becoming a Person. Boston: Houghton Mifflin Co.,
    1961.
Russell, Bertrand: Speaks His Mind. N.Y: Bard Books, 1960.
                Why I am Not a Christian. N.Y: Simon & Schuster,
                1957.
                Marriage and Morals. N.Y: Liveright Pub. Co., 1968.
The Essential Rumi. Tr. Coleman Barks. Edison, N.J: Castle Books,
    1997.
Poems from the Sanskrit. Tr. John Brough. Baltimore: Penguin Books,
    1968.
Sartre, Jean-Paul. Existentialism and Human Emotions. Tr. B.
                Frechtman.N.Y: Philosophical Lib., 1957.
                The Words. Tr. B. Frechtman. Greenwich, CN:
                Fawcett, 1964.
Schaff, Philip. History of the Christian Church. Vols.1-3. Grand Rapids,
    MI: Wm. B. Eerdmans, 1952 (orig. 1910).
Schlick, Moritz. Problems of Ethics. Tr. David Rynin. N.Y: Dover, 1962.
Schiller, Friedrich. On The Aesthetic Education of Man. Tr. Reginald
    Snell. N.Y: Frderick Ungar, 1965.
Friedrich Schiller. Tr. Frederick Ungar. N.Y: Frederick Ungar Publ. Co.,
    1959.

Schillers Gaemtliche Werke: Saekular-Ausgabe in 16 Baenden. Berlin: J.G.Gotta'sche Buchhandlung Nachfolger, 1904.

Schleiermacher, Friedrich. On Religion: Speeches to its cultured despisers. Tr. John Oman, 1893. N.Y: Harper Bros., 1958.
Christmas Eve Dialogue on the Incarnation. Tr.T.N. Tice. Richmond, VA: John Knox Press, 1967.

Seneca Epistulae Morales. Tr. R.M. Gummere. Vos. 1 & 3. Cambridge, MA: 1979 (Orig. 1917).

Seneca: Letters From a Stoic. Tr. Robin Campbell. N.Y: Penguin Books, 1969.

Sex and Morality. British Council of Churches. Philadelphia: Fortress, 1966.

Shah, Idries. The Way of the Sufi. N.Y: E. P. Dutton, 1970.

Shankara. Crest-Jewel of Discrimination. N.Y: New American Lib., 1947.

Sharma, I.C. Ethical Philosophies of India. Ed. Stanley M. Daugert. N.Y: Harper & Row, 1965.

Shu Ching. Tr. James Legge, adapted by Clae Waltham. Chicago: Henry Regnery Co., 1971.

Sophocles. Tr. Thomas Francklin. London: 1832. FCL.

Spencer, Herbert. Data of Ethics. N.Y: John W. Lovell Co., 1879.

Spener, Philip Jacob. Pia Desideria. Philadelphia: Fortress, 1964.

Srimad Bhagavatam. Tr. Swami Prabhavananda. N.Y: Capricorn, 1968.

Stamm, Johann J., with Andre, M.E. The Ten Commandments in Recent Research. Naperville, IL: Alec R. Allenson, Inc., 1967.

Suzuki, Beatrice Lane. Mahayana Buddhism. Toronto, Ontario: Collier-Macmillan Canada Ltd., 1969.

Tabori, Paul. Secret and Forbidden: The Moral History of the Passions of Mankind. N.Y: New American Lib., 1966.

The Autobiography of St. Teresa of Avila. Tr. E. Allison Peers. Garden City, NY: Image Books, 1960.

Hesiod and Theognis. Tr. Dorothea Wender. Baltimore: Penguin, 1973.

The Gospel According to Thomas. Tr. A. Guillaumont et alii. N.Y: Harper Bros.,1959.

The Tibetan Book of the Dead. Tr. Lama Kazi Dawa-Samdup (no date) & ed. by W.Y. Evan-Wentz. London: Oxford U. Press, 1927, 1972.

Poems of Tibullus. Tr. Philip Dunlop. Baltimore: Penguin Books, 1972.

Tillich, Paul. <u>The Shaking of the Foundations</u>. N.Y: C. Scribner's Sons, 1948.
> <u>The Religious Situation</u>. N.Y: Meridian Books, Inc. 1960.
> <u>The Courage to Be</u>. New Haven: Yale U. Press, 1963.
> <u>The Theology of Culture</u>. N.Y: Oxford U. Press, 1964.

Tolstoy, Leo. <u>The Kingdom of God is Within You</u>. Tr. Leo Wiener (1905). U.S.A. Noonday Press, 1961.

Trevor-Roper, H.R. <u>The European Witch-Craze</u>. N.Y: Harper & Row, 1967.

Trueblood, Elton. <u>The Predicament of Modern Man</u>. N.Y: Harper & Row, 1944.

<u>The Upanishads</u>. Tr. Swami Nikhilananda. N.Y: Harper & Row, 1964.

<u>Kama Sutra of Vatsyayana</u>. Tr. Richard Burton & F.F. Arbuthnot. N.Y: Putnam's Sons, 1971.

<u>The Vedanta Sutras of Badaralyana</u>. Tr. G. Thibaut (1896). New York: Dover, 1962.

<u>Poems of the Vikings</u>. Tr. Patricia Terry. N.Y: Bobbs-Merrill Co., 1969.

<u>Westminster Commentaries</u>. Gen. Eds. Walter Lock and D.C. Simpson. London: Methuen & Co., Ltd., 1927. <u>The Book of Numbers</u>, by L. Elliott Binns.

<u>Who Shall Live? Man's Control over Birth and Death</u>. A Report Prepared for the American Friends Service Committe. N.Y: Hill and Wang, 1970.

<u>Wisdom of China and India</u>. Ed. Lin Yutang. N.Y: Modern Library,1955.

<u>The Wonder that was India</u>. A.L. Basham. N.Y: Grove Press, 1959.

<u>World of the Buddha</u>. Ed. Lucien Stryk. Garden City, NY: Anchor Books 1969.

Wright, Arthur F. <u>Buddhism in Chinese History</u>. N.Y: Atheneum, 1969.